Fred Sway

JOHN THORNE

WITH MATT LEWIS THORNE

❧ ❧ ❧

POT ON THE FIRE

JOHN THORNE and MATT LEWIS THORNE live in Northampton, Massachusetts, where they publish the bimonthly food letter *Simple Cooking*. John Thorne contributes to *Gourmet, Saveur, Los Angeles Times,* and other publications. The Thornes' *Serious Pig* was nominated for an IACP/Julia Child Award and *Outlaw Cook* won it. Their Web site can be found at www.outlawcook.com.

ALSO BY JOHN THORNE

Simple Cooking

Outlaw Cook

Serious Pig

Home Body

POT ON THE FIRE

POT ON THE FIRE

FURTHER EXPLOITS OF
A RENEGADE COOK

JOHN THORNE

WITH MATT LEWIS THORNE

NORTH POINT PRESS

A DIVISION OF FARRAR, STRAUS AND GIROUX

NEW YORK

North Point Press
A division of Farrar, Straus and Giroux
19 Union Square West, New York 10003

Copyright © 2000 by John Thorne
All rights reserved
Distributed in Canada by Douglas & McIntyre Ltd.
Printed in the United States of America
Published in 2000 by North Point Press
First paperback edition, 2001

Library of Congress Cataloging-in-Publication Data
Thorne, John.
    Pot on the fire: further exploits of a renegade cook / John Thorne with Matt Lewis
Thorne.— 1st ed.
        p. cm.
    Includes bibliographical references.
    ISBN 0-86547-620-9 (pbk.)
    1. Cookery, International.   2. Cooks.   I. Thorne, Matt Lewis.   II. Title.
TX725.A1 T497 2000
641.59—dc21

                                                                          00-038015

The chapter in this book entitled "My Knife, My Pot" originally appeared in slightly different form in *Gourmet Magazine*. Everything else originally appeared in the authors' *Simple Cooking* food letters.

We have made a concerted effort to obtain permission to quote from copyrighted works. Grateful acknowledgment is made to the following:

Andrew J. L. Blank and Judy Landis. "On the Trail of Arnhemse Meisjes," by Andrew Blank and Judy Landis. Copyright © 1997 by Andrew J. L. Blank and Judy Landis. Reprinted by permission of the authors.

Maurice Frechette. "Hobz iz Zejt," by Maurice Frechette. Copyright © 1997 by Maurice Frechette. Reprinted by permission of the author.

Patience Gray. For permission to quote a passage from a letter to us.

Mrs. Nicholas Kelley. For permission to quote a passage from a letter to us by her brother, the late Augustus M. Kelley.

Johan Mathiesen. "Cioppino," by Johan Mathiesen. Copyright © 1996 by Johan Mathiesen. Reprinted by permission of the author.

Maggie Rogers. For permission to quote a passage from a letter to us.

Elisheva Urbas. "Cinnamon Toast," by Elisheva S. Urbas. Copyright © 1998 by Elisheva S. Urbas. Reprinted by permission of the author.

The Crown Publishing Group. Excerpt from *Larousse Gastronomique*, edited by Jennifer Harvey Lang. Copyright © 1984 Librairies Larousse. Copyright 1998 © English text, The Hamlyn Publishing Group, Ltd. Reprinted by permission of the publisher.

Designed by Jonathan D. Lippincott

For Shirley & George
with love

AUTHOR'S NOTE

The "I" that speaks from these pages is mine in every chapter of this book, except in those letters where the contributor is explicitly named—Patience Gray, Elisheva Urbas, Judy Landis and Andrew Blank, Augustus Kelley, Johan Mathiesen, Maggie Rogers—and in "Cakes on the Griddle," the section on making pancakes, which was written by my wife, Matt Lewis Thorne.

Matt, though, has also considered every word of every draft I have written, reacting, suggesting, amending, and, hence, *reshaping* what appears herein. As I noted in our first collaboration, *Outlaw Cook*, this means that the subjective self who speaks out of these pages is a larger, braver, much more interesting person than I am alone—and I honor her for it.

As in my three previous food books, *Pot on the Fire* assembles a selection of essays written over the past several years, most of them originally published in our food letter, *Simple Cooking*. Those who read this book with pleasure might also be interested in subscribing to it. Either write to us at P.O. Box 778, Northampton MA 01061—or, better yet, visit our Web site: www.outlawcook.com.

—John Thorne

CONTENTS

LAST GLEANING

LIST OF RECIPES

Sweets and Desserts

Vegetables (see also Pasta and Pizza, Rice and Rice Dishes, and Salads)

MOVING TO PARADISE—
BY WAY OF A PREFACE

❧ ❧ ❧

Everything has changed; nothing has changed. Thirty-five years ago, I attended Amherst College, just two towns away from where I now write these words, and there's something disorienting about being back. On the one hand, after all this time I hardly know the place. When I left the area in the late sixties, it was just starting to reflect the hipness of those times: a funky food co-op here, a bicycle store there, a scattering of Crabtree & Evelyn wannabes. Now the place is overripe with the hipness of today: body manipulators, nutrition consultants, coffee roasters, microbreweries, feminist gift shops. The effect is not unlike shopping for clothing at a college prep shop at the age of fifty-five: no matter what shape you're in, nothing really fits. You get to be twenty only once.

On the other hand, the atmosphere—the lush, deciduous greenness of so many enormous trees; the college campus with its strange contrast of sobersided patrician architecture and motley youthful inhabitants— triggers long-buried sensory imprinting that is still dank with the humidity of adolescent angst. I take Matt for a quick drive-through tour of the campus . . . and leave it at that. There will be no looking up old professors or revisiting old dorm rooms. Instead, I prefer to delight in our new home about seven miles farther west—the small, sweet city of Northampton.

This place, if you're unfamiliar with it—the city recently got its fifteen minutes of fame with the publication of Tracy Kidder's *Home Town*—is located more or less at the center of Massachusetts, surrounded by fertile farmland and resting beside the—here, impressively wide—Connecticut River. It is the shire town of Hampshire County, with the requisite impressive granite courthouse, but, more important to us, it serves as the commercial hub for four liberal arts colleges (including Smith College, which is situated here) and the University of Massachusetts, a sprawling educational megalopolis.

So, much of the city's commerce is directed at college students and those who teach them. There are countless used-book stores, a host of coffee bars and ethnic restaurants, two independent movie houses, and a quite respectable museum of art. This is a good place to live if you like to rent obscure videos, listen to live music, buy used books or CDs, or just settle into a plush armchair at one of the coffee bars and, a *caffè latte* by your elbow, bury yourself in *Wired* or *The New York Review of Books*.

When famed soprano Jenny Lind gave a concert in Northampton in 1851, she proclaimed the city "The Paradise of America," liking it so much that she honeymooned here in 1852. I have no idea why she made that proclamation, but I do know that Northamptonites have been quite willing to agree with her—on one little side street you can find a Pizzeria Paradiso and a Paradise Copy Shop. In the intervening years, Northampton has certainly come to possess many ideal metropolitan qualities. For instance, its downtown is not only walkable but inviting to walk in, even late at night. Our second or third evening here, we joined a friend at a nearby restaurant for supper and later decided to stroll a few blocks to an Italian pastry shop for dessert. It was after nine, but patrons filled the outdoor tables of the coffee bars and strollers thronged the sidewalks; the air buzzed with the sound of people having a good time.

Even so, drive ten minutes from the center of town in almost any direction and you're in the middle of farmland. Coming back from the post office the other day, I saw a huge, odd, but somehow familiar-looking truck lumbering toward me. As it got closer, I realized it was an open hopper truck, similar to ones we had seen on our trip to Maine's Aroostook County—and, like those, this one was piled high with spuds. Their soddy, tuberous aroma trailed in the truck's wake, a reminder—as is the fact that garden centers outnumber fast-food joints along our Miracle Mile—that this area is still largely farm country, famous, in fact, for its cigar-wrapper tobacco leaf, onions, and (hurrah!) asparagus.

❧ ❧ ❧

All this helps explain why we came here, but not why we left the Down East coast or why our moving entailed abandoning Maine completely. Some of our reasons were entirely ordinary—wanting to be nearer to nephews who are quickly growing up, missing the pleasures and conveniences of urban life, finding we'd had it with winters that begin in early November and end late in April. But others were not.

I had returned to Maine back in 1987 for a last taste of the place where I spent my boyhood summers. While I had to travel much, much farther up the coast to find it, a taste of that world still lingered on. During the first few years of our time there, we could still find old-fashioned grocery and dry-goods stores, local dairies that had never heard of ultrapasteurization, doughnut shops that made cake doughnuts from scratch and fried them in lard, lunch counters that offered homemade pies and real beanhole beans, and country stores offering skunk cheese, fish jerky, fresh-churned butter in rough-cut chunks—and none of it for the benefit of tourists.

All this—or near enough—disappeared during our ten-year stay, including many of the places I wrote about in *Serious Pig*. In Brewer, the Buttermilk Donut Shop closed; in Ellsworth, Dick's Restaurant, the Hancock Dairy, the Pine Tree Diner, and the J.J. Newberry five-and-ten-cent store, with its classic lunch counter; in Winter Harbor, The Donut Hole+ (despite a rave review of the place by Jane and Michael Stern in *Gourmet* a few months before it closed—the owner was just worn out); in Bucksport, Duffy's Restaurant; in Eastport and Machias, two vintage A & Ps.

Some new, good things arrived to take their places, but they were enterprises of a different order, established by people who had come to Maine because it is lovely there and quiet and, for the moment, still affordable enough to offer them—as it had the potters, the bell casters, and the stained-glass-window makers who arrived decades before—a chance to turn an avocation into a living. We ourselves, of course, were part of this crowd, but we were not really *of* it. I had come to Maine to find something I had lost there; they had come, many of them, to participate in the founding of the New Green Age.

I love trees and organic vegetables as much as anyone, but I take them as symbolic of a liveable future, not a direct route to it, and in

Maine, those who believe it *is* the route seem to be marking it with increasingly ominous road signs. For instance, there's been a vendor who's tried for years to sell hot coffee at the Common Ground Fair, a statewide celebration of alternative agriculture, and every year he's been refused a booth—even when he switched over to organic coffee. It seems that caffeine, like animal fat, whatever the source, is simply bad. That is symptomatic of a kind of self-righteousness that appears to swell with the arrival of each new herbalist and dulse harvester.

Northampton, not surprisingly, is rife with such attitudes—"Happy Valley," a friend ironically describes it—but that is only one part of a headily active ferment. The local natural foods supermarket has a meat department that is much better—more varieties of meat, more specialty cuts, all of it organically raised—than most regular supermarkets, and a cheese department that simply blows the competition away. Porterhouse steaks, Cornish clotted cream, and obscure French cheeses coexist peacefully, if a tad bizarrely, with herbal tinctures, locally made tofu, and rice-milk beverages.

Also, as it turns out, this part of Massachusetts has a more robust vernacular culinary life than any we found in Maine, if only because there are more people and more money here to support them. Recently, local dairy farmers formed a co-op to sell their own antibiotic-free milk and found that they couldn't produce enough of it. The area abounds in roadside farm stands and farmers' markets, diners and hot dog wagons, sausage makers, old-fashioned doughnut shops, and such unexpected finds as the brace of penny-candy stores right here in town.

All this is a statement about *me*, not about Maine, a place I continue to love, or about the people who live there, all of whom I wish well. I'm extremely grateful to have been given a second helping of an experience that touched me as living in no other place ever has. And I already miss the stark, soul-cleansing beauty of the Down East coast. But I was becoming a writer whose major subject was fading into nostalgia and regret. To hell with that . . . better to toss myself back into the turbulent waters of today and see if I still know how to swim.

It certainly says something that while about half the essays in this book were written while Matt and I were still living Down East, reading most of them, you wouldn't know it. And none has anything to do with what might be called "Maine cooking"—the dishes, like baked beans and clam chowder, that figured so prominently in my last book,

Serious Pig. I didn't turn against this food, but I found that I didn't want to spend the rest of my life regularly eating it either. After a decade, the knowledge that two or three fifty-pound bags of potatoes were safely cellared at the start of winter had begun to evoke feelings less akin to security than to dread.

After all, my cooking—and, so, my writing about cooking—has always thrived best in adversity, most often the struggle against my own limitations as a cook, but also against the equally real difficulties imposed from without: the opacity of recipes, the rarity of truly decent ingredients, the strictures imposed by lack of money or limitations of place. No wonder, then, that living on the Maine coast, I eventually tired of lobster and freshly harvested scallops and began battling to make a decent pizza crust in a propane-fired Sears stove. And, with all those bags of spuds in the cellar, what else to do but learn how to make perfect rice?

The acute reader will notice the same pattern repeating itself here. *Pot on the Fire* has a plethora of asparagus recipes—and why? Because it is grown locally and, for the first year or two, I just couldn't get enough. The same was true of sweet corn—here the season starts sometime in July and runs until . . . well, I don't know how long, because I ate away my appetite for it sometime in early September. To my surprise, even my craving for the two-inch-thick prime Kansas City strip steaks sold in a local gourmet store's meat department has begun to peak. So, what next? I haven't the faintest idea. I've learned enough about myself in the last few years to know it would be foolish to take a guess.

Meanwhile, about the second Sunday after we moved here, I set some Cornish game hens to cook in our meat smoker, which now resides on our tiny patio. After a bit, some firemen burst into our apartment, fire axes in hand. The neighbors, it seemed, had smelled smoke and sounded the alarm. I took the two out the patio door and showed them the meat smoker, the wood chips, the game hens. They just laughed and left.

And that pretty much sums things up. Whether or not we end up staying here forever, at this particular moment it's paradise enough.

EDUCATION

OF A COOK

MY KNIFE, MY POT

❧ ❧ ❧

I fell into cooking as many do: by accident, by necessity. I was nineteen, a college dropout, living alone in a dirt-cheap fifth-floor walk-up apartment on New York's Lower East Side. I had no experience, no kitchen equipment, no money, but none of that mattered, because I had no palate then, either. Everything I made tasted good to me, because everything I made was an adventure. At that time, frozen corn and frozen peas were five boxes to the dollar; a pound of hamburger was even less. So, until I discovered rice, a weekday meal was simply a box of the one cooked with a fifth of a pound of the other, and I ate it feeling amazed at what a clever fellow I was.

However, even if I didn't know what to think about what I ate, I had definite opinions about the kitchen equipment I cooked it with. Most of my tiny collection had been bought at a store on East Fourteenth Street. It was different from other junk stores only in that everything it sold was brand new—instant junk. My single kitchen knife was far from sharp, but, even worse, it *felt* dull, as if it had been made to look like a knife rather than to be one. It was little better than a toy—and so were the cheap pans that warped at once if put empty on the flame and scorched anything, even soup, if you weren't infinitely careful.

This upset me. I had an adolescent's volatile sensitivity to anything that threatened my *amour-propre*. Aspiring to become a novelist, I knew I needed a decent, solid typewriter, and I had sacrificed everything to get one. Then, when it was stolen from my apartment a week later, I found a way to buy another, and discovered that sacrifice could pull even more out of me than I knew I had to give. Now I yearned almost as much for two things more: one good knife and one good pot.

This was in the early 1960s, and at that time there was a cook's store on the Avenue of the Americas near Twenty-first Street called Bazar Français. I had come across it on one of my city rambles, and I could tell it was the right sort of place as soon as I came through the doorway. The store itself was austere and slightly scary; the other customers and the equipment they were examining looked serious and professional. This was to kitchen stores what the Gotham Book Mart was to, say, Doubleday's; when you came in you felt less welcomed than appraised.

At the Gotham, at least I could afford to buy a book, however unworthy I might be to own it. Here, I faced complete humiliation. The smallest tin-lined copper pot cost more than I made in a week, working as I then did in the mail room of a steamship line. The kitchen utensils—the spatulas, ladles, skimmers—were made for pots whose dimensions seemed larger than life. I couldn't have put one in any pot I owned without causing that pot to tumble off the stove.

Then I came to the knives. Of course, there were many of these that were also beyond the timid reach of my wallet. But this didn't matter. Almost at once I saw a knife that I both intensely desired and could easily afford. Although there was no mark on the blade or handle that said so, the store claimed it was made in France. If it was, it was certainly not at the top of the manufacturer's line. No knife could have been more utilitarian; it had a blade and a handle, and that was it. I don't remember exactly what it cost, but I know that the price was under ten dollars.

This knife, three decades and more later, sits beside me on the desk as I write. It is made of carbon steel, with a full tang—the metal extending the entire length of the knife, with the two halves of the wooden handle clamped to it with brass rivets. Neither in shape, size, nor hauteur would it ever be confused with a chef's knife: it makes no statement whatsoever about the taste or expertise of the person who uses it. It is simply a tool, and all it says is "I cut."

That, it proved, was enough. The synonyms for *cut* in my thesaurus almost all smack of the rough and violent—"gash," "pierce," "slash," "cleave," "sever," "rip," "lacerate"—but with this knife the experience became eerily sensuous. The blade slid through a piece of meat almost as if it were cutting butter, and the slithery ease of it had a giddy edginess to it, since with one slip it would as easily slide into me. No matter how many times you've done it before, picking up a razor-sharp knife puts the nerves on alert, and practice teaches you to extend them to the blade's tip, so that you feel rather than cut your way around gristle and bone.

In other words, that knife brought the act of cooking to life. I don't doubt that a skilled cook can prepare good meals with the crummiest of kitchenware, because I have done this myself. But after the challenge has been met, there is no real pleasure in doing so. Cheap stuff is never neutral; it constantly drags at your self-respect by demeaning the job at hand. And only if you start a life of cooking knowing that dead weight can you truly appreciate the feeling of release, even joy, when you first lay hands on such a tool.

❧ ❧ ❧

The road to my first good pot turned out to be a much longer one. To begin with, pots are far more complicated than knives. Even tucked away in a cupboard, their presence looms in the kitchen the way a knife's never does. Because, while a knife's job is soon over, a pot's work is almost never done. In the end, a knife, however expensive, is just an implement, while a pot is the kitchen itself made small. After all, it is inside the pot that the actual cooking takes place.

Consequently, it is the pot—really, the set of pots—that is the kitchen's pride. The more self-aware the cook, the more those pots take center stage, not hidden in kitchen cabinets but proudly hung from open racks—sturdy, gleaming, clean. And, let's admit it, expensive. Acquired as wedding presents, they are often less participants in the cook's first fumbling efforts than silent, slightly intimidating witnesses. Spouses are easy to please; the cook's real task is to live up to the set of All-Clad or Calphalon.

As a teenager, one of my household chores was to wash the dinner dishes, a task that always culminated in the ritual cleaning of the pans. My mother's pride and joy was a set of stainless-steel, copper-bottomed cookware, and there was no escaping the kitchen sink until these sparkled—a process that began with steel wool, went on to copper polish, and ended with the nervous rush to get each pot dry and put away before its bottom was stained with a single water spot.

I wanted no such bullying presence in my free-and-easy bachelor's kitchen. In fact, the first pan I acquired, a small cast-iron frying pan, was in appearance and temperament the very antithesis of house proud. It entered my apartment greasy inside and rust-stained without, looking as surly as a junkyard dog. I cleaned it up a bit and taught it how to do a few basic tricks—the skillet equivalents to "sit up" and "beg"—and tried to give it as few chances as I could to bite me.

Still, we got along all right. I found that I felt at ease with the lesser breeds of cookware: larger, equally grumpy cast-iron skillets, a cheap aluminum pasta pot, an unmatching assortment of saucepans made of thin steel and coated with cream-colored or blue-speckled enamel— stuff picked up here and there at yard sales or on the back shelves of hardware stores. Such pots had always been around when I was grow-ing up—identical versions could have been found in my grandmother's kitchen—and while they may not have been all that great to cook with, their limitations were a soothing match to my own.

This situation might never have changed had I not, in my forties, fi-nally gotten married. At this point in our lives, the problem was not one of quickly acquiring a *batterie de cuisine* but of merging two very different ones. Since my wife, Matt, owned pots and pans of a much higher quality, I was quite content to get rid of almost all of mine. In re-turn, I was introduced to what would become, for me, *the* pot: a solid, stainless-steel four-quart Italian-made saucepot with a thick aluminum plate welded to its base.

As with the knife, it was love at first sight, perhaps because the pot's serious cookware look was tempered by a pair of jug ears—two over-sized steel handles—that gave it a gawky sweetness. More than that, though, its particular proportions drew me to it. I just loved to feed that pot. Our ideal cooking vessel must surely be shaped in some mysterious way to fit our appetite, and this one was a perfect measure to mine.

Like the knife, it asserted a simple, unintimidating confidence that somehow got transferred to me. By tolerating my capricious kitchen ways—refusing, say, to let a risotto scorch merely because my attention had lapsed at a crucial moment or to boil a cut of beef into shoe leather because I forgot to check how the temperature was holding—it got me to tolerate them more myself and thus to stop letting them get in my way.

It was also a delight to use. The heavy bottom not only made heat spots a thing of the past, it absorbed and then radiated heat in a way that made tasks like searing meat or browning onions seem rewarding rather than tedious, especially since the results were so compellingly delicious. This pot and I had such rapport that after I had used it a few times, I felt I would never want to cook with anything else. All of a sudden, Matt and I found ourselves eating chowder or cioppino, a variety of curries, butterbean soup, or hoppin' John almost every night—dishes that seemed conceived for no other purpose than for me to take that pot through its paces. Finally, I had my pot as well as my knife. My kitchen was complete.

❈ ❈ ❈

Cooks, at least serious cooks, can be roughly divided into two major groups: pot cooks and knife cooks. Of course, each sort uses both implements; it is a matter of which serves as the lodestone of their kitchen—the piece of cookware that, in case of a fire, they would run to rescue first.

There is no doubt that I am a knife cook. While I may have always yearned for the right pot, I actually *needed* the right knife to find myself as a cook. Even today, if I reached under the counter and found my favorite pot missing, I would groan, yes, but I would have no trouble using another one. Take away my knife, however, and all my kitchen skills would go flitting out the window.

The existential philosopher Jean-Paul Sartre once posed a gnomic query that went something like this: "Pierre has a knife. Every year he replaces the blade; every other year he replaces the handle. What, then, is Pierre's knife?" My own experience has given me the answer to this puzzle: my knife is what I reach for when I need to do some cutting. Because, at this point, I am no longer reaching for a thing but reconnecting to a relationship—a relationship that remains more or less the same even if the knife itself has not.

Some time ago I retired that original utility knife. The same metal that could be honed sharp enough to shave with also stained the moment it touched a tomato, rusted if not dried immediately after washing, and gave any onion it sliced the faint taste of metal. When knives made of a new high-carbon stainless steel appeared on the market, with blades that could be kept sharp by regular honing and that were far less vulnerable to everyday use, I searched one out that also felt right—although it looked nothing like the one it was replacing—and retired the older knife to the kitchen drawer. John's knife is different now, but it is also the same: a sturdy, honest worker in whose company I feel entirely at ease.

When Matt introduced her collection of pots into my life, she also brought a handsome set of fully forged German-made knives. I was ecstatic; I had always longed to have such a set of blades. But it was too late. To my complete surprise, I simply never reached for one and, years later, still have not. A knife, it turned out, was a commitment as much as a possession, a true partner. That utility knife isn't the only knife I use, but it is without question the source of my confidence as a cook. If I have it with me, I can make myself at home in any kitchen; without it, I feel like a stranger in my own.

However, to say that I am a knife cook is to tell only part of the story. The truth is, I had a lot of growing up to do before I understood what a good pot was all about. It is about cooking, to be sure, but it is also about patience, about resolving things through mediation, about taking the time to get something just right. The better a pot, the less it can be hurried.

Knives, on the other hand, are about cutting the Gordian knot. They offer immediate gratification, the opportunity to make decisions first and live with the consequences later. The sharper the knife, the quicker that choice is made—almost quicker than thought itself.

Push the pot in the direction of the knife and you get the skillet, cooking over high heat, with all the attendant risk and showy results. Push the knife toward the pot, on the other hand, and you get the spatula, a tool whose edge cleaves without cutting, gentles rather than rips things apart.

Each cook finds the tools that pull their temperament and their kitchen work into some sort of synchrony. I have always been an anxious and impatient person, and this was especially so when I was young. That sharp carbon-steel knife allowed me to grasp anxiety by the handle and point it away from me. I tended to agonize over decisions; here was something that made them for me, lickety-split. To pick up a carrot and cut it into bite-sized chunks was to confront a series of choices, however inconsequential, and resolve them immediately, chop, chop, chop.

Of course, being young, I didn't realize that grabbing anxiety by its handle is like getting a tiger by the tail—the sense of relief is only momentary. There is an old saw that the most dangerous knife in the kitchen is the dull one, and while that has some truth to it, it is not really true. In most kitchens, almost all the knives are dull, and for good reason—a sharp knife can get you into trouble very quickly. I did get into trouble, all the time. But the worst cuts I gave myself—two scars I still bear after fifteen years—came from sharpening my knife, an act that required being careful of my knife and myself at the same time. I was never all that good at either task: the two together were an open invitation to catastrophe.

Some part of me must have known this almost from the start. An uncle of mine had once gone into a butcher's shop and fallen in love with a saberlike knife the butcher was using to dismember a carcass. My uncle bought it out of his hand. Years later, when I found it buried away in my grandparents' cellar, I begged and pleaded until he gave it to me. However, while I have carried it proudly from one kitchen to the next ever since, it has always remained carefully wrapped up and stored away. Here, for once, I recognized the tiger right away.

With my own knife, things were never so clear. Even so, my protective instincts eventually edged their way in. When I replaced that knife with the one made of high-carbon stainless steel, I managed not to notice that, while I could get this new knife sharp, I could never get it *fiercely* sharp. And, as I became accustomed to wielding a less dangerous blade, I began to fall into the tempo set by the new pot. Happiness for me is now somewhere between the two: perhaps one day I'll wake up and grasp the fact that, really, what I am is a skillet-and-spatula cook.

Even so, sharp knives continue to thrill me. Recently, I happened upon my first knife, which, over the years, had worked its way to the back of the knife drawer. Picking it up, I felt as if I were pressing the hand of a long lost friend. How well it fit into my palm. How solid it was. How naturally my fingers closed around its handle. I brought it into the workroom, clamped it into a vise, and scrubbed the metal with a wire brush until the rust was gone and the blade glistened in that nacreous way peculiar to carbon steel. Then I took out the sharpening stone and stroked back the edge that, tested too firmly, will slice the thumb.

As I stood there, turning the blade to catch the sunlight, I found myself swept back to the moment at the Bazar Français when I first laid eyes on it and felt that flash of intense and covetous desire. Despite all I had learned about myself since, I was still glad that this hot-wired adolescent was about to purchase that knife—and that, many years later, I would inherit it from him. I will be honored to have it . . . even if I'm pretty certain that these days I won't find much occasion to put it to use.

PERFECT RICE

※ ※ ※

For most of my cooking life, I paid hardly any attention at all to ordinary rice, except that I thought I did a good job of making it. Early on, I used converted rice, not because I liked it especially but because it kept in all those "essential" vitamins—Wonder Rice—and because I had somehow imbibed the idea that rice, real rice, was difficult to make. Then, during a stretch when I was pinching every dime, I switched over to plain, supermarket-label long-grain rice. This rice was not only much cheaper, it also tasted better. Like frozen vegetables, converted rice has a vague "cooked" taste; all its flavor edges have been rubbed away in some distant processing plant. By comparison, even bargain-basement ordinary rice had a noticeably sweeter, brighter taste.

Consequently, when money started coming in again, I switched, not back to Uncle Ben's but to various premium brands of standard American long-grain rice—Carolina, River, Alma—and stayed with them. I made this rice by following the instructions on the package, performing the ritual so often that I knew the formula by heart: one cup of rice, two cups of water, a tablespoon of butter, a teaspoonful of salt. And so the years went.

Then, one evening after Matt moved permanently into my life, we had my friend Dave over for supper. I don't remember what we cooked up that night, except that it was served with rice. As I was dishing this out over at the kitchen counter, Dave said to Matt, "You know, all the years I've known him, John's always made perfect rice." I glanced over at Matt, expecting, I guess, to see a faint flush of pride or, at least, an assenting nod. Instead, I was just in time to catch, flitting across her face, a look of sheer incredulity.

I was dumbfounded. I looked down at the fluffy white stuff on the plates in front of me and poked it with the serving spoon. So, what was I doing wrong?

❀ ❀ ❀

There are over one hundred varieties of rice grown in Burma. . . . Their price and taste vary. *Nga kywe* is the most expensive and the easiest to digest. It is the favorite for the table of the wealthy. *Nga sein*, which has a harder texture when cooked and is less expensive, is eaten by the farmers. *Londei* is the hardest and cheapest and mainly used in feeding the inmates of prisons and livestock. Many of the other varieties, such as the sweet, pink, and black rices, are used in making snacks and confections.
  —Aung Aung Taik, *Under the Golden Pagoda*

Matt and I were then in the process of integrating our rather different cooking styles. Consequently, when we had dishes like rice and peas or tripe gumbo or dirty rice, I made the rice; when we had other dishes, like a vegetable curry or a kedgeree, Matt made it. Or rather, she made basmati rice, which she much preferred to American long-grain rice—certainly, at least, to my version of it.

Early in her wonderful book on the rice culture of the Carolinas, *The Carolina Rice Kitchen*, Karen Hess explains what she intends by the phrase "rice kitchen." It is meant to capture less a body of particular dishes than the almost spiritual presence that a much loved and entirely depended-on ingredient can have for a cook, serving as the basic ground in which all the other cooking in the kitchen has its roots and in relation to which it finds its meaning.

Ours is not and never can become such a kitchen, even if we wanted this. But when I read that phrase the image immediately came to me of Matt preparing rice. I saw her bent over the spread-out kernels and carefully sorting through them, grain by grain, picking out the tiny pebbles, the strange-looking seeds, the discolored and broken grains, and the dead (and sometimes not-so-dead) insects. Following this came the washing and soaking rituals, which sluiced away every trace of the stale bran dust and excess milky-white rice starch. Finally, she carefully calibrated the amount of water to add to the cooking pot. When the rice was done the pot was completely dry, the rice itself light, delicate, and fluffy, a collation of distinct and tender grains as different as day is from night to the dense, gummy stuff I made.

Talking to her about it I discovered that her devotion to all this sprang from something more than her natural fastidiousness. She found it calming, even pleasurable, this sorting. Picking through the rice meant not only removing the detritus but establishing an anticipatory connection with the rest. Raw rice has a lovely translucency and rolls under the fingers with the soothing smoothness of abacus beads. To try to put this experience into words is to exaggerate it, she said; it's something that, doing it, you just feel. Even so, it was clear she felt an affinity to rice that I did not. And her complete absorption while preparing it made me, for the first time, begin paying attention myself.

What there was to pay attention to, however, wasn't at first exactly clear. I was already curious about "gourmet" rices like Italian arborio and Asian fragrant rices. But rice itself—the plain, unparticularized fluffy white stuff—was always in the background of my imagination the way it was in my meals, like a slice of sandwich loaf in a peanut butter and jelly sandwich.

In a way, that was the price I paid, coming from a culture so absurdly wealthy that it lacks an essential starch to connect all the basic dishes of its cuisine, framing them within its own distinctive taste. For the Chinese—at least those who come from southern China—that grain is so central, so much the meal, and what is served with it merely the enhancements, that, as E. N. Anderson writes in *The Food of China*:

> the phrase *chih fan* (to eat rice) also means simply "to eat," and the word *fan* (cooked rice, cooked grain) also means simply "food." A southerner who has not eaten rice all day will deny having eaten at all, although he or she may have consumed a large quantity of snacks. A meal without rice just isn't a meal. . . . [A meal] is made up of cooked rice and *sung* . . . , a Cantonese word that may best be translated as "topping for rice" or "dishes to put on the rice." *Sung* includes everything else, all combined into dishes that are, indeed, put on the rice (and in a poor-to-ordinary home are little more than flavorings for it).

If I got hungry an hour after eating in a Chinese restaurant, it was because, ordering some *fan* with my *sung*, I had got the thing the wrong way around. That tiny bowl of rice that came with the roast duck and chicken with cashews and vegetable *moo shi* was ordered out of politeness, a bit of "When in Rome . . ." I hadn't come there to eat rice; I didn't even particularly want it. Consequently, reading that the average Chinese still nourished by the traditional cuisine eats *eight cups* of cooked white rice a day, I unreflectively imagined the stuff as a kind of undifferentiated starchy filler crammed down out of sheer, driving hunger.

This, of course, reveals a naïve (but still embarrassing) cultural prejudice. It never occurred to me that such a Chinese eater might actually look to the texture, flavor, and aroma of rice for the same aesthetic nourishment that I had come to search for in a piece of bread, and, furthermore, might find it there. Having fought my way to that relationship with my daily bread, you would think that by extension this connection would be obvious. But no, if life teaches us anything, it is that such provincialisms must be uprooted one by stubborn one.

Indeed, as I was about to discover, a forest of cultural confusion stood between me and that simple bowl of perfect boiled rice. Matt, reading Julie Sahni, had spent months mastering the art of preparing basmati rice, a naturally perfumed (the word in Hindi literally means "queen of fragrance") long-grain rice with a distinctive "tender spongy" (Julie Sahni's phrase) texture. Although I didn't confess this to her for some time, I was finding it very hard to accept basmati rice as rice. For me, it was always "*basmati* rice." When this finally spilled out, I had to admit further—still more cultural chauvinism—that its sandalwood-tinged aroma and ephemeral texture vaguely irritated me. Basmati seemed to me the rice of a thin people; all fragrance and ephemerality. I wanted our house rice—our rice—to have *body* to it, the familiar, firm resiliency of American long-grain rice.

So, after bringing into the open this secret ambivalence that existed between us—my uncomfortableness with her rice and hers with mine— we were faced with either pursuing a two-rice cuisine or finding a rice and a way of cooking it that brought to table the qualities that both of us wanted from that grain. So, together, we plunged into several months of experiment, trials . . . and errors.

❧ ❧ ❧

The English, or rather the Anglo-Indian, method of boiling rice is more laborious but less likely to yield a glutinous mess. Set on your stove three large vessels of water. When all are boiling cast the rice into the first. Ten minutes later drain the partially cooked grains in a colander. Wash them with the boiling contents of the second pot and then put them into the third to complete their cooking.

—Peter Gray, *The Mistress Cook*

Plain boiled long-grain rice*: how can something be easy to do if almost every cook insists on a different—sometimes *entirely* different— way of preparing it? Pick up a handful of cookbooks and you experience a riot of conflicting instructions. I don't think there's a single step in making rice where you will not find one instruction countermanded by its opposite, argued with equal authority. Wash/don't wash; wash before cooking/wash after cooking; cook in lots of water/cook in just enough water; cook for a long time/cook for a short time . . . and on and on.

Compare rice with pasta, a basic starch that comes with its cooking method already built in. You don't need a cookbook to teach you how to prepare spaghetti. It cooks up fast, it cooks up easy, and it cooks up right. That is why there's no such thing as Minute Pasta or Success Pasta. And it is also why no one tells you what a snap it is to cook. You already know.

Cooking also follows the laws of evolution: successful methods crowd out all others. If there's no simple method for cooking rice, it isn't because the right genius hasn't yet come along to set us straight (there are already too many vying for *that* role), but because rice cooking is attempting the unnatural. It means to force those grains of rice to do something they don't particularly want to do.

If you come from a non-rice-cooking culture and trust your instinct to cook rice right, your instinct will let you down. Toss a handful of those tiny, pearlescent grains into a pot of boiling water and let them do their thing, and the grains become not soft but soggy. Pressed gently with a finger, they collapse to mush. Measure the water so that the grains absorb it all while cooking, and you get that familiar dense, gummy, sticky mass.

What, though, is wrong with that? Abstractly—nothing. The

---

*Long-grain rice is "plain" rice to most non-Asian Americans; short-grain rice requires a very different kind of cooking and so is outside the reach of this discussion.

French, for instance, cultural chauvinists from birth, seem quite happy with it: their description of perfectly cooked rice is *crevé*, or (to translate roughly) "burst." Taste rice prepared by someone who knows what they're doing, however, and your ignorance will lose its bliss. Well-made rice is something else again.

Still, it isn't all that easy to say what, exactly, that "something else" is. The best way to approach it, I think, is to answer an implicit question that has been hovering over this text from the start: why *white* rice at all? I know that readers convinced of the superiority of the unpolished grain have already started muttering, "Brown rice is natural, it is more nutritious, it is obviously less tampered with, and it has more flavor than polished rice."

All these things are true. The problem is that brown rice is also not really rice. Plain boiled rice has become, like bread, an artifact of culture, as much idea as thing. Brown rice, on the other hand, is just another edible seed—one among many equivalent grains that fill the bins of the natural foods shop: barley, millet, rye, and wheat berries, not to mention such exotics as spelt, quinoa, kamut, and hato mugi. Those who find our civilization too much for them turn to such foods as a portal to an unsullied, primal world. But the Thai or Gambian or Chinese peasant who becomes prosperous enough to set aside the coarse, rough stuff for the refined does so to acquire identity with their culture: white rice wraps the family meal with connection to the common way. For them, white rice is a doorway *in*.

This connection is at the heart of what rice is all about. And for the participating cooks of a rice culture, shared agreement on what rice should be lifts its preparation out of the realm of merely boiling and propels it into the platonic. To cook rice correctly requires not only patience and skill but an abstract conception of an idealized form. In perfectly cooked rice, to let one expert speak for all, "each grain is separate and dry, yet tender, not gummy or sticky."

Taken literally, these familiar adjectives most *exactly* describe Quaker puffed rice, or, for that matter, Rice Krispies. In rice cooking, these terms serve to create a tension between what the rice wants to do and what the cook persuades it to do. It is the vegetable equivalent of dingo becoming dog. (This, by the way, is why the dullness of instant rice extends beyond its taste; it is all obedience, its rice spirit broken instead of tamed.)

Every rice culture has its own definition of perfect rice. For the South Carolina cook, the cooked grains literally pour out of the pan like popcorn. For the Chinese cook, they are similarly individually distinct, whole, and dry, but they also hold together, so that the fingers, or chopsticks, can pluck them up in a bite-sized clump. For the Thai or Indian cook, the ideal rice is transcendentally light and soft—and the talented rice cook can take the longest, most fragile grains and cook them until exquisitely moist and tender, but still unbroken and unburst. All these are results that truly deserve that ultimate accolade.

We Americans have no such cultural consensus, which is why our notion of perfect rice is so murky and undefined—and the directions in our cookbooks so contrary. After all, much of the ritual surrounding rice is only superficially about its making. There is a short Japanese nursery rhyme about rice:

Hajimé choro choro	First it bubbles
Naka pa ppa	Then it hisses
Akago naité mo	Even if baby is crying
Futa toru na.	Don't remove the lid.*

On the surface, this is a neat little onomatopoetic lesson in rice cooking (listen carefully and never peek under the lid, even if baby is wailing for its breakfast), but the Japanese housewife who, plugging in the electric rice cooker, chants it to her daughter is really instructing that little girl (and reminding herself) *how nice it is to be Japanese*—and, consequently, how comforting it is, doing this most Japanese of tasks.

We have no such little songs. No part of our American identity is bound to rice. Trying to prepare it, we have no established standards to absorb, no accepted method with which to test our mettle against our neighbor's, no firmly fixed feelings about texture and taste that we want our own rice pot to produce. We don't even, most of us, *have* a rice pot. In other words, we share no oneness through our rice. And so we don't—excepting a few Southerners, many of them black—understand the first thing about cooking it.

---

*Quoted, with slight adaptation, from Elizabeth Andoh's *At Home with Japanese Cooking*.

❧ ❧ ❧

> Unlike spaghetti and potatoes, which have their devoted fanciers
> in lands to which neither is indigenous, rice must be lived with to
> be loved—and well cooked. In non-rice-producing regions the
> grain is a poor thing poorly dealt with, and the passion for it
> which unites all people to whom it has been the cornerstone of
> family life is never quite understood or even believed by outsiders.
> —Sheila Hibben, *A Kitchen Manual*

Well, what is one to do? I knew for sure that I didn't want to build my
rice cooking either on an arbitrary recipe or on a romanticized identifi-
cation with some arbitrarily chosen rice culture/kitchen. So what I
turned to for help was the basic artisanal sense of *task*. Make it simple
by making it particular: what can I do with *this* rice, *this* rice pot, *this*
need, *this* temperament? In other words, to learn to make some facsimile of perfect rice, I had to learn to anchor it to my life.

My starting point was Alma, our choice of the supermarket brands
of long-grain rice. It had the texture I wanted but not the aroma or
taste. We set out to discover which American rice—if any—might possess all three. Soon, the UPS truck began rolling up the driveway with
sacks of rice from Arkansas, Texas, and Louisiana, some sent directly
from rice mills, others from the actual growers.

Simultaneously, we worked on method. We ransacked the literature
and tried out the most appealing-sounding of the techniques, including
Elizabeth David's method of boiling the rice and then putting it,
casseroled and buttered, to dry out in the oven. They all worked well
enough, but none of them produced rice equal to Matt's basmati. The
problem, I gradually realized, was that I wanted to simply follow a set
of instructions, whereas what was required of me was to establish a
close working relationship with a particular cooking vessel—my personal rice pot.

Although it would, in fact, become a pot almost solely devoted to
rice-making, that designation as "rice pot" came from the fact that I
chose it because its shape and weight somehow spoke directly to the
point. I walked up and down the aisle of the kitchen-equipment store,
hefting one pot after another, until a one-and-a-half-quart Calphalon
saucepan made of heavy anodized aluminum, with a tight-fitting glass
lid, spoke out to me, simply and directly: "I can make your rice." I believed it, bought it, and brought it home.

The fact that it *is* a very good pot made my work all the easier—an authentic workhorse, its solidity gave me confidence and its stolidity posed no problems of intervening temperament. Having it as my constant, I learned to be increasingly stingy with the water and more aggressive in the cooking than I had before found nerve to be. Because American cooking shares no common rice pot, rice-cooking directions always counsel moderation—but in this instance, moderation leads to mush.

When I began my exploration of rice, I happened to be baking all the bread we ate. This task required continual consideration, which, in turn, meant a slow accretion of observed detail. Part of the pleasure of eating your own bread lies in contemplating the result of today's efforts, in comparing the crust, texture, and taste of this loaf with the one made yesterday or the day before, which, in turn, brings to mind other flours, other approaches, other loaves.

The same is true with rice. In ways that matter as much as they are hard to quantify, it has gained increasing substance, presence, weight. For an inattentive eater sitting down to dinner at our table, the difference most likely would elicit no more than an appreciative grunt. However, for us, now, the shared discussion of choice of rice and the gradual articulation of a method have lent a quiet but deeply pleasing richness to the meal.

Perhaps our favorite rice right now is the long-grain Della-type grown in Cajun country and called popcorn rice after its familiar aroma (the two share a highly aromatic chemical compound). To our surprise, we found that distinctions could be made between batches of the rice grown in neighboring parishes; they were all delicious, but in subtly contrasting ways. Now when the rice is done, I bring Matt a forkful from the pot, and we taste it together consideringly, the way the mouth works a first sip of wine.

When the rice is good, this tasting is an act of unmitigated pleasure. Part of it, of course, is just whetted anticipation of the meal, but there's something else there, too . . . only more difficult to explain. Dingo into dog—that connection wasn't gratuitous. A dog acquires dogness learning to sit, shake hands, roll over, and other, similar dumb pet tricks. When I got my dog Mick to sit and shake hands (rolling over was beneath his dignity), I felt silly with pleasure—exactly how I felt when I first lifted the lid of that Calphalon pot and saw that the rice had *risen up* of its own accord into a white and fluffy mound.

With Mick, as with rice, I wasn't showing my talents as a trainer (negligible) or his at accepting discipline (laughable)—or even the bond between us (he would do the same for anyone who offered him a biscuit). No, I was simply delighting in what I can only call his "dogness"—in which at that moment I was somehow allowed to participate. That is what the phrase "my dog" is really all about. In the same way, when I bring Matt a forkful of rice at the end of cooking, what we both delight in is neither my rice-cooking talents nor the savor of the thing but—what else can I call it?—its *riceness*. Our rice—we, together, have somehow managed once again to pull off the trick. And now, at least as far as Matt is concerned, I know how to make a pot of perfect rice.

PERFECT RICE

The grain seems to invite controversy. The fight over the proper way to cook it—covered or uncovered, in lots of water or a little, stirred or unstirred—is still being fought. The didactic tone of those instructing others on how to cook rice is evident in the voice of Charles Gayarré, a gourmet writing in the 1880s about an old southern cook: "Who but Valentin knew how to bake rice in an iron pot? I say *iron*, because it must be nothing else, and that rice must come out solid, retaining the exact shape of the pot, with a golden crust about its top and sides."
—*Woman's Day Encyclopedia of Cookery*, Vol. 10

According to Karen Hess, the first rule of good rice cooking is not *over*cooking. Perfectly cooked long-grain rice is tender but resilient, faintly sticky but not gluey or mushy. She also insists that the rice must be left unmolested during its recovery time. This is similar to letting a roast "sit" after it's been brought out of the oven, so that the juices can redistribute themselves throughout the meat. In the rice pot, this resting time allows the moisture to penetrate to the center of each kernel and the excess to evaporate, producing firm-textured, separate grains.

Whether Karen Hess would approve of our method or its results is something we'll discover only should we ever have her over for supper. For us, though, it does the trick. Even so, I want to stress again that every instruction that follows was built on our growing familiarity with our own rice pot. So far as your own "perfect" rice is concerned, surely the right approach is to get a basic grasp of the issues involved and to work them out after your own fashion and to your own satisfaction, and at your own pace.

A BEGINNER'S GUIDE TO RICE

> Anyone from the south of India should be able to recognize at least twenty sorts in the bazaar, rices which differ not only in such obvious characteristics as whether they are long or short grain, polished or unpolished, raw or parboiled, but also in colour, translucency, smell, age, cooking quality and, of course, price.
> —Tom Stobart, *The Cook's Encyclopedia*

All the rices that are most commonly eaten around the world come from the Asian variety *Oryza sativa*. This rice is usually divided into two major groups: indica rices, such as basmati and jasmine, which are more fragile-grained and often fragrant; and japonica rices, which have sturdier, plumper grains and are more tolerant of cold weather and so can be grown in more temperate climates. (A third group, javanica, consists of tropical rices, mostly grown in Indonesia.) Whether a rice is short-, medium-, or long-grain is dependent less on type than on the length of the growing season. Similarly, "sticky," or glutinous, rice may be long-grain or short-grain, indica or japonica.

Arborio and other Italian japonica rices, such as *baldo* and *carnaroli*, are discussed in detail elsewhere in this book (see pages 65–66). Spanish rices, such as Valencia, are very similar to these risotto rices.

Basmati rice, grown in the foothills of the Himalayas in northern India and Pakistan, is the perfumy, fragile, long-grain indica rice most associated with Indian cooking. Dehra Dun is considered the choicest; patna is the more abundant and less expensive, although connoisseurs consider it to be not quite as good. American-grown basmati rice (such as Calmati) is acceptable but does not completely capture native basmati's unique aroma or texture.

Brand names to the contrary, there hasn't been a commercial rice crop grown in South Carolina since 1927. With it went the distinctive Carolina Gold, which had made the word *Carolina* a synonym for quality rice. Said to have originated in Madagascar, it is a fragile long-grain variety described as possessing a distinct if delicate flavor, firm texture, and astonishing whiteness. Recently, Richard and Patricia Schulze persuaded the United States Department of Agriculture, after a hiatus of more than sixty years, to propagate authentic Carolina Gold from the grains stored in its seed bank in order to bring it back into cultivation on their plantation on the Savannah River. The Schulzes grow the rice as an avocation and donate their tiny crop to charity.

Della is an American cross between basmati and standard long-grain American rice. When cooked properly, it produces a fluffy-textured rice with dry and separate grains. Della is often sold as Louisiana "pecan" or Louisiana "popcorn" rice, because its distinctive aroma (but not its taste) is uncannily reminiscent of those two foods.

Japanese rice is of the japonica type, medium-grain and slightly translucent. When cooked, the grains are distinct and firm but slightly sticky. (This rice absorbs much less water than other kinds, which can be confusing to those accustomed to preparing indica-type rices.) Japan does not export its rice; the Japanese-style rice available in America is grown in California. Preferred brands include Kokuho Rose, CalRose, Nishiki, and Matsu. Sushi rice is cooked Japanese rice delicately seasoned with rice vinegar and sugar.

Jasmine is an aromatic, long-grain indica rice native to Cambodia, Vietnam, and Thailand, which export large quantities to this country. Introduced to American rice farmers in 1989, it is now grown in Texas and California. When properly prepared, it possesses a spongier, slightly stickier texture than Della or basmati, but its cooked grains are still firm and easy to separate.

Sticky rice has a predominance of amylopectin, a rice starch that becomes gummy when cooked, causing the grains to adhere. Sticky rice is easy to eat with the fingers because it can be gathered in clumps; the same quality—along with its sweeter taste—makes it perfect for a wide variety of Asian rice pastries. The sticky rice grown in warmer areas, like Thailand, is long-grain; that grown in more temperate areas, like Japan, is short-grain.

PLAIN BOILED RICE
[*serves 2 to 4*]

1 cup (6 ounces) long-grain white rice
1½ cups minus 2 tablespoons (11 fluid ounces) water
¾ teaspoon salt

Choosing the Rice. Although Indians believe that aged rice increases in flavor (and, consequently, let some develop for as long as ten years), in our experience—with rice as with flour—the fresher it comes from the mill, the brighter the flavor notes. Age also affects the amount of water needed to cook it.

Choosing the Rice Pot. Here is Diana Kennedy on this subject, as set out in *The Art of Mexican Cooking*:

> Choose a heavy pot for cooking the rice; it will be less likely to scorch on the bottom. The shape of the pot is also important; if it is too wide, the water will cook off too quickly and the rice will not be as tender; if it is too deep, it is liable to be mushy at the bottom.

As noted, we use a Calphalon one-and-a-half-quart saucepan with a tight-fitting lid.

Sorting the Rice. Matt finds all sorts of detritus (seeds, pebbles, chaff, insects, and, mostly, damaged and discolored grains) in the rice we use, especially when it is processed in small, old-fashioned mills. Spread the rice out on a paper towel and look for yourself.

Rinsing the Rice. Washing rice rinses away polish dust, bran particles, starch, and sprayed-on vitamin powder, so that the grain's own subtle favors can come through. Barbara Tropp argues—and our experience confirms—that mere swishing under running water accomplishes nothing; you have to give it a good *wash*. Pour the rice into a small sieve and insert this into a bowl. Fill the bowl with cold water and stir the rice with your fingers until the water is milky. Lift up the sieve, pour off this liquid, refill the bowl with fresh cold water, and repeat several times, until the water stays clear and the rice grains are translucent.

Cooking the Rice. Again, the secret to perfect rice cooking is to cook the rice aggressively and quickly, so that the grains are given just enough time to swell and soften but not to begin breaking up. Different writers have different strong feelings about when that moment is; I have taken my time from H. Pearl Adam. I add the salt and washed rice to the water, bring everything to a brisk boil, cover the pot, and lower the flame to the point where the tiniest amount of additional heat would cause the pot to bubble over (to make sure this is so, I follow the hint supplied by our electric-rice-cooker experiments and *let* it boil over—just a bit). The rice is allowed to cook in this manner for exactly *12½ minutes*.

Resting the Rice. At this point I remove the pot from the heat, turn the flame down as low as possible, set a flame tamer over the burner, and put the pot back on this. Then, quickly, I remove the cover of the pot, wrap it in a dish towel, and press it back firmly onto the pot, folding the ends of the towel so they sit on top of the pot, out of the way of the burner flame. The rice is allowed to rest for *17½ minutes*, making an even half hour of cooking time. The rice will be dry all through—there should be no wet patch on the bottom of the pot, and hardly any rice stuck to it, either. The rice in the lower part of the pot will be compressed, but not soggy or damp. It will easily fluff up when turned out of the pot into a serving bowl. The result is about 3 cups of cooked rice.

RICE WITH SPINACH, GOAT CHEESE, AND WALNUTS
[for each eater]

It seems unfair to devote a whole chapter of a book to cooking rice without sharing at least one of the dishes we make that pushes it to center stage. Interestingly, once we began to look forward to the rice itself, the things we ate on it or with it began to reformulate themselves to accommodate our anticipation. Unlike pasta, which can handle a slightly soupy sauce, there's no point in preparing a bowl of fluffy rice and then drowning it in a sea of cooking liquid. For us, the ideal rice topping contains a nice mix of complementary tastes and textures, the whole ensemble just moist enough to balance off the delicate dryness of the grain. The following dish spontaneously presented itself as one possible resolution of that equation—and the recipe has been written to sustain its impromptu nature.

6 to 8 walnut halves
1 bunch (or 12-ounce bag) fresh spinach—frozen not
   acceptable (see note)
plain white rice, cooked as in preceding recipe
1 clove garlic
olive oil
generous pinch salt
generous pinch powdered chile (see note)
1½ to 2 ounces fresh goat cheese
freshly ground black pepper to taste

Preliminary to the cooking, toast the walnut halves in a small cast-iron frying pan or similar ovenproof pan in a preheated 450°F oven for about 10 minutes, or until they have darkened in color and become quite fragrant. (Don't burn them, but do *toast* them.) Turn them out onto a cutting board. Meanwhile, pick over the spinach, discarding any less-than-perfect leaves and, with a sharp paring knife, trimming away all split and damaged ends of stems. Rinse carefully in 2 or 3 sinkfuls of cool water, to remove all grit. Place directly, dripping with water from the last rinse, into a large pot, and cover.

At this point, begin cooking the rice.

Put the pot with the spinach on a burner and cook over high heat until it is completely wilted, about 3 or 4 minutes after the water comes to a boil. Empty the pot into a colander or sieve set over a bowl. Press firmly with a rubber spatula or the back of a wooden spoon to remove all excess liquid. (Pour this liquid into a cup, season, and enjoy—cook's treat.) Turn pressed spinach out onto the cutting board.

In 3 separate piles, coarsely chop the spinach and walnut meats and coarsely mince the garlic. Pour some olive oil into a 10-inch nonstick skillet and add a generous pinch each of salt and chile powder. Turn the heat under the frying pan to medium-low. As soon as the olive oil becomes warm, stir in the garlic. Cook, stirring, until the garlic becomes translucent. Immediately add the chopped spinach and mix together well. Turn off the heat as soon as the spinach is heated through.

Serve each portion in a large, warmed soup bowl. Put in a fair portion of the rice, top with the spinach mixture, and over this sprinkle the walnut pieces and crumbled fresh goat cheese. Season with a generous grinding of black pepper and eat at once.

Cook's Notes. Chile: We regularly use a vibrantly flavored but only mildly hot New Mexican chile powder called Chimayo in our cooking. An Internet search should turn up a number of sources; at the time of writing, one of them is, appropriately, www.chimayotogo.com.

Spinach: The amount called for is not a typographical error. When wilted, spinach leaves shrink down to almost nothing—that is, if you like spinach. And if you don't like it, this is not your dish.

ADVENTURES WITH AN ELECTRIC RICE COOKER

We came across so many recommendations urging us to purchase this device during our rice research that we were finally persuaded to order a Chinese model from a mail-order discount firm that specializes in selling off the buying mistakes of other companies at prices too good to refuse. Our unit arrived with a host of accoutrements, including a video tape, which we could not bear to watch, and a set of instructions, written in barely comprehensible *Chinglais*.

Even so, we soon got the hang of its operation. One was to add strictly determined proportions of (carefully washed) rice, water, and salt, plug the thing in (there was no on/off switch), and then stand back while its contents began to boil furiously. Soon the lid was jiggling ominously, the signal, we soon learned, that a steady flow of rice scum would soon be oozing down the side of the machine and creeping across the counter. When, at last, the indicator light changed from "cooking" to "warming" and we removed the cooking insert, we found a thick crust of rice firmly burned onto its bottom and lower sides.

The rest of the rice, however, was the closest we had ever come to preparing genuine Chinese—or, at least, Chinese restaurant—rice. Perhaps our cooker was defective? After a few more experimental runs, each of which resulted in the same behavior, we returned it for another, which behaved in exactly the same way. Our tentative conclusion—as we sheepishly returned this second unit—was that these machines were designed by people who couldn't imagine anyone preparing so *small* an amount of rice as amply feeds us two.

Sources

Ellis Stansel's Rice; P.O. Box 206; Gueydan, LA 70542; (318) 536-6140; www.stanselrice.com. When Ellis Stansel was alive, his Louisiana popcorn rice was the best American rice we've tasted, possessing a superlative texture and an elegantly balanced flavor. However, since his death in 1994, while the rice tastes just as good, the milling, in our experience, has not been nearly as expert. The Stansel family still likes to do business on a personal basis, sending orders with an invoice enclosed. When this book went to press, a ten-pound sack of rice was $10 plus shipping.

Guillory's Louisiana Popcorn Rice; Route 3, Box 55; Welsh, LA 70591; (318) 734-4440. Paul and Anne Guillory's Louisiana popcorn rice had the most distinctly "popcorn" aroma of the varieties we sampled, and it is also the one most likely to be found in local gourmet and natural foods stores. However, you'll get a better price if you order straight from the source. When this book went to press, a five-pound sack of their rice was $5.95 plus shipping.

Lowell Farms; 311 Avenue A; El Campo, TX 77437; (409) 543-4950; www.lowellfarms.com. The organically grown jasmine rice produced by Linda and Lowell G. Raun, Jr., is something special. The grains are almost uniformly perfect, the aroma has delicate floral notes, and the rice cooks dry and slightly sticky—a classic "rice bowl" rice. At the time this book went to press, a twenty-five-pound sack of their jasmine rice (white or brown) was $20 plus $9.95 shipping.

Further Reading

Anyone interested in learning to cook rice should start by reading the chapter "To Boil the Rice" in Karen Hess's *The Carolina Rice Kitchen* (pages 22–35). Karen Hess bestows her insatiable curiosity, articulate attention, and fastidious palate to this task, with the result that no reader will leave her book with complacencies intact.

Barbara Tropp's advocacy of the creamy texture and pleasing plumpness of short-grain rice is only one reason to turn to the rice cooking section in *The Modern Art of Chinese Cooking* (pages 399–404); she, too, brings a passionate intelligence to many aspects of the rice kitchen.

Julie Sahni presents the case for basmati and explains its cooking in *Classic Indian Cooking* (pages 355–361), adding some interesting and useful amplifications in her later *Classic Indian Vegetarian and Grain Cooking* (pages 56–60 and 411–415).

Diana Kennedy has a characteristically crisp and informative section on the subject in her *Art of Mexican Cooking* (pages 119–124).

Although the Japanese also prefer short-grain to long-grain rice, Elizabeth Andoh's charming commentary on rice cooking in *At Home with Japanese Cooking* (pages 68–72) is equally applicable to both.

The section on basic rice cooking in *Dried Beans & Grains*, edited by Richard Olney (pages 22–23), demonstrates three different methods, with detailed color photographs that further augment the lucid text.

Two rice cookbooks of special note are Sri Owen's *The Rice Book*, which has a fascinating introductory section on the large part rice has played in civilizations past and present, and Jeffrey Alford and Naomi Duguid's travelogue *Seductions of Rice*, with its handsome photographs of (and locally gathered recipes from) contemporary rice cultures around the world.

Finally, Tom Stobart gives a world tour of rice types, dishes, and cooking methods in *The Cook's Encyclopedia* (pages 345–350). It's just another example of why that book holds a primary place on our culinary reference shelf.

KNOWING NOTHING ABOUT WINE

❧ ❧ ❧

I've been drinking wine, off and on, for decades now, but until recently the relationship was a difficult one—a few pleasurable moments floating like flotsam in a dark sea of disappointment. For the longest time, I thought the problem lay in the wine itself. But I have gradually come to realize that, instead, it lies within me and that what kept me from coming to terms with it can only be called an especially tenacious ignorance.

Perhaps the ideal way to get to know wine is as a child in a household where drinking it is an everyday—by which I mean entirely ordinary—event. If your parents take an unselfconscious sensual delight in drinking it, you naturally imbibe—along with an occasional taste—the assumption that this pleasure is there to be pursued, when you are old enough to do so, to whatever degree you choose.

In my own family, wine was almost never present at our table. My parents weren't hostile to wine, but having it as an everyday dinner companion was a foreign notion. Instead, wine signaled an event: company dinners (to which we children were not invited) and family occasions, like Thanksgiving or Easter dinner, where its presence was an aspect of ritual and so possessed no intrinsic interest—no more than did the tiny sip I took when receiving Holy Communion.

Instead, my introduction to wine came from reading books, specifically, as my taste was in my early teens, historical novels. In their pages, I learned that beer and ale were the beverages of peasants, wine the drink of warriors and kings. It was purplish stuff, thick as blood, perfumed and fruity, to be drunk between duels or before bedding buxom chambermaids.

When, a little later, I learned that the best, the highest, sort of wine was not sweet but "dry," that was a word I associated with Canada Dry ginger ale, my favorite soda. Good wine, then, was something more piquant than cloyingly sweet, enlivened, if you were lucky, with a bit of fizz. If someone had given me a taste of Riunite Lambrusco, I would have thought I understood everything. I would also have been in heaven.

However, I did not try that particular wine until it was far too late for such innocent calf love. Rather, the summer before my freshman year in college, Nana—my grandmother—conceived the notion to mark this transition to manhood, or, as she probably thought of it, my first step toward becoming a gentleman, by inaugurating my wine cellar. To this end, every month of that summer and into the following autumn, when she telephoned an order in to S. S. Pierce, a fancy Boston grocer, she concluded by asking the clerk to select a half-bottle of French wine that she could send on to me.

Nana herself took only an infrequent glass of port, and her impression of wine connoisseurship, although slightly more formed than mine, was equally romantic. It was her fantasy that I would cellar these bottles in my dorm closet, where, like me, they would gradually mature until I had reached the legal drinking age. Then I would invite in a friend or two, reach under my dirty sweatshirts, and produce a bottle of, say, Baron Philippe de Rothschild Mouton Cadet, vintage 1957, with a seignorial flourish.

As with most of Nana's ambitions for me, I thwarted this one, too. My freshman college roommate and I faithfully polished off each bottle the moment it arrived. We enjoyed the buzz and thought ourselves a couple of swells. But—although I didn't admit this even to myself—I was truly mystified as to where the pleasure lay. It was nicely alcoholic, but it was also sour and harsh and thin. This must, I thought, be like drinking black coffee or taking your bourbon neat: it required an initiation period. And if college wasn't the place to undergo that, what was?

Looking back after thirty-five years, it seems as though I must have caught an exceptionally virulent cultural virus the moment I stepped on campus. During those four short years, I kept trotting off to the theater to see Brecht and Ionesco, to the concert hall to hear Charles Ives and Milton Babbitt, to the cinema to take in Antonioni and Godard. My meager record collection fattened on the likes of Thelonius Monk and Brahms quintets; my dormitory wall sported a print of a Monet railway station. The cure for this disease, it turned out, was a college diploma—as soon as one was shoved into my hands, the fever started to abate. A year or so later, all that remained to mark its passing were a few barely perceptible scars.

However, while it raged, I discovered that I *liked* making judicious distinctions. Not only did they prove a means of understanding why I preferred some things (Fellini, the Rolling Stones, Brie) over others (Bergman, the Who, Gruyère), but they also offered me a way of pursuing what I did enjoy to depths of pleasure heretofore unknown. For instance, I arrived at college a pipe smoker; I left it a pipe bore. I became fussy about the grain of my briars, I nurtured a meerschaum, and, above all, I took a passionate interest in pipe tobacco, talking from personal experience about such esoterica as Old London Pebble Cut, Three Nuns Spun Discs, and Condor Rubbed-out Leaf.

Consequently, when at last I *did* reach legal drinking age, I began making weekly pilgrimages to the town package store (the wine shipments from my grandmother had long ago dried up), expecting that the same transformation of taste that had happened at the local smoke shop would also happen there. The store devoted an entire wall to French, German, and Italian wines (serious California wines were then all but unknown). I would wander up and down the aisle until some bottle shape or label seemed to intimate that its contents were the right stuff. After staring at this bottle for a moment or two in a state of exquisite hesitation, I would seize it up, assume an expression of casual assurance, and bear it to the cash register.

So it went. My purchases remained completely random, since none of these bottles ever made me want to go back and buy its brother. If I left college feeling some sort of connection to serious art, literature, and cinema, I departed on no such familiar terms with wine. And so, for several years afterward, I lost all interest in it.

❀ ❀ ❀

Then, sometime in the mid-seventies, I got interested in cooking—and, even more, in *reading* about cooking. Several of the writers I was most drawn to—Elizabeth David, Robert Courtine, Richard Olney—made

drinking good wine seem such a necessary part of the pleasures of eating that I felt encouraged—well, really, *obligated*—to try again.

This time, though, I was determined to do it right. I sought out the
best discount wine stores in the city. I subscribed to a wine newsletter.
Finally, I bought a tiny loose-leaf binder into which I could enter lists of
wines to search for and record my tasting notes after I had found and
drunk them. It soon contained page after minuscule page of typed wine
lists, definitions of wine terms, and, of course, those tasting notes. In
fact, I put so much work into creating it that for many years afterward,
despite its total uselessness, I was unable to throw it away.

However, I must finally have done so, since it is now not to be
found. I wanted to quote from it here, not to mock but simply to evoke
the pathos of the would-be enthusiast. I plugged away at it for four
years, until, at last, I *did* taste a wine that I wanted to rush out and buy
again. It was a Chappellet Chardonnay, and it had a completely unexpected effect on my wine drinking—besides revealing to me what utter
dross all those reams of previous jottings were.

Before that bottle of Chardonnay, I thought my ignorance about
wine was a matter of my uneducated palate—of not knowing what to
look for and not knowing what to taste for even if the right bottle happened along. But I had no problem at all experiencing the pleasure
of *this* wine; indeed, I was shaken by its accessibility. There was no
mystery here, no secret code that only the initiate could decipher. Its
delicious complexity was not that of a daunting enigma but of the personality of some newfound best friend.

The thing was, that Chardonnay was also the most expensive bottle
of wine I had ever bought—an act of audacity I knew I would not easily be able to repeat. I realized, all in a flash, what the stakes of this
game really were, and that if I continued to play it in this manner I
might very likely not encounter a bottle like this for *another* four years.
In the span of an hour, I went through all the stages of an unrequited
love affair: astonishment, rapture, bitter disillusionment, despair.

The French philosopher Gaston Bachelard once observed that, despite our persistent belief to the contrary, our ignorance is rarely a
blank slate waiting to be written upon. Instead, it has the assured grip
of deeply felt, fully formed (if unarticulated) assumptions that—no
matter how hard we try to shake them—prove dismayingly durable,
even regarding the simplest things.

So, for instance, while I "know" that the earth circles the sun, my perceptions remain faithful to the naïve egocentricity of my childhood, which locates me in a universe where the earth is the center of all attention, the sun a great beaming parent, and the moon a lovely but coolly indifferent one. One of the sobering lessons of maturity is that our school-taught learning has given us as much power over such ignorance as the lady from Niger had over the tiger upon whose back she had decided to ride.

To expect to drink decent wine regularly, you must have a good memory, more than a little canniness, a willingness to spend lots of money, and, even then, a bit of luck. In other words, what getting your hands on good wine is about, more than vintage or *terroir* or type of grape or proper cellaring or anything else, is knowing yourself. This is because the making of wine—unlike the brewing of beer—is an art, which is to say, an extraordinarily chancy business. Even quite talented vintners, more often than not, find themselves with a wine greatly inferior to the one they produced the year before. When this happens, they don't pour the contents of the huge oak barrels (or stainless-steel tanks) down the drain. They bottle it and hope the reputation of last year's vintage will sell this one, too. The wine merchant racks the new bottles in the same slots that held the ones from the year before and leaves the old review pasted above them. *Caveat emptor.*

Consequently, if you are interested in beer, you can take a hundred dollars and try about a hundred different brews. At the end of that romp, you will not only have discovered quite a few that you like, you can expect them to be waiting there for you to enjoy again and again. Spend the same hundred dollars on wine—no, ten times that amount— and nothing like this will happen. A thousand dollars will certainly buy a hundred bottles of wine; but you will come away from tasting them feeling more confused, more lost, than before. Money can get you through the door of this club, but it won't make you a member.

As it happened, this was a time when I was living on a very limited income, and my interest in cooking was fueled in part by a burgeoning ability to search the supermarket for inexpensive vegetables and cuts of meats that a little culinary expertise could turn into delicious meals. I brought this same mentality with me when I set out to buy wine. I was certain—a certainty reinforced by the wine books I was reading—that there were excellent "undiscovered" wines that could be had for a song. And, in truth, there are such wines; it's just that the odds are as-tronomically against you that any of them are in the markdown bin at your local wine store. Here, as with buying lottery tickets, dogged per-sistence is not a virtue but a vice; it is the identifying mark of a loser.

This was the revelation brought about by that bottle of Chappellet Chardonnay. It so discouraged me that I gave up drinking wine for yet another decade—until, in fact, Matt and I began living together.

❋ ❋ ❋

I wanted to be able to go into a wine store and buy a bottle of good wine on my own recognizance—and it angered me that this was nearly impossible. I was being silly, but I wasn't only being silly. There are many more bad books published every year than good books, and lots of those bad books come with glowing testimonials, ecstatic jacket copy, compelling reviews. But in the bookstore you can open those books and sample enough of the wares to make up your own mind. This has saved me from purchasing countless bad books, and also many *good* books that, while deserving everything that was said about them, were not to my taste. If I am unable to actually handle the book—say, when I'm ordering a title from a catalog or on-line—I often end up not reading it. Or, worse, I compel myself to read it because I've spent good money on it—in other words, just what happens when I buy wine I haven't tasted.

In such situations I, like many another, become vulnerable not only to the blandishments of those wishing to sell me these things but also to the force of my own ignorance. When Matt and I set out to buy wine together, it soon became clear that I would have to deal with the near-desperate impulsiveness that had previously defined my wine buying by confronting those aspects of myself which, despite my best efforts, kept leading me astray.

Money. I have always found it very hard to accept the price of any but the bottles in the bottom rank, which was another reason why my buying excursions usually went awry. This is, I think, the result of my Yankee upbringing: part instinctive parsimony, part the belief that be-fore you spend money you should know—and know that you want—what you are paying for. I don't think that this is necessarily admirable—there are many things in this world that can be appreciated at their fullest only by paying more than the experience is actually worth. But it is such a dominant part of my emotional makeup that instead of pushing on past it, I found it easier to fantasize being a kind of Sam Spade, scouring the mean streets of bargain-bin wines for the vinous equivalent of the Maltese falcon.

Memory. This is even more important to the search for good wine than the willingness to spend money. Of course, an excellent sensual memory—the ability to recall and compare the taste of the last bottle (and the one before that) of Cabernet Sauvignon with the bottle you are drinking now—is an absolute prerequisite of connoisseurship. But in this instance I mean merely the capacity to call up particular bits of data on demand. Successful wine-buying forays require a memory at least agile enough to cross-reference vineyards, vintage years, and grape varieties, and to keep in mind specific recommendations—that bottle of . . . what was it? . . . Domaine Délétang 1995 Montlouis Sec les Batisses? I don't possess this kind of memory; names of any sort fly out of my brain as fast as they fly in. Since I also usually lack the stamina to compensate for this condition by writing everything down and making sure it is easily at hand when needed, I tend to arrive at the wine store with canniness as the sole arrow in my otherwise depressingly empty quiver.

Canniness. This quality, though, if possessed in sufficient measure, can do a lot to make up for a paucity of money and memory. Canniness is looking down under the display bottle into the wine racks themselves to see what is being snapped up fast; it is double-checking that the blurb from *The Wine Spectator* or Robert Parker that the wine merchant has pasted up is an exact match—winery, vineyard, vintage year—with the bottles stuck in the slots beneath it. It happens that I *am* endowed with a certain amount of such shrewdness—but, then, so are most wine-store proprietors.

As it turned out, such of these talents as Matt and I possessed were complementary—if I outdid her in canniness, she surpassed me in the matters of memory and preparedness. Going to wine stores in her company, I found that I was at last able to edge away from the old Sam Spade routine—first by making a concerted effort to discover the lowest median price (somewhere between ten and fifteen dollars) at which well-crafted California or other West Coast red wines (our usual preference) with true varietal character could be purchased, and then by assuming the much harder task of learning to feel comfortable spending that much on a single bottle. (Even so, as soon as the price approaches twenty dollars, something in me freezes. I may yet work up the nerve to spend, say, seventy-three dollars for a 1992 Ridge Montebello Cabernet, but it will be the exception that proves, not breaks, the rule.)

Most important, Matt, with some initial resistance on my part, began to create a substitute for the one thing we most needed, even if we hadn't yet articulated it as such: our own wine *négociant*—which is to say, a source of friendly expertise that could be regularly tapped when we found that we had once again lost sight of the forest in the confusing morass of individual trees.

❊　❊　❊

If you are fortunate enough to live in a place where wine making and drinking are integral parts of the culture, knowing the wine is something—even these days, I think—that happens as a matter of course. This is partly because there isn't all that much wine to taste—most people who live in one wine-growing region never even consider drinking the wine of another; it is partly because all the local wine is accessible for tasting. You find your favorite *vigneron* and return to him or her year after year to fill the trunk of the car. Or your local *négociant*—who knows your taste and your income—arrives at your door with an armload of bottles so that the two of you can sample his latest acquisitions.*

In our culture, there is no tradition of the local vineyard, of wine that is good because it is familiar and that can be drunk with anything because it is on as intimate terms with our cooking as it is with us. Instead, for most of us, wine has never been anything other than a merchandised product, one that comes, like most of what we buy, at once from everywhere and nowhere.

At first glance, it might seem that attending tastings at a local wine

---

*W. S. Merwin draws an intimately detailed and quietly affecting picture of the daily life of one such small-town *négociant* in "Blackbird," one of the three narratives that make up *The Lost Upland: Stories of Southwest France*. Each is a richly textured portrait of an anarchically independent inhabitant of the area—Blackbird himself, a stubborn shepherd, and a companionably seedy aristocrat—and through them, an unsentimental exploration of French small-town and rural life.

store would serve this purpose, but these turned out to be of very little use to us. If only you could go into the store and select six or seven bottles of Sonoma County Cabernet Sauvignon that interest you, and then ask the wine merchant to open each of them for you to sample, and perhaps in the bargain have him say, "Well, if you're drawn to these, there's another you should try," and go get *that* bottle, too.

Wine merchants might do this if customers like Matt and me bought our wine, as people did fifty years ago, by the multiple case. Today, however, we buy by the bottle, and on those rare occasions when we do buy a case, it is usually a mixed one, bought simply to get the 10 percent case discount. The wine merchant's task, then, when we come in to buy one bottle, is to see that we leave with three or four—and wine tastings, like store newsletters and the tasting notes pasted about the shop, are geared to that end.

The proprietor of a small and actually rather discriminating local wine store recently introduced a selection of inexpensive red wines by claiming that these were the pick of "literally thousands we've tasted during the past year." Given the profit margin on a five- or six-dollar bottle of wine, the act of tasting *thousands* of such to find the eight most worth drinking suggests—does it not?—that the place must be run solely for the benefaction of fellow wine lovers. So, when the bottles we purchase seem to bear no relationship to his tasting notes—"rich, lushly flavored . . . the bouquet mingles blackberries and herbs . . . the flavors have a rustic, earthy slant and velvety texture"—well, whose palate must be at fault?

In truth, not necessarily ours. Like used-car salesmen or real-estate agents, wine merchants cannot magically change what they have at hand to match their customers' desires, and so they must maneuver their customers into desiring—and purchasing—what they have. Why should they point us toward a wine that is so good that almost every other wine in the store will seem lackluster by comparison? Far better to encourage us to learn to like the moderately decent wines that fill their bins and about which they write such fulsome encomia.

Still, if our wine merchant was not going to be our Monsieur Boirebien, who was? On these shores, only one sort of person—the wine writer—gets to replicate the experience of what elsewhere is that of the ordinary wine consumer. He or she gets to taste wine freely—by which I mean not only without paying but as a self-directed process meant to promote the education of a particular palate. It is the wine writer alone who is in a position to provide the rest of us with considered, knowledgeable, and honest evaluations.

As I said, I resisted this conclusion. I hated the idea of appearing at the wine store with a copy of *Best Wines! Gold Medal Winners from the Leading Competitions Worldwide* tucked under my arm. But Matt felt differently, and in her persistence had begun to select some very decent bottles. It was already obvious that ours would necessarily be not a real but a virtual *négociant*—where else were we going to encounter him? Thus it was that we began to acquire the rudiments of a wine library.

As I dipped into these books, however, I soon discovered that a number of wine writers seem to have confused unlimited access to wine with some sort of inherent superiority over the rest of us. They've set themselves up as wine explainers in the way that—years ago—those with a college education, when such was a privilege limited to the wealthy few, used their "higher" education to become a now extinct breed of popular explainer (of opera, poetry, classical music, the Great Books of Western Civilization).

Take, for instance, Matt Kramer's highly recommended series of books on "making sense" of the wines of Burgundy, Bordeaux, California, et cetera. I'm sure these books do that, as well as provide pleasant reading for those searching for some sort of contact with the vineyards that produce their favorite wines. But how do we separate the fantasy of visiting these places from the fantasy of being Matt Kramer visiting these places?

More important, how much do we want to confuse wine itself with wine as the subject of a book? Wine exists to be drunk, not read about, and we should be careful not to bury this simple purpose beneath more than we ever need to know about grape varieties, the history of various wine producers, or the life of the *vigneron*.

The same is true for books that purport to teach us the "basics" of wine. The mouth learns by tasting, not listening—drink enough truly good wine and you'll find you can connect the dots as easily as anyone. These books exist because good wine is so difficult for the beginner to get hold of, but they lack the necessary specificity to help find it. Better, then, to push such distractions aside and devote all our energy to the search for the elusive bottle.

Here, books like *Parker's Wine Buyer's Guide* and *The Connois-*

seur's Guide to California Wine—which provide ratings of specific wines—can be of real help, since they offer succinct descriptions of the style that a particular wine maker strives to achieve (powerfully rich and intense, say, versus smooth and well balanced) and an objective judgment as to how well, year by year, this vision has been realized.

Disappointingly, though, the actual ratings turned out to be of surprisingly little use. By the time these books reach the bookstores, they are already out of date. What you find instead is the same wine but of a later vintage than the one in the book. Because your appetite is already whetted by the description of that wine, you buy this one instead—and find it not nearly as good. It is the rare wine maker who charges ten or so dollars for a wine that is dependably excellent, year after year—and then produces enough of it to reach your local wine store.

The problem of availability plagues the recommendations in wine magazines as well. Their ratings are current enough, but—because their imperative is to keep turning up undiscovered "finds"—their top ratings are often given to wines produced in hundreds, sometimes dozens (rather than thousands) of cases, which means that the chances of finding any are very slim indeed.* In the end, these ratings do little more than provide a gloss to their real purpose, which—like any other lifestyle publication—is to encourage their readers to spend money . . . on wine, yes, but also on official wine-tasting glasses, thermostatically controlled wine-storage systems, ingeniously devised wine racks, posters of grape varieties, tours of the California wine country. And this is as it should be, because most wine drinkers, even serious ones, prefer the sweetness of wine myth to the dryness of wine truth.

All this time Matt and I were slowly learning what I have come to believe is the single most important lesson about buying wine: *there is nowhere near enough good wine to go around.* It is a lesson that I have never seen spelled out in a beginner's guide; indeed, almost everything in the world of wine writing seems to conspire against our learning it at all.

---

*Conversely, when general-subject magazines publish wine ratings, quality is almost always given a backseat to guaranteed availability. This is why the October 1997 issue of *Consumer Reports* bestowed their only "best buy" recommendation upon Napa Ridge's 1994 Central Coast Cabernet Sauvignon, certainly a good buy for the money, but not a wine that deserves to be placed at the top of any budget-minded aficionado's list.

This became almost painfully obvious to us when we came across a little wine publication uniquely tailored to our needs: the *Quarterly Pocket List of Top-Rated Wines for $15 or Less.* Its editor, John L. Vankat, searches through the latest issues of selected wine publications (*The Wine Advocate, Smart Wine, The Wine Spectator,* and so on), selecting only bottles in the stated price range that have received a rating of B+ or higher, arranges them by grape varietal, and prints them up in an easily consulted, thirty-six-page-long, pocket-sized publication—and he gets this out to his subscribers before those wines have vanished from the shelves.*

At the time our first issue arrived, we were buying our wine at three places: two specialty shops and a giant supermarket. This last devoted one side of a whole aisle to it, more than two-thirds of which—several hundred bottles—were at least one cut above jug wine and many of which were several cuts above it. Even so, there were fewer than a *dozen* bottles in the entire aisle that our guide rated at B+ or better. Since these were spread among the varietals, there were few of each (sometimes just one) to choose from. Only four bottles in the whole aisle received an A-, and just one received an A: a 1993 Chateau Ste. Michelle Cabernet Sauvignon. (*Very* few wines are rated A+ in the *Quarterly Pocket List,* and we have yet to come across one.)

The more carefully selected collections at the specialty stores did a little better—we found some particularly good wines there, including a memorable Benziger 1994 Cabernet—but not *that* much better. Over time, this has proven to be a depressing rule of thumb: no matter how large or carefully chosen a store's selection, you can count on one hand the wines of any particular varietal—Sauvignon Blanc, Zinfandel, Pinot Noir—priced at fifteen dollars or less that have been rated B+ or better.

To understand the full import of this, you also have to realize that we've found most wines rated B+ to be not—as that rating is supposed to indicate—"very good" but something more like "moderately pleasing" or "hey, not bad." The wines that actually taste *very* good have almost always received at least an A- rating, or, according to one estimate, about *1 percent* of all available wines.

---

*At the time this book was published, subscriptions were $25.95 a year from Grapevine Associates; P.O. Box 6003; Oxford, OH 45056; (800) 524-1005; www.winepocketlist.com.

When you think about it, this makes complete sense. If good wine were commonly available, very few bottles would be priced over twenty dollars, and wine drinkers would be as unsnobby and democratic a lot as beer drinkers—as they mostly still are in places where good wine can be taken for granted. Underlying any serious interest in wine is a gnawing awareness of scarcity, which can transform a wine collector into a vinous miser, with a cellarful of bottles that have become too good, too valuable, to drink.

Scarcity, indeed, is the subtext of the wine business in all its aspects, which is why it celebrates the pleasure of drinking wine while at the same time subtly keeping us from seeking out the few bottles that are truly good. This can be most clearly seen in the comically conflicted attitude that many wine stores have toward wine ratings. Even the most respectable stores seem to have no inhibitions about milking the consumer's response to positive ratings by such deceptive practices as leaving old ratings over bottles of a newer vintage, creating fake reviews by enclosing unattributed comments in quotation marks, and—as on video boxes—unabashedly flaunting a good rating no matter how lowly its source . . . all this to give the impression that about half their stock has received outside—hence, objective—acclaim.

This means that these stores believe that wine ratings are a good thing, right? On the contrary. As the wine manager of a highly regarded local wine store (whose wine racks glitter with fluorescent-colored rating notes) sanctimoniously stated in a recent newsletter, "We have always thought poorly of numerical ratings, used by ineffectual writers to create a false shorthand for customers in a hurry."

I beg to differ. The whole *point* of wine ratings is to help us to judge a bottle without tasting it ourselves. And it is at best disingenuous to criticize the practice by pointing an accusing finger at the wine writer and the consumer, when it is the wine trade that gives us no choice but to buy first and sample later, often on the strength of their own spurious or misleading recommendations.

Furthermore, it's worth asking whether numerical ratings are as reductive as critics often claim. If a friend tells us a thriller she has just read is terrific, we don't demand an entire book report to justify that claim. In the same way, the bottom line for the wine drinker is not whether a wine has nuances of cherry blossom and tobacco but how much it has to offer in comparison to the bottles in the racks on either

side of it—information that can be clearly and unambiguously con-
veyed by a simple number.*

Needless to say, wines with the same rating don't taste equally good
(Malbec, for instance, is a varietal that tastes rather like ink; a highly
rated one tastes like delicious ink); nor do these ratings protect you
from the occasional unpleasant encounter. Some publications overrate
wines (especially those that sell the wines they rate), and all who rate
wines have their biases (like Robert Parker's notorious weakness for
"big"—"gobs of fruit"—wines). But it has almost always been our experience that even when we don't care for a highly rated wine, we find
drinking it instructive rather than baffling; we can see why others may
like it, even if we do not. And the more rigorously we restrict our purchases to such highly rated bottles, the more we find true delight in
what we drink.

❧ ❧ ❧

The sort of deep-seated ignorance that is the subject of this essay
does most of its damage by encouraging us to indulge in such venial
flaws as envy, cynicism, self-pity, even—paradoxically, pathetically—
self-congratulation. These character flaws regularly infect my system,
along with what may be the worst of them all: the perennial hope that
the condition that has tormented me for so long has somehow finally
gone away. I know this, and so it has occurred to me that my obsession
with finding the best possible bottles of wine might be more a symptom
of my ignorance than part of its cure.

Wouldn't a real wine lover be more willing to take each bottle as it
comes, to find its flaws as interesting, revealing, and ultimately almost
as enjoyable as its virtues? If I believe—as I do—that a man interested
only in beautiful women is not really much interested in women themselves, then, by analogy at least, this belief should reveal something

---

*Not surprisingly, Robert Parker, the wine writer who has done the most to popularize the
numerical rating system, has also generated an enormous amount of hostile criticism for doing so. The real problem is that so many wine drinkers subscribe to his publication that a high
recommendation of a reasonably priced wine (a rare event—most of the ones that interest him
cost a lot more than ten or fifteen dollars) means that every bottle of it will be bought up in
the next several days. (At the time this book went to press, *The Wine Advocate* was $50 a
year from P.O. Box 311; Monkton, MD 21111; www.wineadvocate.com.)

telling about my relationship to wine. And, on reflection, I think it does.

The truth—and this is something that many readers may already suspect—is that I don't much like wine. What I like—and sometimes very much like—are a few *good* wines. When I take a sip from a glass of, say, Rabbit Ridge Zinfandel or Marietta Old Vine Red, I find the experience one of concentrated, complex voluptuousness. But because love of the grape is part of neither my patrimony nor my body's chemistry—my palate, which adores the salty and greasy, has always had a problem with the sweet and sour—it *has* to be about that good before I want to drink it at all.

One important aspect of wine that one often looks for in vain in the higher reaches of wine writing is that it is a potently alcoholic beverage (it has twice the alcohol of beer) and that this is the fundamental reason why people drink it. If it were just grape juice—no matter the location of the vineyard or the spectacularity of the growing season—there would hardly be any interest in it at all. To rephrase a remark of Bertold Brecht's: first the buzz, then the *terroir*.

And the buzz is something that I don't really care about. I am already anxious and fuddled by nature; inebriation only makes that worse. My taste in narcotics leans toward those that leave me mentally sharp and emotionally calm—famously nicotine (I smoked furiously for about twenty-five years), but also caffeine. My image of mind and body at absolute sensual ease is not a snifter of cognac after an elegant dinner but a cigarette and a second mug of coffee after a good breakfast.

So, if I'm offered some coffee and then told it will be made from a year-old jar of instant, I groan inwardly but still say "Okay." For me, bad coffee is better than no coffee, and that makes me, pure and simple, a coffee lover. In the same way, a true wine lover drinks Gallo Hearty Burgundy if that's what it takes to ensure a glass or two with every meal. Not me. I'd rather have a glass of water.

All this is probably enough to guarantee that my relationship to wine will remain problematic, but there's something else that guarantees it—my inability to establish true feelings of connection to a place.

I have visited only one vineyard in my entire life—in New York State, yet—but it made an impression, since the memory of it remains clear even after twenty years. The day was a lovely sunny one in late September. The winery was situated at the top of a hill. Row after row of grapevines flowed down its side, with grape harvesters trudging back up, the baskets strapped to their backs heaped to overflowing with fresh-picked bunches of green grapes. Each basket was emptied into a large open hopper cart that stood in the winery's courtyard. The air was full of the buzzing of yellow jackets and a deliciously tart yet syrupy aroma of crushed fruit.

The winery itself was housed in an enormous barn, and tastings were offered on the lower level in a large and open room with a cement floor and walls of rough-hewn granite blocks. Crates of wine were stacked helter-skelter; under the one window was a massive, grape-stained wooden table littered with half-empty bottles and used paper cups. The vintner, also huge and grape-stained, stood behind it, sipping his own wine and chatting to some customers who had driven from Manhattan for the afternoon.

I slunk up as inconspicuously as I could to try some and, as usual, found myself stumped: to my mouth, the stuff was simply awful. Suddenly, I felt the eye of the vintner upon me and reluctantly turned in his direction.

"So, what do you think?" he asked.

"Very interesting," I stammered, and, picking up a single bottle, added, "I guess I'll take this." Meanwhile, the New Yorkers were loading case after case into the trunk of their black Cadillac Seville.

At the time, I thought them dupes, too much wanting to boast of their "own little vineyard" to actually taste what it produced. However, at this point in my voyage of wine discovery, I think differently. The connection those visitors felt to that vineyard might have been tenuous, but that doesn't make it laughable—as anyone who has ever spent a week in Paris can attest to. One trip there may not make you Parisian, but it gives you more of a handhold on the place than a lifetime of book reading ever could.

That vineyard wasn't Paris, of course, but it was about the only one that was a pleasant afternoon's drive from New York City. That made it local enough, and what is local can be as legitimately, if differently, good as that which possesses objective distinction (although it's especially nice when the two converge). Otherwise, most of us would be unable to feel any loyalty to our own high school but would wear AN-DOVER or BOSTON LATIN sweatshirts instead.

When it comes to wine, what makes "local" delicious is only partly a matter of flavor. This kind of deliciousness is based (as already noted) on familiarity—which is itself a concatenation of a complex and diffuse range of experiences. The production of wine is rife with particularly evocative experiences, which is one reason why exploring wine country can be so much fun. But a visit offers nothing compared to the presence of a local vineyard. Then you get to know the vintner, see the vineyards in the first flush of springtime green, earn spending money as a teenager helping with the harvest, join the party when that year's wine is pronounced ready to drink.

The making of wine melds together two of the most potent middle-class American yearnings—to connect to a particular piece of land and to possess a totally absorbing, challenging, and, at the same time, very competitive avocation. This is why airline pilots, brain surgeons, and corporate lawyers emerge from their midlife crises as vineyard owners: it's the same stress level as before, only now they're having much more fun.

This isn't to say that inside every wine drinker lurks a potential vintner (although maybe there does), only that wine itself—as well as the bottles it comes in, even the corks that plug them up—is charged with evocative significations of place, at least for those who can tune in to that wavelength. I can, a little, but I mostly feel it passing me by. I can love a place but cannot wholly entrust myself to it, because—as I explain at length elsewhere in this book—I lack the capacity to sink down roots, even pretend ones. My loyalty is to the individual, never to the whole.

This, then, is where I've gotten in my struggle to know wine—and where I haven't. I've found some bottles that I enjoy tremendously; I've found much to think about along the way. But I now know that wine drinking will never become as intimate a part of my life as, say, reading or cooking. Wine wants something of me that I'm simply unable to give. Because of that, I'm destined to remain on the outside looking in . . . which is to say, knowing wine only one bottle at a time.

BANH MI & ME

✦ ✦ ✦

There are at least three small Asian markets in easy driving range of our apartment here in Northampton, but my favorite sits in a tiny, shabby minimall just across the bridge over the Connecticut River. There it shares space with an adult-movie rental outlet, whose much larger road sign is usually defaced by advocates of family values. As I wait beside it for a break in the traffic to ease my car back onto the highway, I endure knowing looks from occupants of passing vehicles who have appraised me—middle-aged, bearded, white, male—and passed their judgment. But the bright pink plastic bag that sits beside me on the front seat is the only lurid aspect of my shopping trip. Its contents are exotic in an entirely different sense: packets of rice noodles, a bottle of oyster or fish sauce, a few cans of coconut milk, and, if I'm very lucky, one or two Vietnamese sandwiches trucked in that day all the way from Boston.

When, on my second or third visit to the store, I first came across a small pile of these sandwiches in the store's drinks cooler (I was burrowing around for a can of a Taiwanese coffee beverage called Mr. Brown—another story), I had no idea what they were. I also had no hesitation in giving one a try. It would be nice to write that I already knew that the Vietnamese had acquired a taste for French bread and French charcuterie during the colonial occupation and that what I held in my hand might be a sample of both. But the truth is that I have a weakness for anything that comes packaged in a French roll. I bought one, took it out to the car, ate it, and went straight back in and bought another. One bite and I knew that I was onto a good thing.

Exactly what *sort* of good thing, though, it would take me a while to determine. The roll—the size and shape of a small sub roll—had a resilient crust and a light, chewy interior. It enfolded a slice each of two different kinds of cold cut—one pink-colored, the other grayish-white, both of them unfamiliar to me. On top of these were slices of carrot and cucumber, and lots of fresh coriander. The inside of the roll was spread on one side with mayonnaise and on the other with . . . something else.

Since by the time I noticed this I was on the road, I could only analyze the other substance with my tongue. It was gelatinous and full of little bits of what tasted like crumbled chicken liver. When I got home, I examined a smear of it left on the wrapping. It was opaque, a light-tan color, and as utterly baffling in its composition as it was delicious to eat. This was definitely something that required serious investigation.

It goes almost without saying that I returned to the market for another round the very next day; it also goes almost without saying that there was not a sandwich in the store—not that day, nor for several following days. Soon the Vietnamese clerk, a brusque young man who spoke exactly enough English to suit himself, simply assumed a "him again" expression when the large bearded white man came rushing in, stood for a moment disconsolately staring into the drinks cooler, groaned, and slunk back out the door.

Then, one day, there they were. I swept up an armful and carried them over to the cash register. I held one up and asked the clerk what it was called. He gave me the sort of look reserved for askers of truly stupid questions and answered shortly, "SANN-wich." And, to this day, between the two of us, things have advanced no further. (Me, on the telephone: "SANN-wich today?" Him, in response: "No, no. Maybe Thursday.") But I had other resources. I had cookbooks. And, of course, I had the Internet.

❀ ❀ ❀

The first question that comes to mind when encountering a new dish is, What am I eating? But in this instance that "what" was a very complicated matter. Here was something completely familiar—a sandwich—given a series of intriguing twists. The vegetables, cut into long, thin strips, added a pleasing crispness; the coriander provided an electric herbaceousness. The cold cuts were unfamiliar, but it was an unfamiliarity characterized by mildness rather than unusual flavor—they lacked the sour/bitter aftertaste that mars so much American charcuterie. If, at that moment, I had been asked to put all this into an equation, I would have offered the following:

> fresh coriander + carrot & cucumber slices + good French-style
> roll + delicate cold cuts + mayonnaise + ???? = X

with "????" representing the mystery substance with the chewy bits. I had been a terrible algebra student, God knows, but I learned enough to know that an equation with two unknowns is a fearsome thing. It was time to go on-line.

I had already e-mailed a few people who I thought might be able to help me out. Jim Leff, ace New York restaurant explorer, pointed me to a series of interchanges at his chowhound.com bulletin board. I myself might have written the query that had started the chain: "What is a Vietnamese sandwich? Has anyone got a recipe?"

There was only one reply—but it was enough to set me on my way, and to warn me that the water I was about to enter was deeper than I had thought:

> Ah! *Banh mi* in detail. French rolls/baguettes with five-spice
> chicken, pork, or meatballs with grated carrot, some kind of sliver
> of a white vegetable (daikon radish?), jalapeño pepper (optional),
> with classic Vietnamese dipping sauce poured onto the sandwich.
> I don't think there's any lettuce. They're kind of small. Usually it
> takes two to fill me up. Vietnamese iced coffee is a good accom-
> paniment.

Five-spice chicken? Meatballs? Daikon radish? "Classic" dipping sauce? My equation was clearly going to need some tweaking. But at least I now had the thing's name: *banh mi*.* I e-mailed Bob Lucky, writer/editor of *The Asian Foodbookery* (see page 58), and asked him if he could tell me what the two words meant. He could. *Banh mi*, he told me, meant "wheat bread." At least, *banh* is a word that denotes "cake,"

---

*Vietnamese is an inflected language; a word's meaning often depends on how it is "sung." To show this in print, a complex system of diacritical marks has been adopted—marks that I have not attempted to replicate here. *Banh mi* is pronounced "bagne mee," with "bagne" more or less rhyming with the French pronunciation of *champagne*.

"pie," "bread," or "pastry," and *mi* is the word for "wheat"; by itself, it can mean simply "wheat noodle," as in the Chinese word *mein*.

Perhaps "baked wheat thing" better captures the multiple meanings inherent in the phrase, while "French-style bread/roll stuffed with something good" is probably the connotative meaning for many Vietnamese. *Banh mi*, in other words, is the way they say "sandwich"—the exact translation offered to me by the Vietnamese grocery clerk.

However, in the short distance the word had traveled from him to me, its meaning had subtly changed. In Vietnam, as in other Third World countries, the focus of the meal is the starch, in this instance the bread. Here, when we order a sandwich, our attention is directed to what fills it; the word, after all, takes its name from the Earl of Sandwich, who delighted in the fact that this arrangement allowed him to eat his roast beef and play whist at the same time.

I had wanted *banh mi* to be like "cheeseburger," a unique descriptive term that I could utter in any Vietnamese sandwich joint and be reasonably confident as to what I would receive. This, as often happens in life, would prove to be at once true and untrue.

Since my Vietnamese cookbooks were of little help in my *banh mi* research, I went back to the Internet. There isn't exactly a treasure trove of information waiting there to be discovered, but if you keep on searching, you do learn some things. One of my more interesting finds was a piece by *Los Angeles Times* reporter Barbara Hansen on her eating experiences in Vietnam in the early nineties. Most mornings, she wrote, she breakfasted on

> a plate of silky rice dough wrappers stuffed with ground meat, topped with bean sprouts, cilantro and other greens, and slices of what the Vietnamese call pork pie, a finely textured cold cut. . . . But one morning I stopped instead at a wooden cart laden with French rolls. The quality of the French bread here is astounding. Nowhere in Los Angeles have I found bread that can compare. Racks of it were set out here and there in Ho Chi Minh City. At this cart, I ordered *banh mi*. The woman vendor split the bun, dabbed on pâté, added bits of charcuterie, marinated carrot, jicama strips, cucumber slices, cilantro, a cloud of pepper, and thin chile sauce. It was a fantastic bundle of food for fifteen cents.

Jicama, if you haven't tried it, is a root vegetable that, when eaten raw, has a crisp, bland succulence somewhere between a radish's and a water chestnut's. That a sidewalk vendor might not add mayonnaise (or

"American bean paste," as one Vietnamese endearingly remembers calling it as a child) comes as no surprise; that in Vietnam *banh mi* is considered breakfast food does, a bit. It turns out that in America, as well
as in Ho Chi Minh City, many *banh mi* places open at the crack of
dawn to serve the *banh-mi*-and-coffee crowd, hurrying to work.

Most of the other mentions came from restaurant reviews. In the
best of these, an exploration of Vietnamese sandwich shops in San
Francisco written for www.sidewalk.com, Sharon Silva pretty much describes the lay of the land for the novice *banh mi* enthusiast:

> At midday in the tiny, simple Saigon Sandwich Shop on Larkin
> Street, hungry yet patient customers waiting in a long line slowly
> make their way to the counter to order from among a half-dozen
> choices: *banh mi thit* (roast pork), *banh mi xiu mai* (pork meat-
> balls), *banh mi cha lua* (so-called "fancy pork," a kind of steamed
> pork loaf—and an acquired taste for some Westerners), *banh mi
> pate gan* (a liver pâté), *banh mi ga* (grilled chicken) and *banh mi
> thit cha pate* (a pork/pâté combination). No matter which version
> you order, the construction is basically the same: a large, crusty
> French roll (sometimes lightly toasted) smeared with a flavorful
> mayonnaise knockoff, then layered with pickled carrot and
> daikon slices, white onion rings, sprigs of coriander, fiery cross
> sections of green chiles, and your choice of meat. Sometimes a lit-
> tle cucumber and tomato turn up, too, as well as a shake or two
> of Maggi Sauce, the Swiss condiment that traveled to Vietnam
> with the French and is found in every Vietnamese pantry from
> Hanoi to Houston.*

However, it was Pittsburgh research librarian Jeff Fortescue who actually got me out on the road, pointing me to a review at boston.
citysearch.com of a small take-out Vietnamese restaurant in downtown
Boston called Banh Mi:

> The real draw here is the freshly prepared Vietnamese sandwich, a
> crisp French roll laden with pork and fresh vegetables. The roll is
> first heated, then a ground pork pâté is slathered on, followed by
> slices of two different types of Southeast Asian pork cold cuts

---

*Maggi Seasoning looks and tastes like a sort of Western soy sauce. To the Vietnamese, the la-
bel and bottle shape were French and exotic, but the taste of its contents was comfortingly familiar.

(one looks like headcheese, the second like liverwurst), shredded
carrots, sliced cucumbers, shards of fresh chile pepper, and
sprigs of cilantro. The result is texturally pleasing and appetite-
appeasing. If you find mystery meat unnerving, they also serve a
vegetable sandwich, sans pork.

Shortly thereafter, I was standing at that counter myself, ordering
half a dozen to go, at two dollars apiece. The Vietnamese proprietress
offered me the choice of chile pepper hot or not, and since I would be
sharing this bounty with two nephews, I chose three of each. As she assembled the order, I looked around, trying to take in as much as I could.

In this sort of situation, I am always bombarded by an overload of
impressions that I need time and distance to sort out. Here that feeling
was aggravated by the fact that I was double-parked outside (downtown Boston is your worst parking nightmare). I had been in the store
barely a minute, and already my brain was reeling.

I had expected to find something like a deli counter—with cold cuts
and cooked meats on display. Instead, beside the counter was a large
glass case holding a huge assortment of those pastel-drenched Asian
pastries that look as if they glow in the dark. Beneath these was a refrigerator case containing, among other things, loaf-shaped, string-tied
packages, with labels in Vietnamese. These parcels, I would come to realize later, contained various kinds of Vietnamese charcuterie. But right
then they were nothing more than elements of that rush of confused
impression whose name is foreignness. Dazed, I took my plastic sack
stuffed with *banh mi* and fled.

However, once the car was nosing its way back to the suburbs, my
head began to clear. Or, more accurately, that peculiar *banh mi* aroma
of hot French bread and fresh coriander had started to work its magic,
comforting the spirit even as it drew my right hand into the bag. How
warm and crusty these sandwiches felt. How accessible they were, in
their loose waxed-paper wrapping secured with a tiny rubber band. A
moment later my shirt front was covered with brittle flakes of crust,
and my mouth was experiencing a slow burn. I had grabbed one of the
three sandwiches laden with slices of raw chile pepper.

The burn in my mouth only increased my happiness. *This* was how
banh mi was meant to be eaten: absolutely fresh from the making. The
outside of the roll was toasty and crisp; the interior was cool and full of
flavors, a complex mix of the soft and the crunchy, the brightly (fiery!)

piquant and the unctuously rich. The cold cuts were definitely an element of the sandwich's goodness, but, in truth, perhaps not the most important one. Western cold cuts are meant to dominate a sandwich; these were meant to fall into harmony with everything else. If you left them out, you might lose the backup group, but the sandwich itself would go right on singing.

Right then, I understood something about *banh mi* that made me laugh. It was, after all, the Vietnamese translation of a common French snack, and here I was, with my meat hunt, trying to translate it back into French, or really into American Vietnamese French. This, of course, was the tug of my appetite and fifty-odd years of cultural conditioning, but I was being yanked past what I actually *liked* about *banh mi*. If this kept up, I would find myself right back at French bread spread with pâté, with maybe a sprig or two of fresh coriander to add a touch of—what would one call it?—well, maybe *Vietnamienerie*.

❀ ❀ ❀

A week or so after this event, a friend and I drove over to the Vietnamese neighborhood in Springfield. I had gone there looking for pâté, but it was lunchtime and the view through the window of Saigon Pho was very enticing—a small room full of Vietnamese, alone or in groups, hunched over bowls of noodles and broth. Inside, we found that the menu offered a few different versions of *pho*—Vietnamese beef noodle soup—one distinguished from the other by the number of different sorts of beef cuts included. I ordered the *pho* with everything: beef brisket, beef tendon, beef meatballs, and strips of rare steak.

In a few moments, our waiter brought us a plate heaped with bean sprouts, whole branches of basil leaves, lime quarters, and slices of hot pepper, to be added as we wished to our soup. Then he brought the *pho* itself: two large steaming bowls of clear broth in which floated rice noodles, strips of scallion, fresh coriander leaves, and paper-thin slices of those different kinds of beef.

If I had been in a beef-craving mood, I would have been rather disappointed—one or two determined swoops of my porcelain spoon would have caught up every meat shred in the bowl. In fact, I was quite happy with what I received—it was delicious and filling—but I did think about this paradoxical situation as I ate.

The versions of *pho* the restaurant served—and the prices charged for them—were determined by the variety, not the amount, of beef you got in a bowl. Meat was central to the dish, to be sure; it was just that that centrality had nothing especially to do with quantity—which, to a Westerner like myself, seemed a very Zen-like notion. The meat was as much a spiritual as a physical presence in the dish. I silently renamed it "meat-blessed noodles in broth."

I finished my Vietnamese iced coffee (two glasses are brought to your table, one filled with ice, the other with an inch of condensed milk at the bottom and a small metal drip coffeemaker set on the top. When the coffee finishes dripping onto the condensed milk, you stir the two layers together and pour this over the ice in the other glass. The result is unexpectedly delicious) and we drove over to Saigon Market, several blocks away. There I found a refrigerator case full of *banh mi,* packaged in plastic bags and set vertically into milk-bottle cases. Each bag held—separate from the sandwich—a bright red, fresh Thai hot pepper and some shredded carrot packaged in a little plastic bag.

It was a hot Saturday afternoon, and the atmosphere was quiet, even sleepy. I felt free to root around. In a freezer case I found a hoard of Vietnamese cold cuts, mostly various brands of the notorious *cha lua* ("fancy pork"), a mild pork loaf seasoned with *nuoc mam,* as well as a few other similarly shaped but differently named pork loaves. I bought one made of pork and pig's ear.

However, I didn't see any pork liver pâté. I asked the pleasant-faced woman at the checkout counter about this, and she led me to a freezer case. "I buy by whole loaf and slice here," she explained, pointing to a stack of plastic-wrapped anonymous-looking slabs that I had utterly missed during my survey. I promptly added one to my shopping basket. By the time I set out for home, I was feeling a kind of Sherlock Holmesian satisfaction: the pieces of the puzzle were finally falling into place.

※ ※ ※

Two days later, a little plate of Vietnamese charcuterie sits beside me as I write. *Cha lua,* it turns out, has the pinkish-gray color, slightly rubbery texture, and unremarkable flavor of chicken loaf, albeit chicken loaf flavored with fish sauce. I don't dislike it, but nothing draws me to it, either. Under its foil packaging, the pork and pig's ear loaf is

wrapped in real banana leaves and has been made with the same attention to detail. It is dotted with bits of mushroom and whole peppercorns, as well as chunks of the promised pig's ear. The latter is
pleasantly chewy rather than gristly and tastes of nothing much. This is
probably the headcheese-like cold cut mentioned by the Boston re-
viewer. It's very good.

However, the liver pâté is far and away the best of the three, with its
delicate crumbly texture and clean, fresh liver taste. And, at five dollars
a pound, it's a terrific bargain—reminding me again of how much extra
we are forced to pay for anything that can be packaged in the tinsel
wrappings of gourmet pretentiousness.

No surprise, then, that the Saigon Market *banh mi* was the best one
yet. The shredded carrot had been "pickled" in a marinade of rice vinegar and sugar; it was crunchy, tangy, and sweet. The inside of the roll
was spread on one side with that delicious liver pâté, on the other with
garlicky *nuoc cham,* the classic Vietnamese dipping sauce that also contains fresh lime juice, fish sauce, and chile paste. In the cold-cut department, *cha lua* was playing for the gray side and a Vietnamese version of
boiled ham for the pink. There was fresh coriander aplenty. And this
time I knew to put the sandwich in a low oven until the roll was warm
and crusty again.

At the beginning of this adventure, my goal had been to figure out
the contents of that mysterious spread and then find out something
about the cold cuts: what were they made of? what were they called?
where could I buy them? More or less, over the span of several months,
I accomplished all this. I even believe I deciphered the secret of the
spread (although I may well be corrected on this): I suspect that the
makers of that first version of *banh mi* simply crumbled up some liver
pâté and mixed it with mayonnaise or salad dressing to make it easier
to spread (and to practice a little economizing at the same time). A nice
trick, but now that I've eaten *banh mi* with the pâté spread on straight,
I'm not quite as interested anymore.

Also, although I'm glad to have tried what Vietnamese charcuterie
I've managed to track down, it was even better to learn how little the
goodness of a *banh mi* depends on it. Vietnamese cooking has many
dishes that could happily become part of a *banh mi,* and often do—
crunchy skewer-cooked meatballs, barbecued strips of pungently seasoned pork or beef, fried chicken morsels, and so on. Pages containing

some of these recipes are already marked in my Vietnamese cookbooks.

The important thing, however, was the realization brought on by that bowl of *pho*. Compared to meat-blessed noodles in broth, *banh mi* is carnivore heaven—which, of course, is a reflection of its Franco-Vietnamese roots. Still, there's no denying that it is infinitely closer to a bowl of *pho* than to, say, an Italian sub—the American sandwich that, in temperament and balance, it most resembles.

I know this because last night Matt and I stopped at the local natural foods store to do some shopping, and I found myself staring meditatively at a block of tofu that had been "wood-smoked in a real New England smokehouse." This, I caught myself thinking, might be very good in a *banh mi*. Now, that sandwich had certainly not made me love tofu more; what it had done was allay my need to stuff a sandwich with meat, which is almost as much of a miracle.

This has come about, I think, because the feeling of amplitude in both dishes, *pho* and *banh mi*, derives from an artful combination of flavors and textures: in the one, the limpid, delicious broth, the slippery strands of noodle, the crunchy bean sprouts, the pungent fresh herbs, the chewy bits of beef; in the other, the crusty bread, the crisp, moist cucumber and marinated carrot, the tangy dressing, the suave meatiness of the cold cuts, the nostril-clearing astringency of the hot chile, and fresh coriander. All the senses have been stimulated, hunger has been satiated, and yet, in the end, not all that much has been eaten. Enough, yes, but no real surfeit. It makes you think.

Meanwhile, for the *banh mi* enthusiast, where next? I got a hint when Matt came across an article in an old issue of *Saveur* about a return visit to Cambodia by the expatriate owners of Boston's Elephant Walk Restaurant, Longteine and Kenthao de Monteiro, with their daughters, Launa and Nadsa. Much there had changed since their exile, and mostly for the worse. Even so,

> at a Chinese-owned restaurant in the middle of Phnom Penh's commercial district, Launa and Nadsa rediscover one of their own childhood delights: a baguette filled with liver terrine and pork pâté, cucumber slices, chiles, and pickled carrots and green papaya. It is *nom pang pâté*.

Gentlemen, start your engines.

BANH MI

The Bread. This can be an entire French (or Italian) light crusty roll or a wedge cut from a *bâtard* (the next bread size up from a baguette). If it's not fresh from the bakery, heat it for 5 minutes in a warm oven before making the sandwich.

The Spread. Choose one or more of the following: mayonnaise, hot sauce, pork or chicken liver pâté, sweet butter, Maggi seasoning, a drizzle of *nuoc cham* (see recipe below). I like pâté spread on one side and *nuoc cham* mixed into mayonnaise on the other.

The Topping. Consider these mandatory: thinly sliced European cucumber, marinated slivers of daikon and carrot or carrot alone (see recipe below), and lots of fresh coriander. Optional extras include sliced jicama, a few basil or mint leaves, some slivers of scallion (or very thinly sliced onion), and slices of fiery hot chile pepper.

The Filling. One or more different kinds of Vietnamese cold cuts (look in the freezer section of your Asian grocery), preferably from a pork loaf (white) and a cured ham (pink). A reasonable supermarket substitute would be a few slices of chicken loaf and boiled ham. Those leery of cold cuts in general might try thin slices of roast pork, grilled mushrooms, or slices of firm tofu, drained and then marinated in *nuoc cham* overnight. The more adventurous should seek out recipes for other options mentioned in the essay.

NUOC CHAM
(Vietnamese dipping sauce)
[*makes ¾ cup*]

The secret to this sauce, says Mai Pham in The Best of Vietnamese & Thai Cooking, *is to add plenty of lime pulp as well as lime juice, especially when—as here—it is to be used for dipping.*

    1 clove garlic
    ½ teaspoon ground chile paste
    1 Thai chile pepper, seeded (optional—see note)
    2 tablespoons fish sauce (see note)
    1 tablespoon fresh lime juice with pulp
    ⅓ cup hot water
    2 tablespoons sugar

Put the garlic, chile paste, and optional Thai pepper into a mortar or food processor and pulverize into a paste. Combine this mixture with the rest of the ingredients in a small bowl and stir until the sugar has dissolved. This sauce can be kept in the refrigerator for one month.

Cook's Note. Thai chile peppers are small and intensely hot. Any small fiery (or not so fiery!) chile pepper can be substituted.

Fish sauce, *nuoc mam*, is an essential element of Vietnamese cuisine. It is made by packing anchovies in salt and drawing off the brine; the best brands contain no other ingredients. Apply with a light hand.

CU CAI CAROT CHUA
(Carrot and Daikon in Vinegar)
[*makes ¼ cup*]

1 medium carrot
1 small daikon (sweet white radish)
1 cup water
2 teaspoons rice vinegar
2 teaspoons sugar
1 pinch salt

Peel the carrot and radish and cut each into 2-inch lengths. Either grate coarsely into long strands or, with a sharp knife or vegetable peeler, cut each length into paper-thin strips. Put the rest of the ingredients in a small bowl and stir until the sugar completely dissolves. Marinate the strips of carrot and radish in this mixture for at least 1 hour or as long as overnight. Remove the vegetables from the liquid before using. If marinated carrots alone are preferred, omit the daikon and cut the marinade proportions in half.

Further Reading

I didn't find *banh mi* recipes in my Vietnamese cookbooks for the same reason that no bologna sandwich recipe appears in *Joy of Cooking*: most of us don't make cold cuts at home. In Vietnam they are sold at local charcuterie shops, where large electric mortars pummel the meat into the perfect consistency. The one exception to the rule was *The Classic Cuisine of Vietnam,* by Bach Ngo and Gloria Zimmerman, written before Vietnamese charcuteries were well established in this country. It contains recipes for a few basic pork terrines, like *cha lua*. Look in it and the following for *banh mi* fillings: *Café Vietnam*, by Annabel Jackson; *The Best of Vietnamese & Thai Cooking*, by Mai Pham; and *The Foods of Vietnam*, by Nicole Routhier.

And, last, a grateful tip of the hat to R. W. Lucky, who generously searched his files and queried his informants for information on *banh mi*. Bob is the editor of *The Asian Foodbookery*, and his witty, knowledgeable reflections on recently published Asian food books—and his insightful annotations to the sample recipes he selects from them—are, in our opinion, essential reading for anyone interested in the many fascinating cuisines of that continent. At the time of writing, subscriptions are $16 a year (four issues) from *The Asian Foodbookery*; P.O. Box 15947; Seattle, WA 98115-0947; lucky8rice@aol.com.

DESPERATELY RESISTING RISOTTO

❋ ❋ ❋

There are certain dishes that can quietly haunt your life. They are the ones that seem at once gloriously appealing and somehow—for no apparent reason—perpetually out of reach. For me, one such dish is *osso buco*. The phrase is Italian for "marrowbone" (literally, "bone hole") and in this instance refers to veal shanks cut about two inches thick. These bones are quite meaty, but the essence of the dish lies in what they contain, a generous portion of meltingly delicate marrow. Prepared in the classic Milanese manner, the shanks are browned in a mixture of butter and olive oil, then simmered for hours with minced aromatics in stock, white wine, and, controversially, tomatoes until the meat is falling off the bone. Finally, the dish is sprinkled with a *gremolata* of lemon rind, garlic, and parsley, and served forth.

Osso buco draws me enormously, and yet . . . and yet . . . I don't go to restaurants that prepare it, I don't shop at markets where veal shanks are sold. Of course, with some effort on my part, these obstacles could be overcome. However, when the subject is denial, there is usually something darker and more tenacious at work. Perhaps *osso buco* is just a little too imperious for me to be comfortable with it. In any case, there it is—a dish I may go to my grave still desiring and never having tasted.

Because the traditional accompaniment to *osso buco* is *risotto alla milanese*—which when I started cooking was pretty much the only risotto in town—it looked for a long while like I might never make a risotto either. There was no way I was going to leapfrog the entrée for the side dish, especially when *it* seemed haughtier still. Saffron-flavored, stock-enriched, marrow-and-butter-freighted, *risotto alla milanese* de-manded expensive and exotic ingredients, and a facility at what was by all reports not only a mysterious and daunting cooking technique but a test of character as well.*

As time passed, such cooking became more within the reach of my talents and my wallet. However, I had also become less inclined to master complex dishes that wouldn't be making a regular appearance at our table. If I were the sort who cooks for company, I suspect *osso buco* and *risotto milanese* would now be part of my repertoire. But I cook to give each day a little sweetness of expectation and to treat my-self to the mind-calming focus that comes from working with familiar foods. The dishes we prepare most often are old friends, or new ones in the making—enjoyable company, still capable of the occasional sur-prise, but with ways that are in some kind of keeping with our own.

I also came to know that there were many risottos other than *alla milanese*, some quite similar in kind to dishes I already happily made. Even so, the whole risotto family seemed to share one off-putting trait: turn to the risotto section of most Italian cookbooks and you'll hear the intake of a deep breath—preface to a flood of advice, instruction, cau-tion, and critique, and not always from the author, as Loyd Grossman recalls in his *Italian Journey*:

> Many years ago, an Italian friend pulled me aside and whispered conspiratorially that he had seen one of our more well-known Italian chefs stirring a risotto with a metal spoon rather than a wooden one. "How could he do such a thing?" he asked me in horror and despair.

The prospect of opening my kitchen to the scrutiny of a gaggle of Ital-ian cooks . . . *grazie—ma no*. So, while I had long ago learned to make, say, the Venetian specialty *risi e bisi*—a tasty stew of rice and green peas, made in a related but more relaxed way—and had even managed to collect a few cookbooks devoted solely to risotto, I found myself still tiptoeing around it . . . the way you treat someone everybody says you'll really like, but toward whom you're afraid to make a move until they give some indication of wanting to know *you*.

---

*According to Arrigo Cipriani, for instance, in *The Harry's Bar Cookbook*, "If you're a cold person, you are not going to make a perfect risotto." Now, I don't consider myself a cold per-son, but neither do I see any reason to put myself in a position to find out differently.

Then a set of propitious coincidences broke the ice. As it happened, we had on hand some good Parmesan, some first-rate chicken broth, and, most important (thanks to the generosity of our favorite spice merchants, Bill and Ruth Penzey), some superlative saffron. So, strangely enough—as these things happen in life—my initial encounter turned out to be with the grande dame herself, *risotto alla milanese*. *Osso buco* was one thing. But rice dishes—dirty rice, kedgeree, rice and beans—figure largely in our way of eating, and it seemed time to give risotto a try. We consulted the proper authorities, got ahold of some marrowbones, and set to.

                              ❀ ❀ ❀

> But the Italian is more abstinent than the Frenchman, and often lives in the simplest fashion. . . . He delights in made dishes, in his own macaroni, and in stews of many orders—above all, the many forms of *risotto*, a preparation of rice, in which the grains are first browned in butter and then boiled so perfectly that each grain holds its shape. . . . Often this makes the second breakfast, with a flask of wine and a bit of cheese.
> —Helen Campbell, *In Foreign Kitchens* (1892)

For those who are not already way ahead of us in familiarity with risotto making, here is a brief but lucid description of what it involves, extracted from Anna Del Conte's entry on the subject in her *Gastronomy of Italy*:

> The basic method of making a plain risotto, called *risotto in bianco* or *risotto alla parmigiana*, is as follows. The rice must first be sautéed in butter or butter and oil, usually with onion. This has to be a gentle operation, or the grains will harden. The simmering liquid must be added a little at a time—about [half a cup]—and the next addition made only when the rice has absorbed the liquid that was added previously. . . . At the end, more butter and some Parmesan are always added. The risotto is left for two or three minutes, then stirred vigorously, transferred to a dish, and served. It should be eaten as soon as it is ready. Risotto needs a good amount of butter and cannot be left to cook by itself; it must be watched and stirred very frequently.

Although rice has been grown in Italy for centuries, the earliest printed recipes for risotto appeared around the beginning of the nineteenth century. Two of these, quoted at length in Waverley Root's *The Food of Italy*, while both completely recognizable as direct ancestors of the current dish, are also different in the same distinctive way. Neither calls for what is now the dish's signature technique: the addition, ladleful by ladleful, of the cooking liquid. Instead, after the rice receives its initial turn in the hot butter, the broth is poured in all at once and the rice cooked in the ordinary way (simmered until done).

This isn't surprising. Risotto began as a home-style dish, and it's hard to imagine that many cooks had the time to spend just before the family meal was served, when everything was at its busiest, standing over a risotto and giving it her undivided attention. Risotto as we know it now was most likely developed by restaurant chefs at a time when kitchen labor was plentiful and cheap: "Here, kid, stir this until I say stop—and if you look away for a second, I'll box your ears!"

Whether this is true or not, a foodstuff with the ability to both retain its inherent character and give substance to a delicate, flavorful sauce is—for a cuisine in which sauces play so central a role—a stupendous gift. Italian cooks, high and low, were quick to make the most of it—as any casual perusal of Italian cookbooks will reveal—if also, perhaps, a bit trapped by it. Lidia Bastianich, in her *La Cucina di Lidia*, after pointing out that what makes risotto rice unique is its abundance of soluble starch, which "coats each grain of rice with a light, savory sauce of its own cooking liquids and fats," goes on to insist (wrongly, as will be revealed elsewhere in these pages, in the chapter on *riso in bianco*) that

> For this reason, risotto [rice], unlike long-grain rice, *never* [emphasis mine] is cooked in plain water, but always with gradual increments of broth or stock.

Italian cooks are so adamant that stock is a necessary component of risotto that if none is on hand, they turn without hesitation to bouillon cubes—and some, in fact, turn to them as a further enhancement even if stock *is* on hand. (For more on the mysterious relationship between Italians and their beloved *brodo di dadi*, see pages 70–73.)

I balk at this. In truth, I balk at it so entirely that if it hadn't been for the series of coincidences related above, risotto might forever have remained a stranger to our kitchen. And this would have been too bad, for several reasons—not least among them my slowly growing realization that the Italian way is not the only way to think about the matter.

Meanwhile, there I was making *risotto alla milanese*. Not surprisingly, it turned out to be a pretty delicious dish, but my memories of eating it have been obscured by the adventure of producing it. You know that kid I just mentioned—the one dragooned into stirring the pot? Well, at least for the first few months, he's going to have a ball.

Making a risotto isn't all that different from turning out a béchamel—except that blending flour into hot fat and then gradually working in hot milk is tricky and tedious, while doing the same with rice, butter, and stock is easy and fascinating. Where flour is nothing more than a thickener, added for effect, not flavor, rice is something else. You develop the dish by developing *it*.

Raw, risotto rice looks a lot like other rice, if bulkier than most. But once you begin to stir it into melted butter, it quickly takes on a lovely, translucent sheen, revealing the opaque heart of the rice—*la pèrla*—buried within a hard, pellucid layer of starch, now as clear as glass. When you inhale that delicious toasty odor, the immediate temptation is to go on stirring the rice until that clear coating turns a golden amber. Waverley Root mentions a Lombard dish called *ris in cagnon*, in which the rice is fried in butter, garlic, and sage (and finished with plenty of grated cheese). It gets its name, he tells us,

> because a minute drop of butter blackened in the frying clings to each grain of rice, making it resemble a certain type of small white black-headed worm called . . . *cagnott*.

I was achieving this effect—it's quite easy to do—by my third risotto. Perhaps "making *ris in cagnon*" is also a slang phrase in Lombardy for "not knowing when to stop."

Then comes the first splash of liquid, which produces a great sizzling and a burst of heady steam. As you continue adding it, splash by splash, the grains of rice, the bits of onion, anything else in the pan, are gradually coated with a naturally creamy sauce—one made even more unctuous by a final addition of more butter and a generous amount of cheese, everything then receiving a furious beating to make it even creamier (as they say in Italy, *all'onda*—like a wave).

By the time the dish was ready, I was completely enchanted. This is what cooking is all about.

❊ ❊ ❊

It is, in short, the rice itself and not the additions, the stocks, the flavourings, which make the northern Italian risotto unique.
—Elizabeth David, *Italian Food*

The reason I resisted risotto for so long was partly a matter of my own culinary traditions speaking and partly one of temperament. My cooking is based more on my various relationships with the stuff of our larder than on the myriad kinds of business with which cooks transform these things into this or that dish.

Thus, for me, Elizabeth David cuts directly to the heart of the matter. It was only when I was able to shove aside the mythologies that surround risotto and begin to experience the possibilities of the rice— the *"riso"*—itself that my way became clear. If you are a certain kind of cook, you need to become captivated by a particular ingredient's character, and even the humbler varieties of risotto rice have an integrity that draws you to them. The stock, the wine, the Parmesan—it isn't as if these things don't make their contributions, but they are, in the end, items of wardrobe, there to dress the rice only to the extent that they are wanted and prove a comfortable fit.

As for ourselves, risotto fits most easily into the way we eat when it is the meal, not just an accompaniment. There were, we knew, many risottos in which the rice is combined with something else, but often this something else—even if it's a vegetable—is cooked separately and stirred in at the end. We wanted, instead, to cook it with the rice for as much of the cooking time as possible, taking full advantage of that wonderful sauce while adding its own quiet complementarity. Volunteers immediately stepped forward: carrots, kale, leeks, parsnips, celery root, butternut squash, portobello mushrooms. As it turned out, most of these were good, but the last two produced results so memorable that we wanted to share them here.

First, though, listen: cooking risotto is both easy and a lot of fun. Easy because, unlike an equally well-made pot of plain boiled long-grain rice, there's no mystery about measurements or timing; you simply keep pouring in boiling liquid, stirring all the while, until the dish tastes done. Fun because doing this breaks all the rice-cooking rules I know. Cooking long-grain rice is a matter of keeping out of the way; cooking this rice is all hands-on. The more vigorously you stir, the creamier the results—without any damage to the *amour-propre* of the grains themselves.

NOTES ON ITALIAN RICE

Although arborio is the Italian rice best known and most frequently used by cooks outside of Italy, I don't think it's the best rice for risotto. [These] are vialone nano semifino, which is grown in the province of Mantova, and carnaroli, which comes from Novara and Vercelli.

—Arrigo Cipriani, *The Harry's Bar Cookbook*

According to Burton Anderson—who, in *Treasures of the Italian Table*, recounts his visit to the Lomellina area of Lombardy, where many of Italy's choicest rices are grown and where he talked at length to agronomists, rice farmers, processors, and chefs—all the varieties of rice now specifically used for risotto date back no further than to the middle of the nineteenth century, when traditional Italian rice (known simply as *nostrale*—"ours") was crossbred with short-grain japonica rice, imported from Asia. Today, all such Italian rice is divided into four groups based on grain size, from small to large: *comune* (common or ordinary), *semifino, fino,* and—the choice for risotto—*superfino.* (In America, we would say something like "jumbo gourmet.")

However, he then notes that most of the rice sold in Italy doesn't reveal either the variety *or* the size on its packaging, content instead to attract customers by cheap price, fancy packaging, or just a snappy name. Certainly this applies to the rice from our local supermarket that we used for our early risotto experiments. I had assumed it was arborio, but the Pastene Company, which packages it, makes no other claim for it than that it is "Italian rice"—which, it seems, is about as helpful a description as *vin rouge.*

Well, like many another, I've drunk a lot of *vin rouge* in my day, and Matt and I have gotten a good deal of pleasure out of this "Italian rice." Even so, we fired off an order to Zingerman's Delicatessen in

Ann Arbor, Michigan, whose excellent mail-order catalog offers three different high-quality risotto rices—arborio, *baldo*, and *carnaroli*—with prices ranging from about five to seven dollars a pound. All three are imported from the Principato di Lucedio, a rice-growing estate in the Piedmont.

When these arrived, each packed in its own attractive cloth sack, they proved to be something of an eye-opener—and, at the same time, at least distant kin to our supermarket arborio rice. The *carnaroli*, especially, was impressive: its grains a bunch of sturdy *contadini*, with appealing, rough-hewn, husky exteriors that hid what would prove to be deliciously chewy kernels. The arborio actually did resemble the Pastene rice, but was less processed-looking; the *baldo* was, compared to all, distinctly smaller—tiny little nubs encased in a coating of clear starch.

Although the importer describes *baldo* as "a new *superfino* variety," Burton Anderson describes it as a *fino*, and visual examination bears this out. Indeed, I expected it to practically dissolve during cooking, but instead it produced a good-tasting rice with a yielding texture that was the closest of the three to that of ordinary long-grain rice.

All three rices are worth trying and, taken together, give some sense of the range of character in Italian risotto rices. However, the *carnaroli* stood out head and shoulders above the rest. It's hard to imagine a risotto rice producing a creamier sauce or offering a more impressively resilient texture. Rice lovers will find it a revelation.

However, thanks to the popularity of Italian cooking in this country, good-quality arborio has become more and more available on supermarket shelves at increasingly competitive prices. This is the sort of rice that most native Italians cook with, and it is what we mostly use, too.

MAKING RISOTTO
Basic Information

The Rice. For the most spectacular results, track down a bag of *carnaroli*, but even a supermarket risotto rice provides better than adequate results.

The Pot. Although I had always imagined that risotto was made in a saucepan, many Italian cooks recommend a deep skillet, since this provides the stirrer with more control and accelerates evaporation. Following this logic, we found that a nonstick wok was the perfect choice—at least for our small-sized propane burners.* It allows us to do the initial toasting of the rice with less butter, ensures an even distribution of heat, and helps corral flying grains. Our second choice would be a large nonstick skillet.

The Liquid. Fill the teakettle and set it to boil. If you have a quart or so of good homemade chicken stock on hand, by all means start with it. You'll probably still need some boiling water to finish up. If we're in the mood for wine, we open a bottle of Sauvignon Blanc and add a glass to the pan.

Cook's Note. Italian cooks often add a spoonful or so of butter along with the cheese during the final stirring (called the *mantecatura*— "beating into a pulp"), which emphasizes the creamy richness of the dish. For us this is an option, but occasionally an irresistibly attractive one.

RISOTTO WITH BUTTERNUT SQUASH
[*serves 2 or 3 as a meal, 4 to 6 as a side dish*]

Italians make a similar risotto with pumpkin, but they steam and purée it first. In our version, the squash is added raw, so that the finished dish is full of tiny, molten orange cubes. We look for smallish, tubular (thick-necked) squashes with unblemished skin and a feeling of heft. Butternut improves in flavor when stored well, which makes this dish increasingly enjoyable as fall segues into winter.

1 small butternut squash (about 1 pound prepared weight)
2 or 3 tablespoons butter or butter and olive oil
1 teaspoon salt, plus more to taste
1 onion, chopped small
1 clove garlic, minced

---

*We currently use a thirteen-inch wok made by Farberware as part of their "Millennium" series. It is made of a very lightweight metal, but the nonstick surface seems all but indestructible—whereas the rice grains annealed to the more attractive and substantial Joyce Chen nonstick Peking Pan, leaving behind an indelible pattern of pockmarks.

small sprig of fresh thyme or winter savory, minced
1 cup (8 ounces) risotto rice
½ cup dry white wine (optional)
1 ounce (a heaping ¼ cup) grated Parmesan cheese
freshly ground black pepper to taste

Peel the butternut squash, scrape out its seeds, and cut it into dice-sized cubes. Fill a kettle with water, bring it to a boil, and then keep it simmering. Melt the butter (with the olive oil, if using) in a large nonstick wok or skillet set over a medium flame. Stir in the salt, onion, garlic, and herb. As soon as the onion turns translucent, add the rice. Now, stirring continuously with a wooden spoon or spatula, sauté the rice until its coating of starch has turned clear and the rice itself releases a toasty aroma.

Stir in the cubed butternut, then immediately pour in the wine—or, if this is omitted, the first splash of boiling water from the kettle (or ladleful of hot stock). As soon as the liquid evaporates, pour in more, about half a cup at a time. Stir regularly but not necessarily continuously (this is a good time to wash everything used for prep).

After 20 minutes, begin tasting the rice and squash for doneness. When the rice is pleasantly chewy and the squash tender, remove the pan from the heat. Add the Parmesan, a bit at a time, stirring quite vigorously (this develops the creaminess). Taste for salt, adding more if necessary, and season generously with freshly ground black pepper. Serve at once.

RISOTTO WITH PORTOBELLO MUSHROOMS
[*serves 2 or 3 as a meal, 4 to 6 as a side dish*]

Portobellos are the darker-colored cremini mushrooms allowed to mature and produce gills, thus developing their flavor to the fullest. The noted mushroom chef Jack Czarnecki in A Cook's Book of Mushrooms says—and I think rightly—that "portobellos are the only [supermarket mushrooms] that possess the size and succulence of the larger wild mushrooms, such as porcini." Choose undamaged specimens with fully opened but not yet deliquescing gills.

3 or 4 whole portobello mushrooms (about ¾ pound)
4 to 6 tablespoons butter
¼ teaspoon ground hot red pepper
1½ teaspoons salt
6 to 8 shallots, chopped small
1 clove garlic, minced
1 cup (8 ounces) risotto rice
½ cup dry white wine (optional)
several sprigs of Italian parsley, minced
1 ounce (a heaping ¼ cup) grated Parmesan cheese
freshly ground black pepper to taste

Carefully brush the mushrooms clean of any detritus, cutting away the humus-coated stem bottoms. Gently detach the stems from the caps. Cut the stems into small-sized dice and the caps into larger bite-sized cubes. Divide the butter equally between a 10-inch nonstick skillet and a nonstick wok, or into two skillets—one for sautéing the cubed mushroom caps and the other for preparing the rest of the dish.

Fill a kettle with water, bring it to a boil, and then keep it simmering. Set both pans over a medium flame. As the butter melts, add the hot red pepper and half a teaspoon of salt to the skillet and a teaspoon of salt to the wok. Turn the cubed mushroom caps into the skillet and the shallots into the wok. When the mushroom caps have wept their liquid and begun to turn brown, remove them from the heat.

Meanwhile, as soon as the shallots turn translucent, stir in the minced garlic and then pour in the rice. Stirring continuously with a wooden spoon or spatula, sauté the rice until its coating of starch has turned clear and the rice itself releases a toasty aroma. Turn up the heat to medium-high. Stir in the minced mushroom stems, then immediately pour in the wine—or, if this is omitted, the first splash of boiling water from the kettle (or ladleful of hot stock). As soon as the liquid evaporates, pour in more, about half a cup at a time. Stir regularly.

After 20 minutes, stir in the sautéed mushroom caps and the parsley. Begin tasting the rice for doneness. When it is tender and pleasantly chewy, remove the pan from the heat. Add the Parmesan, a bit at a time, stirring quite vigorously. Taste for salt, adding more if necessary, and season generously with freshly ground black pepper. Serve at once.

RISOTTO AL SALTO

In Italian this means "sautéed risotto," but "risotto pancakes" would be a better name for this dish, which is a memorable way of using up any remaining risotto from the night before. I don't usually like to eat leftovers for breakfast, but I make an exception here—this is ultimate breakfast fare. Since there's no telling how much leftover risotto will be at hand, the recipe here is necessarily somewhat sketchy, but the idea is simple enough. The challenge is to make one big crusty pancake, but if your flipping skills are negligible, make smaller ones instead.

Pour ½ tablespoon olive oil into a nonstick skillet or pan. Tilt the pan to coat the entire surface lightly with oil. Put the leftover risotto into the pan and flatten it evenly with a spatula. Now put the pan onto a low flame and cook the pancake(s) slowly until a golden crust forms underneath. Then flip it over and let the other side become golden and crusty. (A little more olive oil brushed on before turning it helps along the crisping process.) To serve, slide onto a plate and cut into wedges. Eat at once.

ITALIAN BOUILLON CUBES—A TASTING

Nowadays, brodo is made from scratch mainly as a treat, and the *bròdo di dadi*, the stock made from bouillon cubes, has triumphed in the Italian kitchen. Even quite elegant recipes allow it as an ingredient; and I've never met an Italian cook who felt guilty about using bouillon cubes in daily cooking, for they are quick and economical. . . . In all fairness it must be said, however, that Italian bouillon cubes are much more flavorful than ours.
—Nika Hazelton, *The Regional Italian Kitchen*

Bouillon cubes are perhaps the most basic method of seasoning in the Italian home kitchen. Italian cooks use them to give broth, soup, sauces—almost anything—added flavor, much the way Americans use salt and pepper. We achieve the best results with Knorr brand. . . . Keep a large supply on hand since their uses are infinite, and they can be stored on the shelf indefinitely.
—Efrem Funghi Calingaert and Jacquelyn Days Serwer,
Pasta and Rice Italian Style

Although it's not at all unusual to come across quotations like the ones above, I didn't take them seriously until a few years ago, when I read an interesting piece in a prominent food magazine in which several food writers were queried about what they stuffed into their suitcases when they headed back home from their trips overseas. A *very* famous writer confessed that, for her, *brodo di dadi* (literally, "broth from dice") topped the list. Dried *porcini*, capers from Pantelleria, estate olive oils, tiny bottles of vintage *balsamico*—all these things I could understand. But *bouillon cubes*?

In Italy, it seems, it isn't just housewives in a hurry who are addicted to them. Top-flight chefs use them all the time. At the Osteria Cascina dei Fiori, a rustic inn specializing in Piedmontese cuisine, Burton Anderson watched the chef, Massimo Milan, demonstrate the making of a true risotto. He reported the following little trick without thinking it worth a comment (although in an earlier chapter he had lambasted Neapolitan *pizzaioli* for using canned tomato sauce):

> The broth had been made without salt, so that it remained clear, although Massimo added some bouillon to heighten flavor, even shredding a bit of the cube directly into the rice.

Could there, then, be something to the rumor that foreign—and, especially, Italian—bouillon cubes have some unique quality that lifts them out of the realm of the meat-flavored salt cubes available here? I was intrigued enough by this question to importune anyone I knew heading for Italy to smuggle some packages back for me. And so eventually I assembled an informal tasting of twelve—two from Mexico, a few from Switzerland, but the majority (seven) from Italy.

The Tasting

In appearance, these cubes were all much larger than their American cousins, each weighing twelve grams, or almost half an ounce. But where most American bouillon cubes are meant to be dissolved in a cup of water, the directions for these called for twice that amount. (The Mexican ones, although the exact same size, called for a quart.)

Bouillon cubes, there as here, come in a variety of flavors. The group I had assembled I divided into five categories: beef, chicken, mushroom, vegetable, and "broth." Consequently, the tasting was divided into five rounds. Bouillon was made from a cube taken from each of the packages. This was tasted by itself, and then compared with the others in its category. Additionally, the beef- and chicken-flavored bouillon cubes were compared to a standard canned broth of the same flavor.

The Results

Anyone trying to decide on the merits of bouillon cubes must first come to terms with their feelings about monosodium glutamate, because MSG is what makes a bouillon cube tick. Comparing canned chicken broth with chicken-flavored broth made from a bouillon cube, one immediately discovers that the bouillon-cube broth, while it may have some chicken flavor, tastes nothing at all like chicken broth. However, at the same time, it has more "flavor" than chicken broth—so much so that, in order to understand what I was tasting, I mixed a quarter-teaspoon of MSG into the cups of canned beef and chicken broth. These mixtures, in all but one instance, tasted like—but also tasted *better* than—the bouillon-cube broths.

Of course, salt and MSG were ingredients I was expecting to find. What I wasn't prepared for was the high proportion of animal and vegetable fat. In several of the cubes it was the second ingredient listed, directly after salt. This fat gave the broth a more authentic-seeming "mouth feel" but universally left in its wake a greasy aftertaste.

The all-around *worst*-tasting cubes were those purporting to make beef bouillon. I tasted two: one from Knorr (*caldo de res*), made in Mexico, and the other from Maggi (*bouillon de bœuf*), made in Switzerland. Both had a strong "bouillon-cube" flavor and a very greasy aftertaste, but the only hint of beefy flavor was the dominant tone of stale Bovril—along with, in the Maggi cube, dried parsley.

Only slightly better were Maggi's *bouquet de légumes* and Knorr's *brodo ai funghi ("speciale per risotti, sughi, umidi")*. Maggi's mixed-vegetable broth had the taste of cooked yeast (it did, in fact, contain yeast extract) and left a tallowy coating on the tongue. The mushroom-flavored cube did have a perceptible taste of cèpes, but it was also too salty and the mushroom taste was unpleasantly coarse. I can imagine it—although I wouldn't *want* it—as a flavor agent in a gravy (*sugo*) or a stew (*umido*), but it would be a disaster in a risotto.

A further step up were the chicken-flavored bouillon cubes, again one from Knorr (*caldo de pollo*), made in Mexico, and one from Maggi (*bouillon de volaille*), made in Switzerland. These had a distinct chicken taste, but their bouillon-cube taste was much stronger. The MSG–chicken broth mixture was superior to both.

The last batch I tasted proved to be far and away the most interesting: the Italian "broth" cubes. I tasted five of them: *brodo "classico,"* made by Liebig, in Perugia; *brodo di lusso sovrano* ("supreme luxury") and *brodo di gusto classico* ("classic taste"), both made by Knorr; Brodo Star; and Brodo Maggi. The last four were all made in Milan.

Among these, two stood head and shoulders above the rest: Knorr *brodo di lusso sovrano* and Brodo Maggi. However, the Knorr broth, while it had a notably good taste, was marred by the recognizable (and lingering) flavor of boiled bones. On the other hand, the best of the lot—Brodo Maggi—although greasy tasting, was not tallowy and did not, in fact, contain animal fats (the only brand that didn't). It was also the only brand without a bouillon-cube taste. Instead, it had a rich, complex flavor that was quite good—better even than the canned broth—perhaps because it contained dried onion, carrot, celery, and leek. If I were bringing bouillon cubes back from Italy, Brodo Maggi are the ones I would stuff into my suitcase.

Still, I doubt that I'd ever bother to do so. Tasty as it is, the effect created by Brodo Maggi is accomplished not by some kind of magic but by massive infusions of MSG, salt, and vegetable fat. I suspect that the allure these cubes have for Italian cooks, who use them even to enhance real stock, reflects that old and hard-to-argue-with culinary maxim: more is more. However, those of us for whom the taste of a highly concentrated meat broth is not the be-all and end-all of good eating might do well to leave this kind of dice playing to those who understand the game.

THE BREAKFAST CHRONICLES

It's been more than fifteen years since I last held down what many people disconcertingly refer to as a "real" job. Which is to say that for more than a decade I haven't shaved before going to bed, taken my shirts to the laundry ("iron but no starch"), or put on a sports jacket before noon. I can no longer find the snooze button on my alarm clock while fast asleep. I'm not sure that I still know how to tie a necktie—or, for that matter, where exactly my neckties are.

What I can't forget, however—what I continue to dream about regularly—is the trauma of the workday morning. It was such a mysterious thing—I went to bed wrapped in the quiet solitude of my personal life; I woke up to find my bed down the corridor from my office door. It was a long corridor, to be sure, and it took a lot of effort to drag myself down it—splashing my face with water, donning work clothes, and swilling coffee as I went.

I would have given anything at the time to make that hallway much, much shorter. I had to face cheek-nipping cold, subway cars so crammed with riders that I had to hammer myself in to escape being crushed by the closing doors, and the predictable but always mortifying late arrival, a good twenty minutes after everyone else. If only I could have woken up sitting in my office chair, scrubbed clean and fully dressed, to find that some considerate soul had left on my desk a jeroboam of steaming coffee and a cheese Danish the size of a pizza.

Instead, if I wanted such things, I had to make a quick detour to obtain them for myself. Although surely, most mornings, I must have eaten breakfast before I left home, I can't for the life of me remember doing so or what I might have eaten if I did. (No time to cook. No appetite for dry cereals. Toast? Instant oatmeal? My mind is a blank.) All I remember is a world of pre-Starbucks coffee-and-pastry take-out joints and doughnut shops, with their half-evocative, half-repellent odor of boiled coffee and stale frying grease, filled with jostling patrons fighting for the counterperson's attention.

I worked in downtown Boston for several years, and by the time I left I knew all the breakfast dives in the area and every item on their take-out lists, from almond croissants to Chinese crullers to the sausage rolls sold at an outlet of a British bakery chain trying to establish a beachhead on this side of the Atlantic. Then I left my job . . . and never entered one of those places again.

What surprises me on reflection is not the abruptness of this change but my total obliviousness to it. There was no sigh of relief heaved nor "good riddance" muttered. One day, there I was with my mouth full of cranberry-walnut muffin, and the day after, it was as if I had never known such things existed. From the moment the working world and I went our separate ways, I haven't eaten a single jelly doughnut or raspberry turnover or anything else much resembling them.*

I suppose I shouldn't be surprised by this. Of all our meals, breakfast is the one in which form most relentlessly follows function. The workday breakfast is eaten with one foot already out the door—which means that the outside has already planted *its* foot right in our kitchen. In the television sitcoms of my youth, Dad ate standing up, a cup of coffee in one hand, his briefcase in the other. Now Mom is standing there with him, and the dirty cups sit in the sink until one or the other of them returns home at night.

The backlash hits once we arrive at the office, where a force as strong as gravity draws us toward the box of doughnut holes some well-intentioned soul has left beside the coffee machine. "Take three," our inner quack prescribes, "one chocolate, one rolled in coconut, one dusted with multicolored sprinkles, wash them down with a hit or two of java . . . and you might just survive until noon." By then, of course, we will know all too well how the day is—or, rather, *isn't*—going. Our

---

*I except a brief addiction to the bear claws made at a certain Down East bakery and a life-long fondness for old-fashioned Maine buttermilk doughnuts. But that's another story for another time.

earlier resolve has been for naught: today has turned out to be no different from any other. The iron-willed may still lunch on salad and cottage cheese; the rest of us sink our teeth into an overstuffed pastrami sandwich, happy enough to have arrived at the top of the slope. From here, quitting time is downhill all the way.

The coffee break, the midmorning treat—these are nothing more than an all-too-ephemeral antidote to that white-collar malaise compounded of boredom, stress, fluorescent light, and recycled air. My interest in such treats vanished once I stopped perversely trying to move my bedroom closer to my office and instead found a way to shift my office into intimate proximity to my bedroom. These days, rather than waking up to find—as I had once wished—that the painful transition from private to public self had already taken place, I open my eyes knowing it doesn't have to happen at all.

❋ ❋ ❋

Even so, I was still a long way from discovering a breakfast of my own. After I left my job, I moved to the coast of Maine, where Matt soon came to join me. For most of our time there, we lived off a dirt road in a house tucked into a pine woods. The deep silence that greeted us every morning all but mandated the house-livening presence of breakfast baking—pancakes, popovers, cranberry clafoutis, blueberry coffee cake. Indeed, such baking became so routine that Matt eventually had her biscuit making perfected to the point where she had them in the oven in five minutes flat and out of it before the coffee had finished dripping through the biggin.

I fed on the pleasure that Matt took from making these things, on the warmth of the hot range on a chilly winter's morning, on the rich aromas that filled the kitchen as they baked. But as time passed, I began to discover that my pleasure faded about halfway through the actual meal. It's hard to explain this experience—eating something good that is still somehow not the thing for you. Each bite is delicious, but deep inside you keep wanting the next spoon- or forkful to arrive holding something else. When the murmur of city life replaced the quiet of the pine woods outside our windows, I was more than ready for a change.

At the same time, without the isolation pushing us together we became less dependent on each other's constant company. Dormant personal rhythms began to reassert themselves. I hate to go to bed at night and hate to get out of it in the morning, but Matt is often up at dawn. Eventually, we surrendered to the obvious. Now, although we spend the rest of the day together, most mornings we breakfast by ourselves.

As it turned out, Matt had also begun to tire of all that morning baking. These days she prefers a very simple breakfast—hot buttered toast with honey, or sometimes Grape-Nuts and yogurt.* But my morning appetite, however lazy, is too restless to settle happily into so regular a gig. Initially, I thought otherwise. At first, my solitary breakfasts reflected a need to compensate for years of suffering from FEDS (fried-egg deprivation syndrome—Matt has never been much of an egg lover). But after several months, this everyday routine of fried or scrambled eggs began to pale. I needed some fresh inspiration.

Unfortunately, however, my breakfast instincts had atrophied, or perhaps I had never developed any to start with. True, I had always seemed to know what I *didn't* want—but while this ruled out whole aisles in the supermarket, it didn't really bring me any closer to an answer. Here I was, at last able to have anything I desired for breakfast . . . except *anything* wasn't what I wanted. I wanted *something*, and that something had a name I didn't yet know.

❊ ❊ ❊

The word *breakfast* seems to me not quite right for our first meal of the day. Whatever you want to call that stretch of time since supper, most of us don't exactly think of it as a fast. We're hungry when we wake up in the morning, no doubt about it. But we're also groggy, vulnerable, feeling as though our brain is encased in nothing more solid than tissue paper. That mouthful we seek, blindly groping our way across the kitchen, bare feet padding on the cold linoleum, needs to be a very special sort of sustenance.

For the farmer who gets up at five to milk the cows, breakfast is not the hearty meal of flapjacks and sausage waiting for him when he gets

---

*Here for the record is her keep-'em-crunchy Grape-Nuts breakfast: Take a flat soup plate and spoon in a thick layer of plain yogurt. Scribble honey over its surface. Shower this with Grape-Nuts until the yogurt disappears from view. Lightly drizzle on more honey. Do not stir. Eat immediately.

back from the barn; it is the scrap of bread he grabs from the bread box as he passes through the kitchen, bucket and lantern in hand. And from that crust we can extrapolate what matters most for the rest of us when we sit down to the day's first meal—minimum effort, maximum return. At breakfast time, we are all babies, yearning for our mother.

Admittedly, it can be a rather torturous road back to the metaphysical breast. For the truly innocent, a bowl of hot pap is all the occasion requires, whether that be porridge and milk, a doughnut dunked in coffee, or a bowl of steaming noodles steeped in beef broth. These days, though, most of us need some sort of psychic calmative as well, embodied in the jujube-esque megasupplement, the frothy protein drink, the vitamin-drenched, premasticated flakes of grain.

And what of the divide between the sweet and the savory breakfast lover? Is this a matter of body chemistry, or is it another way of handling primal discontent? Does the one keep adding sugar in hopes of returning to a half-remembered, now unattainable state of sweetness and bliss? Does the other keep salting and peppering to give savor to what has otherwise proven drearily bland?

Well, whatever the answer, we hardly want it to intrude on our breakfast. It's enough to notice that the essence of the perfect morning meal, no matter how we season it, is the soothing feeling of imbibing energy without expending any. The golden rule of morning eating is simply this: breakfast is *before* work. If there has to be any cooking at all, we want it to be nothing more than an appetite-enhancing form of play.

This is only possible, of course, if someone else has done all the necessary prep. And until the advent of the processed-food industry, that person was usually a hen. The egg is the original prepackaged breakfast, a meal that—at least before salmonella worries—could be sucked right from the shell. (I had a college friend who breakfasted every morning on two fresh raw eggs, which he broke into a glass, seasoned with salt and pepper, whipped up with a fork, and drank straight down.) Otherwise, they can be cooked easily and quickly in any number of pleasant ways—poached, fried, scrambled, boiled, coddled, baked, even, if it comes to that, deep-fried.

The problem—at least for savory breakfast lovers like myself—is that after the egg comes . . . what? Cheese, to an extent. It is soft; it melts pleasingly when laid over a plate of home-fried potatoes—in fact, it would prove to be a crucial ingredient in many of my new breakfasts. But as the featured event, a slice of Gorgonzola or farmhouse Cheddar quickly begins to cloy. It turns out that the world abounds in ideas for one-shot epicurean breakfasts—the wedge of pâté, the smoked duck breast, the tureen of menudo, the brace of marrowbones. Far harder to find is the unremarkable but always welcome sort—the savory equivalent to a bowl of granola or a sticky bun.

Or so I feared when I first started pushing our grocery cart into some unfamiliar areas of the supermarket, searching for clues, toying with foods that otherwise would never have caught my eye—individual pork pies, frozen beef and bean burritos, Chinese ravioli, finnan haddie. At one point or another, I tried them all. I made lots of mistakes. But gradually the field narrowed, and I began to approximate my ideal morning meal.

BAGELS AND CREAM CHEESE

This as a breakfast subject might seem to require hardly a mention, let alone a page of prose, but bear with me. I first sampled real bagels during my youthful stint living on New York's Lower East Side, so I learned early on that they are a lot more than a roll with a hole. The interior should be dense and chewy, the crust shiny, resilient, and tight—as if it had been shrink-wrapped around the crumb. Bagels—like croissants, another ideal breakfast item too often spoiled in the making—require communion between knowledgeable bakers and knowledgeable eaters; if that's not there, all you're getting, no matter what it looks like, is just another bun.

Northampton has a bagel bakery—part of a chain called Bruegger's—where surprisingly decent bagels are boiled/baked all day long, and after a decade of bagel . . . *wantage* must be the word . . . you can get a feeling close to ecstasy hoofing it home through the snow with a sackful of warm bagels sheltered within your winter coat.

Bagels—warm, fresh bagels—exist to be split in half and spread with cream cheese, and it can stop right there. I love cream cheese; it has more attitude than butter, damned if it will melt in your mouth. And people who think of it as bland haven't really bothered to let it sit in their mouths long enough to taste it. Good cream cheese is tangy, rich, and slightly sour, with a lingering clean dairy aftertaste. But, really, its role is to play the straight man of a two-man team—the nice cop who sets you up for his partner's punch, and then soothes you down so that the next one will also catch you off your guard.

On the sweet side, cream cheese makes preserves come alive—guava jelly, famously. But even old familiars like strawberry jam or grape jelly get a fresh charge in its company, since it has no trouble standing up to their cloying sweetness and bringing out the taste of the fruit. For me, however, where cream cheese best works its magic is on the intensely salty: smoked salmon, thin slices of prosciutto, dried salt beef.

One morning, as I was waiting my turn at Bruegger's, I noticed that they were introducing a new green-olive-flavored cream cheese spread. This sounded tempting, but in appearance it proved to be not unlike their smoked salmon spread, except that where that was a solid mass of white speckled with tiny, pathetic orange wisps, this was a solid mass of white flecked with mingy bits of green.

As it happens, Northampton is home to the legendary Steve Herrell, inventor of the "smoosh-in." I remember being taken to his original ice cream parlor in Somerville, Massachusetts, by the historian/writer Theodore Rosengarten, back in the early seventies, and watching with conflicting surges of incredulity and naked lust as the counterperson plopped scoop after scoop of Steve's lusciously rich homemade ice cream onto a giant marble slab and muscled in whatever items the watching customer wanted: M&M's or salted almonds, broken bits of Oreo cookies or Heath bars, big chunks of chocolate or peppermint candy.

If the smoosh-in has endured over the decades, it's because there's no quicker way to win an eater's heart than by trumping expectation. And if Bruegger's couldn't take the hint being waved right in front of their faces and start mashing generous portions of salmon or chunks of olive into their cream cheese instead of allowing some tight-fisted comptroller at the factory to ration those things by the pinch, well, by God, I could. I left the store with a bag of hot bagels clutched to my breast and an even hotter desire burning inside it. I was heading straight for my first . . .

CHUNKY OLIVE-AND-ONION CREAM CHEESE MASH
[serves 1]

> 2 ounces cream cheese
> 3 or 4 imported black and/or green olives
> 1 teaspoon dried onion bits (see note)
> generous dash hot pepper sauce

The night before, put the cream cheese on a cutting board. Pit the olives and tear into small bits. Work these, the dried onion bits, and the pepper sauce into the cream cheese with a butter knife. Form into a block, transfer to a plate, and cover with a small bowl. Refrigerate overnight, before spreading on a sliced warm bagel the next morning.

Variation. Chopped bits of dried tomato also soften nicely overnight in cream cheese and provide a fruity-tasting but still savory mash. Add a pinch of dried oregano and a grind of black pepper to this blend, plus—unless you have a dental appointment the next day—some minced garlic.

Cook's Note. I fell in love with dried onion bits years and years ago, when I first met them pressed into the center of onion bialies made at an East Fourteenth Street bakery. In my innocence, I thought these delicious chewy little shreds, potent with onion flavor, were the result of some mysterious process known only to bialy makers. It would be decades before I discovered they were simply dried onion bits rehydrated in a little water. Their advantage lies in their resilient texture and convenience (and the fact that the hydrating process makes them more digestible than raw onion bits). The disadvantage is that their flavor has been reduced to a single onion-loud tone; they possess no finesse at all. (If you want the convenience without the vulgarity, substitute pricier but subtler freeze-dried shallots.) They can be found at most supermarkets; be warned, though, that if they're only available in a little spice jar, you'll be paying an obscenely inflated price. I buy mine in bulk and keep about half a cup in a plastic container in the refrigerator, moistened with a splash of Scotch whisky. They keep like this for weeks, ready to supply a pinch whenever I need one. As this book goes to press, a pound is only $6.40 (plus shipping) from the Spice House; 1031 Old World 3rd St.; Milwaukee, WI 53203; (414) 272-0977; www.thespicehouse.com.

✹ ✹ ✹

Western Massachusetts has a strong Polish contingent, and there are several locally made Polish specialties at the supermarket, including some splendid kielbasa. What caught my eye during my breakfast browsings, though, was Millie's pierogi, looking genuinely hand-shaped and prepared from good, simple ingredients, sitting freshly made in the dairy case.

Pierogi are very basic half-moon-shaped dumplings, not dissimilar to Chinese pot stickers, but pierogi dough is made with melted butter and egg instead of plain water, which means that the dumpling skin itself is far tastier. This is a good thing, since the fillings have none of the panache of the Asian variety—Millie's, for instance, come in four rip-snorting flavors: farmer's cheese, farmer's cheese and potato, cabbage, and prune. (The dough's utter simplicity means that pierogi are also laughably easy to make, but the process is time-consuming, especially since the usual recipe—based on one egg—is for four to five *dozen*.)*

Also like Chinese dumplings, pierogi can be steamed or boiled, but nothing compares to cramming a bunch of them into a skillet and sautéing them lovingly in sizzling butter, with bits of onion and dried mushroom. On a good morning, they all puff up into plump little balloons and slowly turn an extremely appetizing tawny gold. I find that six of the plain farmer's cheese sort make a good breakfast, brought straight to the table in the pan, which keeps them hot. At first, I took them with a dab of sour cream on the side, but lately I've been having them dressed in nothing but their cooking butter, seasoned as directed in the following recipe.

PANFRIED PIEROGI WITH BITS OF ONION AND DRIED MUSHROOM
[*serves 1*]

2 tablespoons unsalted butter
1 teaspoon dried onion bits (see page 81)

---

*Those living in areas of the country where fresh pierogi are not a supermarket staple will find that frozen varieties serve as a passable substitute in the recipe that is to follow.

1 or 2 pieces of imported dried bolete (porcini), rinsed
    quickly in cold water and chopped into tiny bits
hot pepper sauce, salt, and freshly ground pepper to taste
8 cheese pierogi (if frozen, defrost on a plate in the
    refrigerator overnight)
sour cream (optional)

Melt the butter in a 10-inch nonstick skillet over medium heat. Sprinkle
in the dried onion and mushroom bits, add a dash or two of hot pepper
sauce, and season with a pinch of salt and a few grindings of pepper.
Stir this gently with a spatula so that the seasonings are evenly distributed. Add the pierogi one by one and, as you do, dip one side quickly
into the seasoned butter and then turn it over so that the unbuttered
side goes facedown. After 5 minutes, start peeking at the undersides—
turn them when their surface is anywhere from golden yellow to crusty
brown around the edges, according to taste. When the other side is
cooked to the same doneness, bring the skillet to the table and set it on
a trivet. Sour cream is optional.

BIRD'S NEST

Although this was one of my favorite breakfasts when I was a little boy,
I've rarely made it since, perhaps because you need a child's innocence
not to think it slightly silly. To make a bird's nest, you tear a slice or
two of buttered toast into pieces and put these in a small soup bowl
or (as I remember it) a stoneware custard cup. This is the nest. Into
that you spoon one or two soft-boiled eggs, add a pinch of salt and
a grind of black pepper, and there you are. You eat it with a spoon;
the soft white, the molten yolk, the buttery bits of toast, all get mixed
up together without exactly melding, at least until they reach your
mouth.

When I made it recently, I found it just as tasty as my memory of
it—a lovely breakfast. But something isn't quite right when you prepare
it for yourself. A breakfast dish that forces you to wash your hands before you eat it—which you have to do after tearing up that buttery
toast—just doesn't cut the mustard. One possibility might be to cut the
bread into cubes and fry these in butter to make croutons, which is not

a bad idea. But before I had a chance to try it, another solution proposed itself.

Recently, the produce section of our supermarket has been offering a variety of already prepped and minimally precooked potato products imported from Canada—among them, small cubes for making pan fries and matchstick silvers for making hash browns. I've never been a big fan of hash browns, which too often turn out to be a slab of glueytextured potato shreds encased in a crust. But if you panfry the same shreds loosely in butter until they get nicely (but not necessarily totally) browned, they make an absolutely transcendental bird's nest.

The temptation here is to mold them into little nests in the skillet and fry the eggs right in them. This is easier, yes, but not better, since too much melding takes place in the pan. Do it this way instead:

BIRD'S NEST WITH MATCHSTICK POTATOES
[*serves 1*]

1 or 2 tablespoons unsalted butter
salt and freshly ground pepper to taste
6 ounces (⅓ bag) already prepped matchstick-cut potatoes
   (for whole potato, see note below)
2 eggs

Melt the butter in a small skillet and season it with salt and pepper to taste. Add the potatoes and, over medium heat, sauté until golden all over and edged with brown, about 10 minutes or so.

Have a small pot of gently boiling water waiting. When the potatoes are all but ready, lower the eggs into the water and cook for 3 minutes (or however long you like to cook a soft-boiled egg). Lift them out with a slotted spoon and briefly immerse them in cold water. Meanwhile, transfer the fried potatoes to a small bowl or large Pyrex custard cup and form them into a nest. Scoop the soft-boiled eggs into this, season to taste with salt and pepper, and eat at once.

Cook's Note. If prepped potatoes aren't available, peel a mediumsize all-purpose potato and coarsely shred it through the large cutting holes of a hand grater onto a clean dish towel. Wrap the towel around the shreds and squeeze firmly to extract as much moisture as possible, then transfer them to a skillet and proceed as directed above.

GOYA FROZEN TAMALES

Matt and I had made a quick family visit to the eastern part of Massa-chusetts to present her nephew with a computer game for which he'd been waiting a year and a half (or, as I pointed out to him, one-eighth of his life). Everyone then decided to make a celebratory lunch trip to our favorite barbecue joint, Blue Ribbon BBQ in West Newton, where we feasted on Kansas City burnt ends with assorted sides. Impulsively, on the way out, I ordered some cheese grits to go.

A few mornings later, back home in Northampton, I decanted the grits from their tub, cut them into thick slabs, and panfried them in hot butter. This, with some sausage links, was a truly fine breakfast, and the obvious thing to have done next would have been to dig out the address in Alabama for Adams Mill, order their speckled heart grits, and make up a batch myself.

I truly meant to do this, too—cheese grits is a dish you can make in your sleep, and a loaf pan full would provide many a happy breakfast. But . . . well . . . first I would have to wait for them to come from Alabama. Then I would have to make a batch, mix in the grated cheese and Tabasco sauce and garlic, and let it set overnight. Surely some prescient entrepreneur had already foreseen such cheese-grits yearnings and had some waiting in the frozen-food section of the supermarket?

No, they had not—not in these parts, anyway. However, anticipa-tion whetted my interest in what I did find, a sort of cheese grits South-of-the-Border cousin—Goya brand frozen tamales. What connects cheese grits to tamales (and distinguishes them from both plain grits and polenta) is that each is enriched with fat: one with cheese and the other with lard and bits of cured pork. The tamales weren't quite as tasty as the grits, but they were still very good, with the texture of a sa-vory corn pudding and a clean if unemphatic corn taste. (They also come individually sealed in boilable plastic wrappers, which makes preparing them a snap.)

It probably helped that it's been a long time since I've eaten a hand-made tamale, so nothing lingered in memory with which to compare them. When Matt suggested I pull down Diana Kennedy to see what she had to say about them, I spontaneously blurted out, "Good Lord, I don't want *her* to know what I'm eating," but really, in this instance it's probably best to leave well enough alone.

In their native habitat, tamales are often formed around a filling and served lapped in chile sauce; in my breakfast world, they are eaten so:

TAMALES, ROASTED PEPPERS, AND CHEESE
[*serves 1*]

2 frozen tamales
2 slices of a mild white cheese like Monterey Jack
1 whole roasted red pepper (see note)

Heat the tamales as directed on the package. Meanwhile, slice the cheese. Split the roasted pepper into 2 halves and—if fresh from the fridge—warm them up a bit. (I put them on a saucer and slide this into our toaster oven, turned down to its lowest setting.) Slip the tamales from their packages directly onto a plate. Set a slice of cheese on each and top with a pepper half. Eat at once.

Cook's Note. In the past several years, roasted red peppers have become much easier to find in supermarkets. Make sure the label actually says they are roasted (they also come pickled in brine). They are most likely to be found in the Italian foods aisle, but the ones I use—packed in a jar with huge garlic chunks—come from Bulgaria.

❀ ❀ ❀

So, there you have it—my current breakfast lineup. On the one hand, you might exclaim: What variety! Pierogi, tamales, hash-brown egg nests, pungent olives mashed into cream cheese. But you might just as easily remark: How boring! A year of rooting around for the perfect breakfast and all you've accomplished has been to find a few fresh visages for the same old morning pal: something salty, soft, rich, and, almost always, crisp around the edges. (Once I perfect the panfried tamale, the *almost* will be deleted from that description.)

That both of these insights are equally true tells us less about me, I think, than about what makes a meal a breakfast. The needs food fulfills when eaten directly after waking are too primal to allow much room for gastronomy, which quickly shifts the elegantly constructed engine of our appetite through every notch in the gearbox. First thing in the morning, however, we lock that shift lever in bottom gear, needing plain brute force to drag consciousness out of the primeval swamp and onto the rutted dirt road that leads to the business of the day.

I read a thriller before I go to sleep because it slips a leash around the free-floating anxiety bubbling in my brain and takes it for a run around the block, tiring it enough to allow sleep to come. I want that thriller to be sufficiently literate and inventive to draw me in, but not so much that it would interfere with its ability to play on those subliminal cords of fight or flee. In other words, I want to have my cake and eat it, too—the plot always different, the story always the same.

And so it is with breakfast. The mulish rigidity that governs what we want then signals something visceral at work that has no patience with such fripperies as true variety, let alone brunch menus or nutritional guidelines. On the other hand, once you start giving it free rein, there's no saying what unholy places you may visit or in what strange company you may find yourself.

I don't find this prospect disquieting. After all, if you think about it, you'll see that, once again, breakfast form has been shaped by breakfast function, which these days is to gently shove this solitary writer—clinging tightly to his pierogi- or tamale-shaped life preserver—each morning out onto the dark and turbulent waters of his own imagination.

QUINTESSENTIAL TOAST

"*Buttered* toast!" said Mr. Jeffries. "I suppose we might manage that. . . ." His voice trailed away, leaving in its wake a note of doubt, perhaps even mild alarm. Indeed, he had taken on the appearance of someone reluctantly forced to the verge of a personal confidence.

"The thing is," he began hesitantly, "Wilkins is such a dab hand at *dry* toast. He has the patience, you see. The stuff is crispness incarnate, and yet the surfaces are of the most delicate brown. It is like . . . ," he closed his eyes, "the tastiest breadcrumb you've ever nibbled, except . . . ," here a discreet but suggestive gesture, "of course, one is allowed an entire *bite*."

He opened his eyes and bent toward me in what was now a frankly conspiratorial manner. "To tell the complete truth, I worry that Wilkins might find making *buttered* toast rather demeaning," he said. "Or worse, suspect a certain waning of confidence on our part in his toasting skills. . . ."

"Dry toast it is," said I.

—Nigel Strangeways, *Toaster Agonistes* (1923)

It's early morning. We're on the road for once, and we've just spent the night in a motel. Matt is in the shower; I'm fiddling with the television's remote control, looking for The Weather Channel. To my exasperation, I find it just in time to miss the local forecast and have to sit through the entire cycle until it appears again. Someone details the weather situation in California; someone else prepares the international businessman for storms in Eastern Europe. A flood of commercials. I'm shaken from my drowsy state by one for Sunbeam toasters: something—but what?—is missing in this picture. Lots of people eating toast—no surprise there—but it's all *dry* toast. No butter, no jam, no setting a ring of half-slices around a plate of ham and eggs.

Then, as all things do on television, the image fades. I absorb the local weather (cold, cloudy, chance of snow) and switch off the set, and we then head off together to the lounge, where a complimentary continental breakfast is being served. This, it turns out, surpasses our rather meager expectations: hot decent coffee, a choice of fresh fruit juices, a variety of bagels and breakfast pastries, and a very nice American home-style loaf, hand-sliced, ready for toasting.

I pick out two pieces that are cut almost too thick to fit into the waiting toaster, pop them in, and start opening little butter packets. As I do, the television commercial comes back to mind. Sunbeam obviously thinks that for toast—and with it, of course, the toaster—to survive the Health Age, it must be pitched as a kind of heat-crisped, handheld breakfast cereal. Plain toast: faster to make than instant oatmeal, and not one iota of worrisome fat or sugar. You don't even have to sit down at the table to eat it—and no dishes to wash, just a few crumbs to brush off the kitchen counter at the end of the meal.

Back in the 1970s, I read an article in *The New York Times* about the conditions in a particularly notorious welfare hotel. The reporter made passing reference to one of the tenants, who, with no money left for food, had been forced to feed her children on toast for an entire week. I can still feel the impact of this brief but graphic portrayal of desperate poverty and a mother's love: there might be nothing but the cheapest kind of sandwich loaf to eat, but she would at least make it into toast. Hold this next to that Sunbeam commercial and you can't help but feel something—whether irony or pathos I'm not quite sure—regarding the times in which we live.

However, there remained one final twist to this train of thought. Very recently, and unexpectedly—for reasons that had nothing to do with either poverty or fear of fat—I myself had become a devourer of dry toast. Here in this motel lounge, eating the buttered variety in the old familiar way, I realized that I had experienced a sea change similar to the one that happened when I first stopped drinking my coffee mixed with plenty of sugar and cream—hot-coffee ice cream, Matt's father calls it—and began to take it black.

❈ ❈ ❈

October 7th, 1794. We had for Breakfast, Chocolate, green &
brown Tea, hot Rolls, dried Toast, Bread & Butter, Honey,
Tongue and ham grated very small.
　　—The Reverend James Woodforde, *Diary of a Country Parson*

But there is another kind of bread and butter usually eaten with
tea, which is grilled by the fire and is incomparably good. It is
called toast.
　　　　　　　　—Charles Moritz, *Travels, Chiefly on Foot,*
　　　　　　　　　　through Several Parts of England in 1782

Dry toast, let me start by saying, is not—at least in its ideal form—
merely *unbuttered* toast. To the uninitiated the two may look the same,
even seem to taste the same, but for the aficionado there is between
them all the difference in the world. Unbuttered toast is a substance
half complete, and to be forced to eat it in that state is necessarily to
feel deprived. Dry toast, from the moment it is sliced, has a destiny
wholly its own.

To comprehend this destiny, we must spend a moment with the
word *dry*. In America, where volume and lightness are the virtues of
good bread, commercial bakers make their money by pumping up our
loaves with air. In Britain, where buyers still expect an honest heft, bakers comply by making bread damp—water, of course, being cheaper
than wheat.*

Consequently, in this country, it is the rare piece of bought bread
that *doesn't* emerge from the toaster as "dry toast." In Britain, on the
other hand, considerable effort has always been required to accomplish
this—as can be gathered from Isabella Beeton's careful instructions in
Mrs. Beeton's Book of Household Management (1869):

> To make dry toast properly, a great deal of attention is required;
> much more, indeed, than people generally suppose. Never use new
> bread for making any kind of toast, as it eats heavy, and, besides,
> is very extravagant. Procure a loaf of household bread about two

---

*Elizabeth David, writing in 1979 in *English Bread and Yeast Cookery*, rejects the average
British loaf of sliced white bread as all but untoastable: "There is too much water to get rid of
before the toasting process starts, and steamy bread sticks to the toaster."

days old; cut off as many slices as may be required, not quite
¼ inch in thickness; trim off the crusts and ragged edges, put the
bread on a toasting-fork, and hold it before a very clear fire.
Move it backwards and forwards until the bread is nicely
coloured; then turn it and toast the other side, and do not place it
so near the fire that it blackens. Dry toast should be more gradually made than buttered toast, as its great beauty consists in its
crispness, and this cannot be attained unless the process is slow
and the bread is allowed gradually to colour. It should never be
made long before it is wanted, as it soon becomes tough, unless
placed on the fender in front of the fire. As soon as each piece is
ready, it should be put into a rack, or stood upon its edges, and
sent quickly to table.

In other words, "dry toast" is a bit of a misnomer, since we are talking about something different from a piece of rusk, even a warmed
piece of rusk. True, with the English loaf, dampness is *the* daunting ob-
stacle to be hurdled, but dryness is only a by-product of the actual goal:
a piece of toast that is in-and-out, fully, intensely *crisp*. As Col. A. R.
Kenney-Herbert ("Wyvern") tartly observes in *Culinary Jottings for
Madras* (1885),

The easy process of toasting is frequently slurred over carelessly,
and the bread is scorched, not toasted. If you watch a servant in
the act of toasting, you will generally find that he places the slice
of bread as close to the glowing embers as possible. Setting aside
the risk that the bread thus incurs of catching a taint of gas from
the live charcoal, it cannot be evenly and delicately browned, neither can it attain that thorough crispness which is a *sine quâ non*
in properly made toast. The slice of bread must be kept some little
distance from the clear embers, being gradually heated through,
crisped, and lightly and evenly browned by degrees.*

*Taint of gas, indeed. You don't have to immerse yourself all that far in the literature to be-
come aware that the difficulty of making crisp toast with British bread created a new breed of
English eccentric: the toast bore. Col. Kenney-Herbert is as robust an example as any collector could hope for, but I also treasure my encounter with Sir Henry Thompson, who instructs
us—as quoted in Florence White's *Good Things in England* (1932)—to take each piece of
toast as soon as it is done and carefully slice it vertically to produce two half-toasted slices,
the untoasted surfaces of which are to be returned to the fire. Such toast, he assures us (and
who would doubt him?), will be genuinely crisp, and not "scorched outside and flabby inside,
as is toast [made] according to the general custom."

Crispness versus dryness: this may seem a distinction hardly worth making, let alone brooding over, but there is a morsel of understanding here that will repay worrying out. Toast, after all, is a peculiarly British institution, and none of the usual explanations for this seem quite on the mark. Take, for instance, the oft-quoted thesis floated by H. D. Renner in his idiosyncratic but beguiling *Origin of Food Habits* (1944):

> One of the best examples of a habit originating from village conditions is the toasting of bread. The flavour of bread can be revived to some extent by re-warming, and even new flavours are created in toasting. Village life makes stale bread so common that toasting has become a national habit restricted to the British Isles.

An appealing vision, yes, but the truth is that stale bread is part of country life all over Europe. However, outside Britain such crusts are more commonly used as sops—either dunked into soup or wine or dipped into an eggy batter and fried. For centuries, this was also what the English did with their stale bread, except that they developed a taste for toasting the bits they dropped into their drink. This may be because toast complements the taste of ale much more than it does wine, or it may be for a reason we will get to in a moment. But it was so much the case that the word *toast* was then as often coupled with brew as it now is with butter—and an old soak (or, as the *Oxford English Dictionary* tactfully puts it, "a brisk old fellow fond of his glass") was called an "old toast"—a phrase that, today, would be met with an uncomprehending stare.

So, what caused the British taste in toast to turn from sopped to dry? Well, the first quote the *O.E.D.* uses to example this new trend provides us with a clue: "Sweeten your tea, and watch your toast" (Jonathan Swift, 1730). Instead of quaffing down a quart of ale for their breakfast and another for dinner, the British cottagers, imitating their betters, began brewing up a pot of tea. And, since tea—especially the cheaper sort, where the leaves are fired to a darker color to increase their flavor—is already "toasty" (the word is a venerable and quite favorable adjective in the tea trade), toast itself has no place *in* the cup. But toast is as comfortable set beside it as is the toasting iron next to the kettle on the hob.

Tea and toast—the phrase alone is enough to summon up the scene: the murmuring fire, the bubbling kettle, the table laid with tea things, the sugar bowl and creamer, the butter crock. The curtains are drawn tight against the draft, but if we should happen to pull them aside, our eyes would be met by an ocean of well-trimmed grass of the softest and greenest of greens, wet with rain as fine as mist, and just as penetrating. It was in the chilly draft that pursued you down the hallway to this room; now, inside, closed windows and doors can barely keep it out.

"The damp little island" Britain is called, and damp it is, the winters especially marked by chill and endless drizzle. In the days before central heating, that damp insinuated itself everywhere—through walls and bedclothes, through layer after layer of woolen clothing, right through to one's very bones . . . the marrow of those bones. If you can remember what it was like stepping out of the shower at gym only to discover that the person before you had taken the last dry towel, then you can begin to imagine why, for the English, the word *dry* might not only shake off some of its less appealing attributes (arid, sapless, dusty, sharp-tongued) but also take on an almost spiritual glow. And to be dry *and* warm: is there any more evocative word for this condition than . . . *toasty*?

Remember, dry toast is not really dry in the sense that a rusk is dry: parched to the point of desiccation. The toast rack—a device designed to hold several pieces of dry toast on edge and separate from each other—was invented because when the slices are just piled in a heap, they almost immediately become soggy. During the toasting process the heat permeates the tiny air pockets—the nooks and crannies—within the bread, vaporizing their moisture and crisping the inner surfaces that surround them. But it does not draw the moisture out of the crumb itself. No, dry toast is dry the way *we* want to be when we step away from the fire: with the damp and chill driven out of every molecule of our being, our body having soaked up so much warmth that we begin to radiate it ourselves. And the phrase for this condition? *Warm as toast.*

If it weren't a bit too twee, dry toast might more precisely be called *toasty* toast, and we can see from this that there is a not-all-that-hidden subtext to the act of making it. Esther Copley pointed a wagging finger at it when she wrote, in *Cottage Cookery* (1849), "As to toast, it may fairly be pronounced a contrivance for consuming bread, butter, firing, and time"—firing and time, the less puritanical among us might rejoin, that has rarely been put to better use.

Also in toasting's favor is its inherent egalitarianism. To assign the task to a servant is almost to guarantee that the job will be hurried and the toast scorched, because—for the already warm—toast making is hot and tedious work. However, for those of us just in from damp and chilly weather, what better way to warm ourselves slowly, deliciously, and completely than to volunteer to make the toast? Let someone else go fill the kettle—we'll pull a stool up to the hearth and reach for the toasting fork. And once the toast rack is full, we can settle into our favorite armchair, drawn up to that same fire, with hot toast and a steaming cup of tea, stretching out our legs to toast our toes. . . .

❋ ❋ ❋

If allowed to stand and become sodden, dry toast becomes indigestible. From the fire to the table is the thing.
—Lizzie Heritage, *Cassell's Universal Cookery Book* (1894)

Matt and I put in a long morning—no lunch until sometime late in the afternoon—so coming up with the right midday snack for myself has become a matter of some urgency, and one that I never seem able to resolve for long. For reasons both logistical and calmative, this snack must be something I can look forward to, with the occasional break, day after day after day. Unfortunately, since I like to continue writing while I eat, all the usual favorites are ruled out: no potato chips or pork cracklings (they get grease on the computer keys); no salted peanuts in the shell (they leave a mess all over the desk). And, since I don't have much of a sweet tooth, I rarely feel like ducking out for a molasses doughnut, an apple fritter, or a bear claw (to name just three of the local coffee-break treats).

Then a baker named Stephen Lanzalotta built a wood-fired bread oven in nearby South Brooksville and started turning out the best bread—to my mind—anywhere north of Boston. I was especially drawn to his variations on *pain au levain,* hefty, flavorful loaves that kept nicely for more than a week. These, I was sure, would make wonderful toast, and at last provide me with the quintessential *casse-croûte.*

However, it quickly became apparent that my years of making toast for buttering were no qualification for making toast to be eaten dry. In fact, this was so much so that after several attempts—and despite the goodness of the bread—I began to lose heart. I was abusing the bread by treating it this way: it kept coming out of the toaster with a crisp veneer laid over a totally untoasted, steamy-moist interior. A dousing of olive oil made it palatable—but it didn't make it right.

In desperation, I went to the bookshelf to consult some cookbooks that were written before the electric toaster arrived on the scene to convert toasting from an art to a techno-snap. I was met with a blast of admonitions. In my greedy way, I'd been cutting the slices as thick as I could and still get them to fit into the toaster slot. In my hasty way, I'd been sliding the timing lever all the way right (toast to the max)—and, even so, had been frustrated because I had to go and push the toast down for a second run.

Totally wrong. So, first, I reluctantly began cutting my thick slice into two thin ones, since this is the only way to toast the bread all through. And then, to keep the edges from burning, I learned that I had to make my toast very, very slowly. The timing lever started moving farther and farther to the left, until it finally came to rest at "1." This meant that to get the toast just right I had to run it through four or five short cycles with a brief rest between each.

Is all this worth it? I think it is. The act of toasting changes bread, and toasting it so thoroughly transforms it. Mary Lincoln writes that this method produces "pure wheat farina," by which she means an aggregation of lightly roasted crumbs, and a slice that possesses not only a penetrating toasty flavor but a lighter, drier, chewier texture, through and through.

When I, following Matt's example, started to take my coffee strong and black, it wasn't because I thought it tasted better that way. At the time, we were working hard to find a bean we really liked and a brewing method that brought out the best it had to offer, and it gradually dawned on me that I had been missing out on another kind of pleasure: getting to know coffee—good coffee—on its own terms. I still use cream and sugar when I have coffee in a restaurant, and on other occasions simply for the treat. The thing is, I now know that coffee can be its own treat. And in the past few months I've learned the same thing about toast. I still love it buttered, but a snack of plain dry toast can be pretty great, too—a realization that had nothing to do with dietetic fashion and everything to do with Stephen Lanzalotta's bread, and my learning how to toast it perfectly.

There's one last thing I haven't told you about dry toast: it has the most amazing aroma. I used to work in an office cubicle about twelve feet square. That was almost fifteen years ago, but when I started making dry toast I found myself fantasizing about what it would have been like if I had had a toaster on my desk.

Ten minutes before coffee break, I slip two slices of bread out of their sandwich bag and into the toaster slots, and push the lever down. During the first cycle, the toaster emits the delicately yeasty smell of warm bread. I go on about my work. When the bread pops up, I press the lever down again. This time the aroma is stronger, crisper. The yeastiness is gone, as are the undertones of steam. The bread isn't toasted, but it begins to smell of toast. Up come the slices and back down they go. Now the whole cubicle begins to fill with the deep and penetrating fragrance of wholly toasted bread—every particle of crumb adding its mite. The slices pop up for the third time and are sent back down for a final round while I take my cup and head off to the coffee machine. The aroma seeps out after me to torment the others gathered at the snack cart. What jelly doughnut or cheese Danish can compete with even the *smell* of hot toast? In a week there is a toaster on every desk; at coffee break the air in our corridor is good enough to eat . . . with butter, or without.

> "Toast," said Berry, taking the two last pieces that stood in the rack. "I'm glad to get back to toast."
> —Dornford Yates, *Adèle & Co.* (1931)

DRY TOAST
How to Make It

To make the best kind of dry toast, you must start with the right kind of bread: a loaf with a dense, moist crumb. A *pain de campagne* or *pain au levain* is the perfect bread for this, but so is a whole-grain loaf. To get the proper texture, cut the bread into slices that are about ⅓-inch thick.

For a toaster. Turn it to its lowest setting and keep pushing down the toasting lever until the toast is golden brown. Some rotation of the slices may be necessary to keep the edges from burning. Ideally, you'll not be standing by the toaster the whole time but engaged in some other business so that the slices can rest a few moments between trips (thus the advantage of keeping a toaster by your desk or VCR).

For a toaster oven. Preheat to 350°F and then set the slices on the toasting rack and bake them until they have turned a golden brown. Again, some adjustment may be necessary.

In either instance. If the toast burns, *chuck it* and start over. As Sarah Tyson Rorer, in *Mrs. Rorer's New Cook Book* (1902), emphatically puts it: "Burned bread is objectionable, and has a bad flavor, no matter how much of the outside is scraped away." Hence Harry Graham's heartfelt lament in *Ruthless Rhymes for Heartless Homes* (1901):

> *Making toast by the fireside,*
> *Nurse fell in the grate and died.*
> *And what makes it ten times worse,*
> *All the toast was burnt with nurse.*

How to Eat It

In winter, salt butter would be sent for and toast would be made and eaten with celery. Toast was a favourite dish for family consumption. "I've made 'em a stack o' toast as high as up to their knees," a mother would say on a winter Sunday afternoon before her brood came in from church. Another dish upon which they prided themselves was thin slices of cold, boiled streaky bacon on toast, a dish so delicious that it deserves to be more widely popular.

—Flora Thompson, *Lark Rise to Candleford* (1945)

Plain. About this, surely, enough has been said. But the innocent simplicity of the following recipe, with which Eliza Acton concludes *The English Bread Book* (1859), delights me.

BREAD CRISPS

TO SERVE INSTEAD OF BISCUITS FOR DESSERT: Cut thin shavings of bread from a stale loaf, spread them on a dish, or lay them singly on the tin tray of an American oven, and dry them very gradually until they are perfectly crisp; then bring them to a pale straw colour; withdraw them from the fire, and, as soon as they are cold, pile them on a napkin, and serve them without delay. They require an extremely gentle oven to produce the proper effect on them; but, if well managed, will retain their crispness for several hours; and it may always be renewed by heating them through afresh. By many persons they are much preferred to biscuits, being considered far more delicate. A small American oven answers for them extremely well if placed at a distance from the fire: they require quite half an hour to dry them as they ought to be done.

Buttered. We've seen that dry toast is not unbuttered toast, but a deeply crispy *kind* of toast. So there is no reason on earth not to eat it buttered, as long as the toast is kept hot and crisp. Here again Sarah Tyson Rorer gives us succinct advice: "Send at once to the table. Butter while eating."

Dipped. "Toast that is to be served with anything turned over it, should have the slices first dipped quickly in a dish of hot water turned from the boiling teakettle, with a little salt thrown in." So direct the authors of *The White House Cook Book* (1915), who follow up with almost four pages of examples: tomato toast, baked eggs on toast, oyster toast, reed birds on toast.

This may seem to go against all I've written, but consider—dipping (or dunking!) the toast only anticipates what is about to happen in your mouth, that moment when crispness collapses into succulence. The trick is to move quickly in both the dipping and the eating. So, for instance, cook some broccoli florets in lightly salted water while you make dry toast. Lift out the florets and toss them in a little garlicky olive oil, seasoned with both red and black pepper. Then dip the dry toast into the still boiling broccoli water for a scant second, set it in a bowl, spread the florets over it, along with a scattering of grated cheese. Another notion: dip the toast into homemade beef or chicken broth and heap with sautéed mushrooms.

Sopped in Cream. Finally, this little extravagance—"Cream Toast"—from Janet McKenzie Hill's *Practical Cooking and Serving* (1902):

> Prepare four slices of toast; dust with salt and pour over 1½ cups of cream heated to 160°F for 15 minutes. With cheese: Sprinkle hot toasted bread with grated [Cheddar], and set in the oven until the cheese melts; pour over hot cream, and serve at once. A beaten egg may be added to the cream.

CINNAMON TOAST

Elisheva S. Urbas

When Avital, my three-year-old, wants nothing else for breakfast, she will happily eat cinnamon toast. I have made hundreds of slices over the past months, but increasingly more of them are for myself, to eat at my desk while she's in nursery school. I vividly remember my own very first slice of cinnamon toast, offered as a snack by the mother of a boy I had a crush on in my kindergarten class, and my description of this memory was what persuaded my daughter that it was, at least, worth trying. But now she'll eat it anytime (as long as I cut the crusts off, to be sure, but there's only so much one can hope for before one's child's fourth birthday).

Cinnamon toast is a treat because, of course, it is covered with cinnamon and sugar. But it is, as Avital says, "a treat that is food," meaning that I don't need to feel guilty about giving it to my children for breakfast, because it is at its best made with whole-wheat bread. Unlike French toast, whose fluffiness is best complemented by eggy challah, or the French schoolchild's snack where chocolate is laid into bread of strongly contrasting whiteness, cinnamon toast is supposed to taste *brown*. After some experimentation we have all found our favorite to be the same presliced whole-wheat loaf we buy in the health food store for sending peanut butter sandwiches to school. It is not a distinguished bread, but one with some wheaty flavor and no fake-food taste.

Here's how we make it. First, toast your bread to just a bit lighter than you normally would your plain toast. In my case that is pretty dark and crunchy, whereas Avital likes hers, as she says, "more tender," meaning barely warmed and staled. *Chacun à son goût.* When your toast is ready, spread it immediately with butter. How thickly you spread it is up to your taste, but be sure to cover the whole surface, right up to the edges of the crust, with at least a light layer.

Next, sprinkle cinnamon and sugar surprisingly heavily over the entire buttered surface. This does not take very much of either. When Avital and I began making cinnamon toast last year, we first shook cinnamon from the spice jar onto the bread, then stood the bread up and tapped it so that the excess cinnamon in some spots fell and spread to cover others. Then I half-filled a teaspoon from the sugar jar and sprinkled it lightly—but again thoroughly—over the whole slice, as Avital said, "just like snow."

This is easy but slightly fussy, and eventually, when I realized I was doing this twice a day, I invested $1.49 at my local housewares store in a spice-jar-sized shaker, which has speeded up the process. Mix the cinnamon and sugar up well, remembering that a teaspoon of the former is enough for a shakerful of the latter, and you can thereafter shake the two together over the whole slice with no tapping, spooning, et cetera.

Then it's back into the toaster oven. Most recipes I've seen assume you'll do the first part in a pop-up toaster and the second under the broiler, which is what you really need to melt the sugar into a glaze with the butter and cinnamon. However, using a toaster oven at home, I've found that if the bread is slightly undertoasted the first time through, you can just put it back to toast on the lightest setting and the final result will be perfect.

The melted sugar is wickedly hot when it first hits the plate, and the toast itself still melted-butter soft, but within moments it will have cooled into a crisp slice of toast that has died and gone to heaven. Avital likes hers in quarters, no crust. Her baby sister, Ronit, still working with toothless gums, needs hers cut into tiny pieces. But I wait until they're all out of the house and eat mine with strong black coffee.

HOW RESTAURANTS MEAN

❀ ❀ ❀

What are we looking for when we go out to eat? I don't mean when necessity forces a pit stop for a quick bite; I mean when we head for a restaurant with no other expectation but pleasure. If the answer to this question seems entirely self-evident . . . consider.

Matt and I drive miles and miles through the darkness of the Canadian woods to a restaurant in a tiny hamlet in the middle of New Brunswick where we have a reservation for supper. When we arrive, the place is so dark and silent that, instead of just walking in, we ring the doorbell. The door is opened by a very young woman—the owner-chef's daughter, she later tells us—who ushers us to a table in a dining room about the size of a spare bedroom. Ours is the only table in it. A menu, short but appealing, is written out on a chalkboard.

Shortly thereafter, in the ghostly quiet, we hear the *pad-pad-pad* of footsteps as the young woman comes to take our order. We give it to her—we have already decided that we drove too far through too much wilderness to back out now (*flee* is actually the word in our minds)— and listen to the *pad-pad-pad* of her footsteps as she heads back down the hall to the kitchen. Then . . . silence. No voices, no sounds of cooking, nothing. The stillness is finally broken by a somehow familiar but not quite placeable *ping*. A moment later, we hear the *pad-pad-pad* again and our appetizers arrive, along with a carafe of the house red (this turns out to be Carlo Rossi Burgundy, a name forever after associated with this evening).

We begin to eat. Again, the retreating footsteps, the total silence in the kitchen, followed by that telltale *ping*. Now it dawns on me where

I have heard this noise before. "Matt," I whisper, "it's a microwave oven. *There's no one here but her and us.*" We look at each other and then at the chalkboard menu, which our server has left propped up on its little stand. All the dishes—soups, appetizers, and entrées (including the lamb stew Provençale that we have both ordered)—however otherwise various, either require no cooking (smoked salmon) or can go straight from freezer to microwave.

The cook our restaurant guidebook had so lavishly praised had indeed made the meal we were eating, but she'd prepared it—and dozens of others exactly like it—days ago. Matt and I are nothing more than two strangers eating in her empty house. We drive back to our hotel in an unsettled state, feeling, if not swindled, at least betrayed.

When we think of restaurants, we think of food. We go to them because we like to eat, and there are certain dishes that only taste good—or taste good in a way that can't be reproduced at home—when we eat them in a restaurant. But saying that restaurants are about food is like saying a job is about money: it's the reason we're there, yes, but that says nothing about the work we have chosen to do or the salary that we end up earning. When we first set out to look for a job, we encounter powerful, unarticulated forces that push us in one direction and keep us, even against our will, from heading in another, whatever our dreams or ambitions.

The same with restaurants. This is why most of us have favorite places that would not fare all that well in a serious restaurant review, and why when we do decide to treat ourselves to dinner at a four-star restaurant, we are—at least secretly—somewhat disappointed. You can't just turn up—least of all at those places—and expect to have a good time. Restaurants give us something more than food, and that means they ask for something more than money in return.

Two books have recently been published that cast an illuminating light on the mysterious intimacy between restaurants and those who eat there: Robert Cornfield's *Lundy's—Reminiscences and Recipes from Brooklyn's Legendary Restaurant* and Frank Pellegrino's *Rao's Cookbook—over 100 Years of Italian Home Cooking*. Both books not only tell a fascinating story but, even more interestingly, manage to make reading about the experience of eating in these places almost as compelling as it was—and, at least in one instance, still is—to the actual customers.

LUNDY'S

This happened in the late sixties: my date and I had ordered the
famous Shore Dinner. My lobster was served to me, but it wasn't
cracked well enough to get at the meat of the body and claws. We
called the waiter over and explained the problem to him. He took
my lobster, wrapped it in my dinner napkin, and smashed it
against the nearest wall. He returned to our table, unwrapped my
dinner, placed it on my plate, and said, "How's that, lady?" That
was the essence of Lundy's.

—Lydia Greenblatt*

Lundy's is the sort of restaurant that can generate longing in those who
never ate there (or, for that matter, have never in their lives been to
Brooklyn) simply because it evokes such a powerful burst of nostalgia
in those who did. This is important: if Lundy's story were told without
their testimony, it would hold your complete attention, to be sure, but
you wouldn't understand why anyone ever patronized the place.

The restaurant's owner was Irving Lundy, born into a family of oys-
termen who lived in Sheepshead Bay, then a lively and attractive stretch
of Brooklyn's southern shorefront. His first seafood restaurant, which
he opened in 1926 at the age of thirty, was a shack built on the Lundy
family pier. But Irving was ambitious, for both himself and his restaurant, and—thanks to income from bootlegging during Prohibition and
a windfall from public shoreline redevelopment—he was able to purchase a choice piece of waterfront property. There he built, in the then-
fashionable Spanish Mission style, what might without exaggeration be
called the Lundydrome: a stucco-covered two-story leviathan topped
with a red tile roof. It could accommodate 850 diners on the first floor
and as many on the second, where you could sit on a veranda with a
panoramic view of Manhattan Beach across the bay.

Such a restaurant could be only one of two things: a dismal failure or
a spectacular success. For decades, even during the Depression, Lundy's
was the latter, mobbed on summer weekends, serving ten thousand

---

*All quotations that have to do with Lundy's, unless otherwise attributed, come from Robert
Cornfield's book, which contains a whole section of reminiscences from Lundy patrons. I
should disclose here that Bob is our friend and literary agent. However, while this may be why
I opened the book, it isn't the reason I've read it through, spellbound, twice—Bob takes a
great story (only part of which is recapitulated here) and runs with it.

meals on a typical Mother's Day, and, indeed, usually so crammed with noisy families that, as one patron remembers, "The roar of thousands of conversations all but pushed the new arrival back onto the avenue."

If the customer were truly new, he or she would encounter something much more unusual for a restaurant that size than noise: Lundy's had no one assigning seating. It was all catch-as-catch-can, with newcomers scouting the enormous dining hall for tables where the patrons had reached the stage of dessert and coffee, then surrounding that table—both to encourage its occupants to finish up and to discourage anyone else from even thinking they could claim it.

Knowledgeable customers would scan the room for anyone they knew who had a table, then pull up a chair and join them, while their families stood in the background, waiting for the signal that the table was about to be theirs. Then they would fight through the crowd to their seats, dodging waiters bearing huge trays—called Big Berthas—heaped with food and crockery, and busboys struggling to clear away the remains of the last meal and reset the table.

The moment everybody had settled in, someone at the table would start calling out for one of Lundy's specialties—the heaping basket (or, as some describe it, the towering pyramid) of fresh-baked biscuits, which arrived at the table still hot enough to melt a pat of butter instantly. The appearance of these was a matter of great anticipation—an anticipation charged with an undercurrent of anxiety. To get your biscuits you first had to get the attention of your waiter, which in Lundy's hectic atmosphere was almost as challenging as claiming a table.

The waiters, all black, all male, all dressed in a special Lundy's uniform, which at one time included mint-green jackets and tan pants with a pink stripe down the side, were brusque, efficient, imposing, and extremely busy.* It paid to get to know one and stay in his good graces,

---

*A waiter's lot at Lundy's was not an enviable one, especially on weekends, when shifts ran for twelve hours with no breaks, starting at eleven in the morning and ending, with luck, at midnight. Like the patrons they served, former waiters also recall the size of both the dining room and the portions at Lundy's, but from a very different perspective. As one waiter told Cornfield, "Let's say you had a party of six, and they were all having the Shore Dinner. You'd be carrying from almost a block away six orders of steamers covered with heavy bowls and the butter and broth. During the summer sixty percent of the customers would order watermelon for dessert, and they'd each get one-fourth of a melon. With six people you'd have close to two watermelons on a tray."

or else to bring a pack of cards and play gin rummy while waiting for your meal. It wasn't until you got your waiter to bring that first batch of biscuits that you could be really sure your meal at Lundy's had begun.

It's almost impossible to reconcile the image that seaside eating places usually summon—the white tablecloths set flapping by the cooling ocean breeze, the mingled aromas of salty sea air and boiling lobsters—with the claustral pandemonium that was Lundy's. Indeed, everything about the place seemed wrong: there was no air conditioning (it was so hot in the summer that waiters had to change their jackets seven or eight times during their shift), and there was such a clamor that the only way to carry on a conversation was to shout. So shout you did. But mostly you ate . . . and then, with new arrivals literally breathing down the back of your neck, you got out.

The food, you think, must have been terrific.

Certainly this is how those who ate there remember it. "I believe the fried onion rings were the most delicious I ever had." "The pumpkin pie . . . could not be duplicated." "My father would always start with a wonderful lump crabmeat cocktail." "The thick, golden-brown Manhattan clam chowder . . . was delicious." "Lundy's was the only restaurant that could broil a lobster without drying it out." "Lundy's always had the best clams."

Most of all, people remember those biscuits. "The hot biscuits on the table were a family favorite." "Food: the biscuits were to die for!" "Those biscuits were unequaled anywhere on this planet." "I could hardly wait for the little warm muffins to come out." People recall smelling them the moment they came through the door, the number of baskets their family would eat, and how they filled their pockets with them, only to discover that they were never as good the next day.

The particular intensity with which these biscuits are remembered provides us with an unexpected insight into what eating at Lundy's was all about. The people who ate there were immigrants and the children of immigrants. To them, baking-powder biscuits were something new, an emblem of America and American food. They were hot; they were tasty; they were rich; they soaked up melted butter; they were free. You could eat all you wanted of them and nobody cared. It was almost like finding gold bricks lying around on the streets.

Patrons look back on the menu selection as vast, but in truth it was rather limited. Fish was served broiled, fried, or made into chowder. Shellfish could be had the same ways, or pan-roasted or on the half-shell. Shrimp, crab, and lobster meat could be eaten as a salad, in a Newburg, or au gratin. Those who didn't care for seafood could order steak, ground steak, or lamb chops. Potatoes in various forms were the standard accompaniment; vegetables were few; dessert was ice cream, pie à la mode, or watermelon.

However, for those who ate there, these offerings seemed more than sufficient. Lundy's was democratic in the best sense of the word: it was inclusive, affordable, and pleasurable, and the menu was easy to understand. Remembering his own childhood as part of an immigrant family, Jerry Della Femina writes in *An Italian Grows in Brooklyn*,

> We didn't go to restaurants, because we thought we'd be made fun of. Maybe we wouldn't be able to read the menu and the waiter would laugh at us.

The Della Femina family would have felt at ease at Lundy's. There, such customers were made to feel not like bumpkins but like real Americans. Instead of the foods they had at home—pasta and tomato sauce, chicken soup with matzo balls, boiled beef and cabbage—they dined on huge boiled lobsters, thick slabs of steak, hot buttered biscuits, fat wedges of blueberry pie, all served by a black waiter . . . a waiter, that is, who might intimidate but never patronize them.

On the contrary, because of their race, these were waiters with whom Lundy's customers could feel quite comfortable—perhaps even discern a certain commonality. This, in turn, prompted generosity. Customers prided themselves on leaving big tips and not only remembering their waiter's name but buying him drinks, giving his children snowsuits at Christmas, and referring to him as a family friend—none of which would have been true had the waiter been white, Protestant, and Anglo-Saxon.

What Lundy's did was turn the immigrant's struggle to become American into a kind of game—even better, into the kind of game where everyone wins. Everything was part of it: the restaurant building itself, with its grandiose size and ostentatious design; the roar of confusion as newcomers plunged into unfamiliar chaos and found themselves pushed aside by the aggressive hustle of everyone else.

Wasn't this exactly like their first encounter with the streets of New York? No one had told them anything; they had had to pay attention, watch how others succeeded, in order to figure out how they could, too. Learning the ropes at Lundy's—finding the order in the chaos and then summoning the brazenness to claim a table and thus join the feast—transformed what in real life often had a bitter edge into something wholly sweet. No wonder patrons delighted in playing that same game over and over again.

None of this, of course, was what Irving Lundy had in mind when he started his restaurant; little of it is articulated by those who share their reminiscences of eating there. But this is what made the place a success, and it also meant that the more acclimatized the customers became to America, the less eating at Lundy's would provide that old familiar thrill. Lundy's began to falter as the decades passed; Irving was now too old to change it and too loyal to his customers not to keep it running, at an ever-increasing loss, until his death in 1977. Soon thereafter, Lundy's closed its doors.

But it refused to die. Through the efforts of former patrons, the building was declared a historic landmark in 1991, keeping it safe from destruction. In 1995, it reopened under new management: same name, same Shore Dinner, same hot biscuits. Cornfield writes:

> The old-timers return, driving from Long Island, New Jersey, and Connecticut. . . . Many begin to cry when they remember what the old days were like. Lundy's stands for vanished youth, family bonds, happier times. Before patrons order, they ask for the manager, Steve Gattulo, to show him where their table was in the old days, to talk of clams thirty cents a dozen, to recall the waiter who was their friend.

If most of the old clientele fail to notice that what was once a kind of Ellis Island plus great American food is now just another fancy Brooklyn restaurant, this should come as no surprise. They would be in for quite a shock if they were magically transported back to the Lundy's of their youth. From the perspective of today, it would seem so noisy, so hot, so . . . uncouth. What aging in oak casks does to wine, time does to memories: polishes and refines, mellowing harsh flavors and smoothing out the tannins. The name may be the same, but it isn't Lundy's Restaurant at all—it's the Lundy's Restaurant Museum.

RAO'S

> When you mention Rao's to someone, you can see their eyes light
> up. Probably they've never been there—you can't get in the
> place—but they've heard about it: the location, the ambience, the
> mystique, all those stories. You can only imagine what it's like.
> And then one night, you get lucky. You get in and find out it's all
> true.
>
> —Regis Philbin

Rao's (pronounced "RAY-o's") might best be described to those who
have never heard of it as the greatest Italian neighborhood restaurant
you'll never eat at. In contrast to Lundy's, Rao's six booths and four tables are permanently reserved by a small group of regulars whose hold
on them only death and bankruptcy will ever break. Rao's is the tough-
est place in Manhattan to get a table; the few guidebooks that mention
it also tell you not to even bother trying.

This fact alone is enough to whet the appetites of certain highly
competitive American alpha males. In fact, everything about Rao's—its
obscure, distant location in East Harlem; the fact that there is only
one seating each evening (Monday through Friday; the place is
closed weekends); the Italian grandmotherly nature of the cooking; the
tough-guys-can-be-suave, Frank Sinatra atmosphere—nurtures a very
particular kind of masculine self-image. Lundy's was a family restaurant, but you see no children in the photographs of Rao's. There,
mostly, you see guys—well-dressed, successful guys. Sure, they bring
their ladies as well as their buddies, but there's no mistaking it: this is
their place.

Their place, not surprisingly, started up as a saloon. When Rao's
opened its doors in 1896, East Harlem was the largest Italian community in the United States. Rao's was just another neighborhood joint
where, in the days when bottles were unaffordable luxuries, folks
would line up in the evening to have their beer pails filled. It wasn't
until 1958, when Vincent Rao took over the family business, that the
place began to evolve from a bar that served food into a restaurant
with a bar.

Vincent liked to cook; more specifically, he liked to grill steaks, veal
chops, and chicken over charcoal on a brazier set up on the street beside the saloon door. The customers began to come as much for the

meat as for the drinks, and eventually Vincent persuaded his wife, Anna, to bring her pots and pans and recipes over from where they lived in the house next door. As it happened, Vincent was born, grew up, lived all his life, and died in that house. He and Anna were a wholly unselfconscious part of a neighborhood where people liked to eat well and had at hand abundant resources with which to do so. As Nicholas Pileggi writes in the introduction to *Rao's Cookbook*:

> Italian food stores sold macaroni in bulk and lined their walls with glistening golden gallon cans of imported olive oil. Fish stores sold dried cod, or baccalà, stacked like cords of firewood near the door, and bushels of snails, baskets of live crabs, and barrels of eels were always available. Cheese stores made their own mozzarella in the mornings and it was bought warm; the ricotta was so fresh it had to be sold in tall tin cans with holes in them to drain away the excess water. Loaves of freshly baked bread—both long and round, with seeds or without—came out of neighborhood bakery ovens two or three times a day.

In such a community, restaurants serve home cooking prepared at its best to customers who think there is no better eating than the dishes their mothers used to make. Well, Anna Pellegrino Rao *was* that mother, and, under her iron rule in the kitchen, Rao's became known for what Mimi Sheraton would describe in a glowing, three-star review as its "simple, honest, and completely delicious Italian food."

That review appeared in *The New York Times* in 1977, at what, it turned out, could not have been a better moment. The neighborhood was already undergoing the traumatic conversion that would end with the Italian community all but entirely dispersed to the city's outer boroughs, leaving Rao's one of a few holdouts in an area now predominantly populated by Puerto Ricans and African-Americans. If Sheraton had not reviewed Rao's—had not given Rao's the review she did—it's unlikely that the restaurant would have lasted for long.

Of course, neither Vincent Rao nor his nephew Frank Pellegrino—then a waiter and now the restaurant's proprietor—want to see it that way. Frank, who was a professional singer until he was persuaded to join the family business, often entertains patrons with his renditions of old standards. Among them, you can be sure, is Sinatra's "I Did It My Way." Pellegrino tells Rao's story with the modesty of a man utterly convinced that his family got where it did just by being true to itself, no matter the odds against it.

The family take on the impact of the *Times* review was that it was a monstrous, unsought, and unwanted intrusion, producing an avalanche of calls—many from wealthy, famous people—demanding reservations at a tiny local restaurant already booked to capacity every night.* Vincent Rao was sure that giving all these people reservations, even in the distant future, would mean—as Thomas McNamee writes in a recent piece on the restaurant in *Saveur*†—that

> the fancy people would take over—regulars were not the sort to plan dinner three months ahead—and then the fancy people would run on to their next infatuation, and Rao's would be screwed. [Consequently,] they worked out an understanding with their regulars: Tony and Larry, this is your table every other Tuesday, okay? No matter what. You just come. . . . From then on, every table at Rao's has been "owned" every night, by a regular customer.

According to McNamee, this arrangement has continued, to ensure that "the fancy people . . . are comfortably outnumbered . . . by regular customers." This seems to me a bit disingenuous: you can still fit in a lot of high rollers if the regulars' claim to those ten tables is, as he also says, often limited to a "monthly . . . bimonthly . . . even quarterly" basis.

Be that as it may, this policy made Rao's the restaurant into Rao's the legend. The regulars were thrilled to rub shoulders with the likes of Woody Allen, Tony Bennett, Rob Reiner, and Vic Damone, while the glitterati were equally delighted to be in the same room as Jimmy Cigars, Johnny Roastbeef, Little Jerry, Father Pete, and Nicky the Vest. (Frank Pellegrino himself has received the sobriquet "Frankie No" for his practiced ease in turning down reservation requests.)

---

*The comedian Alan King, in his culinary autobiography, *Is Salami and Eggs Better Than Sex?* (answer: no), advises his readers to "wait at least six weeks before going to a restaurant that has had a favorable review. It's got to be a madhouse, the way Rao's was when Mimi Sheraton gave it three stars. They went so crazy trying to handle everyone they finally tore the phone off the wall."

†"The Hangout," by Thomas McNamee. It appears in the July/August 1998 issue, pages 62 through 72. McNamee buys the restaurant's version hook, line, and sinker, but he recounts it with gusto, and the photographs by Maura McEvoy are astonishingly effective in capturing Rao's peculiar self-congratulatory charm.

In a sense, you could say that each half of the room is there to flatter and entertain the other—and at no cost to the management. Writers about Rao's like to point out how democratic this arrangement is: barbers, delicatessen owners, and plumbers on the one hand; on the other, what *The Washington Post* has described as "billionaires, beautiful people, politicians, guys in dark suits, corporate moguls, entertainers, and sports stars."

But, really, there's nothing democratic about Rao's. A stroke of luck gave the restaurant the opportunity to skim the cream from the dining public—i.e., to take the celebrities, the big spenders, and the owners' cronies and shut the door in the face of everyone else—and they grabbed it. Even so, you gotta love 'em for it, right? I mean, everybody loves a winner—why else would you want to share table space with Chuck Barris and Dick Clark?

There it is. To "own" a table at Rao's is to savor power, something even tastier than the best-cooked Italian food. The aura of this place in New York City is such that to have eaten there even once is for many the experience of a lifetime. To be "lent" a table for an evening costs the giver nothing even as it reaps eternal gratitude from the recipient—who in turn does some reaping of his own from the people he (as it most likely is) chooses to bring with him.

What about the food? Once again, they say it's terrific, and, once again, you and I will never know. As a cookbook, this one is better than Lundy's, if only because Kathy Gunst, who did the recipes for that book, was denied access to the original Lundy's recipe file—a rather insurmountable handicap. In *Rao's Cookbook*, you get an appealing collection of Italian-American recipes, many of which Rao's actually serves: not only old standbys, like shrimp scampi, veal parmigiana, and *pasta e fagioli*, but also less familiar traditional neighborhood dishes, like risotto with veal sauce and fillet of sole with fennel and white wine.

Still, to prepare this food at home, however expertly, is one thing; to eat it at Rao's is another. A restaurant's food—the making of it and the eating of it—is the medium, not the message. At Rao's, you aren't handed a menu; instead, the owner himself sits at your table and discusses what you'll have. The food, like the best home cooking, is comfortingly familiar and straightforwardly good, cooking that puts eaters, whatever their level of sophistication, at their ease. The customers know each other, so conversations ramble from table to table. The jukebox is the best in town. And, after your meal, Jimmy Cigars sends over a smoke with his compliments.

Rao's, in other words, is the sort of great neighborhood joint you can't find in the real world anymore, because the neighborhoods necessary to support them are no longer around. The experience of eating there is very like that of eating at Lundy's, but with a reverse twist: a meal at Rao's lets Americans feel like immigrants, or, as Frank Pellegrino would put it, like part of the family.

If Lundy's aging customers welcome the return of that restaurant so they can show their children what the old days were like, Rao's is the place to which their children—should they be so lucky—would love to take their parents, to show them how far they've come, and, at the same time, with great unconscious irony, how faithful they've remained to their roots. Put these two restaurant stories together, and what the result says about the immigrant experience in this country is so emotionally powerful and complex as to be beyond words.

What it also says about the experience of eating in restaurants in general is almost as volatile and difficult to grasp. People eat all kinds of stuff and think it good, which is why restaurants that serve indifferent—even bad—food are a dime a dozen, and those that serve truly delicious food are a statistical anomaly. If a restaurateur honestly thinks his food is good, the chances are his customers will, too.

To understand what makes a place succeed, you have to take the forces that drive the owner to want to feed us and those that drive us to want to eat there, and then see what happens when the two collide. This isn't always pretty—but, in a real restaurant, it's always richly human. That's why Matt and I left that New Brunswick restaurant in such a state of shock—the food itself may have been real, but the cook was not. It was as if we had wandered into a haunted house and been fed by a ghost. Even a take-out meal, hot from a real kitchen, is more redolent of human connection.

Then again, surely there are diners who would *prefer* that much distance from the cook. Perhaps the restaurants that don't seem odd to us are merely the ones that are odd in the same way we are. Going out to eat can be a very pleasurable experience, but—perhaps because of this—it is also at bottom a very mysterious one.

In one of my favorite reminiscences from Bob Cornfield's book, Roberta Temes tells of how, when she was a junior in high school, her parents moved from a Bronx tenement to an apartment in a two-family house on a quiet, tree-lined street in Brooklyn. Their first Sunday in the new neighborhood, they all took a stroll down to Sheepshead Bay, where they were stunned to see what seemed like an endless line of cars up and down Emmonds Avenue, waiting patiently to get into Lundy's parking lot. On the way back home, Temes recalls,

> my parents wore their serious faces and talked to each other, not to us. They were proud of their new sunny and spacious four-room apartment. But their notion of upward mobility did not include the strange concept of "eating out."

RAO'S FAMOUS LEMON CHICKEN
(adapted from *Rao's Cookbook*, by Frank Pellegrino)
[*serves 6*]

1 cup fresh lemon juice
1 large clove garlic, minced
½ cup olive oil
½ teaspoon dried oregano
½ tablespoon red wine vinegar
salt and freshly ground black pepper to taste
1 2½- to 3-pound broiling chicken, halved
3 or 4 leafy sprigs of Italian parsley, minced

Preheat the broiler for at least 15 minutes. Meanwhile, make the lemon sauce by whisking together in a small bowl everything but the chicken and the parsley.

Put the chicken halves on a rack over the broiler pan. Put this under the broiler and cook, turning the chicken once, for about 30 minutes, or until the skin is golden-brown and juices run clear when the bird is pierced with a fork.

Remove chicken from broiler, leaving the broiler on. Using a very sharp knife, cut each chicken half into about 6 pieces (leg, thigh, wing, 3 small breast pieces). Remove the rack from the broiler pan and pour off any grease. Coat each piece of chicken generously with the lemon sauce and place it back in the pan skin side down. If any sauce remains, pour it over the chicken.

Return the pan to the broiler and broil for 3 minutes. Use tongs to turn each piece skin side up and broil for an additional minute. Remove the chicken pieces from the broiler and arrange them on 6 warmed dinner plates. Pour sauce into a heavy saucepan. Stir in the parsley and place over high heat. Bring to a boil, cook for 1 minute, then pour the sauce over the portioned chicken. Serve with crusty bread to sop up the sauce.

KITCHEN DOINGS

BEANS IN A FLASK

※ ※ ※

Recently, while making my way through Paolo Scaravelli's *Cooking from an Italian Garden,* I came across the following rather evocative passage:

> When I was a child bread was baked once a week at the villa. Since the brick oven was large, it took time and lots of wood to heat it, so that it was practical to bake other foods at the same time. One of the real treats was beans baked in a flask, *fagioli al fiasco.* Beans were placed in a large chianti flask . . . [along with] water, oil, garlic, and sage. Fresh sage leaves were placed . . . in the neck of the flask to seal in some of the vapors. The flask was deposited in the oven on the smoldering embers and left for a few hours. When retrieved, the water was absorbed, the beans cooked, and the flask intact. We would eat the beans cold with lemon juice, olive oil, salt, and pepper. Beans cooked in this simple manner were light, tender, and richly flavored.

The flask in the fireplace! The very phrase can still evoke an echo of the shiver of excitement I felt when, back in the late seventies, I first came across the dish in Ada Boni's *Italian Regional Cooking.* It is illustrated there with a color photograph, and this, especially, my imagination seized hold of and embellished into something more akin to a vision than an image—a vision, moreover, that remains almost as clear now as it was then.

It is centered, of course, on the flask itself, made of thin, bubble-pocked, green-tinged glass, its long, narrow, graceful neck reaching up from an unsteadily bulbous body. It is tucked in the corner of a handsome stone fireplace among the glowing embers, its mouth stuffed with a tuft of straw, its belly with a mass of beans flecked with bits of herb and garlic and red pepper, all cheerfully seething away.

I discovered, when I returned to the book to check this memory, that I had actually conflated two pictures. The fireplace with its hot embers appears in another photograph on the same page showing the grilling of a Tuscan steak. The *fiasco* with its *fagioli* is nestled instead into a very sweet, tiny, square charcoal brazier designed, the caption informs us, especially for the purpose of cooking this dish.

What a complex business cooking really is. After all, even at the time of which I write, I had garnered enough experience as a cook at least to suspect that cooking beans in a wine flask was less a culinary method than an invitation to disaster—as the very name of the dish suggests. *Fagioli al fiasco*—that last word is not a misprint. I just didn't care. And why? Because I had then and still have now a terrible weakness for anything made of glass.

Matt bears with patience my collection of old milk bottles, oddsized jam jars, clunky drinking glasses, cruets, and the like. Empty, cork-stoppered, dark-green-glass olive oil bottles multiply like rabbits in the cupboards. I'm not sure I know why this is so. Part of the reason is purely tactile—that cool, smooth surface—and visual—the teasing way glass takes invisibility and makes it visible, takes fragility and makes it hard as nails. But it is also, I think, because of the tension inherent in glass, every jar and bottle an explosion waiting to happen.*
No wonder the idea of using an extremely fragile glass flask as a *cooking pot* made me dizzy with pleasure.

In those days, I was without a fireplace (or, for that matter, a charcoal brazier), which was probably just as well, but Chianti flasks were easy to come by, and it was only a matter of days before I was popping beans into the first of what would prove to be many. This, as it turned out, wasn't because the flasks kept on breaking but because the first one

---

*The Italian word *fiasco* means both "a straw-encased flask"—such as a Chianti bottle—and "an utter failure," "a ridiculous breakdown"—in other words, a fiasco. *The Random House Dictionary of the English Language* finds the connection between the two meanings obscure, but the phrase "to make a bottle" (as the complete Italian expression goes) implicitly suggests an inexorable Humpty-Dumpty trajectory, especially if one thinks of the hand-blown, infinitely delicate things these flasks once were.

did—spectacularly—the second or third time I used it. (You don't know the full meaning of the word *explode* until a flask of boiling-hot beans goes *ka-poof* in your kitchen.) So I deduced a helpful rule of thumb: reheating untempered glass over a flame makes it increasingly unstable.

Eventually, however, I found a flask-shaped, heavyweight clear glass vase that succeeded where the Chianti flasks had failed, and I made beans in a flask until I wearied of the thrill—or, really, of burning my fingers while shaking the cooked beans down and out the narrow neck. This proves to be an almost impossible dish to decant at table, which, in a way, defeats the whole purpose of the enterprise; emptying the bottle in the kitchen robs the event of all its éclat.*

❈ ❈ ❈

Looking back on my initial experiences cooking beans in a flask, I suspect that the major reason I let the dish slip out of my repertoire was that I didn't ever truly understand what I was doing. Transfixed by the bottle, I never spent much time thinking about the point of what was going on inside it. Or, rather, I all too readily thought that this was entirely obvious: the point of cooking beans in a flask was to keep their flavor in.

At its simplest, which also seems to be at its most traditional, the dish contains only five or six ingredients, depending on whether you decide to cook the beans with salt: fresh white Tuscan or cannellini beans, olive oil, sage leaves, garlic, and water. Many Italians, like cooks the world over, believe that adding salt to the flask will toughen the beans; others (also like cooks the world over) are more sanguine. Here is a representative recipe.

---

*Giuliano Bugialli, in *The Fine Art of Italian Cooking,* is so enraptured with the idea of bringing this dish to table in a *bagno maria* (bain-marie)—preferably "a beautiful one of antique copper"—that he manages to persuade himself that the beans can be served from the flask with a *spoon.* Unless you also have a marrow spoon the length of a bath brush—and very patient dinner guests—it might be best to think of another way to show off your antique *bagno maria.*

FAGIOLI AL FIASCO

(adapted from Anna Martini's *The Mondadori Regional Italian Cookbook*)

[*serves 4*]

¾ pound shelled fresh cannellini beans or ½ pound dried
cannellini beans, picked over, washed, and soaked for
8 to 12 hours
⅓ cup extra-virgin olive oil
2 cloves garlic, crushed
5 or 6 fresh sage leaves
salt and freshly ground pepper

Drop the beans into a large Chianti flask, the straw wrapping removed
and reserved, or some other wine bottle. Pour in the olive oil, the
crushed garlic, the sage leaves, a little freshly ground pepper, and 3 cups
of water. Stuff a plug made of the straw wrapping or a wad of cheesecloth into the mouth of the bottle. This should be loose enough so that
steam can slowly escape.

Place the wine bottle on smoldering charcoal embers or in a slow
oven and cook for 3 hours, or until all the water has evaporated and
the oil has been mostly absorbed into the beans. Empty the flask into a
preheated serving bowl. Salt to taste. The beans can be eaten as a meal
in themselves or served as a side dish. They are equally good hot or
cold.

When, recently, Matt and I came across some very handsome-looking
dried cannellini beans at our supermarket, I found I wanted to bring
them—and beans baked in a flask—back into our daily eating. By mutual consent, the glass vase remained firmly categorized as a flower and
not a bean container—we had a very nice, and nicely smallish, locally
made bean pot to serve instead.

However, as I began to cook them in it, I discovered that, no matter
how careful I was, the beans tended to break apart. I love to cook them
until their interiors are silky smooth, but I also want that tiny resistance
as the skin bursts in the mouth. When the beans are allowed to fall
apart during cooking, their insides disintegrate into mush. Was there
any way to cook these beans so that they would stay whole and yet be
rendered completely tender? It was this question that brought back my

memories of beans in a flask—and sent me digging through our collection of Italian, and specifically Tuscan, cookbooks.

In Italy, "Tuscan" is nearly synonymous with "bean eater." When Waverley Root notes in *The Food of Italy* that

> the bean is ubiquitous in Tuscany. There are bean antipasti; beans in soup (*minestrone di fagioli*, in which they are accompanied by celery and tomato); beans with rice (*riso e fagioli*); beans with fish (*fagioli col tonno*, tuna); and even beans with beans (*lenticchie e fagioli*, lentils and beans) . . . ,

he is barely scratching the surface. The Tuscans adore beans of every sort—*borlotti* (cranberry beans), lentils, chickpeas, black-eyed peas. But it is the cannellini—as you might guess from the fact that Italians also call it the Tuscan bean—that is closest to their hearts.

One day an idea occurred to me: the fact that Tuscans concoct so many glorious bean dishes might mean that they also possess *opinions* about the cooking of beans that would be well worth consulting. So, there in Grazietta Butazzi's *Toscana in Bocca* (one in a series, published in Palermo, devoted to regional Italian cooking, written in the local dialect, but also offering standard Italian and somewhat nonstandard English translations), under the heading *Fagioli lessi alla fiorentina*— perhaps best understood as "How to cook beans as the Florentines do"—I found the following (which I have polished up somewhat from the original):

> To boil beans seems easy, but in order to get excellent results you should follow certain rules of preparation. First of all, when using dried beans, don't put them in water to soak. On the contrary, they must be put directly on the flame, preferably in an earthenware pot, with a little cold water, some cloves of garlic, and two sprigs of fresh sage. Put some water in a second pot of the same size and set it over the first to serve as its cover. The steam rising from the beans will heat this water, which should then be added, bit by bit, as necessary, when the cooking liquid in the first pot has all but boiled dry.
>
> The cooking time will depend on the age of the beans, but should take from 2 to 3 hours, always over a low flame. The beans are done when they are on the verge of melting. Add salt only during the last 30 minutes of cooking time. Drain and dress them with olive oil and freshly ground pepper. The same proce-

dure is to be followed when using fresh beans, except, of course, the cooking time will be much shorter. In this case you can also put in the pot a little olive oil and some peeled and seeded fresh tomatoes.

At first glance, this method may seem to you, as it initially seemed to me, to have gotten everything assbackwards. In essence, the cook has taken a double boiler and put the beans in the bottom and the hot water in the top—*not* the usual way of doing things. However, set this method next to the one for cooking beans in a flask, and the pieces of the puzzle start falling into place.

Here, despite my infatuation with glass, is the lesson I had failed to absorb during my first encounter with *fagioli al fiasco*. Just as the dangerous frangibility of the flask commanded attention then, the inversion of the double boiler pushes the cook toward caution, ensuring that the beans receive the most delicate treatment possible.

Especially if one uses an earthenware pot—which is thought to impart an incomparable flavor to the beans*—the flame must be kept low, and, by letting its contents heat the water in the second pot, which is being used as its cover, one can be sure that this water will remain no more than moderately hot and will encourage the vapors released by the cooking beans to recondense and fall back into the pot rather than escape in the form of steam.

As this understanding began to shape itself in my mind, I found that certain other confusions were also resolved. Leslie Forbes, whose recipe for *fagioli al fiasco* in *A Table in Tuscany* has the distinct feel of personal use, directs that, lacking a fireplace full of hot embers, one should

> put the bottle in a warm place, such as an airing cupboard, the warm place on a stove, or beside the boiler or solid fuel cooker [by which I think she means an Aga].

Clearly, what she has in mind is not hot but *warm*. The other interesting thing about her method is that she calls for an equal weight of wa-

---

*Hence the legendary savor of Mexico's primal peasant dish, *frijoles de olla*, or "beans from the clay pot." In modern times, the pot has universally become the pressure cooker and the dish has suffered accordingly. However, more recently still, Mexican cooks have taken to cooking their beans in a clay pot *put into* the pressure cooker—about as nice a definition of postmodernism as anyone could want.

ter to (fresh) cannellini beans—which, as bean cooking goes, is a very small amount of cooking liquid. Here, too, the idea is to have, at the end of the cooking period, all the liquid evaporated and the beans lightly coated in the garlic-and-sage-flavored oil. Thus do the two Tuscan bean-cooking methods we are discussing draw even closer together.

❧ ❧ ❧

> Besides the minestrone with beans, there is *zuppa di fagioli alla toscana*, where the beans are not just *in* the soup, they *are* the soup, the only other ingredients being seasonings: salt, pepper, garlic, olive oil. After having been soaked overnight, the beans are cooked, half of them puréed by being forced through a sieve to make the thick soup, into which are put the remaining whole beans—beans in beans.
>
> —Waverley Root, *The Food of Italy*

As I began to work out my own strategy for preparing *fagioli al fiasco*, I soon realized that this would require several trials, each with its share of errors. So Matt and I arranged that I would cook a single portion of these beans every day in an appropriately bean-pot-shaped coffee mug and eat them for my *merenda*, or midday snack. Consequently, for a week or so, when I sat down to write each morning, there would be a mug of savory beans simmering not only in the kitchen but—much more importantly—in the back of my mind.

Until now, for us, a pot of beans baking in the oven brought with it the pleasant expectation of a particular meal. My mug, however, was emitting a different and more enticing promise. Flipping through our Tuscan cookbooks, I kept encountering dishes that, on closer examination, turned out to be not so much free-standing recipes as just one more way of enjoying a batch of *fagioli al fiasco*: tossing them with pasta or broccoli or canned tuna; spreading them on *bruschetta*; turning them into a bean salad with a squeeze of lemon and some raw onion; mashing a portion of them—as Waverley Root directs—into a thick broth for an instant bean soup. Quite conceivably, a cook can put such a pot in the slowest of ovens in the morning as she sets off for work, only to return in the afternoon still happily undecided as to exactly what tasty impromptu meal she will make of its contents.

Of course, none of this would mean a thing if there weren't something special about the beans themselves. But there is. Unlike the very similar-looking Great Northern bean (which is often suggested as a substitute), the cannellini responds to such exaggeratedly careful cooking in its own inimitable fashion: it all but melts away. Indeed, the Italian phrase for judging their doneness—*disfarsi leggermente*—means precisely that: "lightly melted." Some of them do fall apart anyway, but most remain whole just long enough to reach the mouth, where they then dissolve on the tongue like a cool piece of butter. (This analogy, while obviously not exact, does capture the pleasing *density* of the bean; it melts because it is not already mush.)

Furthermore, my first bite made me deeply regret that last fall—contrary to my usual custom—I decided not to bring the sage plant in from the herb garden to winter with the thyme, rosemary, and bay in our warm and sunny living room. Sage, it turns out, is an herb favored by Tuscans over almost any other, especially in peasant cooking, the third of a trinity with olive oil and garlic. They especially love what this simple seasoning does to beans, and, indeed, it is a perfect flavor match. Fortunately, I did at least pluck the plant clean and dry the leaves, and that little herb jar suddenly found itself basking in totally unaccustomed regard (although I suspect that rosemary has the right character to replace it in a pinch).

So it was that the days went pleasantly by as I inched closer to a workable method. Since both Tuscan techniques emphasized slow cooking with just enough liquid to cover, I adapted and melded the other instructions so that this could be done as unfussily as possible. The result, detailed below, is—not at all accidentally—very close to Russ Parsons's basic bean cooking method (see pages 127–28), with two exceptions.

First, I further reduced his already low cooking temperature from 250°F to 200°F, thus ensuring that the beans would never boil. Second, both because of that fact and because I was using dried (sometimes, *very* dried) beans instead of fresh ones, I found that presoaking was absolutely necessary. Otherwise, the beans took much longer to cook and—at least during the early part of their time in the oven—quickly absorbed, again and again, all their cooking liquid.

I still have not quite managed the trick of getting the beans to absorb all the cooking liquid and the olive oil—perhaps this represents a lack in my technique or perhaps the description is more a shared Tuscan culinary fantasy than it is a realized fact. Practice, I hope, will tell.

Meanwhile, here's our recipe. It is named in honor of our stolid Maine bean pot, which has been delighted to exchange its aura of salt pork and molasses for one of sage and garlic. We hope you'll find that the results elicit the same response as the one described in a popular Tuscan rhyme—

> *Serve such cooked white beans to a Florentine*
> *And he'll lick his bowl and his napkin clean.*

TUSCAN BEANS FROM THE OLD CLAY POT
[serves 2 to 4]

½ pound dried cannellini beans, picked over, washed, and
    soaked for 8 to 12 hours in spring water to cover amply
¼ cup robust-flavored extra-virgin olive oil
2 cloves garlic, finely minced
3 or 4 sage leaves, fresh or dried
½ teaspoon black pepper
½ teaspoon ground hot red pepper
½ teaspoon salt (or to taste)

Preheat oven to 200°F. Drain the beans, reserving the soaking liquid. Remove and discard any beans that have failed to rehydrate (they will be distinctly wrinkled and ornery-looking). Put the beans and everything else, except for the bean-soaking liquid, into a small earthenware bean pot (or similar vessel) and stir gently. Pour the bean-soaking liquid into a saucepan and heat to boiling. Add enough of this to the bean pot to barely cover its contents, reserving any remaining liquid.

Cover the pot, put the beans in the oven, and cook at this very low heat (they should never come to a boil) until they are nicely done, about 4 to 5 hours. Check the water level periodically during the first 4 hours, adding the remaining bean liquid, then plain boiling water, as necessary to keep the beans covered.

Serve the beans hot or at room temperature, dressed with a little more oil and a squeeze of lemon juice. This amount will provide a side dish for 4 or a meal for 2. Or, if you wish, use the beans as the foundation for one of the dishes listed below.

Fagioli con prosciutto. In his recipe for *fagioli al fiasco* in *The Fine Art of Italian Cooking*, Giuliano Bugialli instructs that an ounce or two of diced pancetta, good country ham, or prosciutto be included with the other ingredients at the start of cooking. A few links of Italian sausage seem another likely option.

Fagioli bianchi. Dress the cooked beans with some minced raw onion and olive oil to taste.

Fagioli al tonno. Flake the contents of a 6-ounce can of Italian-style tuna in olive oil into the cooked beans, dress with minced parsley, and eat as is or toss with a tubular pasta.

Zuppa di fagioli alla toscana. Use a spatula to work half the cooked beans through a sieve. Dilute, if you wish, with a little boiled water to make a rich broth. Stir in the remaining whole beans and serve in warmed bowls with a dribble of olive oil.

Pasta e fagioli. Toss the beans with a corkscrew-shaped or tubular pasta. Dress with a minced sprig or two of Italian parsley and, if you like, freshly grated Parmesan.

Fagioli e broccoletti. Blanch bite-sized pieces of broccoli (or broccoli rabe) until just tender and stir into the cooked beans.

Fagioli con salsicce. Cut a large onion into small pieces. Heat a little olive oil in a skillet and sauté the onion bits and two or more links of Italian sausage until the edges of the onion are crusty and the sausage is cooked through. Remove and thickly slice the sausage. Spoon out and discard any unwanted fat. Combine the cooked beans, sliced sausage, and the remaining contents of the skillet and serve at once.

Fettunta con cannellini e pancetta. Spread the cooked beans—mashing them slightly—on grilled slices of Tuscan bread and top with pieces of fried bacon or pancetta.

Fagioli all'uccelletto (beans in the manner of little birds). There are various arguments as to why the dish has this name, but there are none at all as to its merits—if an Italian cookbook has only a few bean dishes, this will surely be one of them. To make it, simply remove the bean pot from the oven just before the beans are done and stir in 2 tablespoons of good tomato paste or ½ cup crushed canned tomatoes (or, in summer, two ripe tomatoes cut into small chunks). Return the pot to the oven and let the beans continue to cook for another 15 minutes or so, until the remaining bean liquid and tomato have amalgamated into a sauce. *Fagioli all'uccelletto in bianco* can be made by replacing the tomato with a generous portion of sautéed onion. In either instance, dress the dish at the table with a drizzle of your finest olive oil (Anna Del Conte: "This is the touch that makes all the difference!") or, for a change, balsamic vinegar (Anne Bianchi: "In certain towns in Versilia [where *fagioli all'uccelletto* is considered a local specialty] it is customary to add this just before serving. Try it").

A NOTE ON RUSS PARSONS'S
BEAN-COOKING REVOLUTION

If you cook dried beans, chances are you know that success depends on your obeying at least three inviolate rules, the catechism of which goes like this:

1. Beans must *always* be presoaked, preferably overnight, but at least brought to a boil and let stand for an hour.
2. The bean-soaking liquid must *always* be discarded—and, preferably, changed several times during the soaking period—to avoid flatulence.
3. Salt should *never* be added to the beans during the first hours of cooking—otherwise, the skins will toughen.

The gospel of the well-cooked bean: a few food writers have vigorously challenged aspects of this accepted wisdom, but it would be hard to find someone who doesn't believe any of it. Diana Kennedy, for instance, who famously rails against the first two—*don't* presoak, but, if you must, *don't* discard the water—completely accepts the third. And most, myself included, have bought all three hook, line, and sinker.

Thus, it came with the force of a revelation when, in the February 24, 1994, issue of the *Los Angeles Times*, food editor Russ Parsons blew the whole business out of the water. Here, in essence, is his refutation of those rules:

1. Unless they are very old, presoaking the beans accomplishes little beyond saving some cooking time—about a half hour or so—and this at the cost of flavor and texture.
2. Neither cook nor eater can do much to reduce the problem of flatulence, except to eat *more* beans. (The more you eat, the better your digestive flora can handle them.)

3. Salting the bean-cooking water not only has no effect on the beans' texture but allows the salt to penetrate the dish better, since the beans absorb it from the start.

Bean cooks—again, myself included—may find these statements hard to accept, but they are based on extensive kitchen testing, on much interrogating of authorities, and, it must be admitted, on common sense as well. He draws some other conclusions, too: cooking beans in an earthenware pot adds nothing to their flavor; covering the pot with a lid greatly reduces cooking time; and the choice between stovetop and oven cooking is largely a matter of the cook's convenience.

Here, in brief, is his own preferred method:

Clean the beans of any pebbles, clods of dirt, and other detritus, rinse them of dust, and put them in a large pot with a teaspoon of salt for every pound of beans. Top them with three inches of boiling water, cover them, and put them in a preheated 250°F oven. Cook until done, adding more boiling water occasionally to prevent them from boiling dry.

All this is pretty terrific. It has cleared the air, replacing dubious lore with a basic method of cooking dried beans that is simple, direct, and good. However, it's also important to bear in mind that cooks often do not themselves know why they do the things they do, and so the reasons they give may be completely off the mark. Taste a spoonful of bean-soaking liquid sometime and you'll discover that there is barely any flavor to it at all. Diana Kennedy's resistance to discarding it was primarily a visceral one, an act of allegiance to the Mexican cooks who taught her their bean-cooking secrets. It was this, not the truth of any rule, that flavored her pot.

Similarly, Matt and I *like* to presoak our beans (we also cook them in that water), and so—despite the above—we still do. Not only is it a pleasure to watch them plump up during the course of the day, but the sense of connection that comes from this coddling adds to our anticipation of the meal. Consequently, I value Russ Parsons's piece less for its new rules than for the way it calls back into consciousness rote behavior that kept me from noticing that different beans have different needs—and reminds me that my job as cook is, before all else, to attend to them.

EXISTENTIAL PIZZA

❀ ❀ ❀

In the summer of 1936, two budding French intellectuals, Jean-Paul Sartre and Simone de Beauvoir, traveling together through Italy, paid a visit to Naples. The city fascinated them both, and each night in their hotel, Sartre poured out page after page of impressions in the letters he sent back to Paris. He was especially entranced by the dreamlike intermingling of public and private life. In hot weather, the poor simply lived in the street, dragging out chairs, tables, even beds. In the afternoon, entire streets would fall sleep, the inhabitants—even passersby—just dropping off wherever they happened to be: waiters on top of their tables; musicians slumped against their instruments; a young man curled up among the stems and leaves in the same flat basket from which he had just been selling fruit. The few people who remained awake appeared to be caught between naps, with "reddened eyes and a pensive look, as though remembering one dream or just embarking on the next."

And, everywhere, people ate and ate. De Beauvoir had remarked of Rome that it was a city without a stomach; in Naples, however, the stomach was always evident. Bowls of tomato paste were stuck out into the street to dry; onions hung in thick ropes. Although these were neighborhoods plunged into direst poverty, the street food available there was so cheap that it seemed almost no one was denied it. Children in rags wandered about gnawing on huge chunks of bread stuffed with cooked peppers or with their faces buried in thick wedges of watermelon. Vendors could be found in every alley, selling "nuts, boiled ears of corn, grilled fava beans, fish, crustaceans, small squid."

What poverty did mean was a blurring of the usual distinction between vendor and customer. Anyone with a little money would buy
something and try to sell it to his or her neighbors to make a little more
money. Often, that something was food or drink. A vendor of lemon-
ade was someone who had bought two lemons, filled a bucket with
water, and sat down on a bench with these, two glasses, and a lemon
squeezer. Sartre observed:

> You give him two cents, he wakes up, squeezes the lemon into the
> glass, pours in a bit of water, and *voilà*: lemonade.

Sartre found the *napoletani* to be neither a resentful, downtrodden
proletariat nor a merry band of opera-singing paupers. They defied cat-
egorization and, for that matter, caricature by their ability to take nothing and make it into something. Poverty might force them to live in
squalor, but the ways in which they utilized that squalor could be delightful and profound. The streets abounded in surrealistic juxtaposi-
tions:

> a basket of fruit beside a barrel organ . . . a plate of tomato paste
> drying beneath a picture of the Virgin . . . an oven drawer, full of
> hot coals, laid on a rickety chair.

At one point, de Beauvoir wanted a bite to eat, so they entered a
pizzeria. It was little more than a tiny white room with a counter and
four tables covered with white cloths, one of which was occupied by
four fat naval officers in white uniforms, consuming pizza with glasses
of red Vesuvius wine. However, most of the pizzas were sold from a
stall in front of the shop.

> Through the store window and open door we could [hear] the
> pizza vendor, with red hair and long decaying teeth . . . singing, in
> an odd and very Neapolitan sort of nasal singsong, with flourishes
> and scoops, to attract customers. . . . A mass of tattered, squealing
> little boys would crowd around him; the cook, a handsome young
> Neapolitan, would bring out the steaming pizzas. . . . [The] ven-
> dor would take up a pizza, fold it in two, and put a thick slice of
> cheese inside. It's more rudimentary than in Rome, where the
> cheese is melted into the pizza.

If Sartre had been more interested in pizza,* he would soon have noticed that it isn't only in Rome that the cheese is melted on top; what he saw served at this place was certainly not "authentic." Even so, it was *real* Neapolitan pizza, and if, as Sartre would come to claim, existence does indeed precede essence, his account casts an illuminating light on the narratives of two more recent travelers, Edward Behr and Burton Anderson, both food writers and, in this instance, both in hot pursuit of *la vera pizza napoletana.*

❊ ❊ ❊

Burton Anderson, who devotes a chapter to the subject in his book about Italy's most famous foodstuffs, *Treasures of the Italian Table*, arrived in Naples confidently expecting to confirm his belief that "the supremacy of pizza *napoletana* is founded on the quality of local products." When, instead, he discovered that his favorite Neapolitan *pizzaiolo* used canned tomato pulp instead of fresh tomatoes—and, worse, *seed* oil instead of olive oil—to make what Anderson himself had to admit was a completely delicious pizza, his whole thesis quietly self-destructed.

The truth is that Neapolitan pizza is good for reasons that, while not indifferent to the quality of the ingredients, are not entirely dependent on it, either. Edward Behr, in his essay "Pizza in Naples," is ensnared in the same belief, and at times it is hard to tell how much of what he says is the exception today—"The tomatoes that go on pizza are traditionally used raw, whether cut up or crushed in a simple purée, although some are now canned"—and how much the rule. When he asks a producer of *mozzarella di bufala*—the authentic stuff—how much he sells to *pizzerie*, Behr is astonished by the answer: "None." Pizzerias don't use it; it is too expensive and, anyway, when it melts, it reduces to a translucent sheen—not what the customer expects.

Even so, Behr's observations of the *pizzaioli* at work touch the heart of the mystery.

---

*In fact, they both made the mistake of ordering something else: Sartre, a bottle of mineral water—"One does not drink mineral water in Naples, sir," their indignant waiter expostulated. "One drinks *water*"—de Beauvoir, a plate of pasta. Although this was on the menu, her request caused some consternation—and a long wait. "They obviously had to get it from some old box in the cellar," and it tasted like it.

> The *pizzaiolo's* only secret is experience. All his work except the preparation of dough and lighting of the oven is done in full view of those who come to eat.

He watches the expert shaping of the dough, the final addition of the topping, the small shovelful of wood shavings tossed on the fire when the pizza is pushed into the oven. This makes the flames leap up, a burst of heat that helps raise the edge of the crust—the *cornicione*—and cook the top in the single minute it is in the oven. When it is brought to his table,

> the surface of the pizza is here and there flecked with black; sometimes, without apology, it is blacker than that. The underside has tiny charred spots as well.

Notice the charred bits on the crust, but also consider the import of that phrase "without apology." This, I think, gives us the essential clue.

Anderson, in another chapter of his book—this one on the Tuscan artisanal baker Carlo Cocollino—describes in minute detail the making of his loaves, which are hand-shaped and baked in a wood oven. When Carlo extracts them, they emerge

> the size of pillows with mottled shadings of tan, powdery buff, and charcoal amid welts, ripples, craters, and crevices that resembled relief maps of the surface of the moon.

These loaves demand a social interaction that factory-produced loaves do not. They encourage customer participation at least to the extent that they offer a choice among objects that, were they identical, would offer none. Some people, in fact, *do* prefer a bit of char on their crust.

However, I think this interaction involves something more than choice. We can see it best by considering the pizza that most of us are familiar with from years of patronizing our local pizza parlor. The formula for American fast food plays on our naïve delight in having something good given to us over and over again in the exact same way. The problem with this, as it turns out, is that the only way to improve on this pleasure is to intensify the sameness. The cheeseburger becomes the double cheeseburger becomes the double cheeseburger with bacon.

So, too, the pizza with sausage and cheese becomes the pizza with double sausage and double cheese. This approach gradually polishes away all the edges from what was once real street food. I mean here, literally, the crusty edges of the grilled burger, the burned onions—the chef pushing things to the limit. At an Italian pizzeria, intensification of sameness—although many of the pizzas *are* the same—is not the issue. Eaters there relate to the spin that a particular *pizzaiolo* gives to his pie.

That spin can be a general statement—thin crust versus thick crust, real mushrooms versus canned mushrooms, real tomatoes versus canned tomato purée—but it is also something spontaneous, personal, that makes this pizza just that much different from that pizza. The result is pizza with personality, and you don't get personality just by heaping on the cheese. You can find such pizzas in serious pizza cities in this country—New Haven, say, or New York—where pizzas manage to be good, better than good, and still remain, like the guys who make them, tight and muscular.

If I myself had ever had the chance to go to Naples, I also would have visited pizzerias, torn crusts apart, sniffed cheese, rolled the tomato topping around in my mouth, looking for something—a clue, a technique, a special ingredient—to bring back home. But is this the point? If I had looked around, I would have realized that, as much as it is food, pizza is a social event, a way *napoletani* have of enjoying life— the *pizzaiolo* as well as the customers. They might live entirely for the moment, but out of that moment they know how to squeeze a lot.

Given this, perhaps we can propose a definition that wraps Sartre's, Anderson's, and Behr's pizzas in the same fraternal embrace. Authentic pizza is, first of all, delicious crust. It is a topping that complements, even enhances, that crust. It also somehow embodies—even radiates— the craft that made it. Finally, it absorbs and momentarily resolves the tension between limited means and a desire to relax, have fun, eat something good. In the best possible situation, it is all these things. In America, pizza is most often a routinely made take-home food. Perhaps double cheese and double sausage is not meant as enhancement, after all, but rather as solace for something missing in our lives.

❀ ❀ ❀

Crust. The center of the classic Neapolitan pizzeria is a dome-shaped *forno*, or baking oven, fired by wood to about 750°F, which can bake a pizza in one or two minutes. (A similar pizza in a professional American pizza oven takes about five times as long.*) This near-instantaneous baking provides the *pizzaiolo* with a constant, and at the same time constantly varying, challenge.

As the day's orders rapidly mount from a trickle to a flood, his work rhythms also gain momentum—an intricate *pas de deux* with a mercu-rial, temperamental, even dangerous, partner. And always, of course, there is the audience to please, not as a group, but one by finicky one. The fact that his customers hardly pay attention to him is not impor-tant. It is the pizza that speaks for him, and what it says is far more in-teresting than anything most American pizzas have to say—including homemade pizzas.

How does one bring this spirit of controlled risk, of authentic en-gagement, into the home kitchen? "The *pizzaiolo*'s only secret is expe-rience." To understand that sentence, we have to remind ourselves that a hard-working *pizzaiolo* will probably make as many pizzas in a day as you or I will in a year—even a year when there is a homemade pizza on the table two or three times a week. A recipe—especially one as sim-ple as that for pizza dough—is only the starting place, and, to the ex-tent that a recipe is repeated over and over, very little experience can accrue.

When I wrote a pamphlet on pizza back in 1981, my project was to amass as much information on the subject as I could. I wanted to drench myself in origins, history, and ingredients, i.e., authentic ways of making it. This, given the situation and the sources, I did the best I could. Still, when I went into the kitchen, the only experience I had to draw on was my own. Flour, water, yeast, salt: I could make a dough all right, but what was it that made it a *pizza* dough?

I had no real answer to this question. Consequently, my pizza crust was mediocre, dull, not comparable even to the pizza at the nearby Villa Rosa. It was less a pizza than a secondhand account of a pizza. As often happened to me in a situation like this, I persuaded myself that my failure was caused by lack of a real pizza oven, or, at least, real Ital-ian pizza flour. I gave up pizza making for almost a decade.

Then, a few years ago, while developing a moist dough that would

---

*The fact that an oven heat of 750°F is *illegal* in restaurants in this country makes the con-trast all the more telling.

produce a light-textured, crisp-crusted loaf of bread, it occurred to us to try it for pizza. Again, the initial results were not promising: a wan-complexioned crust with the texture of leatherette. However, I was now baking all our bread and had some thoughts about where to go. To spell out what happened next would be to produce a narrative too much dominated by details—super-hot ovens, ceramic bricks, blends of various flours—that are, I think, finally incidental. Where I was head-ing was a destination that can be reached by many routes. What they all have in common, though, is learning—mostly by trial and error—how to sense the minute differences that make a mediocre crust into a decent one.

What I want to stress about this experience is its complex social quality: a relationship built up out of a series of interactions between the two of us, the baker and the baked. You don't ask dough a question and get back an answer; attending involves a kind of prerational ab-sorption and intuitive adjustment. I shaped the dough, but the dough also shaped me. It taught me to give it what it needed—to find answers to questions I hadn't even thought to ask.

For instance, a hand-stretched dough has a tenderness and a charac-ter all its own, but for the longest time I was unable to hand-stretch this one completely because of its tendency to tear. Then, without at first noticing any connection, I developed an interest in making fresh pasta. Same flour minus the yeast and water and plus two eggs, and I had a dough that could be stretched so thin I could read a newspaper through it.

Once I was aware of what in other circumstances this flour could be made to do, some inarticulate percipience prompted a new, wholly in-tuitive response. The next time I made a pizza, I gave the dough a thor-ough drubbing with a rolling pin before I stretched it out—and found it had acquired a silky texture and was much more willing to be shaped.

For me, this act had a decisive significance, quite apart from whether the technique will stand the proof of time. I had pursued my pizza dough beyond the realm of recipe—anyone's recipe—to the point of intimacy. Authentic? The result didn't look like any pizza dough I had ever seen. It glistened slightly because of its stickiness; the pound-ing gave the strands of gluten a quilted texture. I added the topping and slid it into the oven. What came out was no *vera pizza napoletana*, but it was our pizza, and it was finally very, very good. To the question—

what was it that made it a pizza dough?—I now knew the answer. For better or for worse: me. I had become like a *pizzaiolo napoletano* in this one way: I had accepted responsibility for my crust.

✳ ✳ ✳

Poverty may not be the issue for Matt and myself that it is for the *napoletani*, but limitations are. And each time we learn to play off instead of sidestep these, our pizzas get that much better. When we lived in Maine, two of the three basic ingredients of the traditional topping posed serious problems for us. Fortunately, good olive oil was easy to come by, but fresh mozzarella was available only occasionally. And because I've never been a big fan of canned tomatoes, I wanted only fresh ones—locally grown fresh ones—on my pizza, which meant making it tomato-free ten months of the year.

A pizza without mozzarella or tomato sauce? Well, there was pizza in Naples before there was tomato sauce, and there was pizza there before and after for people who couldn't afford the cheese. Indeed, the problem isn't that it's difficult to come up with such pizzas but, rather, that it's all too easy. Pizza books are full of good-sounding suggestions: pizza topped with pesto, say, or with roasted peppers.

But once you decide to roast the peppers on the grill instead of taking them from a jar, chances are you'll prefer to have them with a loaf of fresh-baked bread—which won't obliterate their surprisingly delicate thunder and will soak up all their delicious juice. Similarly, if you prepare your pesto from scratch, you may wonder if baking it on a pizza is really how you want to treat what is, after all, a fresh herb sauce. Nothing gets on one of our pizzas without an argument—whether it belongs there at all and, if so, what it belongs there with. Consequently, any topping, however ordinary, that finds a place with us is also autobiography.

To return to the beginning: you might say that Matt and I comprise a mini *pizzeria napoletana* of our own—at least our pizzas are certainly holding up *their* end of the conversation. They are, in other words, genuinely themselves, not an imitation, however clever or ingenious, of anything else. Even so, I would hesitate to label them "authentic." The longer I work in the kitchen, the more confused I am about the whole subject of authenticity. I don't dismiss it, but I am more inclined to think of it as something, like virtue, best cultivated indirectly—visible through the eyes of others, not your own.

After all, the difference between the pizza of a Neapolitan *pizzaiolo* and that of the guy who makes them at Pizza Hut is not necessarily that the former takes his work more personally but that his craft still *allows* him to personalize his work. What authenticity is best used for is to help us think our way back to that permission by trying to understand and reimagine for ourselves the conditions under which it thrives. Sartre finally did find a word to sum up the *napoletani*: they were, he said, *insouciant*. In French, the word has overtones of bravado as well as fecklessness, of laughing in the face of fate. Now, when I think of *pizza napoletana*, I think of that.

THE CRUST

What follows is not a recipe so much as an explanation of how we have melded certain techniques to produce what we consider an exceptional pizza crust—a crust, that is, that has good wheat flavor and is chewy but also cracklingly crisp. It makes a pizza that is as good as—and in many instances better than—those produced in most American pizzerias. However, if you have never made a pizza before, you should start by using a reliable introductory recipe (see pages 147–48 for recommendations). Then, when you feel you have gone as far as you can with it, use what follows below as a suggestion for ways to develop your strategy.

Our method involves blending three flours, letting the dough rise slowly to develop flavor, hand-stretching it, and using a ceramic pizza brick at the top of a very hot oven. What this narrative does not discuss much are approaches we have tried and discarded, such as the use of olive oil and/or milk to tenderize the dough, oven baking tiles, different oven-shelf positions, other flour blends, fresh yeast, and so on. The following should be considered a *snapshot* of how, at this particular moment, we make our pizza dough. Tomorrow, I'm sure, it will already be slightly different—as it will also be for you.

The Oven Arrangement

We bake our pizza in a gas oven, adapted to replicate as closely as possible the effect of a brick pizza oven. This is done by raising the oven shelf to a high position, placing on it a thick rectangular pizza stone, setting the oven at its highest baking temperature (approximately 550°F), and allowing it to preheat for about forty-five minutes while the pizza dough and the topping are prepared. The stone we chose is a large (14 x 16-inch), extra-thick (half-inch), coarse-textured ceramic brick, made of the same material used to line pizza ovens. Such a stone absorbs oven heat during the long preheating and radiates this into the small space above it at the very top of the oven with even intensity during the actual baking time. The pizza is fully cooked in five to six minutes—or one-third of the time that many cookbooks say is necessary and much closer to the baking time of a professional American pizza oven—with a crisp, golden bottom crust and brown, puffy edges.

Special Tools

Apart from the pizza stone described above, we use an electronic digital scale to weigh our flour—far more accurate than measuring by cup—a *wooden* pizza peel (invaluable), and a professional, heavy-duty pizza cutter.

The Flour and Yeast

We buy our flour in fifty-pound bags from a food-service company. The foundation of our pizza blend is King Arthur's Sir Lancelot, an unbleached, unbromated, high-gluten (14.2 percent protein), hard red spring wheat flour. This makes a crust that browns quickly and has an appealing chewy texture. These qualities are enhanced by a small amount of durum wheat flour, which adds some additional crispness and flavor depth. To these two hard flours we add an equal portion of Round Table, an unbleached, unbromated, low-gluten (7.6 percent protein) pastry flour milled from New York State soft white winter wheat, which we have on hand for other baking. This gives us a tender crust without resorting to the addition of olive oil or milk. Blended together, these three flours approximate all-purpose flour in strength but not in character, since all-purpose flours tend to average out the qualities (flavor and texture) of hard and soft flours rather than combining them. We currently use French SAF instant yeast ("instant" means the yeast can be mixed directly into the dough rather than proofed first in hot water), but other granulated yeasts are fine.

THE METHOD
[*makes 1 12-inch thin-crust pizza*]

scant teaspoon fine sea salt
4 ounces soft unbleached pastry flour
3 ounces hard unbleached bread flour
1 ounce very fine durum flour
½ teaspoon instant dried yeast
4½ ounces tepid water (about)

Initial Preparation. Into a large mixing bowl, measure first the salt, then the flours, and finally the yeast, sprinkling this evenly over the top. Pour in the water and work everything into a cohesive dough, kneading until it is elastic and muscular-feeling, or about 10 minutes. The dough should be slightly sticky. Dust it lightly with flour and put it in an ungreased bowl. Cover the bowl with plastic wrap, prick this with a fork, and set in a cool, draft-free place to rise for 4 or 5 hours. The dough will triple in bulk. Deflate, then let rise again for about an hour, or until it has doubled in bulk. (*If you do not have a scale,* add first a generous ½ cup water to the bowl and mix in the yeast and salt. Put ¼ cup of the durum flour in a 1-cup dry measure, then fill with the bread flour and stir this into the yeast–salt water mixture. Now, bit by bit, work in just enough pastry flour [about 1 cup] to form a cohesive but *slightly* sticky dough. Then proceed as described.)

La Battitura. Preheat oven as directed below. After the dough has risen for a second time, deflate, reform into a ball, dust well with flour, and set on a clean empty counter. Using a rolling pin or similar implement, beat the dough into a flat disk. The beating should be done firmly and methodically, with the pin lifted up only a few inches above the counter and brought down smartly onto the dough. Rotate the disk and turn it over, to ensure that the blows are evenly distributed over its entire surface. Dust regularly (although lightly) with flour, both over and under, to keep the dough from sticking. The blows should fall flat across the surface of the dough. This is especially important toward the end of the beating, to avoid pinching the dough (or denting the counter). The dough should now feel distinctly silky and yielding.

The Hand-stretching. When the dough has been flattened to a disk about 9 inches wide, dust it lightly with flour. Then, using the palms and fingers of your hands, gently but firmly stretch it, shaping it into a round about 12 inches in diameter. Move the hands about the surface so that the stretching is done evenly. (Never grasp it by the edges and pull it.) This method should result in a pizza-shaped dough with a natural ridge around the edge and a stretched, irregularly textured surface. Scatter coarse semolina or cornmeal onto the surface of a wooden pizza peel and set the dough out on this. Then let it rest and rise slightly while the topping is prepared.

The Baking Process. Begin preheating the oven before shaping the dough. Raise the shelf in the oven to a high position. Set the pizza stone on this and preheat the oven to 550°F or its hottest baking temperature. If you have an electric stove with a broiling element at the top of the stove, be sure this is *not* turned on. Add the topping to the pizza directly on the peel, first giving it a gentle shake to make sure the dough has not adhered to the peel's surface. Then slide it directly onto the preheated (and now *very hot*) stone. Bake until the crust is a golden brown, or about 5 to 6 minutes. Remove the pizza carefully to a cutting board, slice, and serve.

SOME FAVORITE TOPPINGS

BROCCOLI RABE
[*makes 1 12-inch pizza*]

This is, perhaps, our favorite pizza. With its "ferocious pungent-bitter taste" (Elizabeth Schneider), broccoli rabe, even sautéed with garlic in plenty of olive oil, has overwhelmed any pasta dish we've tried it in. Put it on a pizza, however, and something magical takes place. Pizza wants aggressive flavors, and it makes a perfect setting for this one. Broccoli rabe (also known as rapini, cime di rape, *and broccoli raab) is available from late fall into early summer, and is at its best in the colder months. Look for resilient (rather than limp) stalks and tight buds with only a sprinkling of yellow blossoms.*

> dough for one 12-inch pizza, made as described above
> 1 bunch (about 1 pound) broccoli rabe
> 1 large clove garlic
> 2 tablespoons olive oil
> ½ teaspoon pure hot red chile powder
> ¼ teaspoon salt and black pepper to taste
> 4-ounce ball fresh mozzarella, cut into small cubes
>   (see note)
> ½ cup freshly grated Parmesan

Preheat oven and pizza stone and prepare pizza dough as directed above. Put dough in a warm place to rest.

Pick over the bunch of broccoli rabe for wilted or damaged leaves and trim away the very bottoms of the stalks. Wash well. Immerse in a large pot of boiling salted water. Cook until the largest stalks are tender but not soft, about 3 to 5 minutes, depending on the size of the stalks.

Meanwhile, trim and mince the garlic clove until it is reduced to a moist pulp. Pour the olive oil into a skillet and set it over medium-low heat. Add the minced garlic, chile powder, and salt. Stir well. Turn off the heat as soon as the garlic is translucent, about 1 minute.

Empty the cooked broccoli rabe into a colander and press the leaves gently with the back of a wooden spoon to remove excess moisture. Arrange the drained pieces on a cutting board so that the stalks are together. Cut these into small rounds, about ¼-inch long. Then coarsely chop the leaves. Add all this to the hot (but not still heating) oil and mix well. Spread this mixture over the pizza dough, grind over black pepper, and sprinkle with the cubed fresh mozzarella and the grated Parmesan. Slip the pizza onto the preheated stone and bake until crusty and brown, or about 5 to 6 minutes. Cut and serve at once.

Variation. Swiss chard, prepared the same way, makes a less lusty, but still delicious, pizza.

Cook's Note. Fresh cow's milk mozzarella floating in a bath of salty whey is becoming more and more available in supermarkets, although some searching may be required to find it. (At one of our local supermarkets it is in the cheese section; another includes it in the self-serve olive bar.) Unlike the hard-rubber familiar in the dairy case, fresh mozzarella has the delicate, yielding texture of gently compressed curd and a fresh dairy taste. On a pizza it less melts than swoons. Once you try it, you'll never go back to the other, faux kind.

PEPPER, ONION, AND SAUSAGE
[*makes 1 12-inch pizza*]

dough for one 12-inch pizza, made as described above
¼ pound fresh Italian sausage, store-bought or homemade
  (see note)
½ large green bell pepper, seeded and cored
½ large red bell pepper, seeded and cored
1 medium onion, peeled and cored
1 tablespoon olive oil
½ teaspoon pure hot red chile powder
¼ teaspoon salt
1 large clove garlic
freshly ground black pepper to taste
½ cup freshly grated Parmesan

Preheat oven and pizza stone and prepare pizza dough as directed above. Put dough in a warm place to rest.

Remove the sausage meat from its casing. Flatten into a large patty and fry in a lightly oiled skillet until browned on both sides. Remove and cut into small cubes.

With a sharp knife, slice the bell pepper halves as thinly as possible. Cut the onion in half and slice each half as thinly as possible. (This helps keep everything on the pizza.) Add enough olive oil to the skillet in which the sausage was cooked to make 1 tablespoon, including any grease already in the pan. Turn on the heat to medium and add the chile powder and salt. When this has heated, add the slivers of pepper and onion and sauté gently until softened, about 6 or 7 minutes.

Meanwhile, mince the garlic clove until it is reduced to a moist pulp. Stir this into the vegetable mixture. Cook until the garlic is translucent, about 1 more minute.

Spread the pepper-onion mixture over the prepared pizza dough.

Dot with cubes of the sausage. Generously grind over black pepper and sprinkle with the grated Parmesan. Slip the pizza onto the preheated stone and bake this until crusty and brown, or about 5 to 6 minutes. Cut and serve at once.

Variation. Substitute a few anchovy fillets and/or pitted and halved black olives for the pork sausage and ¼ pound cubed good mozzarella for the Parmesan.

HOMEMADE SAUSAGE
[*makes 1 sausage patty*]

Although our supermarket makes an acceptable fresh Italian sausage, we find this basic—and less fatty—sausage mixture better tasting, easy to make, and amenable to adaptation. If fresh sage is unavailable or unwanted, mince the garlic by itself and, if you like, add ¼ teaspoon fennel seeds.

    1 medium clove garlic
    2 fresh sage leaves
    ¼ teaspoon pure hot red chile powder
    ⅛ teaspoon freshly ground black pepper
    2 tablespoons grated Parmesan (optional)
    ¼ teaspoon salt
    ¼ pound ground pork

Mince the garlic and sage leaves together until reduced to a moist pulp. Mix this and all other listed seasonings into the ground pork and, with the side of the mincing knife or your palm, flatten into a patty.

Variation. To make lamb sausage, substitute ground lamb for the pork and 3 or 4 rosemary leaves for the sage. Omit the cheese.

SPINACH AND MUSHROOM
[*makes 1 12-inch pizza*]

    dough for one 12-inch pizza, made as described above
    1 bunch (or bag) fresh spinach (about 12 ounces)
    8 ounces cremini (brown) mushrooms

2 tablespoons olive oil
½ teaspoon salt
1 large clove garlic
½ teaspoon pure hot red chile powder
4-ounce ball fresh mozzarella, cut into small cubes (see
    note on pages 141–42)
½ cup freshly grated Parmesan
freshly ground black pepper to taste

Preheat oven and pizza stone and prepare pizza dough as directed above. Put dough in a warm place to rest.

Pick over the spinach, discarding any less-than-perfect leaves and, with a sharp paring knife, trimming away all split and damaged ends of stems. Rinse carefully in two or three sinkfuls of cool water, to remove all grit. Place the leaves, still dripping with water from the last rinse, in a large pot, and cover. Put this on a burner over high heat. Turn the flame off the moment steam emerges from under the cover. (If using an electric range, remove entirely from the burner.) This should take about 3 or 4 minutes. Let this sit with the cover on.

Cut away any moldy or soil-impregnated stem bottoms from the mushrooms and gently brush off any loose bits of dirt. Slice thin. Pour the olive oil into a large nonstick sauté pan and sprinkle in ¼ teaspoon of the salt. Cook the mushrooms quickly over high heat, turning often, until their edges are brown. Remove and reserve.

Trim and mince the garlic clove until it is reduced to a moist pulp. Stir the minced garlic, chile powder, and remaining salt into any remaining oil in the sauté pan. If there is none, just add these to the pan.

Empty the spinach into a colander or sieve set over a bowl. Press firmly with a rubber spatula or the back of a wooden spoon to remove all excess liquid. (Pour this liquid into a cup, season, and drink—cook's treat.) Turn the pressed spinach out onto the cutting board and coarsely chop it. Transfer to the frying pan and stir gently to distribute the garlic and chile throughout the spinach.

Spread the spinach over the prepared pizza dough and then dot with the sautéed mushrooms and mozzarella cubes. Sprinkle with the grated Parmesan and pepper generously. Slip the pizza onto the preheated stone and bake until crusty and brown, or about 5 to 6 minutes. Cut and serve at once.

Variation. Omit the mushrooms and replace them with crumbled fresh goat's cheese and a scattering of coarsely chopped pine nuts.

EGGPLANT AND LAMB SAUSAGE
[makes 1 12-inch pizza]

Sautéed eggplant makes a terrific pizza. Many recipes encourage you to do without the salting, soaking, and subsequent wringing out of that vegetable. We do it, however, because the process transforms the eggplant's texture (as it also does zucchini's).

> 1 small to medium eggplant (about 12 ounces)
> salt
> dough for one 12-inch pizza, made as described above
> ¼ pound homemade lamb sausage (see page 143)
> 1 large clove garlic
> 2 tablespoons olive oil
> ½ tablespoon balsamic vinegar (optional)
> ½ teaspoon pure hot red chile powder
> ½ teaspoon dried oregano
> ½ teaspoon salt
> ½ red or yellow bell pepper, cut into strips
> freshly ground black pepper to taste
> ½ cup freshly grated Parmesan

An hour or so before the pizza preparations begin, trim the stem ends of the eggplant and then peel it. Cut the flesh into French fry–sized strips. Place these in a colander and sprinkle with about ½ tablespoon of salt, mixing this through the eggplant pieces. Set over a large bowl and let rest for at least an hour. Discard the collected liquid and put the eggplant strips in a sink full of cool water. Swirl them around to rinse, then lift them out, handful by handful, squeezing hard. Put them in an old but clean dish towel, gather its ends together, and twist it tightly, squeezing out as much liquid as possible. (Note that this may permanently stain the towel.) Reserve.

Preheat oven and pizza stone and prepare pizza dough as directed above. Put this in a warm place to rest.

Prepare the lamb variant of our homemade sausage. Flatten into a large patty and fry in a lightly oiled skillet until browned on both sides. Remove and cut into small cubes. Meanwhile, trim and mince the garlic clove until it is reduced to a moist pulp.

Add enough olive oil to the skillet in which the sausage was cooked to make 2 tablespoons, including any grease already in the pan. Turn on the heat to medium and add the minced garlic, balsamic vinegar, chile powder, dried oregano, and salt. Stir well. As soon as the garlic softens, about 1 minute, add the eggplant and strips of red or yellow pepper. Sauté until the eggplant is limp and translucent and the pepper strips tender, about 6 minutes.

Spread the sautéed vegetables over the prepared pizza dough. Dot with the sausage. Generously grind over black pepper and sprinkle with the grated Parmesan. Slip the pizza onto the preheated stone and bake until crusty and brown, or about 5 to 6 minutes. Cut and serve at once.

SUMMER TOMATO AND FRESH MOZZARELLA
[*makes 1 12-inch pizza*]

When we lived Down East, fresh mozzarella was available only when there were enough summer folks around to make a market for it. This meant that mozzarella season and tomato season arrived pretty much at the same time, and we celebrated that fact accordingly. This is our one tomato pizza. It's hardly original, but the method is not the usual one, and it results in an especially tasty version—one worth waiting most of the year to make.

   3 small or 2 medium ripe red tomatoes
   dough for one 12-inch pizza, made as described above
   4 ounces good mozzarella
   1 large clove garlic
   1 tablespoon olive oil
   ½ teaspoon pure hot red chile powder
   salt and freshly ground pepper to taste
   several leaves of fresh basil

An hour before general pizza preparations begin, core, quarter, and cut the tomatoes into bite-sized chunks. Lay these out on paper towels (see note).

Preheat oven and pizza stone and prepare the pizza dough as directed above. Put this in a warm place to rest. Cut the mozzarella into small bite-sized cubes. Trim and mince the garlic until it is reduced to a moist pulp. Heat the olive oil in a skillet. As soon as it is hot, turn off the heat. Sprinkle in the ground chile, add the minced garlic, and stir together well. Turn in the tomato pieces and mix quickly so that they are all flavored with the garlic, hot pepper, and oil. Season with salt and pepper.

Spread the seasoned tomatoes and pan juices evenly over the pizza dough and then dot it with the cubes of mozzarella. Slip the pizza onto the preheated stone and bake until crusty and brown, or about 5 to 6 minutes. While the pizza cooks, tear the basil leaves into small bits. When the pizza is done, remove it from the oven and slide it onto a cutting board. Sprinkle the fresh basil evenly over the hot pizza, then slice and serve slightly cooled.

Variation. Scatter the pizza with torn bits of Mediterranean black olives after spreading the dough with the tomato-garlic mixture.

Cook's Note. The trick to this pizza is to keep as much juice in the tomato pieces as possible, since it is the juice that contains the flavor. To prevent the pizza from swimming in juice, cut the tomato into chunks rather than slices. Then—at least in our quick-cooking method—the pizza is done and out of the oven before these chunks collapse. However, be warned that the chunks emerge scalding hot; take your time scattering the bits of basil over the pizza to give them a chance to cool.

Sources & Further Reading

Our pizza flours and baking stone are available from the King Arthur Flour Baker's Catalogue (see page 212), an admirable source for baking supplies and high-quality specialty flours. (But avoid their aluminum pizza peels; the dough adheres to them.)

Edward Behr's essay "Pizza in Naples," which contains his recipe for authentic Neapolitan pizza, appears in the spring 1992 issue (no. 22) of *The Art of Eating* ($9.00 from P.O. Box 242; Peacham, VT 05862).

The novice pizza maker might start with Marcella Hazan's *Essentials of Classic Italian Cooking*, Carol Field's *The Italian Baker*, Pamela Sheldon John's *Pizza Napoletana*, which contains a wealth of color photographs taken in the city's pizzerias (who would ever have believed that *napoletani* eat pizza with a knife and fork!), or Arthur Schwartz's section on the subject in his *Naples at Table*, a splendid account of the cooking of that city in particular and the region of Campania in general.

CRUSTACEANS & CRUMBS

❀ ❀ ❀

Sometime during the Great Depression, the crab cake leapt from obscurity to the status of an American gastronomic icon. There's no question that crab cakes were eaten before that time by those who lived near the Chesapeake Bay,* but it seems that even there this was a dish relegated to the back of the recipe box. In the early decades of this century, the area's famous oyster beds were beginning to vanish from overharvesting and pollution, and the watermen were turning to crabbing to earn their living. But crabmeat was only slowly acquiring a reputation as a delicacy. It was the poor who, finding oysters priced beyond their reach, would embrace it first, replacing the oyster roast with the boiled-crab dinner as the region's signature seafood dish.

The Chesapeake is home to the blue crab, the meatiest and best-tasting Atlantic crab, and to eat a boiled-crab dinner is to experience that crustacean in as direct a way as possible. It is also to step back in time to when working-class eateries—beer gardens, oyster houses, barbecue pits—offered generous portions in a convivial, even boisterous, atmosphere to customers who took an uninhibited delight in both.

To dine on boiled crab, you sit down at a table covered with brown paper; your eating implement is a wooden mallet, with your fingers

---

*The culinary essayist Edward Behr traced published recipes for crab cakes as far back as the 1897 revised edition of a Baltimore cookbook, Marietta Hollyday's *Domestic Economy*. The recipe—"Crab Cakes for Breakfast. (Very nice.)"—calls for the crabmeat to be seasoned "high with red pepper and salt." The cakes are bound with flour and butter, then dipped in egg and cracker crumbs and fried in butter or lard.

playing outfield. The waitress arrives with a pitcher of beer and a tray piled with boiled crabs, and you fall to. Shells crack, juices splatter, the mess on the table gets messier, and your fingers get smellier. The room is noisy with the crunch and thud of mallet on shell and the hubbub of people drinking lots of beer and having a good time. The novelist Jean Rhys got this atmosphere exactly right when she wrote: "They [ate] with gusto and noise after the manner of simple-hearted people who like their neighbors to see and know their pleasures."

To such eaters, the crab cake would seem, at best, an appetizer to this feast and, at worst, an intrusion from their great aunt's bridge club. However, as the century progressed, the economics of the restaurant business and the general genteelizing of society conspired to bring such eating places to extinction's brink. What replaced them was something new: the turbocharged vernacular meal. Chili joints, fish-fry shacks, pancake houses, burger havens, hot dog carts: each specialized in a dish that might by necessity come from inexpensive ingredients but was prepared and promoted with such unalloyed enthusiasm that eating it made you feel like a prince. It was as if the raucous-tinged ambience of the hash house, now outlawed, transmuted itself into an aura that embraced the food itself. With the lip-smacking already injected into the foot-long hot dog or fried chicken in a basket, eaters could be persuaded that there was no need for *their* lips to make any noise at all.

The revolutionary force that transformed the Salisbury steak napped with cheese sauce into the cheeseburger had the same liberating effect on the crab cake. At the time, crabmeat was dirt cheap, and the dishes that utilized it had names—crab cutlets, crabmeat de Luxe, crabmeat à la king, crabmeat imperial—designed to help the hostess obscure the fact that it was, in culinary prestige, only a few steps up from dirt itself.

The crab cake took over several of the techniques that made these dishes tasty—it was well seasoned with Worcestershire or Tabasco to make it spicier and was bound together with a sauce—or sometimes heavy cream—to make it richer. But it broke almost entirely away from the tradition of refined dissembling. Its name and its unadorned presentation declared, "I *know* I'm good, and, as far as I'm concerned, you're a snobby fool if *you* don't know it, too." The crab cake was the Clark Gable of crabmeat dishes: it didn't wear an undershirt and it didn't give a damn who found out.

Like its beefy cousin the hamburger, the crab cake's simplicity focuses rather than diffuses our appetite. Sit down to a boiled-crab dinner and you have to winnow out your pleasure bit by bit. Sit down to a crab cake and the pleasure is immediate and intense. The crabmeat has already been picked—you can take as big a mouthful as you want. In fact, the crab cake goes the burger one better in concentrated taste experience. It provides its own bun and—unless you're the sort with a ketchup bottle instead of a left hand—its own relish, too.

Crab cakes are so delicious you don't have to like crab to love them. In fact, you don't even need crab to make them—salmon or shrimp or minced clams will work nearly as well. However, the crab cake was first, and for a very good reason: the common denominator of most crab cookery is the container of picked meat. And crab cakes serve that meat best because they mess with it least.

❦ ❦ ❦

Before there was the crab cake, there was the crab croquette, an extremely popular dish at the turn of the century. Bits of meat or seafood were bound together in a thick sauce, formed into shapes—balls, mostly, but also pyramids, ovals, what have you—breaded, and deep-fried. What we call the crab cake today is the sum of inspired improvements made to it by countless unknown cooks over a span of decades. The crab cake recipe in Sheila Hibben's *The National Cookbook*—published in 1932—shows us the first step in this evolutionary process, namely, flattening and then panfrying the crab croquette.

CRAB-FLAKE CAKES (BALTIMORE-STYLE)
[*serves 4*]

2 tablespoons butter
2 tablespoons flour
1 cup milk
1 egg yolk
1 teaspoon Worcestershire sauce
½ teaspoon onion juice
2 cups crabmeat, flaked

salt and pepper to taste
bread crumbs for coating
lard or butter for frying
rich cream sauce

Melt the butter in a saucepan and add to it the flour; when well mixed, add the milk gradually, stirring constantly until smooth. Add the egg yolk, beaten up with the Worcestershire sauce and onion juice, and the crab flakes, seasoning to taste with salt and pepper. As soon as this mixture is cool enough, put it in the icebox to get very cold. Form into flat cakes; dredge in finely sifted bread crumbs and fry on both sides in either lard or butter. Serve on a hot platter with rich cream sauce (a white sauce made with cream instead of milk) poured over the cakes.

Although there are other things worth noticing here—Hibben is unable to shake off the fussiness that has always clung to the croquette (that drenching with rich cream sauce!)—what strikes me most is how unappetizing this early crab cake seems. Tasty as it may have been when turned out by the right cook, to read the recipe is to feel one's tastebuds wilt.

Others must have agreed with that assessment, for it was right about this time that the great tidal wave of white sauce, then the universal culinary lubricant—a gluey amalgam of butter, flour, and milk—began at last to roll back out to sea. Younger readers may not even know what white sauce is, but older ones surely will, since even into the second half of this century basic cookbooks devoted pages to it and its many variations. Here was a sauce that any cook could make, and so almost every cook did, in one or another of its many forms and with varying amounts of success: celery sauce, cheese sauce, curry sauce, onion sauce, pimiento sauce, Newburg sauce, brown sauce, orange sauce, and so on, ad infinitum.

One thing that helped change all this was the discovery by the delicatessen owner Richard Hellmann at the beginning of the twentieth century that there was an unexpected market for his bottled mayonnaise. By 1915, he gave up the delicatessen business entirely to make it; by 1927, he had factories up and running in Astoria, Chicago, San Francisco, Atlanta, Dallas, and Tampa. His Hellmann's Blue Ribbon mayonnaise had taken the country by storm.

And why not? Where few white sauces managed to rise much above library paste, mayonnaise offered instant voluptuousness and piquancy. Of course, recipes for mayonnaise appeared in period cookbooks, too, but making it oneself was a challenge rarely accepted by most home cooks. Hellmann's, however, could be spooned straight from the jar, and this easy deliciousness was immediately embraced by our vernacular cooking, producing such delicacies as potato salad, the club sandwich, and the BLT. Also, since mayonnaise is a cold sauce, our national taste began to shift away from dishes like lobster Newburg to ones like lobster salad. Where the white sauce tradition *was* maintained, it, too, was no longer made at home; its effects were accomplished by canned cream soups.

Although it took cookbook writers a long time to admit that their readers weren't, in fact, *making* all this mayonnaise—the commercial version isn't even mentioned in *Fannie Farmer* until the tenth edition (1959)—recipes utilizing it as an ingredient began to exfoliate in the thirties, and it was quickly recognized as the ideal binder of the crab cake. Here is an early version that the Brown clan managed to wheedle from Getz's, a premier Baltimore seafood restaurant whose crab cakes were legendary—and this in a city already famous for them.

GETZ'S BALTIMORE CRAB CAKES
(adapted from *America Cooks* [1940], by Cora, Rose, and Bob Brown)
[*serves 4*]

1 pound crabmeat
½ teaspoon salt
1 teaspoon white pepper
1 teaspoon chopped parsley
1 teaspoon dry English mustard
2 teaspoons Worcestershire sauce
1 egg yolk
1 tablespoon mayonnaise
flour for dredging
1 egg, beaten
dried bread crumbs

Put the crabmeat in a large bowl. Blend the salt, white pepper, parsley, powdered mustard, Worcestershire sauce, and egg yolk into the mayonnaise and gently but thoroughly mix into the crabmeat. Form this mixture into 8 cakes, pressing well together. Dip each into the flour, then into the beaten egg, and finally into the bread crumbs, coating the crab cakes all over. Fry these in a hot greased skillet until golden brown on both sides. Serve with potato salad or coleslaw.

Now, these are good—in fact, they're so good that you can still find crab cakes in Maryland today made precisely in this way. However, they also show that eschewing the white sauce doesn't mean you've escaped the croquette. When the croquette was fried in boiling fat, its protective crumb coating quickly crisped, keeping it intact and preventing it from absorbing any grease. The panfried crab cake—unlike a hamburger—still needs a binder to hold it together, but—very much *like* a hamburger—it doesn't need any coating to protect it from the fat. I believe that until the crab cake shed this croquettish coating, it didn't truly come into its own.

Those who disagree with this opinion should ponder why panfried crab cakes have remained universally popular, while the crumb-coated deep-fat-fried ones have all but disappeared everywhere except on their native turf. If deep-fat frying is still the preferred method for frying chicken, it is because the crusty coating provides an ideal contrast to that bird's tender but relatively insipid flesh. But when it comes to something as delicate as a crab cake, that sort of crust only gets in the way.

❋ ❋ ❋

The quintessential crab cake should be buttery crisp on the outside, to be sure, but its integument should hold it together only up to the moment when a forkful reaches the mouth. Then it should collapse—not melt, not crumble—into moist, tender crabmeat, its assertive flavor balanced by the piquancy of the seasonings and its richness enhanced and broadened by the mayonnaise. It is the succulence of crabmeat that makes the crab cake so special and explains why other seafood cakes— good as they can be—are of a lesser breed. And it is the ability to retain this succulence that is the mark of the superlative crab cake cook.

To become such a cook, you need to acquire a light, deft hand in forming and then cooking the cakes. This comes with practice. You must also acquire a certain resolution in avoiding the crab cake recipes in most cookbooks—even Maryland cookbooks. Because of its simplicity, the crab cake tends to suffer more than most from the American tendency to make things easier than they ought to be and to improve a good thing out of existence. As Euell Gibbons confesses in his classic guide to shoreline foraging, *Stalking the Blue-Eyed Scallop:*

> Crab cakes can be excellent if one is generous with the crabmeat and severely limits or completely eliminates the other ingredients. At one time I added such things as chopped parsley, minced onion, chopped peppers, chopped celery, breadcrumbs, and other things to my crab cakes, but by experimenting I gradually made the amazing discovery that crab cakes are much better when made of crab.

Compared to most, Gibbons's approach *is* amazingly spartan: he mixes his crabmeat with a beaten egg, shapes this into one-and-a-half-inch balls with dampened hands, lets these firm for an hour or so in the refrigerator, then rolls them in crushed cracker meal and deep-fries them. Unfortunately, in this case, what simplicity gives with one hand it takes away with the other. Call these "crab nuggets" and heap them into a pita pocket lined with shredded lettuce, spoon over a generous dose of tartar sauce, and you would certainly have something to give falafel a run for its money.

But this is not the way to make a crab cake. Beaten egg is the easy way to bind them together, but it solidifies during the frying and makes the crab cake rubbery and dry. As Mary Seymour, a Maryland cook who grew up at the very edge of the Chesapeake Bay, observes to Jean Anderson in *The Grass Roots Cookbook* (1977):

> Most people use eggs in their crab cakes, but I don't like to. If you don't use a lot of mayonnaise or something in the mixture to loosen it up, the eggs dry the crab out and make it tough. The mixture should be juicy and soft but still thick enough to hold together . . . but try not to handle it too much or the crab will pack down too tight. Now I remember when I was a girl, my mother didn't even bother to pat out the crab cakes—with eight children, she didn't want to take the time. She just dumped the crab mixture in a great big skillet and stirred it over the heat—sort of like

crab hash. But I do take time to shape the crab cakes. I make right good-sized ones—about 2-½ inches across and I guess 'bout an inch thick. Of course, I never was accused of making my crab cakes all the same size.

It was by following the thrust of Mrs. Seymour's advice that I produced my first truly successful crab cake. Before, I had made my crab cakes the same way I made my codfish cakes—patted into the shape of a hamburger—which all but guaranteed that they would be overhandled and overcooked. Molded gently into the shape of a baking-powder biscuit, they retained both their moisture and their collapse-in-the-mouth texture. Her recipe is a good one, but during my time in Maine I've wandered away from it, for reasons spelled out in the following.

CRAB CAKE BASICS

The Crabmeat. Commercially picked blue crabmeat is sold by the grade, the most expensive of which is "lump"—big pieces from the back fin—and the least expensive "special" or "regular"—a mass of tiny meat slivers picked from the body. It's no strain on the brain to guess the grade most likely to end up in crab cakes—which is fine, but it does pose a problem for the cook. The finer the bits of crabmeat, the drier it is, so a way must be found to add moisture back. But because Maine crab has nothing much in the way of lump meat, pickers almost always give you a mix of claw and body meat, which is usually quite moist. Your crab cake strategy should be based on whether your crabmeat is chunky and moist or fibrous and dry. Or, if you have no trustworthy access to crabmeat at all, consider substituting either salmon or one of the tender, easily flaked, white-fleshed tribe of cod. Gently poach it until just done, flake it, and proceed from there, using a little of the poaching liquid to moisten it. Although hard to find even in Maine these days, a good cod cake can make for a memorable repast.

The Binder. Those who claim that the truly authentic binder of crab cakes is a handful of crushed Saltines are mostly boasting that they have a friend in the crab-picking business and get to make their crab cakes from big, flavorful chunks of meat. The dry Saltines soak up the crab juices and keep the crab cakes from losing moisture and flavor. However, as noted above, those faced with a container of crab shavings have to find some way to remoisten the meat—usually in the form of milk-sopped bread bits (i.e., the next size up from crumbs).

In either instance, the amount should be minimal: a couple of crackers or a slice or so of bread torn to bits and lightly moistened with milk or cream. Mrs. Seymour finds this sufficient as a binder and adds no mayonnaise, but most everyone else uses both, plus, in many instances, a raw beaten egg. If, on the other hand, using none of the above seems the most inviting option, consider the recipe for Crab Norfolk, on page 162: it's at once simple and over-the-top.

The Seasonings. In your basic, no-frills crab joint, these are usually a tablespoon of prepared mustard and half a teaspoon of Worcestershire sauce, with perhaps some minced parsley for color. (Those who no longer deign to keep Worcestershire sauce in their larder substitute a high-toned vinegar or fresh lemon juice.) Mrs. Seymour adds a tablespoon of grated onion to this list and specifies Gulden's spicy brown mustard. Tabasco sauce and—less often—grated horseradish are also used. Recently, Old Bay Seasoning has been appearing in Maryland crab cake recipes to give them the stamp of "authenticity"—but in my opinion, that stuff has too many ingredients to belong in a crab cake. Better to season the crab cake lightly and add the appropriate zip via some homemade tartar sauce.

PIGEON HILL BAY CRAB CAKES
[makes 8 cakes to serve up to 4]

Pigeon Hill Bay comes to an end in a small cove a little more than a stone's throw from our house. Along its shores we saw seals basking, bald eagles fishing, and humans engaged in any number of tasks— clamming, catching elvers, digging for bloodworms to sell as bait. Crabs aplenty were to be found there, too, and not a few of them ended up in the following recipe.

1 pound crabmeat, checked for shell fragments
2 or 3 Saltine crackers, crumbled in the fist
2 tablespoons mayonnaise
generous dash Tabasco sauce
½ teaspoon spicy brown mustard
1 tablespoon minced parsley

¼ teaspoon salt
freshly ground black pepper to taste
3 to 4 tablespoons butter for frying

Put the picked-over crabmeat in a mixing bowl and crumble the Saltine crackers into it. Blend the mayonnaise, Tabasco sauce, mustard, and parsley together, turn into the crabmeat mixture, and sprinkle this with the salt and black pepper. Using your fingers or a rubber spatula, gently toss to produce a loosely textured crab salad.

Take a biscuit cutter or a small, clean topless-and-bottomless can about 2½ inches in diameter and set it on a large plate. Spoon approximately one-eighth of the crab mixture into the ring, tapping the ring gently when full to settle it. Then remove the ring, set it elsewhere on the plate, and repeat the above process, continuing until you have formed 8 crab cakes. Put the plate in the refrigerator and let the crab cakes firm for 1 to 2 hours.

Meanwhile, to prevent burning the cakes, put the butter in a heat-proof measuring cup and place it in an oven turned to its lowest setting. After 15 minutes—or when the butter has turned clear and the butter solids have settled to the bottom of the cup—using an oven mitt or a pot holder, carefully pour the liquid butter onto a griddle or large skillet, leaving behind—and then discarding—all of the butter solids.

When it is time to cook the crab cakes, remove the plate from the refrigerator. Heat the clarified butter in the griddle over medium-high heat. When the butter is hot, slide a thin-edged spatula under each crab cake and, with a gentle shake, slip it onto the hot griddle. Fry the cakes until the bottoms are golden brown, about 2 minutes, then turn them over to cook on the other side. Serve at once with coleslaw and potato salad or a dressed green salad and hot boiled rice, and pass the tartar sauce.

TARTAR SAUCE

As ketchup is to French fries, so tartar sauce is to crab cakes.
—John Shields, *The Chesapeake Bay Crab Cookbook*

One more way to divide the world is into those who put tartar sauce on their fried fish and those who squeeze lemon over it. (There is, I know, the tiny minority who use neither and that other, perhaps not so small one, who use both.) Store-bought tartar sauce can be deliciously vulgar stuff, great with fish and chips, but crab cakes deserve something with more gumption.

Eliza Acton is said to have introduced tartar sauce to English-speaking eaters in *Modern Cookery* (1845), and her version is not nearly as sweet and bland as ours. It is doubtful that Acton knew anything about Tartar cooking; the word was then commonly used in England to evoke their rebarbative reputation—"swear like a Tartar"—and here to signal that this sauce was pretty fierce stuff. Nor is her recipe based on mayonnaise but on a salad dressing called English sauce, made by thickening fresh cream with cooked egg yolks. This is lighter and creamier than mayonnaise, and quicker and easier to make.

ENGLISH SAUCE
[makes about ½ cup dressing]

1 large hard-boiled egg yolk
⅛ teaspoon each salt and cayenne
¼ teaspoon sugar
½ cup whipping cream
1 teaspoon lemon juice or tarragon vinegar

Put the hard-boiled yolk into a shallow soup bowl and use the tip of a rubber spatula to mash it to a lumpless paste, working in a few drops of cold water toward the end to make it as smooth as possible. Blend in the seasonings, then, bit by bit, stir in the cream. Finally, add the lemon juice or vinegar. Set in a cool place for a few hours so that the lemon juice or vinegar has time to help thicken the cream to the right consistency. Taste again for seasoning before serving. (Elizabeth David blends a *raw* egg yolk with the hard-boiled one to make an even smoother sauce.)

Those who like creamy salad dressings will delight in the way this one accepts all sorts of flavorings. Eliza Acton herself recommends adding chopped fresh herbs, anchovy fillets, finely grated horseradish, prepared mustard, and/or minced garlic to taste when dressing salad greens or composed salads of seafood, chicken, or cooked vegetables. In making tartar sauce, she pulls out all the stops. The following recipe is taken straight from the pages of her book.

TARTAR SAUCE

Add to the above amount of English sauce a teaspoonful or more of made mustard, one of finely minced eschalots, one of parsley or tarragon, and one of capers or of pickled gherkins, with a rather high seasoning of cayenne, and some salt if needed. Good French mustard is to be preferred to English for this sauce, which is usually made very pungent, and for which any ingredients can be used to the taste which will serve to render it so. Tarragon vinegar, *minced tarragon*, and eschalots, and plenty of oil, are used for it in France, in conjunction with the yolks of one or two eggs, and chopped capers, or gherkins, to which olives are sometimes added.

Of course, if you prefer, you can also make Tartar sauce with prepared mayonnaise—not as authentic as the above, but still a distinct cut above the commercial product. Into 1 cup mayonnaise blend any or all of the following: 2 tablespoons each minced raw onion and parsley, 2 or 3 minced gherkins, the juice of ½ lemon, and a few dashes of Tabasco sauce. Let this sit in the fridge for an hour for the flavors to meld, then give it a quick final stir before bringing it to table.

Further Reading

For a thoughtful, evocative essay on blue crabs and those who catch and cook them in the Chesapeake Bay, turn to Edward Behr's essay "Maryland Crab" in the summer 1992 issue (no. 23) of his food letter, *The Art of Eating* (the single issue is $9.00 from Box 242; Peacham, VT 05862). Those seeking crab cake recipes will find a wealth of vernacular ones in John Shields's excellent *The Chesapeake Bay Crab Cookbook*.

A NOTE ON CRAB À LA NORFOLK

The late Augustus Kelley, whose seminal writings on chowder under the pseudonym "Theophrastus" are discussed at length in *Serious Pig*, occasionally wrote to us about his other favorite seafood dishes, including one for which he had never found a printed recipe.

> I was in the secondhand book business for many years, specializing in the field of economics. In my day, Washington, D.C., was a terrific book town, mainly because when congressmen or senators lost their bid for reelection, they quite often sold their books to the Washington book dealers before returning home. I used to look forward to these Washington trips. There were so many good restaurants; one in particular, O'Donnell's, in the heart of Washington, used to feature all kinds of shellfish "à la Norfolk." Everything else there was good, but the Norfolk dishes were supreme. The waiters were terribly nice, but none would reveal the receipt. (O'Donnell's finally moved to Bethesda, and though the food was still good when I was last there, it was not quite *as* good). I did a lot of searching for a Norfolk, Virginia, cookbook but never found one. I wish I had—the recipe for shellfish à la Norfolk would be a great prize.

Our curiosity piqued, we set out to find what we could about the dish. Norfolk, Virginia, is perched at the mouth of the Chesapeake Bay. Before World War II transformed it into the world's largest naval base and the Atlantic headquarters of NATO, it was a quiet Southern shipping port already famous for this simple but ultrarich seafood dish. In his *North Atlantic Seafood* (1979), Alan Davidson writes that crab or lobster

> prepared Norfolk style, which is to say with nothing else but butter and seasoning, is too rich for some. I have been eating it on and off at Martin's restaurant in the Georgetown district of Washington, D.C., for nearly thirty years, but I plan to give it up on my sixty-fifth birthday.*

We eventually found a more detailed account of "Crab Norfolk" in two cookbooks, the most recently published of which was Craig Clai-

---

*That birthday having since come and gone, Davidson may now regret putting this pledge in print.

borne's *Southern Cooking* (1987). It is all but identical in both its simplicity and buttery richness to one given forty years earlier in Sheila Hibben's *American Regional Cookery* (1947). Claiborne also tells us something more of its history:

> Crab Norfolk is a specialty of Norfolk, Virginia, where it was first created by W. O. Snowden of the once popular, now defunct, Snowden and Mason Restaurant, which opened in that city in 1924. The dish was originally cooked in specially designed small oval aluminum pans. In some establishments in Norfolk it is still cooked and served in those pans.

Here, somewhat adapted, is his recipe.

CRAB NORFOLK
[*serves 4*]

1 pound lump crabmeat
⅛ cup white or cider vinegar
¼ pound (1 stick) unsalted butter
dash of Tabasco sauce
salt and black pepper to taste

Pick over the crabmeat to remove any trace of shell or cartilage. Put it into a bowl and toss it with the vinegar. Melt the butter in a skillet. When the butter is bubbling, add the Tabasco, swirl to mix, and then stir in the seasoned crabmeat. Stir the crab gently until it is heated through, being careful not to break up the larger lumps of claw meat. Lightly season with salt and black pepper to taste. Serve hot, with buttered rice on the side.

Hibben uses the juice of half a lemon instead of the vinegar, which seems a good move to us, and she heats the crabmeat in a double boiler instead of a skillet, which doesn't. Part of the defining character of this dish is the sizzle, and it's surprising that Claiborne doesn't make more of this in his recipe. Consequently, I was immensely drawn to Joe Hyde's version of the dish in his *Love, Time, & Butter* (see page 226 for more about him), where panache (and timing) is everything and the ingredient list cut to the bone.

Hyde simply spreads the pound of crabmeat evenly over the bottom of a buttered baking dish and slips it into a preheated 400°F oven. Five minutes later, he melts a stick and a half of butter in a skillet over medium-high heat until it has browned and has a nutty smell—don't let it burn. The crab is removed at the ten-minute mark, sprinkled with parsley, and rushed to the table, with the melted butter, in a small, warmed pitcher, set at its side.

RISO IN BIANCO

❧ ❧ ❧

Anyone setting out to learn to make risotto, as I did recently, will find that the hardest part is sorting through the abundance of information and recipes. Risotto may or may not be the most famous rice dish in the world, but it is the only one I know that has had several entire books devoted to it; in fact, one food writer, Judith Barrett, has written *two*.

However, as risotto follows risotto, the attentive reader gradually becomes aware of a strange absence lurking behind all this amplitude and begins to wonder: do Italians shun all other ways of preparing rice? As I searched through our Italian cookbook collection, I discovered that, in them at least, rice cooking and risotto making are all but synonymous. There are rice-based soups, fried rice balls, rice molds, and rice salads (new to Italian cuisine, but very popular), but you have to look long and hard for any discussion about what in other rice-centered cuisines is the focal point of most any meal, whether it be eaten by rich or poor—plain steamed or boiled rice.

Apparently, this is because the Italian way of showing respect to the central starch is to serve it separately, traditionally as the first course. Here, pasta points the way: it's impossible to imagine a bowl of plain boiled spaghetti being set on the table, no matter what else is being served. And this is also true of rice. Consider, in this light, the recipe for "Rice As a Side Dish" in the godfather of modern Italian cookbooks, Pellegrino Artusi's classic *Science in the Kitchen and the Art of Eating Well* (1890):

> To avoid using too much broth, first blanch the rice in water, and
> then finish cooking it in chicken broth. Make the rice firm and

when nearly done, flavor it with butter and a little Parmesan cheese. If you are using [half a pound] of rice, bind it with one egg, or better still, with two yolks as you remove it from the fire.

If you are serving the rice with a stew of milk-fed veal or veal chops, rather than with boiled chicken, in addition to the ingredients mentioned above add two or three tablespoons of spinach which you have boiled and passed through a sieve. In this way your rice will be green and have a more refined flavor.

In Italian cooking, it seems, the simplest starch dish has to restrain itself from becoming the entire meal. And with so many Italian rice dishes already heading down the road that leads to risotto, you have to admire the few plain rice dishes that have stubbornly refused to do so. The two peculiar qualities of Italian rice that make a risotto unique—the ample starch that provides its luscious creaminess and the resilient interior that resists being cooked to mush—can be utilized more simply (see Patience Gray's recipe for "*La Peperonata con Riso*" on pages 175–77) or individually. For instance, a few handfuls of the rice can be used to thicken soups or cooked into a savory porridge, or a large amount can be tossed into boiling water until the starch is cooked away, leaving behind the pleasingly chewy center of the rice kernel. Such *riso al dente* is treated like pasta, drained and then tossed with a small amount of sauce, or, even better, tossed without it, as Elizabeth David says in *Italian Food*:

> One of the nicest ways of eating plain rice [*riso in bianco*] is, it cannot be denied, with plenty of grated Parmesan cheese and an unlimited quantity of good fresh country butter, and this is a dish which may be eaten to perfection in northern Italy. The rice of Piedmont is so good and so full of flavor that it is almost a pity to pour a sauce over it.

Such dishes fall under the loose rubric of *risi in bianco*. In Italian, *bianco* has two meanings: "white," and "blank" or "empty." Consequently, in culinary parlance, the term *in bianco* not only means "unadorned" or "served plain" but implies additionally an absence that is itself a kind of presence (as in the suggestive phrase "blank check").

This absence can be literal—*in bianco* is often used to indicate that tomatoes have been left out of a dish that usually includes them, not in an attempt to cheapen it but to make it into something different. However, it can also mean something a little more metaphorical, as Biba Caggiano explains in *Italy al Dente*:

Italians turn to *mangiare in bianco* when they are a bit under the weather, when they want to lighten up on their diet, or when they have partied a bit too much the night before. It is believed that a plate of pasta or rice, dressed only with a bit of fresh butter and cheese, restores body and mind. Certainly, it is a basic comfort food.

And this is exactly the case when Italians prepare "white" rice.

❋ ❋ ❋

It was Matt who brought *riso in bianco* into my life. Back in the early seventies, reading Marcella Hazan's *The Classic Italian Cook Book*, she had come across a simple version in which the boiled rice was tossed with butter, torn basil leaves, shredded mozzarella, and plenty of grated Parmesan. Unlike the many pages of risottos that had come before, this dish was something that immediately sparked her interest. In fact, it awakened a longing that wouldn't be satisfied until she moved to New York City a few years later, where both arborio rice and fresh mozzarella were easier to come by.

However, it wasn't until Hazan's second book, *More Classic Italian Cooking*, appeared, with a variant of the original recipe—in which ribbons of parboiled savoy cabbage were sautéed in olive oil with minced garlic and tossed with the cooked rice along with mozzarella and Parmesan—that the dish became a regular part of her cooking. Not only was it surprisingly good with the cabbage, it positively invited improvisation, drawing to it whatever was in season or especially appealing at the produce stand. By the time we began to live together, she had made it with, among other things, tomatoes, fennel, zucchini, and asparagus.

It was with asparagus that Matt first prepared the dish for me, and to this day I wonder why she was ever willing to cook for me again. I can't think of another meal whose making filled me with so much dismay or brought about so much impulsive acting out. This wasn't because the resulting dish wasn't any good—on the contrary, it was delicious—but it was a deliciousness achieved in a way that had me transfixed with dread.

First, there was the asparagus issue. A lifetime of acute asparagus deficiency had rigidly shaped my cooking of that vegetable: if necessary

I would peel it, I would even trim away obviously dry and woody ends, but otherwise I always cooked the whole spears—so that I could gnaw off everything edible. Matt, on the other hand, working up from the butt, found the point where the spear would easily snap in two and then discarded the lower part. When I realized what she was doing, I couldn't keep myself from snatching these from the refuse pile and cooking them separately. Then, while she continued her work at the stove, I sat at the kitchen table, sullenly sucking at my collection of cellulose-infarcted discards.

And that wasn't all. I had long ago perfected a method of cooking asparagus in a contained environment that allowed no flavor mote to escape (see page 224). Incredulously, then, I watched Matt blithely toss the spears into a huge pot of boiling water as if they were strands of pasta, letting all that asparagus flavor leach away.

Then came the final straw. The cooked asparagus was removed from the pot, to be replaced there with the risotto rice. I could barely stand it. This was rice for which we'd paid a premium, supposedly because of its raison d'être—the thick, creamy, delicate sauce produced by all that lovely starch, which would now be *completely dissolved*. As I stood there staring disconsolately, unbelievingly, into the pot, what I saw there was not cooking water but a kind of elemental cream of asparagus soup.

So, while Matt was busy tossing the rice and asparagus pieces together in a buttery, eggy, lemony sauce, I was at the kitchen sink, blowing fiercely on a mug of boiling-hot, starchy, asparagus-flavored liquid that I had retrieved as the rest went swirling down the drain. By the time we sat down to supper, I had already made a first meal for myself out of the garbage.

A writer who can't discard a sentence—however cleverly crafted—for the good of the piece is a writer who has lost (or has never gained) control over his writing. The same is true of a cook. I knew this, but to act on it I had to overcome a fiercely stubborn resistance to "wasting" anything desirable, a resistance that was, in fact, a manifestation of my fear of deprivation. So, potato peelings, despite their high nutritional value, have always been thrown away without a tremor of regret, while cheese parings, meat scraps, even chunks of gristly fat, are more likely to end up in my mouth . . . if I haven't already adapted the dish to include them (as I did later devise a version of *ris e latt con parmigiano e*

sparagio that included every bit of rice starch and asparagus flavor—
see page 178).

Paradoxically, what in northern Italy had sprung from a cooking
based on economy of means became possible for me only after a period
of surfeit. As Italian rice got cheaper and easier to find, we began to eat
it more often, and my deprivation anxieties began to ease. Then, our
move to what is sometimes called "Asparagus Valley" meant that for
the first time in my life, I actually had *enough* asparagus, something I
had thought as much an impossibility as getting too much sleep.

So, slowly but surely, I was won round, Matt was vindicated, and
riso in bianco found a place in our everyday eating. What I discovered
was that cooking risotto rice like pasta didn't make it the same as
pasta. With its starchy integument boiled away, Italian rice develops a
honeycombed texture that sponges up the sauce that on pasta would
only be a coating. This quality can be drowned in a sea of sauce—but
there is no better way to set off a small amount of a rich and delicate
one than to toss it into *riso*.

Also, of course, it *tastes* like rice, and there are certain foods and assorted aromatics that make a match with rice as they do with nothing
else. In my opinion, asparagus is better with rice than with pasta, and
so are—for instance—fresh peas, ham, chicken livers, and shrimp.
Sauté some celery in butter, stir it into *riso in bianco*, and you'll never
think the same way about that vegetable again. And rice is to sage
what pasta is to oregano: the starch that gives that herb its reason for
being.

Mozzarella, on the other hand, is good with rice in a different way
than it is with pasta. When small cubes of that cheese are mixed into
the hot rice, they produce long filaments that adhere to the cooked
grain, resulting in a deliciously chewy tangle of rice and cheese—something that doesn't happen when mozzarella is tossed with pasta. There,
the slick surface of the noodles doesn't give it anything to grip, and so
it clumps together instead.

The recipes that follow show how we have adapted *riso in bianco*
to provide a variety of simple one-dish meals. Consequently, they are
heartier and contain more ingredients than the traditional versions,
which are intended to be eaten as a separate course. At the same time,
ours are less rich in butter and cheese—although anyone succumbing to
Elizabeth David's siren call will receive no scolding from us.

Risi in bianco are like risotti without the fuss. These dishes, built upon the simplicity of plain white arborio rice, although little discussed in America, are an excellent alternative to pasta and represent Italian cooking at its simple, hearty best.

—Gioietta Vitale, *Riso: Undiscovered Rice Dishes*
of Northern Italy

Cooking term. A *pioggia* ("like rain")—to add rice to boiling water in a thin, steady stream so that the water continues to bubble throughout. A simple way to accomplish this is to put the rice in a pitcher and, tilting it carefully over the cooking pot, slowly sprinkle the kernels out of the pouring spout into the rolling water. And do remember that the purer the cooking water, the more the taste of this delicious rice will come through.

RISO IN BIANCO (BASIC RECIPE)
[*serves 2 as a main course, 4 as a side dish (see note)*]

3 or 4 quarts water
pure sea salt
½ pound (about 1 cup) Italian risotto rice

Bring the water to a boil in a large pot and salt as you would to cook pasta. Pour in the rice *a pioggia* (see above) and stir once with a big wooden spoon. When the water returns to a roiling boil, lower the heat and simmer the rice until it is just al dente, 15 to 18 minutes. When the rice is done, drain it gently in a sieve or colander, letting the liquid run out of its own accord but not shaking it dry.

Cook's Note. Calculate serving sizes as you usually do with pasta— if you serve 6 with a pound box of spaghetti, you'll find a pound of rice cooked in this manner does the same service. If you mean to serve the rice as a side dish or as a first course, cut the measure in half.

CLASSIC RISO IN BIANCO DISHES

RIS IN CAGNON

This traditional rice dish was a regular *primo* for most Milanese families before rice gave way to the more fashionable pasta.
—Anna Del Conte, *Gastronomy of Italy*

½ pound Italian rice, prepared as directed above
1 clove garlic
4 sage leaves
4 tablespoons (½ stick) unsalted butter
1 cup grated Parmesan

While the rice cooks, carefully press the garlic clove with the flat side of a cleaver or chef's knife to crush it as flat as possible. Bruise the fresh sage leaves with the spine of the knife to release the herb's fragrant oil.

Melt the unsalted butter in a small saucepan over medium heat. Add the flattened garlic and bruised sage leaves and cook, stirring, until the butter is golden brown and smells like toasted hazelnuts (it is, in fact, called *burro nocciola*—hazelnut butter). Take the pan from the heat and remove and discard the aromatics.

Some cooks toss the cooked rice with the seasoned butter and Parmesan, and others invert it onto a platter or into a shallow serving bowl and top it with the butter and cheese. Either way, it should be served at once.

Variations. For a more potent version of this dish, finely mince the garlic and sage leaves together and leave them in the butter.

To make *Riso al Burro Nocciola*: omit the sage and garlic.

To make *Riso al Salvia e Fegatini*: cook 2 or 3 chicken livers, cut into small pieces, in the butter with the garlic and sage and reduce the amount of Parmesan by half.

RISO CON LIMONE ALLA PIEMONTESE

[*serves 2 as a meal, 4 as a side dish*]

Risotto made with lemon appears in almost every Italian cookbook that ever there was, and for good reason—the sharp bite of the lemon helps keep the essential richness of the dish at bay. Here, conversely, the delicate creaminess of riso in bianco *tempers the acidity of the lemon without crowding its bright citrus flavor. If you know this combination only as a risotto, you're in for a delightful surprise.*

½ pound Italian rice, prepared as directed above
2 egg yolks
2 tablespoons freshly squeezed lemon juice
1 cup freshly grated Parmesan, plus more for the table
2 or 3 tablespoons unsalted butter
salt and freshly milled pepper to taste

While the rice cooks, separate the yolks into a small bowl and beat with a fork until frothy and well blended. Beat in the lemon juice and then stir in the Parmesan. When the rice is done, pour it into a sieve or colander and gently shake out any remaining liquid. Immediately return it to the saucepan and, with a large cooking spoon, stir in the egg-yolk-and-cheese mixture. Put the lump of butter on top and press it into the rice with the spoon. Then put the pot on the burner over the lowest possible flame and let it sit there for 2 or, at most, 3 minutes—just long enough for the butter to melt completely. Mix it gently all through the rice, taste for salt, and mill over a generous amount of pepper. Serve at once in a warmed bowl with the reserved Parmesan.

Variation. Omit the lemon juice and you have *Riso all' Uovo.*

RISO CON MOZZARELLA E POMODORO FRESCHI
[serves 2 as a meal, 4 as a side dish]

½ pound Italian rice, prepared as directed above
2 tablespoons good fruity Italian olive oil
1 clove garlic, minced
sprig of basil leaves
¼ teaspoon salt
freshly ground black pepper to taste
1 teaspoon balsamic vinegar (optional)
2 or 3 large, ripe summer tomatoes, cut into chunks
1 egg-sized ball fresh mozzarella, cut into tiny cubes

While the rice cooks, heat the olive oil in a large skillet over a low flame. When it is hot, stir in the minced garlic. Tear the basil leaves into bits with your fingers and sprinkle them in while the garlic cooks. As soon as the garlic is translucent, turn down the flame as low as it will go and mix in the salt, pepper, balsamic vinegar (if desired), and chunks of tomato, including any juice. Gently turn the tomatoes once or twice to coat them with the flavored oil. They should be warmed through but not cooked.

Drain the rice and turn it into a large bowl. Immediately toss in the cubes of mozzarella, being sure that they are distributed evenly throughout the rice. Then gently mix in the contents of the skillet and serve.

RISO CON MOZZARELLA E PEPERONE ROSSO
[serves 2 as a meal, 4 as a side dish]

½ pound Italian rice, prepared as directed above
2 tablespoons good fruity Italian olive oil
1 teaspoon black olive paste (see note)
1 onion, coarsely chopped
1 red bell pepper, cut small
1 clove garlic, minced
¼ teaspoon salt
freshly ground black pepper to taste
1 egg-sized ball fresh mozzarella, cut into tiny cubes
½ cup grated Parmesan

Set a large heat-proof bowl to warm in the oven, preheated to its lowest setting.

While the rice cooks, heat the olive oil in a large skillet over a medium flame. When it is hot, stir in the black olive paste and then the onion and bell pepper bits. When these are tender, add the minced garlic and continue cooking until it is translucent. Season to taste with salt and a generous grinding of black pepper. Keep warm.

Drain the rice and turn it into the warm bowl. Immediately toss in the cubes of mozzarella, being sure that they are distributed evenly throughout the rice. Then gently but thoroughly mix in the contents of the skillet.

If serving as a side dish, stir in the Parmesan cheese. If the dish is to be eaten as a main course, divide the dressed rice into warmed bowls and bring the cheese to the table separately, to be added to taste by each eater.

Cook's Note. Black olive paste, sometimes labeled "olivada," is a simple mash of black olives packed in olive oil. Recently, our supermarket has been carrying a version made in Greece with Kalamata olives that is very good and very reasonably priced.

RISO CON MOZZARELLA E SALSICCIE
[serves 2 or 3 as a meal]

1 tablespoon good fruity Italian olive oil
2 links sweet Italian sausage, casings removed
2 carrots, peeled and cut into small cubes
1 large onion, coarsely chopped
1 clove garlic, minced
1 teaspoon balsamic vinegar
½ pound Italian rice, prepared as directed above
1 egg-sized ball fresh mozzarella, cut into tiny cubes,
    preserving brine reserved
¼ teaspoon salt
freshly ground black pepper to taste

Set a large heat-proof bowl to warm in the oven, preheated to its lowest setting.

Heat the olive oil in a large skillet over a low flame. Pull the sausage meat into small bits and add these to the skillet as the oil heats. Stir the mixture with a spatula, turn the heat up to medium, add the carrot cubes, chopped onion, and minced garlic, and stir in the balsamic vinegar. Cook, stirring occasionally, until the onion is translucent and the carrot tender.

After the carrots and onions have been cooking for 10 minutes, start the rice. While it cooks, smell the brine that surrounded the mozzarella. If it has no off odors—it should be tangy but clean-smelling—stir ¼ cup of it into the skillet with the sausage and vegetables. Otherwise, stir in ¼ cup of cooking liquid, scooped from the rice pot.

When the rice is done, drain it and turn it into the warmed bowl.

Immediately toss in the cubes of mozzarella, being sure that they are distributed evenly throughout the rice. Then gently but thoroughly mix in the contents of the skillet. Season with salt, if necessary, and plenty of black pepper. Serve at once.

RISO CON ASPARAGI
[*serves 2 as a meal, 4 as a side dish*]

Matt drew on her experience with pasta alla carbonara—*where raw eggs are "cooked" when they are tossed with hot pasta—and Greek av-golemono* sauce—*where egg yolks and lemon juice are beaten together into a simple lemony sauce—to come up with this dish, which sets off fresh asparagus like few others.*

> 3 tablespoons unsalted butter
> 1 pound asparagus, trimmed
> ½ pound Italian rice
> 1 egg
> juice of ½ lemon (about 2 tablespoons)
> 1 cup freshly grated Parmesan
> freshly ground black pepper to taste

Put the butter in a large heat-proof bowl and set this into the oven, preheated to its lowest setting.

Bring 3 or 4 quarts of water to a boil in a large pot and salt as you would to cook pasta. Toss in the spears of asparagus and cook them until barely al dente, about 4 minutes. Remove these from the water, drain, and transfer to a cutting board. Sprinkle the rice into the boiling water and cook as directed in the basic recipe (page 169). Once the asparagus is cool enough to handle, cut it into bite-sized pieces and place these in a colander or large sieve. In a small bowl, beat together the egg and lemon juice.

When the rice is done, drain as directed, using the same colander or sieve containing the asparagus pieces (thus reheating these). Turn both into the now melted butter in the warmed bowl. Toss well and then stir in the egg-and-lemon mixture. Note: be aware that if eating raw eggs is a health concern, this one will be only barely cooked by the hot rice.

If serving as a side dish, stir in the Parmesan and season generously with black pepper. If the dish is to be eaten as a main course, divide the dressed rice into warmed bowls and bring the cheese and pepper mill to the table separately, to be added to taste by each eater.

Variations to all the above recipes. It must be clear by now that these dishes invite improvisation. For instance, cabbage or fennel can replace the carrots in the sausage recipe. Cubes of tender summer squash can be sautéed along with the red pepper in that dish. As for the asparagus recipe above, substitute strips of julienned zucchini for the asparagus, sprinkling these with salt and letting them sit in a bowl for 30 minutes. Then squeeze them firmly to extract as much water as possible. Substituting a generous pinch of chopped fresh marjoram leaves for the lemon, sauté these in 2 tablespoons olive oil and stir them into the rice at the same time as the beaten egg.

☀ ☀ ☀

It is hot in August in southern Italy. Patience Gray, writing a letter to us very early one morning in August 1998, said that for lunch that day she and her husband, Norman,

> can choose between a *peperonata con riso* or the Catalan dish *la verdura* (potatoes, onions, mange-tout beans). Dawn cooking, as during the day the heat of the stove is the *last straw*.

When we wrote back and begged for the rice recipe, Patience replied in part:

> It is the same as the one for *peperonata* in *Honey from a Weed*, with the addition of *riso per risotto* . . . only that this summer I use red and *green* [instead of yellow] Italian peppers (cheerful colours) and owing to the drought they are not large (stretch thumb and middle finger for length). When the rice is initially stirred it is coated with the olive oil and juices from the quietly cooking peppers and onion. The addition of the water to the tomato pulp should be sufficient to arrive at *riso al dente*.

The following recipe is exactly as Patience wrote it out, except for the explanatory matter placed in brackets and in the cook's notes at the end.

LA PEPERONATA CON RISO
[serves 2 as a meal, 4 as a side course]

3 each red and green Italian or Cubanelle peppers
1 red or green chile pepper
1 large sweet white onion
olive oil (see note)
salt to taste
4 handfuls Italian rice (see note)
1 pound plum tomatoes
a sprig each fresh thyme and oregano
1 small glass red wine (optional)
2 cloves garlic
parsley and basil leaves

Slice the peppers in half, remove stalks and seeds, then slice each half again into substantial strips. Do the same with the hot red or green chile pepper, only slice this rather finely. Slice the onion horizontally into thin rings.

For this dish I use a quite heavy Swedish iron frying pan (about 10 inches diameter at top and 2 inches deep). Cover the bottom with good olive oil, then put in the strips of pepper, skin side down, and cover with the onion slices. Sprinkle with a little salt, put the lid on the pan, and set over low heat. When the peppers begin to soften, lift the lid and add the rice handful by handful, stirring it into the pan with a wooden spoon. Now you raise the heat a bit.

I use the small Leccese tomatoes that we grow in quantity, adding them at this point because, being ripe, if added earlier they would overcook. First, put them separately into boiling water for a few seconds. Then put them through a food mill directly into the frying pan [see below for an alternative method]. Pour in twice the amount of cold water as rice—the use of cold water is unorthodox, but it is my way and also Catalan—and bring to a simmer.

Lower the heat, sprinkle the surface with the thyme and oregano leaves, put on the lid, and stop worrying for a quarter of an hour. When the liquid is absorbed, the rice should be cooked. If it isn't, add a little more water or a small glass of red wine.

Pound the garlic in a mortar with some chopped parsley and torn basil leaves. Liberate with a little oil and pour into the pan. Cover with a cloth for 5 minutes and serve.

Cook's Notes. The Olive Oil: "I use our own virgin oil (*not* extra virgin)."

The Amount of Rice: When asked for an approximate cup measure, Patience wrote back: "A woman's hand grabs three or four 'handfuls,' and stirs these into the pan. I have no experience of *cups*."

The Food Mill: If you lack such a device, cut the tomatoes in half and, pressing the cut side against the mesh of a strainer, rub the pulp through it into the pan, discarding skins and seeds.

RIS E LATT

The whitest, the creamiest, and the simplest of all *riso in bianco* dishes is *ris e latt*, in which Italian rice is sprinkled into a mixture of one part water to five parts milk that is already simmering in an open pot. A disproportionately large amount of liquid is used, since rice takes about twice as long to cook in milk as it does in water. During this long cooking time, the dish slowly thickens (and the kitchen becomes saturated with gentle, comforting aromas) as the milk evaporates and the starch is released from the cooking grain, eventually producing the ultimate bowl of cream of rice. Here is an example of the traditional version, adapted from Mila Contini's *Milano in bocca*:

> RIS E LATT. Mix together 10 cups of milk and 2 cups of water in a large saucepan and bring to a strong simmer. Sprinkle in four fistfuls rice (a scant ¾ cup, measuring by my fist), a pinch of salt and *una noce* (a nut) of unsalted butter. Reduce the heat until the mixture barely bubbles and cook until the rice is soft but still chewy, about 40 minutes. Pour into soup bowls and let these stand for ten minutes to allow the creamed rice to cool enough to eat.

Here is how I adapted the dish to make rice with asparagus . . . my way.

RIS E LATT CON PARMIGIANO E SPARAGIO
[serves 2 as a meal]

4 cups whole or low-fat milk
1 teaspoon salt
½ cup Italian rice
2 tablespoons unsalted butter
a dash of Tabasco sauce
1 pound asparagus, trimmed and cut into pieces
1 cup freshly grated Parmesan

Pour the milk into a 3-quart saucepan (I don't dilute this with the traditional fifth part of water). Set over medium heat and bring to a gentle simmer. Stir in half of the salt and then sprinkle in the rice, keeping the milk at a simmer. Cook uncovered, stirring often enough to keep a skin from forming on top of the milk. Gradually, as the rice swells and the milk thickens, increase the stirring to keep the mixture from sticking (and burning) on the bottom of the pan. Keep at this for about 40 minutes, or until the rice kernels are chewy but tender and the mixture has thickened into a densely creamy rice pudding.

Meanwhile, melt the butter in a 10-inch skillet over medium-low heat. Stir in the remaining salt, the dash of Tabasco sauce, and the asparagus pieces. Cook until the asparagus is just tender, turning occasionally with a spatula. When the rice is ready, blend in the Parmesan and then the contents of the skillet. Taste carefully for seasoning (this stuff is hot!) and then let cool for 10 minutes before serving.

STICKS-TO-THE-POT

❧ ❧ ❧

The Gohyang Korean Restaurant is a hard place to find. It shares one of three tiny storefronts in the shabbiest, mini-est minimall on a highway lined with them, hidden behind a curve in the road, its signage (in Korean) blocked by a telephone pole. This is why, although we knew that it existed somewhere on Route 9 in Hadley, Massachusetts, we had driven past it countless times without ever spotting it. When we finally did I was so shocked that I made an immediate U-turn, pulled into its eight-slot parking area, and sat there staring disbelievingly at the place, as if it might yet vanish before my eyes. Then I noticed the proprietor looking out the window at *us*, his face expressing very similar sentiments. Matt and I were, in fact, on our way to a doctor's appointment, but we agreed that we would have to come back afterward for lunch.

When we returned, at about half past one, there were no cars in the lot and the interior seemed *very* dark. Still, the OPEN sign was lit, so we got out of the car and went hesitantly in. The restaurant was totally deserted. We stood together in the empty room, looking around. To our left, demarcated by a short wooden divider, was a raised-floor banquet area where several foot-high tables were turned up against the wall. Before us and to our right were ordinary tables and booths, made of varnished pine, not one of them set for dining.

"What should we do?" Matt whispered to me nervously. Suddenly, just a few feet away, a young man scrambled to his feet. He had been napping on the floor on the banquet cushions, hidden from view by the wooden divider. He looked at one and then the other of us in sleepy-eyed confusion, opened his mouth, shut it, and fled into the kitchen.

A moment later, the same door burst open and a crowd of welcomers appeared, settling us in, laying the table, bringing us menus and pouring us tea. We placed our order, and soon it was all before us: *goon mandu** (panfried dumplings); *jopchae* (stir-fried glass noodles with meat and vegetables); and eight tiny bowls of pickled vegetables, including, of course, *kimchi*, as well as chunks of spicy potato, marinated cucumber, a Korean version of coleslaw, and threads of grated daikon tossed in a fiery dressing.

The food, although good, wasn't memorable; what was—starting with the potboy sleeping on the cushions—was the feeling of *hominess*. I use that word not only in the sense of "like home" but "like it is in Korea." Our meal progressed in a succession of little surprises, from the earthenware cup of rice tea† that began it to the complimentary muskmelon ice pop with which we were ceremoniously presented at its conclusion. (This unanticipated generosity seems to be fueled in part by a cultural imperative of mutual gratitude: at Gohyang, most of the conversation—for server and served alike—consists of saying "Thank you!")

The bowls of pickled vegetables weren't even mentioned in the menu, but they appeared magically and were instantly refilled when emptied; the plate of *goon mandu*, although a single order and an appetizer, held a dozen good-sized, handmade panfried dumplings. These, as soon as I saw them—even before I lowered the tip of one into the dipping sauce and brought it to my mouth—seized my entire attention.

Matt and I are both dumpling lovers, and we rate Asian restaurants in part on how well they turn them out: the panfried dumplings at Taipei & Tokyo; the steamed Thai version at Siam Square; the wontons with sesame sauce at the late, lamented Rasa Sayang; and the *gyoza* at Ichiban. But none of these, however much they brought us back to a restaurant, ever drew us into our kitchen. Like a croissant, they carried with them the aura of professionalism: something you bought, not something you made.

---

*Other transliterations include *goonmondu, goon mandoo, koon man too*, et cetera. None seems any more authoritative than another. As to the meaning, *mandu* is the Korean word for "dumpling," and presumably *goon* means "fried." I consulted a Korean-English dictionary in an attempt to confirm this but managed only to discover that the colloquial Korean expression for pot sticker is "fried dog."

†Called *genmai cha* by the Japanese, this is a blend of green tea and kernels of roasted and popped brown rice. I found it both tasty and disconcertingly reminiscent of Quaker puffed rice.

The Gohyang's *goon mandu*, however, said something quite different. The wrappers had the slightly uneven thickness that comes from being flattened out by hand; their pleats still bore the impression of the maker's fingers; the beef and vegetable filling they contained was delicate and yet firmly textured. The result was something that spoke so directly, so emphatically, to me—*You like me . . . then go make me yourself*—that I had no choice but to listen. I went home and began to figure out how to do just that.

As it happened, beginner's luck was with me, and I found a recipe for *goon mandu* in the Korean section of *The Encyclopedia of Asian Cooking*. The catch was that it called for commercially made wonton wrappers—and *I have* had enough experience in East Asian cooking to know I wanted nothing to do with those soulless things. This started a search for the right wrapper recipe in our collection of Asian cookbooks, and thus I was unwittingly launched on a voyage of culinary discovery. *Goon mandu*, it turns out, are the Korean version of dumplings that can be found all over Asia but especially in China. There they are called *chiao-tzu*, and much has been written about them, some of it very fascinating indeed.

❋ ❋ ❋

Peking is famous for its "small eats" as well as for its classic dishes. Indeed, in Peking today you can probably eat better at sidewalk stalls and cafés than at the fancy restaurants that cater to tourists. Street vendors sell fruit and wheat dumplings stuffed with sweet or savory fillings. Noodle shops abound. *Chiao-tzu* halls sell millions of those marvelous dumplings. They are boiled or shallow-fried without stirring, in which case they are "potstickers," because the bottoms toast themselves onto the pan, becoming exquisitely crisp.

—E. N. Anderson, *The Food of China*

Chiao-tzu* translates approximately as "three-sided (crescent-shaped) dumpling"; Chinese restaurant menus in this country usually call them

---

* 餃子 Also spelled *chaotse, jao-tze, jow-tse, jiaoz, jiaoze,* and *jiao ji*. For the sake of consistency, I have used the *chiao-tzu* spelling throughout, including in quotations. My favorite of various explanations of the phrase's meaning is the Zen-koan-like one offered by Fu Pei Mei in *Chinese Snacks & Desserts*: "In the Szechwan province, Won-ton is called *Chiao-Tzu* in that the way the Won-ton is wrapped looks like two hands that are folded in opposite sleeves."

either "meat dumplings" or "Peking ravioli," after the city that is famously passionate about them. According to the culinary food historian E. N. Anderson, this dumpling originated among the nomad peoples of Central Asia, who unintentionally spread a taste for them during their incursions both east and west. He explains that *chiao-tzu* are but one member of a family that includes

> the *ashak* of Afghanistan, *mu-mu* of Tibet, Russian *pelmeni*, Jewish *kreplachs, samusa* of Arabia and South Asia, and Italian ravioli.

Anderson could have added the Japanese *gyoza*—which shares an identical ideogram with its Chinese sister—and, of course, *goon mandu.*

You might think that a cuisine that already possessed a wealth of delicious dumplings—*ch'iao-mai*, for instance, the Cantonese open-faced pork-stuffed purses; that perennial *dim sum* favorite *har gau*, the delicately translucent wrappers of which encase a mixture of shrimp bits and bamboo shoots; and the omnipresent *hun t'un*, wonton, deep-fried, of course, but perhaps even tastier when savored floating, tender and succulent, in clear broth*—would hardly bother to open its arms to this simple, rustic dumpling barbarian.

In truth, however, the reverse has been the case. *Chiao-tzu* have become so popular among the Chinese that native food writers, when they turn to the subject, almost always strike an especially nostalgic note, as does Ken Hom, for instance, in *The Taste of China.*

> Of the many other popular snack dishes, some of the most cherished throughout China are *chiao-tzu* dumplings. These are wonderful snacks which are sold boiled, fried, or less often, steamed. Filled with meats, vegetables, garlic, scallions—each region has its own touches and variations. Really a well-balanced, light meal, I have eaten more of these dumplings than I care to count and enjoyed every one.

Read this quote closely and you will have a major clue as to their popularity. Since they can be eaten as either a snack *or* a meal, there is often a pleasant confusion about which of the two is taking place. Set-

---

*Thus living up to its name, since *hun t'un* means, literally, "swallowing clouds." As A. Zee, in his book of that title—a delightful meditation on Chinese ideograms—writes: "To Joni Mitchell, clouds are 'ice-cream castles in the air.' To me, they are wonton in the sky."

tle yourself into a table at a *chiao-tzu* parlor, and once the heaping platter of these delectable, inexpensive dumplings arrives, no one is going
to tally how many of them you eat.* As Ellen Schrecker remembers:

> A mammoth plateful of them accompanied by a bowl of spicy dip
> sauce was a feast for the whole family. The children competed
> among themselves to see who could eat the most; the adults
> stuffed themselves without counting.

For grown-ups this is pleasurable enough, but for children it can be
ecstasy. They delight in the moppet size and the juiciness, and they love
the abandon that comes with being allowed to eat all they want.
"When I was young I could eat thirty at one meal, and I never tired of
them," writes Mai Leung in *The Chinese People's Cookbook*, words to
which many Chinese would nod a wistful assent.

As it turns out, this festive aspect carries over into the making of
chiao-tzu. It is a tradition for extended families to gather together during the Chinese New Year. In northern China especially, men, women,
and children sit around the dinner table together and, laughing and
gossiping, make—then eat—hundreds of *chiao-tzu*.

Ordinarily, Chinese rules of propriety would frown on such behavior,
so it is important that the character of *chiao-tzu* undermines these rules.
It does so via another aspect of their slippery identity, this time regarding
culinary status. As happens in all cuisines, the Chinese bestow various
rankings to their primary cooking methods. Boiling, the most common,
sits at the bottom of the totem pole, steaming clings to the middle, and
frying roosts at the top. Not only are *chiao-tzu* prepared by all three
methods, but, in the form popularly known as pot stickers—*kuo teh*—
they are both boiled *and* fried, acquiring, as Irene Kuo puts it, "a dual
texture: they are fluffily soft on top and crunchy-crisp on the bottom."

This duality brings together two qualities of great importance in
Chinese gastronomy—the two basic textures, *tsuei* (crisp, crunchy) and
nun (soft and tender)—even as plain boiled or steamed *chiao-tzu* have
already united the two basic foodstuffs, *fan* (the all-important starch)
and *t'sai* (the civilizing, i.e., "Chinese-making," filling, the deliciously
consonant melding of various tidbits).

---

*Compare them—in this regard—to the White Castle chain's hamburgers. Eaters order them
by the sackful because they're so cheap and so tiny that it makes no sense to buy just one—
but then they have to decide how many it *does* make sense to buy.

They also unite the two flavor elements, *hsien* (sweet, natural)—the dumpling itself—and *nung* (potent, heady, concentrated)—the salty, tangy dipping sauce. Such auspicious harmony can only help in drawing everyone—including distant, sometimes poor relations and household servants—into the family circle to participate in the New Year ritual of their making. This is why *chiao-tzu* is the one dish that Chinese men and little children know how to prepare.

Sometimes, the more you learn about a dish, the less you feel inclined to make it. You become intimidated; you become confused; you find your interest to be all worn out. But with these dumplings, the opposite happened. As I read, I slowly began to realize that the resonant hominess of the Gohyang's *goon mandu* resided in the nature of the dumplings themselves. *Goon mandu, chiao-tzu, gyoza*—the distinctions between them are interesting, but what is essential is what they all have in common. Their tastiness and ease of making means that their time-consuming preparation invites participation, and, with everyone gathered around the table, the feast has, without their knowing it, already begun.

> Chiao-tzu are served mostly by the dozen; the steamed ones are snuggled in bamboo steamer trays; the boiled ones gleam in tasty soup; and the fried ones show off by lying in rows on the plate with their crusty sides up. Accompany them with a cup of tea or a bowl of soup and a bottle of good Chinese beer (we have great beer), and who can leave the table not contented.
> —Mai Leung, *The Chinese People's Cookbook*

MEAT-FILLED DUMPLINGS

> Amy [Tan]'s mother had always wanted to open a restaurant, a specialty place that offered only pot stickers or chiao-tzu. And, indeed, her dumplings were famous among family and friends. She would make the dough from scratch, roll it out into a long roll, then cut off pieces and roll them out into doughy circles. These she would fill with pork, shredded squash, ginger, and other ingredients. She had no recipes. She simply tasted, looked, smelled, felt, and hefted the dough to decide whether it was right. And it always was, even if it was a little different each time.
> —Ken Hom, *Easy Family Recipes from a Chinese-American Childhood*

Despite the fact that homemade *chiao-tzu* wrappers are almost always made with nothing more than flour and water, it's hard to find two Chinese cookbooks that agree on a recipe. The proportion of flour to water varies widely, to be sure, but the essential disagreement concerns whether the water itself should be boiling-hot or cold (with many compromisers filling the ground in between).

None of the texts we consulted offered a persuasive reason to use one or the other of these methods, but practice did—and immediately. The cold-water dough, even though it absorbed much more flour than the hot-water one, remained soft and sticky and proved much more fragile. The hot-water dough, in contrast, became firm and smooth when kneaded. It felt much like traditional pasta dough and, like it, could be rolled out into a very thin but resilient sheet. It was strong enough to hold together when the dumplings were poached, and it became translucent enough to reveal the filling—a very appetizing sight.

Chinese cooks of the old school pride themselves on producing the thinnest possible dumpling wrappers with their hands (no rolling pin); Chinese cooks of the new school buy factory-made wonton wrappers. Both have a point. Wrappers that are handmade possess much more character and *délicatesse* than the doughier, additive-laden commercial ones. However, rolling the wrappers out one at a time in the traditional way is a time-consuming and—after the novelty wears off—excruciatingly boring task. Our nonauthentic solution is to roll out the dough into sheets and then cut out the wrappers with a round, three-inch biscuit cutter. These may not look quite as handcrafted as the ones produced by the one-at-a-time method, but they are just as pliable and delicate, and the amount of time saved in what is already a very lengthy business is, frankly, awesome.

THE DUMPLING WRAPPER
[makes about 100 dumplings: a meal for 4 or a snack for 6]

1 pound (about 4 sifted cups) all-purpose flour (see note)
¼ teaspoon salt (optional)
1½ cups boiling water

Put the flour in a large mixing bowl. Dissolve the salt in the boiling water. (Salt is not a traditional ingredient, but we prefer the wrappers made with it. Omit it if you wish.) Form a well in the center of the flour and gently pour the salted water into it. With a pair of chopsticks, stir the water into the flour to produce a crumbly-textured mass. Let this cool for 1 or 2 minutes and then knead for about 10 minutes, or until you have formed a smooth, pliable dough. Wrap this in plastic film and let it rest for 30 minutes. (This is a good time to assemble the dumpling filling.)

Cook's Note. The Chinese like their dumplings to be as white as possible, which, I think, is a primary reason why Eileen Yin-Fei Lo, in *The Dim Sum Book*, recommends Gold Medal all-purpose, bleached flour as the closest supermarket equivalent to Chinese dumpling flour. However, we use King Arthur all-purpose, unbleached flour with splendid results.

THE FILLING

½ teaspoon Szechwan peppercorns (see note)
2 bunches (12 to 16) scallions, washed and trimmed
1-inch slice fresh ginger, trimmed and peeled
2 cloves garlic
½ tablespoon peanut oil
3 tablespoons dark soy sauce (see note)
1 tablespoon toasted sesame oil (see note)
1 pound ground pork (see note)

Put the Szechwan peppercorns into a small cast-iron or other indestructible skillet and heat dry over medium flame, shaking regularly, until they begin to release their odor. Empty into a mortar or onto a cutting board and let cool a few minutes. Then, with a pestle or the side of a cleaver, pulverize them.

Coarsely chop the scallions, including the green part. Either slice, then finely mince, the piece of ginger or cut it into quarters and squeeze it through a garlic press, reserving the juices and soft pulp and discarding the remaining fibrous mass. Prepare the cloves of garlic the same way.

In the same small skillet used for the peppercorns, heat the peanut oil over medium-low heat, then add the chopped scallions and garlic.

Sauté gently for no more than a few minutes, stirring often, until the skillet's contents have softened and turned translucent.

Turn the sautéed garlic and scallion, the pulverized peppercorns, and the prepared ginger into a small mixing bowl. Pour in the soy sauce and toasted sesame oil and mix well. Add the ground pork and use your fingers or a rubber spatula to work the seasonings through the pork thoroughly.

Meanwhile, bring some water to a simmer in a small pot. Take a pinch of the filling, roll it into a small ball, and poach it gently in simmering water for a few minutes until cooked through. Remove, cool, and taste, adjusting the seasoning of the remaining filling as necessary. Cover the bowl with plastic film and refrigerate while you roll out the dumpling wrappers.

Cook's Notes. Szechwan peppercorns: These are not true peppercorns but the dried berries and husks from a type of ash tree. They have a peppery, complexly spicy flavor.

Dark soy sauce: The Chinese name for this condiment—*lao toe cho*—means "old-head soy," indicating something more mature than the ordinary, or "light," variety. It is intensely salty, with a distinct molasses-y taste and aroma (it contains more of both those ingredients than it does soybeans). Dark soy provides some extra flavor when used in cooking—it will overpower any dipping sauce—but in this recipe it is not essential. Substitute a good brand (such as Kikkoman) of ordinary soy sauce.

Toasted sesame oil: This oil comes from sesame seeds that are roasted before their oil is extracted, producing what Bruce Cost in *Bruce Cost's Asian Ingredients* calls "a prime contender for the world's most seductively flavored oil." He might have written "most seductive flavoring oil," since it is not used for cooking but as a seasoning agent, almost never added to a dish until it has been taken off the heat, and is always used sparingly, since only a few drops are needed to make its suave and nutty presence known. Kodaya pure sesame oil is very good. Keep it refrigerated.

Ground pork: I find the ground pork sold at our local supermarket to lack the texture necessary for a truly good dumpling; mincing it with a cleaver quickly reduces it to a glutinous lump. However, I noticed that the pork in the store's Italian sausages was much more coarsely ground, and I asked the butcher about this. He told me that the ground pork was put through the grinder twice, but the sausage meat only once. He did a "one grind" with the same cut (pork butt); the result had exactly the right balance of texture and succulence.*

MAKING THE WRAPPERS

The dumpling-making process from the kneading of the dough to sitting down at the table takes from 3 to 4 hours. The best way to shorten this is to do as the Chinese do and get everyone who plans to eat them to help make them.

Traditional Method. Take the rested dough and divide it into 2 equal portions. Rewrap one of these and roll the other between floured hands into a foot-long cylinder. Fold this in half and cut it into 2 equal portions. Again wrap one of these portions in plastic film and continue rolling the other until it is about a foot long. With a sharp knife, cut this into 6 equal segments, and each of these segments into 4 equal parts, producing 24 pieces in all.

With floured hands, form each of these pieces into a round ball and, on a floured surface, use a rolling pin to flatten it into a thin dumpling wrapper about 3 inches in diameter. Repeat this entire process, using all the dough, until 96 wrappers have been produced. Set each as it is made on a cutting board or platter, slightly overlapping the one before. Keep these loosely covered with plastic film to prevent them from drying out.

Faster Method. Take the prepared and rested dumpling dough and divide it into 4 more or less equal portions. Cover 3 of these with plastic film. Flatten the remaining portion with floured hands and, with a rolling pin (ideally of the wooden baton sort used to make pasta), roll the dough out on a floured surface until it is as thin as you can roll it

---

*Another prized quality in Chinese gastronomy is *yu-er-pu-ni*, which means "to taste of fat without being greasy." Ken Hom writes that his mother, when she made dumplings, especially sought out pork fatty enough to keep "the filling moist and flavorful. Lean fillings meant a dry and tasteless dish—a grave error in my mother's eye. An often heard criticism was that a dish did not have enough pork fat—the equivalent of an Italian's saying there is not enough olive oil, or a Frenchman's saying there is not enough butter or goose fat." Bear this in mind when choosing your pork.

without tearing it, lightly flouring either side as needed to prevent stick-ing. Then take a 3-inch biscuit cutter (or a can or drinking glass with the same diameter) and cut out as many rounds of dough as you can, laying these out on a large platter. (These can overlap slightly, but be careful that they don't stick together.) Reserve the scraps under plastic film.

Repeat with the 3 other portions of dough, completing the process by kneading all the scraps into a fresh ball and rolling this out as well. By the end you should have close to 100 wrappers.

PREPARING AND COOKING THE DUMPLINGS

Take the filling and divide it roughly into 4 parts. Using about ½ tea-spoon per dumpling, put some filling into the center of the first wrap-per. Lift the edge that is closest to you and stretch the dough over, using the middle fingers of each hand to tuck in the filling as you do. Seal it by firmly pressing the edges together, using your fingertips to hold the filling in place. Finally, turn each one seam side up, fold its arms around its tummy, then press it down gently to slightly flatten its bottom. Con-tinue, setting each dumpling as it is made onto a lightly floured surface and lining them up in ranks of 12.

When you have filled 2 ranks (24 dumplings), you should have used approximately one-quarter of the filling. If not, adjust the amount of filling you are using per dumpling. Check this again when you have filled 4 ranks and then again at 6, awarding yourself a pat on the back if you finish up with no filling or wrappers left over.

To Boil. Fill a (preferably nonstick) 12-inch skillet about three-quarters full with water and bring this to a boil. Slide in as many dumplings as can fit comfortably without crowding. They should soon float to the surface—use a spatula to gently dislodge any that stick to the bottom. Bring the water back to a bare simmer—do not boil or the dumplings may break apart—and cook for 15 minutes, or until the dough is tender. Remove them with a slotted spoon to soup bowls and then, if you like, ladle over some steaming hot, seasoned chicken broth in which bok choy or another leafy Chinese green has been cooked un-til tender.

To Steam. These dumplings can be steamed in any covered pot that has a steaming insert. Lightly oil the insert, layer the dumplings in it one deep, and steam them for 20 minutes over boiling water, repeating the process until all are cooked and moving them when done onto a heat-proof dish in a warm oven. Serve with dipping sauce (see below).

To Panfry (*Kuo Teh*/Pot Stickers). Heat 2 tablespoons of peanut or other cooking oil in a (preferably nonstick) 12-inch skillet. When the oil is hot, tilt the pan to spread it over the entire bottom and a bit up the sides. Then fill the pan with as many dumplings as you can—ideally, half the batch—making sure all their bottoms touch the pan. Let them fry over medium-high heat for 2 minutes and then add 1 cup of water. Cover the pan and turn the heat up high until the water boils. Adjust it until the water is at a simmer and cook—still covered—for 10 minutes. Then remove the cover and turn the heat up again to medium-high. Let the liquid boil off and, shaking the pan frequently to keep the dumplings from sticking (and gently freeing any that do with a spatula), cook until the bottoms are golden brown, adding more oil if necessary. Serve crusty side up on warm plates with dipping sauce.

ASIAN DUMPLING DIPPING SAUCE
[*per person*]

There are countless formulae for these; the one we currently prefer is made simply.

> 1 tablespoon plain (i.e., not dark) soy sauce
> 1 tablespoon chicken stock or water
> 1 teaspoon toasted sesame oil
> ½ teaspoon rice vinegar
> ¼ teaspoon sugar

Mix well and garnish with a smidgen each of minced ginger and scallion.

ADDITIONAL FILLINGS

The following fillings can be used instead of the basic one given above. The method of filling and cooking the dumplings remains the same. Remember to take a small pinch of the filling and poach it gently in simmering water for a few minutes until cooked through. Then remove it, let it cool, and taste it, adjusting the salt and any other of the seasonings in the remaining filling as necessary.

MOSLEM-STYLE LAMB FILLING
(adapted from Barbara Tropp's *The Modern Art of Chinese Cooking*)
[*to fill about 8 dozen dumplings*]

Made with ground pork instead of ground lamb (and, of course, minus the orange peel), this cabbage-and-meat filling is as familiar to Chinese as the pork-intensive version above.

¼ pound Chinese (napa) cabbage leaves
½ teaspoon salt
1 pound ground lamb
1-inch piece of peeled fresh ginger, minced
2 or 3 scallions, minced (both green and white parts)
2 tablespoons regular soy sauce
3 tablespoons Chinese rice wine or dry sherry
2 teaspoons toasted sesame oil
½ teaspoon salt
freshly ground pepper to taste
1 teaspoon freshly grated orange zest (optional)

Rinse the cabbage leaves. With a Chinese cleaver or large kitchen knife, chop these into shreds. Put the shreds into a small bowl and toss with the first ½ teaspoon of salt until it is mixed all through. Let this sit for 30 minutes, then squeeze out as much moisture as possible with your hands or by wringing it out in cheesecloth or an old, clean dish towel. Discard this liquid.

Place the minced cabbage—now much reduced in bulk—into a mixing bowl and add all the remaining ingredients. Use your hands or a rubber spatula to mix these thoroughly and blend the seasonings throughout. Cover and either let sit at room temperature for 30 minutes or in the refrigerator overnight to allow the flavors to meld. Bring to room temperature before filling and cooking the dumplings, as directed on pages 189–90.

PORK AND BOK CHOY FILLING
(adapted from Eileen Yin-Fei Lo's *The Dim Sum Book*)
[*to fill about 8 dozen dumplings*]

4 cups water
1 teaspoon salt
½ teaspoon baking soda (optional)
1 small to medium head bok choy
1 pound coarsely ground pork
6 scallions, trimmed and finely chopped
1 egg
1 teaspoon salt
1 tablespoon sugar
1 tablespoon minced fresh ginger
1 tablespoon Chinese rice wine or dry sherry
1 tablespoon soy sauce
1 tablespoon toasted sesame oil
grinding of black pepper
1 tablespoon cornstarch

Bring the water to a boil and stir in the salt and, if wished, the baking soda (Chinese cooks, among others, use it to retain the color in cooked greens). Cut off the green part of the bok choy leaves and slice these into ¼-inch strips. Coarsely chop the white stems. Add both to the boiling water, stir, and cook until wilted, about 1 minute. Drain in a sieve, refresh under cold running water, shake well, and then use a rubber spatula or the back of a cooking spoon to press out as much water as possible.

Blend these in a mixing bowl with the other ingredients until everything is well mixed. Cover with plastic wrap and let rest at room temperature for 30 minutes to allow the flavors to meld. Then proceed to make and cook the dumplings as directed on pages 189–90.

PORK AND SHRIMP FILLING
(adapted from Ken Hom's *The Taste of China*)
[to fill about 8 dozen dumplings]

5 dried Chinese black mushrooms or fresh shiitake
  (see note)
½ pound Chinese (napa) cabbage, finely shredded
8 ounces coarsely ground pork
8 ounces uncooked shrimp, peeled and finely chopped
2 tablespoons each dark and light (ordinary) soy sauce
1 tablespoon Chinese rice wine or dry sherry
1 tablespoon toasted sesame oil
½ teaspoon salt
freshly ground black pepper to taste

If using dried Chinese black mushrooms, soak these in just enough hot water to cover until they are reconstituted, about 20 minutes. Discard the soaking liquid and the mushroom stems, and chop the caps into small pieces. If using fresh shiitake mushrooms, brush any dirt off the caps and then chop them into small pieces. Put these and all the other ingredients in a mixing bowl and blend thoroughly. Cover with plastic wrap and let sit at room temperature for 30 minutes to allow the flavors to meld. Then proceed to make and cook the dumplings as directed on pages 189–90.

Cook's Note. Chinese black mushrooms are common and inexpensive, and they are available in almost any Asian grocery. They are dried shiitake mushrooms, and, at least in dumpling recipes, the fresh can be substituted for the dried, depending on the preference of the cook.

NIRA (GARLIC CHIVE) FILLING
[to fill about 8 dozen dumplings]

In Japan these dumplings are called gyoza, *and some cookbooks claim that it is the addition of the* nira *that makes them authentically Japanese. But* nira *is their word for the garlic chive, an ingredient widely used in Chinese cooking, including as part of dumpling fillings. Obviously, a dumpling made in a Japanese kitchen will taste differently from one made in a Chinese or an American one, but so far as recipes are concerned, there is no real difference between* gyoza *and* chiao-tzu.

    6 Chinese (napa) cabbage leaves
    ½ teaspoon salt
    1 bunch *nira* (garlic chives) or ordinary chives
    ½-inch peeled fresh ginger, finely minced
    2 large scallions, minced
    2 cloves garlic, minced
    ½ teaspoon salt
    black pepper to taste
    2 teaspoons ordinary soy sauce
    1 teaspoon toasted sesame oil
    1 pound coarsely ground pork
    4 or 5 shiitake mushroom caps, chopped small

With a Chinese cleaver or large kitchen knife, shred the cabbage leaves. Put these into a small bowl and toss with the first ½ teaspoon of salt until it is mixed all through. Let this sit for 30 minutes, then squeeze out as much moisture as possible with your hands or by wringing it out in cheesecloth or an old, clean dish towel. Trim the white root ends from the *nira* and mince the green. (If substituting chives, simply mince.) Turn this and the cabbage into a bowl and blend thoroughly with the other ingredients. Cover with plastic wrap and let sit at room temperature for 30 minutes to allow the flavors to meld. Then proceed to make and cook the dumplings as directed on pages 189–90.

GOON MANDU FILLING (1)
(adapted from *The Encyclopedia of Asian Cooking*)
[*to fill about 8 dozen dumplings*]

Two ingredients, not always combined in the same filling, seem to differentiate goon mandu *from the other Asian dumplings in this family: chopped beef and ground sesame seeds. These dumplings, by the way, will have noticeably more beef flavor and a much more appealing texture if you use a coarse (chili) grind of beef or, better, hand-mince a cut like London broil or sirloin tip.*

1 teaspoon sesame seeds
1¼ pound hand-minced or coarsely ground beef
2 teaspoons toasted sesame oil
6 to 8 scallions, trimmed and minced
1 clove garlic, minced
1 teaspoon salt

Sprinkle the sesame seeds into a cast-iron or other durable small skillet and set over a medium flame. Gently toss the seeds as they heat so that they toast on both sides. Remove from the heat as soon as the seeds release their fragrance and begin to turn color. Thoroughly blend them with the other ingredients in a mixing bowl. Cover with plastic wrap and let sit at room temperature for 30 minutes to allow the flavors to meld. Then proceed to make and cook the dumplings as directed on pages 189–90.

GOON MANDU FILLING (2)
(adapted from Copeland Marks's *The Korean Kitchen*)
[*to fill about 8 dozen dumplings*]

¼ pound each bean sprouts and Chinese garlic chives
   (*nira*—see above recipe) or fresh chives
1 pound hand-minced or coarsely ground beef
1 small onion, chopped fine
1 egg
½-inch piece of fresh ginger, peeled and minced
1 tablespoon cornstarch
1 teaspoon salt
freshly ground pepper to taste
1 teaspoon toasted sesame oil
1 teaspoon toasted sesame seeds (see above recipe)

Toss the bean sprouts into boiling water, cook for 15 seconds, then drain in a sieve. Shake dry and chop coarsely. Chop off and discard the white root ends of the garlic chives and mince the rest. (If substituting plain chives, simply mince.) Thoroughly blend the chopped garlic chives and bean sprouts with the other ingredients in a mixing bowl.

Cover with plastic wrap and let sit at room temperature for 30 minutes to allow the flavors to meld. Then proceed to make and cook the dumplings as directed on pages 189–90.

Further Reading

The aspiring Chinese-dumpling maker will find these books especially helpful: Fu Pei Mei, *Pei Mei's Chinese Snacks & Desserts;* Mai Leung, *The Chinese People's Cookbook; Florence Lin's Complete Book of Chinese Noodles, Dumplings and Breads;* and Nina Simonds, *Classic Chinese Cuisine* and *China Express.*

PASTA AND VEGETABLES

❦ ❦ ❦

A very simple recipe for pasta and pumpkin appears in Vincenzo Buonassisi's compendium of Italian pasta dishes, *Il codice della pasta*. To make it, you take a pound each of the two main ingredients and cook the pasta while you sauté cubes of the pumpkin in a mixture of butter, olive oil, and some minced parsley. The two are then tossed together with grated Parmesan and a little more melted butter, seasoned with salt and pepper, and served. About such a dish, Giuliano Bugialli writes in his *Bugialli on Pasta*,

> If I may reveal my own most personal taste, I would say that a dish made with pasta and vegetables is the most satisfying thing I can eat. It is just the right combination of taste, texture, nourishment and lightness. I feel completely satisfied afterward, and any dishes that might follow are simply an embellishment.

This is one of many similar recipes in a category of pasta dishes that, for the most part, until recently, I had left virtually unexplored. I ate pasta regularly, but in my mind it emblematized a certain kind of hearty meal, and I didn't see any heartiness in a meal of pumpkin and spaghetti. But because this sort of pasta dish attracted Matt, I found myself eating more of them . . . and changing my mind. I realized that, as much as I had been thinking about pasta, there was still a lot I didn't understand.

For example, I had grown up thinking of pasta as an ingredient—as a starch, like rice or potatoes. The Italians, however, think of it as a course—the equivalent of soup, salad, or dessert. I knew this, but I had always treated this information suspiciously, especially because it was often used by writers to justify smaller portions. And yet, a bowl of soup, a plate of antipasto, a salad, even a dessert, in the right circumstances can satisfy all by itself—because, in miniature, it already has the contours of a meal.

When Giuliano Bugialli writes that a dish of pasta and vegetables is "the most satisfying thing I can eat," we know that he means that it is more than a mere vegetable mélange. But none of his explanatory categories—taste, texture, nourishment, lightness—tells us why. For a dish to make a meal it must make the eater feel human, which is the difference between assuaging appetite and placating brute hunger.

Considering our dish of pasta and pumpkin, it is easy to see how it meets Bugialli's criteria: the vegetable furnishes the flavor and texture, the Parmesan some piquant zest, the olive oil and butter a variable sufficiency of richness. The pasta, then, is left with the job of transforming this plain eating into an event.

The word *delicious* has two meanings: the first is simply "pleasing to the mouth"; the other, harder to define, denotes a kind of ticklish mental pleasure, as in the phrase "a delicious sense of humor." Pasta is one of the rare foods possessing both these elements of deliciousness, heightened further by an air of theatricality—those strands and whirls and tubes and bows in which it makes its appearance on the stage. If a roast turkey can be said to possess tragic dignity, lying prone on its platter, pasta is a kind of Papageno—irrepressible, vulnerable, merry, even a little sly.

Bread is the humanizing food *par excellence* and is used to being—expects to be—treated with respect; those who love it break it with their hands at table and use it as a cooking ingredient only when it stales. Pasta, on the contrary, has no dignity, throws itself into anything, and yet manages to remain itself. "What are you doing in *there*, you rascal?" we want to say . . . except, of course, we know: giving the dish this double deliciousness.

✳ ✳ ✳

Pasta and vegetable combinations are often very simple: a vegetable—Buonassisi mentions, among others, onions, zucchini, asparagus, cauliflower, broccoli, and green beans—is tossed with pasta, seasoned, and eaten. At first glance such dishes seem to spring from the cooking of the Italian poor—*la cucina povera*—cut from very much the same cloth as, say, the hearty pasta and dried bean dish *pasta e fagioli*. They are both pastas meant to be eaten as a main course, not a first one; the vegetables are added not to make a sauce but to make the meal.

The difference, however, and it is an important one, is that vegetable and pasta dishes are simultaneously hearty and light. They aren't something, that is, that would sustain a farm laborer or factory worker, as much as they might seem to want to. To separate eaters into delicately picky aristocrats and hearty peasants ignores the fact that one can be genteel and trim and still want to help oneself to something good without chastising oneself, mumbling about sin. Once upon a time there were eaters who, even if careful about overindulgence, found eating a natural and delightful pleasure.

Hence, our *Commedia della Pasta*: a fantasy stage where a comedy of flavor is acted out. The landscape is bucolic; the players are dressed in simple rustic garb. But, because the substance of this delicious illusion is mostly cellulose and water, I found I had to eat a lot not to leave the table feeling empty. At first, it was unnerving to eat something so good that is so innocent of guile, and I suspect that those who are made nervous by appetite will have trouble with these dishes. Those who wish they could exercise theirs more, however, will find them—as I have—a revelation. It is such a pleasant change for the stomach to feel full of something good without any accompanying sense of glut or guilt. It's about as close as you can come to having your cake and eating it, too.

I don't know how Italians would portion these dishes, and—as I have explained in the essay "Mangiamaccheroni" (which appears in *Outlaw Cook*)—I don't trust the portioning given in Italian cookbooks. Because we serve them as a complete one-dish weekday supper, we've simply expanded on the logic inherent in these dishes, amplifying the presence of the vegetables until we had a meal that left us feeling comfortably, happily full. If we were to decide to use the more generous amounts of olive oil that Italian recipes often call for, to eat bread with the meal (or serve dessert after it)—we most often don't—we would downscale the proportions accordingly, and so should you.

❋ ❋ ❋

Nor is liberating generosity all that these pasta and vegetable dishes have to give. Their simplicity makes them easy to adapt to whatever is fresh and best in the supermarket produce section. In Maine, especially in winter, while we can almost always find something good there, we never know exactly what it will be. Suddenly, all the red bell peppers have vanished, but generous bundles of fresh spinach appear instead. On other occasions, there are chubby, tender leeks, bunches of pungent broccoli rabe, giant snowy-white heads of cauliflower, piles of crisp yellow wax beans. Out of these foragings—some of them not at all usual pasta ingredients—we make our meal.

As already noted, in Italian recipes a single vegetable is often used alone. Even at their best, our supermarket vegetables don't really have that kind of presence; except when locally grown produce is available, we get the best flavor using a combination. Something fresh and green-tasting (this can range from a head of romaine or a heap of green beans to a small bundle of parsley) might be combined with something mellow and creamy (flageolets, cauliflower, wax beans) and another something sweetly pungent (leeks, scallions, or onions in generous amounts—plus, occasionally, a red bell pepper), all sautéed in our standard *soffritto* of olive oil, a little hot red pepper, and, usually, garlic and a fresh herb. The results are then tossed with the pasta and served.

Read through the recipe for linguine with green beans, leeks, and flageolets—with its variations—below and you will get a good sense of how we mix and match the best the produce section has to offer. The important thing is to find a balance of flavors and textures in which the whole is somehow greater than—without ever obscuring—its parts. Try them; adapt them. We think you, too, will find them economical, filling, warming, liberating, doubly delicious meals.

PENNE WITH BROCCOLI, RED PEPPERS, AND GARLIC
[serves 2 generously]

1 head broccoli
sea salt
8 ounces penne
2 or 3 cloves garlic
sprig of fresh oregano

1 red bell pepper
2 tablespoons extra-virgin olive oil
½ teaspoon crushed hot red pepper
freshly ground black pepper
grated Romano (optional)

Trim and pare the broccoli. Break the head into individual florets and cut the stalks into bite-sized pieces. Cook these in a large pot of boiling salted water (we use 1 tablespoon sea salt to 4 quarts of water) until tender but still crisp. Remove to a bowl with a slotted spoon. Add the penne to the vegetable water and cook.

While the pasta cooks, mince the garlic cloves and oregano together with a pinch more of salt. Stem, core, and seed the bell pepper and cut it into small pieces. Heat the oil in a medium skillet over a low flame. Stir in the minced garlic-oregano mixture and the hot pepper. Cook this, stirring, for a minute, then add the bell pepper pieces. Sauté these until soft. About 3 minutes before the pasta is done, stir in the broccoli pieces and mix well, adding salt and pepper to taste. Strain the pasta, reserving the liquid. Divide the pasta into large bowls and spoon the vegetable mixture over each, then ladle in some of the cooking water (a few tablespoons to make a sauce or a cup or two to make a delicious soup). Serve with the grated Romano if desired.

Variation. With cauliflower: Prepare as above, substituting cauliflower for the broccoli, adding one chopped onion and minced parsley to the sautéed vegetables, and stirring in a spoonful of red wine vinegar. Or, if desired, omit the vinegar and add a few minced capers and a handful of pitted and coarsely chopped Mediterranean black olives. Use only a few tablespoons of the liquid: it does not make a good soup. Do not use cheese with this version.

LINGUINE WITH GREEN BEANS, LEEKS, AND FLAGEOLETS
[serves 2 generously]

Our natural foods store sells excellent, locally grown flageolets; this is one of our favorite ways to prepare them. In this dish, the green beans and leeks are cut into long, thin strips so that they can be twirled up on the fork with the linguine.

¼ cup dried flageolets
1 pound green beans
2 medium leeks
1 tablespoon butter
1 tablespoon extra-virgin olive oil
½ teaspoon crushed hot red pepper
2 or 3 cloves garlic, minced
sprig of fresh thyme, minced
8 ounces linguine
sea salt and freshly ground black pepper to taste
grated Parmesan (optional)

Pick over and rinse the dried beans. Put to soak in an adequate amount of water for 4 to 6 hours. Drain away and discard this liquid 2 hours before preparing the meal. Put the beans in a small pot, cover with water, and boil for 10 minutes. Reduce the heat to a simmer and cook until the beans are tender. Do not overcook. When done, drain and reserve the beans and the cooking liquid separately.

Trim the green beans and french them—we push them through a "krisker" (an ingenious little device with several tiny razor blades embedded in it that make short work of this task)—into long slivers. Heat 4 quarts of salted water in a large pot. Cook the slivered green beans until just tender, about 6 minutes. Remove the beans but keep the water boiling.

Discard the tough outer green fronds of the leeks and slice the white and tender green parts into long, slender strips. Wash these carefully. Heat the butter and oil in a medium skillet. Add the hot pepper, garlic, and thyme, cook for 1 minute, then stir in the leek strips. When these have softened, start the pasta cooking in the green-bean water.

After 10 minutes, add the cooked flageolets and a little of their liquid to the skillet. Mix the green beans in with the flageolets and leeks a few minutes before the pasta is done, seasoning to taste with salt and black pepper. Drain the pasta and return to the pot. Toss in the vegetable mixture and serve with grated Parmesan if desired.

Variations. This dish has proven especially amenable to substitutions. Scallions are often asked to fill in for absent leeks, and when green beans are old and tough we switch to tender greens, like escarole, romaine, or Swiss chard. Other mild-flavored dried beans can replace the flageolets, but we usually prefer to replicate their texture with some entirely different presence, like the wax beans or summer squash in the first two variations below.

Summer squash, romaine, and leeks with fusilli: Here, summer squash replaces the flageolets; romaine, or some other flavorful green, replaces the green beans; and oregano replaces the thyme. Otherwise, prepare and season as above. Cut 2 or 3 summer squash into bite-sized pieces. Sauté the leeks and summer squash together over low heat in a large skillet. Use a stubby pasta like fusilli or penne instead of linguine and start the pasta cooking only after the leeks are limp. Cut the romaine into bite-sized pieces and add to the skillet during the last few minutes of cooking. Serve as above.

Wax beans, romaine, and leeks with penne: Prepare and season as above, using yellow wax beans instead of the flageolets, and romaine (or other flavorful green) instead of the green beans. Cut the wax beans into bite-sized pieces and blanch in pasta water. Sauté the leeks over low heat in a large skillet. Use a stubby pasta like fusilli or penne instead of linguine and start the pasta cooking only after the leeks are limp. Cut the romaine into bite-sized pieces and add these and the cooked wax beans to the skillet during the last few minutes of cooking. Serve as above.

Escarole and scallions: This simplified version eschews the bean presence entirely. Prepare and season as above, using linguine as the pasta and 2 tablespoons of olive oil instead of the oil/butter mixture. Cut 2 bunches of scallions into long, linguine-like strips and a head of escarole into bite-sized pieces. Start the pasta when the vegetables are prepared. Sauté the scallions until tender, but do not overcook. (If necessary, turn off the heat under the skillet.) Add the escarole pieces a few minutes before the pasta is done, so that they are just wilted through. Serve as above.

SPINACH AND CHICKPEAS WITH FUSILLI
[serves 2 generously]

The following is based on a recipe from one of our favorite vegetable cookbooks, The Cook's Garden, *by British food writer Lynda Brown.*

⅓ cup dried chickpeas
2 bunches fresh spinach
8 ounces fusilli
2 tablespoons extra-virgin olive oil
½ teaspoon crushed hot red pepper
2 or 3 cloves garlic, minced
sea salt and black pepper
grated Parmesan

Pick over and rinse the dried beans. Put to soak in an adequate amount
of water for 4 to 6 hours. Two hours before preparing the meal, drain
away and discard this liquid. Put the beans in a small pot, cover with
water, and boil for 10 minutes. Reduce the heat to a simmer and cook
until they are tender. Do not overcook. When done, drain, reserving
both beans and cooking liquid separately.

Prep the spinach carefully, discarding damaged leaves and tough
stems. Wash 3 times. Put the spinach dripping wet into a large pot,
cover, and wilt over high heat. Turn into a colander and press out the
liquid with the back of a spatula into a bowl. Drink this liquid—cook's
treat—while preparing the rest of the meal. Coarsely chop the pressed
spinach and reserve.

Cook the pasta in boiling salted water. After it has been cooking for
5 minutes, heat the oil in a medium skillet over a low flame. Add the
hot pepper and minced garlic, cook for 1 minute, then stir in the chickpeas, the chopped spinach, and some of the chickpea liquid to make a
sauce. Season to taste with salt and black pepper. Drain the pasta and
return to the pot. Toss in the vegetable mixture, divide into large bowls,
and serve with grated Parmesan.

"THE BEST COOKIES IN THE WORLD"

❧ ❧ ❧

As the quotation marks suggest, this claim comes not from us but from Roald Dahl, who begins his account of these confections in *Memories with Food at Gipsy House** with this typically abrupt and unanswerable assertion:

> This is a true story about the best cookies in the world.

Now, if a phrase like "the best cookies in the world" were as self-explanatory as it might at first glance seem, we could ignore all the introduction and cut straight to the chase. But it isn't. Replace it with, say, "the best little boy in the world," and you see that if you know nothing about the person who is saying this, you can't know what they mean. Such assertions are not statements of fact but volcanic eruptions from the heart.

That this particular eruption comes from the somewhat twisted heart of Roald Dahl, author of (among other wildly popular children's books) *Charlie and the Chocolate Factory* and *James and the Giant Peach,* as well as some hauntingly sardonic short stories for adults, only adds some piquancy to our anticipation—all the more so when we learn that he was writing the book between bouts of illness during the last year of his life (he died in 1990).

---

*Currently out of print in the United States but available in Britain under the title *The Roald Dahl Cookbook* (not to be confused, by the way, with *Roald Dahl's Revolting Recipes,* which is directed at children).

Although he never says this, I believe that he intended it—not so much the finished book as the project itself—as a gift to his wife, Felicity (or Liccy, as she was called). The two of them worked on the book together, and it is, as its title suggests, a celebration of friendship and marriage through the recollection of shared pleasures at the table, pleasures that in their family only began with eating and drinking. Early on in its pages, he unabashedly confesses:

> We are all pigs, but we are, I hope, discerning pigs who care with some passion about fine cooking. No lunch is ever eaten without a discussion or a criticism or an accolade.*

Dahl was an exceedingly complicated person, and, if you prod around a little between the lines of this quote, you can catch some resonances of this. "Treats!" was one of his favorite exclamations, and his role was that of both impresario and final arbiter of the feast. The cooking he left to hirelings, who, it is obvious, sooner or later found all that discussing and criticizing of their efforts too much to take. Even a stream of accolades can wear you down, especially since Dahl's interest in his meals was not restricted to the dining room. He often stood right beside them while they worked, watching and asking questions.

Consequently, cooks came and went at Gipsy House, but that doesn't mean that they necessarily left in a huff. Few cooks have the experience of working for a patron whose curiosity about them, their cooking methods, and their recipes is as lively and perceptive as his appetite. Most (if not all) of them—their personalities, as well as their recipes—are woven into the story here, which gives the impression that some personal connection lingers, however chary these women had become of remaining under the thumb of a demanding old man so completely at ease in having others attend to his comfort that he had no inhibitions about trailing around after them as they did so.

As we are about to see, Dahl's self-centeredness, and the almost regal panache with which he wielded it, play an important part in our story. But first I have to admit to a small deceit. Although born in Wales of Norwegian parents, Dahl was entirely British in sensibility, and so he

---

*How nicely that word *lunch* places the intensity of Dahl's gourmandizing. Had it been *dinner*, he would seem no different from any other food lover; had it been *breakfast*, we might feel that we were getting in over our heads. But lunch! We can only think . . . how *lucky*!

never once mentions the word *cookie* in his narrative; what he writes, instead, is "biscuit"—as in "the best biscuits in the world."

Of course, this *is* the usual substitute when British culinary terms are made American—"aubergine" to "eggplant," "sippit" to "crouton," "liquidizer" to "blender." But things go awry when it is then assumed that "mince" *equals* "hamburger," or that "biscuit" equals "cookie." The substance may be the same, but the gustatory, the cultural, weight is not.

The word *biscuit* in British English means both cracker and cookie, and this points us to a serious difference in connotation. The British feel about their "bikkies"—whether sweet or savory—much the same way we Americans do about crackers. We can get quite worked up over them—as revealed in a recent brouhaha between Mainers and Nabisco over Pilot crackers—but we don't feel that *homemade* crackers are by definition best. Even so, despite our national fondness for Oreos and Chips Ahoy, when it comes to cookies, we absolutely do.*

However, the biscuit about which Dahl writes here has the peculiar quality of being at once a biscuit *and* a cookie, which is to say that it magically transcends, or at least blurs, the distinction between storebought and homemade. The reason I chose to misquote Dahl was not to add a false whet to our tale but to make clear from the outset what was going on. The claim may have been made by a Brit about something that in every way resembles a biscuit, but these are biscuits as worthy as any home-baked brownies or pecan crescents or lemon icebox crumbles to the title of—this time no quotation marks—The Best Cookies in the World.

❊ ❊ ❊

Holland, as it happens, is a country full of bookshops designed especially for children—containing only children's books, yes, but also child-sized chairs, tables, bookshelves, even low-ceilinged rooms that

---

*Contrast here the definition of *biscuit*—"a piece of unleavened cake or bread [that is] crisp, dry, and hard, and in small flat thin shape"—in the British *New Shorter Oxford English Dictionary* with that of *cookie*—"a small cake made from stiff, sweet dough rolled and sliced or dropped by spoonfuls on a large flat pan (cookie sheet) and baked"—in the American *Random House Dictionary*. The first could quite easily have been written more than a hundred years ago and contains not a hint of, say, the chocolate chip cookie. But the lexicographer who defines *cookie* has not only seen a chocolate chip cookie but most probably made one.

only children can enter. Because he loved such places, Dahl agreed to hold book signings in them, something he rarely did outside of Britain. And it was at such an event in the Dutch town of Arnhem that he first encountered the cookie.

As usual, by the time Dahl arrived kids were already lined up around the block, clutching their copies of *Sjakie en de Chocoladefabriek,* and this was just the start. Down the street, Albert Hagdorn, the owner-baker of a small pastry shop at 14 Grote Oord, was watching this endless line of children snake past. He took pity on the madly scribbling author and sent a clerk over with

> a small box of his own special biscuits. While my right hand kept signing, my left hand idly opened the box and fished out one. It was flat and thin and oval, and crystals of sugar were embedded in the top of it. I took a nibble. I took another nibble. I savoured it slowly. I took a big bite and chewed it. The taste and the texture were unbelievable. This, I told myself, is the best biscuit I've ever eaten in my life. I ate another and another, and each one I ate only strengthened my opinion. They were simply marvellous. . . . The lady who owned the bookshop was standing beside me.
>
> "They're wonderful," I said.
>
> "Ah, but they are famous, those biscuits," she said. "They are known all over Holland as the *Arnhemse Meisjes.* The proprietor makes them himself."

Naturally, any cookie with a claim to being the best in the world is going to taste good, even very good, but there must be something else going for it besides that. The cookie also has to have *character.* Character presents itself in cookies in many different ways, but the kind that appeals most to me might best be described as "exuding confidence in its own goodness." That is what drew me in as I read the passage: the way this cookie's self-confidence proved such an equal match to Dahl's own.

This was good, because his own description of it—flat, thin, and oval, with crystals of sugar embedded in the top of it—hardly signaled anything special. It is not a cookie that, in the American manner, wraps its arm around your tongue and becomes its instant best buddy. Yet these *Arnhemse Meisjes*—"Arnhem Misses" or, as we shall simply call them, "Arnhems"—managed to seize the attention of a preoccupied writer in the midst of a crowd of children and make him—or at least his very critical palate—as swoony as a teenager in love.

Now we are about to see why Dahl's personality is as important to this story as his palate. People who expect others to take care of them often also possess the power to induce even complete strangers to do just that. So, when he prevailed on the bookstore owner to go see if she could persuade Hagdorn to part with his famous recipe, she did not come to her senses—as she would have in the normal course of events—the moment she stepped out the door, quite sanely deciding—rather than risk a scornful snub—to take a walk around the block and return to say that *Mijnheer* Hagdorn was sincerely sorry, but this was a proprietary recipe that was *never* to be revealed to *anyone*.

Instead, dazzled by that flash from Dahl's high-beam charm, she went straight to Hagdorn's shop and inveigled the secret right out of him. To get some sense of the magnitude of this accomplishment, you need only know that when we sent our own two intrepid investigators to Arnhem (see page 213), they discovered that no one but Hagdorn's successors at the same shop possesses the secret of *Arnhemse Meisjes* and that the few recipes for them that appear in local cookbooks aren't even close to the mark. As far as the people who worked at Hagdorn were concerned, their recipe still had the status of a state secret.

Last, in true Roald Dahl style, there had to be an amazingly improbable stroke of luck. If Roald and Liccy had cooked for themselves, these precious instructions, written out in a foreign language, would most likely have been lost in a drawer. Instead, they had a cook, and, this one time, she was a Dutch cook—able to decipher Hagdorn's terse notations and then cast them into a workable recipe, which duly appears at the end of Dahl's story. It was at this point that, after giving that recipe a curious but quick glance, I closed the book, put it on the shelf, and left it there for five years. Dahl had persuaded me that this was a great cookie—had I chanced to pass through Arnhem, I would have headed straight to Hagdorn's. But I rarely make cookies these days, and no baking project fills me with greater foreboding than to try to replicate a proprietary cookie from a recipe.

❋ ❋ ❋

Except, except . . . I just couldn't get them out of my mind. Dahl's story had made its impression, certainly, but there was this little burr that had caught hold of me and wouldn't brush off. It was the smallest thing: Arnhems are leavened with yeast, not baking powder; and in this household it is Matt who bakes with chemical leavenings and I who bake with yeast. That scant teaspoon of yeast had claimed me and wouldn't let me go. So, finally, this winter, I gave in. I pulled Matt's vintage Kitchen Aid electric mixer out of storage (it was the first time I had ever used one) and took down *Memories with Food at Gipsy House*.

What I discovered is that great-grandfather Hagdorn had created a buttery, unsweetened dough that was plastic enough to be rolled out almost to the thinness of egg noodle dough and unsticky enough to be rolled out on sugar crystals instead of flour. What this bakes into is the quintessential sugar cookie: buttery, extremely thin and crisp, the coating of sugar crystals adding crunch on top and underneath—where they have completely melted during the long, slow baking into a delicious caramel crust.

They are at once so simple that my version was as like the originals I was sent from Arnhem as to make no difference and so sophisticated that they are like no other cookie: the first time you taste them, your mouth is more astonished than it is delighted. The buttery, unsweetened body of the cookie reaches your tastebuds before the rock-sugar crystals melt on your tongue to provide the completing sweetness, a syncopated beat that tweaks your expectations, and gives the unadorned tastes of butter and sugar an exciting complexity that never stops surprising you, no matter how many Arnhems you eat. They make your mouth happy, but they also make it think.

ARNHEM COOKIES
[makes 1 pound of cookies (i.e., a lot)]

Although Arnhems are in most ways a pleasure to make (and will inspire in the experienced cookie maker all sorts of ideas), mixing the dough requires a powerful, stand-mounted electric mixer: don't even think of using a handheld one or—for that matter—trying to make this dough by hand. (We suspect that a sturdy food processor set with a plastic kneading blade could manage this dough, but we haven't tested that hypothesis.) However, Matt's trusty old Kitchen Aid took it in its stride. Also: Please read through the recipe carefully before attempting to make these cookies; some forethought is required, as the cookie dough should be prepared several hours before you plan to bake the cookies.

1½ cups (7.5 ounces) all-purpose flour

½ cup plus 1 tablespoon (4.5 ounces) whole milk (see note)

⅛ teaspoon freshly squeezed lemon juice

⅓ of a standard .6-ounce cube of fresh yeast or 1 scant teaspoon of dry yeast

⅛ teaspoon salt

1 stick (4 ounces) unsalted butter, cut into 8 cubes

about 1 cup crushed rock sugar or sugar crystals (see note)

a heavy-duty electric mixer fitted with a dough paddle

Combine the flour, milk, lemon juice, yeast (crumbling it into the mixture, if fresh), and salt into the bowl of the mixer or processor. Turn the machine on high. As soon as the contents of the bowl are well mixed, add the first cube of butter. Beat this into the mixture for 1 minute, then add the next cube, beating this into the mixture for 1 minute. Continue in the same way until all the butter has been amalgamated. The dough will be soft and elastic to the touch. Use a spatula or dough scraper to form it into a ball. Place it on a plate, cover it with a bowl, and set it in the refrigerator until cool, or about 2 hours. If you wish, you may leave it overnight.

When ready to make the cookies, preheat the oven to 275°F and line 2 standard cookie sheets with parchment paper (see note). Sprinkle the work surface on which you plan to roll out the dough with a coating of sugar crystals. Uncover the dough and, with a sharp kitchen knife, divide it in half. Form each half into a round ball.

Coat the first ball of dough thickly with sugar crystals and transfer it to the sugared working surface. There, use a rolling pin to gently roll it out as thinly as possible, pausing frequently to sprinkle it and the counter with more sugar crystals. Also, while this is still possible, periodically turn the dough over so that more sugar crystals can be sprinkled on the bottom surface. The thinner and more evenly the dough is rolled, the better (and more authentic) the cookies; it should be almost as thin as homemade egg-noodle dough.

If you wish, use a cookie cutter to cut the dough into ovals, the traditional shape. Otherwise, use a pizza cutter or sharp utility knife to cut them into rectangles, roughly 1 inch by 2 inches. Set the formed cookies onto one of the parchment-lined cookie pans and place this into the preheated oven. The cookies should be baked until their tops are caramel-colored and their bottoms a crisp brown. Dahl's time is 30 to 45 minutes; we used insulated cookie pans, and our baking time was closer to an hour. While these bake, roll out and form the second batch of cookies in the same way.

Remove the baked cookies from the oven and—taking care with the hot pan—slide the parchment paper and cookies onto a wire cooling rack. Remove them from the paper as soon as they are cool enough to handle. They keep well for at least a week in an airtight container—but are best eaten within the first 2 or 3 days. (If your cookies have puffed up and have a chewy rather than crisp texture, they weren't rolled thin enough. They'll be good, but you won't think them contenders for the world's best cookies.)

Cook's Notes. Amount of Milk: The exact quantity will depend on the type of flour you use. If your mixer struggles with the dough, dribble in more milk.

Sugar Crystals: Dahl writes that his own Arnhems were not quite as good as the real thing. This may be because his recipe substitutes crushed sugar cubes for the Dutch *kandij suiker*, amber crystals better known in this country as coffee sugar crystals. We used Billington's amber crystal sugar, which is the ideal size—like fine gravel. But any amber coffee crystals will work well—larger ones should be crushed down to size with a rolling pin.*

Parchment Paper: Don't substitute the new Teflon baking mats for parchment paper; these don't work nearly as well when making these cookies.

---

*When we originally wrote about this cookie, real amber sugar crystals were very difficult to find. However, since then, the good folks at The Baker's Catalogue have taken an interest in the Arnhem cookie and offer these special crystals to interested bakers. (Their catalog photograph of the sugar shows the cookie, too.) As this book went to press, a pound of the crystals is $2.95, plus shipping. And their catalog is a treat. The Baker's Catalogue; P.O. Box 876; Norwich, VT 05055; (800) 827-6836: www.kingarthurflour.com.

ON THE TRAIL OF ARNHEMSE MEISJES

Andrew Blank and Judy Landis

Searching out famous cookies is a tough and thankless job. But someone has to do it, so we selflessly stepped forward to volunteer. This meant heading off to Arnhem to see if the bakery Roald Dahl describes—Hagdorn, at 14 Grote Oord—was still in business and, if so, to sample their wares ourselves. *Arnhemse Meisjes** (or, if you like, Arnhem Girls), while well known in Holland, are a proprietary commodity like *Haagse Hopjes* (coffee candies), not a regional home-baking tradition. You're as likely to find them in a Dutch cookbook as you would be to find a recipe for Pepperidge Farm's Milano cookies in an American one.

Grote Oord lies in Arnhem's "old town," which is tucked into a bend of the Rhine and has been made a car-free pedestrian zone. World War II was not kind to Arnhem, and even in this quarter much rebuilding has taken place since. Where the old buildings have survived you see two or three stories, the top two half-timbered with white plaster, the lower level modernized into a shopfront of glass and brushed aluminum. And gaps have been plugged with entirely new buildings.

However, the streets meander pleasantly and are narrow enough to feel cozy. Just past the wonderfully ornate post office is Grote Oord, a street with a typical jumble of old and new. The eye is drawn to a café selling crisp waffles and ice cream through a sliding window. Next to it is a small pastry shop. The discreet hand-painted sign above the door says HAGDORN. With a start we realize that we're here.

The place is tiny. In the attractive display window, not more than five feet wide, is an assortment of *Arnhemse Meisjes*, the originals in clear plastic bags tied with dull gold ribbons or in metal cookie boxes

---

*As to the pronunciation: *Arnhemse* takes the accent on the first syllable; the *hem* is fairly short, and the possessive *se* is hardly pronounced at all. The Dutch *ei* is an English long *i*, the same as the *i* in *mice*. The diminutive *je* is such a fixture of the language that you can't get through the day without it. It's pronounced "yeh," but again fairly quickly, so you don't linger on the *h*. You have *een kopje koffie met een plakje koek* (a small cup of coffee with a piece of cake). Dutch ten-cent pieces are two fives, hence *een dubbeltje*. *Koekjes* are cookies (small cakes). And so forth. Putting it all together, it's ARNhemse MICEyez. *Meisjes* almost always means "little girls," but teenage boys when crossed in love describe themselves as having problems with the *meisjes*.

decorated with Dutch scenes. There are also a newer variety, made of puff paste, and—for the locals who have had their fill of both varieties—there are some regular cakes and tarts.

The interior is likewise very small and rather dim, thanks to its old-fashioned dark woodwork (the decor has been left unaltered since the 1920s). There is a glass bakery case filled with *Meisjes* and some chocolates and cakes; a freezer case with frozen bavarois and little cocktail snacks; a scale; a cash register; and just enough room left over for a few customers to stand. The kitchen is in the back.

Happily, there is no hype of any kind at Hagdorn, beyond the proud and simple statement that theirs are the *enige echte*, the one and only, Arnhem Girls. This is entirely consistent with the lack of neon around the sign over the door and so completely uncommercial that it wins our hearts. The ladies behind the counter are used to pilgrims coming from all over for their *Meisjes*. They are friendly but businesslike: you wait your turn, state your business, pay for your goods, and leave.

However, we did manage to coax out a little information as to what goes into the cookies (which was fortunate, since there's no ingredient list on the package). *Meisjes*, they admitted, are made with yeast, not chemical leaveners, and do contain some lemon, but they would not divulge whether this was juice or zest. "The recipe is our little secret," they said, firmly putting a stop to our questions. "If you want to know what's in them you should eat a few." And that was it . . . except for the little brochure that comes with each package of Arnhem Girls, which tells the story of how these cookies were created. It reads in part:

> Great grandfather Hagdorn became chief baker at the Van Zalinge Bakery on Grote Oord, a street in the heart of Arnhem, where formerly public assizes were held. As were most master bakers, old Hagdorn was a businessman as well as an artist. He experimented eagerly with all manner of pastries, looking for something "fine on the tongue" and "attractive to the eye," something that might do well at fancy dinners and parties. On a certain day in 1829 he produced a cookie in the form of a miniature shoe sole from a raised yeast dough. It was a crispy, full-flavored *koekje*, generously sprinkled with sugar.

Old Hagdorn's creation must have been quite a success, because he eventually took over the bakery, and it remained the specialty there for the next four generations. Roald Dahl probably had one of the last batches made by great-grandson Albert before he sold out to the current owners—which might be why he was so uncharacteristically forthcoming with the recipe. Certainly, we didn't find a single other baker in Arnhem selling *Meisjes*. They're still exclusively Hagdorn's.

Before leaving town we stopped at the local library, where we uncovered a compilation of pastry recipes by local master bakers. While it contained nothing on *Arnhemse Meisjes*, it did stress the use of two particular ingredients in cookie making: *Zeeuwse bloem*, a flour from the province of Zeeland, right on the North Sea, which makes cookies especially crispy because it binds less moisture than flour from inland-grown wheat; and soft brown *basterdsuiker*, or beet sugar. (You can imagine our reaction when we first found light brown *basterd*, dark brown *basterd*, and white *basterd* sugar in the supermarkets here.)

Bruine basterdsuiker has the texture of American brown sugar and is often used to give a dark color to commercial cookies, including one of our own favorites, LU's Bastognes. However, Bastognes also have a distinctive crunchiness, which derives not from *basterdsuiker* but from another Dutch baking secret—*kandij suiker*. We suspect that it is the thick coating of these amber crystals of rock-candy sugar (made not from beets but from unprocessed sugarcane syrup) that gives *Meisjes* both their shattering crunch and their deep-flavored, mellow sweetness. And, yes, they *are* fairly addictive.

DEPARTMENT OF RANDOM RECEIPTS

❦ ❦ ❦

ESSENCE OF CORN

Down East, locally grown sweet corn won't arrive at the farmers' markets until summer has started to slide into fall. Early August—yes, the days are still hot and the roadsides lined with brown-eyed Susans. But apples are turning red, the leaves of more than one maple are a shock of scarlet, and teachers will soon be holding meetings at the grammar school. In other words, the arrival of sweet corn—Seneca Daybreak, followed soon after by Honey & Cream and Burgundy Delight—is greeted with the little edge of self-pity that flavors any long-delayed anticipation. We buy our first bagful with a resolute determination to make up for lost time.

This, of course, means making an entire meal of it, setting the pot to boil the moment we get home. It is only after we have put at least three such feasts of corn on the cob behind us that we are able to calm down a bit and permit our pleasure in this end-of-summer delicacy to exfoliate. It is one of life's small ironies that when we do we turn to what must be the most unembellished dish of all in that cantankerous compendium of Spartan cookery, Helen Nearing's *Simple Food for the Good Life*, where it is named, starkly, "Uncooked Corn."

To make this, you bring the corn, a large bowl, and a sharp knife with you out to the picnic table in the backyard (this is messy work), shuck the ears, and pull away all the silk. Then take the knife and use the point to cut down the middle of each row of kernels and the back of the blade to scrape the sweet, milky pulp into a bowl. This fresh-scraped custard is served up and eaten as is. You don't have to be of the back-to-the-earth persuasion to find this delicious: no, *more* than delicious—so mysteriously satisfying that even a touch of salt seems unwanted tampering.

The old-fashioned word for this pure corn pulp is *milk*—a word that, until I ate it plain, I felt was a misnomer; if anything, it more resembles watery scrambled eggs. But to eat it in this raw, pure state is to feel something of what a nursing baby must: that you are imbibing not food but food's platonic essence, a substance that by its own pleasing nature—rather than through any subsequent refinement or distillation—is entirely digestible. The experience in the mouth is not so much of eating as of inhaling: the tongue just breathes it in. Nothing I have ever consciously tasted has seemed so light, so delicate and sweet, so effortlessly good.

Indeed, the problem with a bowl of fresh-scraped corn pulp is that it is a little *too* pure to serve as part of an actual meal. It is the sort of thing that, like wild blueberries and milk, you want to eat by itself and by yourself alone, sitting on the porch in meditative silence. Our compromise is to eat a few spoonfuls straight from the scraping bowl, then take the rest and cook up a pot of sweet corn pudding or fill the griddle with the tastiest, most delicate imaginable little crispy puffs: sweet corn fritters.

SWEET-CORN PUDDING
[*per serving*]

3 large fresh-picked ears of corn, shucked and de-silked
⅓ cup whole milk or light cream
a pinch of salt
a grinding of black pepper
a pat of butter

Using the method set out above, slice each row of kernels on each of the three ears and scrape out the pulp (each ear should yield ¼ to ⅓ cup). Put this and the milk or cream in a small pot and set it over a medium flame just long enough for the contents to heat through. Season with salt and a grinding of black pepper, ladle into a soup bowl, and float a pat of butter on top.

Variations. Corn and Seafood Stew: I never thought *anything* could improve on our elemental Maine lobster stew (for that recipe, consult the chapter "Crab Rolls & Lobster Stew" in *Serious Pig*), until one day I stirred in 2 cups of corn pulp during the final reheating. The result was astounding. Conversely, we've added fresh-picked crabmeat to the pudding to make a great corn and crabmeat stew, and I suspect that this would work just as well with oysters or shrimp.

Creamed Corn: Obviously, a small side dish of corn stew would make a transcendental serving of creamed corn, but consider briefly parboiling (2 minutes or so) the ears to set the pulp before scraping it out. This yields something different and quite luxurious: pure corn on the cob . . . in a bowl. Heat this gently and serve it forth lightly seasoned and nicely buttered.

SWEET-CORN FRITTERS
[makes 24 fritters—a meal for 2 or 3 or a side dish for 4 or 6]

    6 large fresh-picked ears of corn, shucked and de-silked
    2 tablespoons butter **or** bacon fat (at room temperature)
    3 eggs (at room temperature), separated
    3 to 4 tablespoons (1 ounce) all-purpose flour
    ¾ teaspoon salt
    black and cayenne pepper to taste
    butter or bacon fat to grease the griddles

Put a heat-proof platter in the oven and preheat at the lowest setting.

Use a patent kernel cutter or the edge of a sharp knife to cut the kernels from 3 of the ears, scraping each stripped cob with the back of the knife to remove any remaining pulp. Then, using the method described on page 216, slice each row of kernels on the other 3 ears and scrape out the pulp. Each ear should yield ⅔ to ¾ cup of kernels or ¼ to ⅓ cup of pulp. All 6 ears will thus produce a generous 2 cups of kernels and about 1 cup of corn pulp.

Put 2 tablespoons butter or bacon fat and 3 egg yolks in a mixing bowl. Stir the fat and egg yolks together gently until they make a smooth emulsion. Add the corn pulp, blending well. In a small bowl mix the flour, salt, and black and red pepper. Sieve this into the batter and stir until well blended. Fold in the corn kernels. Beat the egg whites until they stand in soft peaks. Mix about a quarter of this thoroughly into the batter, then fold in the rest more delicately, to preserve the loft.

Over a medium-low flame, melt a tablespoon of the butter or bacon fat on a griddle or in a large skillet (use half the amount of fat if the pan has a nonstick surface). Drop the batter by generous tablespoons onto the hot griddle and cook until the undersides form a golden crust. Then flip them over until the other sides do the same—about 30 seconds per side. Turn them with care—these fritters are *very* fragile. When the first batch is done, transfer it to the platter in the warm oven, regrease the griddle or skillet if necessary, and prepare the next batch in the same way. Serve the fritters as soon as they are all made. They are a delicious savory side dish but can be a meal all by themselves, topped with sweet butter and, if you like, maple syrup.

A small treasure in our cookbook collection is a tiny book of corn recipes, published in 1917. Called simply *The Book of Corn Cookery*, by Mary L. Wade, it offers many ways of using corn pulp, including the following four easy and very appetizing recipes.

CORN-STUFFED TOMATOES
[*serves 4*]

4 whole tomatoes
1 sweet red bell pepper, cored and seeded
1 tablespoon butter
1 cup corn pulp
salt and pepper to taste

Cut off the tops of the tomatoes; scoop out their centers with a spoon. Pour boiling water over the pepper; remove the seeds and cut into small pieces; cook in the butter for 5 minutes. Season the corn with salt and pepper. Add the cooked pepper. Pack this mixture into the tomatoes, replace the tops, and bake for 30 minutes in a 350°F oven.

CORN OMELET
[*serves 2*]

2 tablespoons flour
½ teaspoon salt
1 cup corn pulp
1 cup milk
4 eggs, whisked together until light
1 tablespoon butter or bacon fat

Mix the flour and salt with the corn pulp; add the milk and the lightly beaten eggs. Heat the butter or bacon fat in a frying pan. When bubbling hot, pour in the egg mixture. Cook slowly on top of the stove or in a 325°F oven about 10 minutes, or until a silver knife stuck into the center comes out clean. Carefully invert onto a hot serving plate and serve at once.

SOUTHERN CORN PUDDING
[*serves 4*]

1 pint rich milk (half-and-half)
1½ cups corn pulp
1 tablespoon butter
½ teaspoon salt
¼ teaspoon paprika
2 eggs, slightly beaten

Heat the milk to just below the scalding point. Add the corn pulp, butter, salt, paprika, and, last, the beaten eggs. Stir gently until the mixture is blended, then pour into a buttered pudding dish and bake in a 325°F oven until set, or about 45 to 55 minutes.

❋ ❋ ❋

We found this recipe in Paola Scaravelli and Jon Cohen's *Cooking from an Italian Garden*, and it immediately captured our hearts. If you like butternut but are tired of it baked or mashed, you'll find that this bright-flavored dish gives it a nice touch of Mediterranean swank, as well as some unexpected matchings of texture and flavor—the union of butternut and basil is especially intriguing. A perfect salad for early fall. Here's how we've adapted it.

ITALIAN BUTTERNUT SALAD
[*serves 4*]

FOR THE VINAIGRETTE:
½ to ¾ teaspoon sea salt
freshly ground black pepper
⅛ teaspoon dried oregano
¼ teaspoon ground hot red pepper
1 to 1½ tablespoons balsamic vinegar
2 to 3 tablespoons olive oil
1 garlic clove, finely minced

FOR THE SALAD:
1 small whole butternut squash, peeled, cored, seeded, and cut into ½-inch cubes
1 red bell pepper, cored, seeded, and chopped
2 large scallions, trimmed, sliced vertically, and chopped
several basil leaves, torn to bits, **or** a handful of parsley, minced

Mix together the ingredients for the vinaigrette in a large bowl. Steam the squash cubes until just tender but not soft (al dente). Turn these out into the vinaigrette. Add the other ingredients and stir gently until the bits of pepper and scallion are evenly distributed and everything is lightly coated with the vinaigrette. Let rest for 30 minutes or so in a cool place before serving so the flavors can meld.

PEASE PORRIDGE

Feb. 28, 1782. Was rather uneasy to-day on Account of being afraid that I have got the Piles coming or something else—unless it is owing to my eating a good deal of Peas Pudding two or three days ago with a Leg of Pork.
—James Woodforde, *The Diary of a Country Parson*

There seems to have been pease porridge as long as there's been an England—although, as C. Anne Wilson dryly notes in *Food and Drink in*

Britain, it was probably not all that much enjoyed until salt was available to season it. There is no dating the moment when some inspired British cook thought to make the porridge into a pudding by tying it up in a sack and boiling this with pickled pork. As the peas swelled, they drew in some of the succulent fat and the savory cooking water, with its delicate taste of pork, salt, and cooking spice. (Unlike ham, British pickled pork is not smoked or dried, and so its subsequently much milder flavor does not overpower the simple pea-and-herb taste of the pudding.)

The taste of pea and pork proved so compelling in combination that by the time of James I, a common street cry was "Hot grey peas and a suck of bacon!"—with the purchaser receiving literally that, for the piece of meat was tied to a string, and the vendor quickly yanked it out of any mouth that was taking more than the paid-for taste.

Pease pudding retains a stronghold in the culinarily conservative northeast of England. Jane Grigson, who was raised on it, remembers butcher shops with "great pots of it in their windows" to be sliced into portions for customers to bring home with the pork. According to Sheila Hutchins in *Grannie's Kitchen*, those pots still exist, each one holding fifty pounds of pudding. "But it soon goes," she notes, to be eaten with "roasts, sausages, white puddings, even sandwiches, with all kinds of pork cuts and with ham and boiled bacon. 'A grand tea we had, boiled ham, pease pudding and pickles,' they say locally."

Originally, the peas for pease pudding were whole. They were put in a sack with a sprig of mint and left to simmer in the pot along with the cut of meat they were to be served with. Today, the usual method is to prepare a more delicate pudding by cooking and puréeing split peas, enriching the resulting porridge with butter and egg, and then either steaming or baking it until firm.

Our version of pease pudding breaks all the rules. The split green peas are soaked overnight and then pulverized in a food processor before being cooked. Almost all other recipes, at one point or another, require a parboiling of the peas instead, a process that cooks out all their flavor. Make it our way and you'll have a pease pudding worth eating, even as a meal by itself.

PENOBSCOT PEASE PUDDING
[serves 4 to 6]

1 cup (½ pound) split green peas
1¾ cups water
2 tablespoons unsalted butter
1 egg, beaten
¼ teaspoon grated lemon zest
1 teaspoon salt
freshly ground pepper to taste
1 cup frozen baby peas (defrosted under cold water)
4 tablespoons (½ stick) butter
a few fresh mint, thyme, or marjoram leaves, minced fine

Wash and pick through the split peas carefully. Put them in a small bowl, pour over the water, and let soak overnight. The next day, pulverize the split peas with any remaining liquid into a coarse-textured gruel in a food processor set with the steel blade. Then work in 1 tablespoon of the butter, melted; the beaten egg; and the grated lemon zest. Season to taste with salt and lots of ground pepper. Stir the defrosted tiny peas into the pudding mixture with a spatula. Use some of the remaining butter to generously grease a 1½-quart earthenware soufflé or similar ovenproof dish. Pour in the pea mixture and dot it all over with small bits cut from what remains of the first 2 tablespoons of butter. If possible, cover with plastic wrap and let rest in the refrigerator a few hours before baking.

To bake, preheat oven to 350°F. Unwrap the cooking dish and put it in the oven. Bake for 1 hour, or until pudding has set. While pudding bakes, melt the additional 4 tablespoons of butter, pour it into a small pitcher, and stir in the pinch of minced fresh herb. Let this steep in a warm place on the stove. When the pudding is done, run a sharp knife around the inside edge of the dish to free it and turn it out onto a serving plate. Serve in slices, bringing the pitcher of melted herb butter to table for each eater to dribble over their own slices as they like.

Cook's Note. Sheila Hutchins suggests that meat drippings make a tasty substitute for all or part of the butter in a pease pudding—an idea that seems to us an immediately appealing use for a big spoonful of drippings from a roast chicken.

❋ ❋ ❋

Confirmed asparagus lovers will immediately see the appeal of the following recipe. Because you can taste as you go, there's no danger of overcooking the spears. Then, the entire meal can be eaten with your fingers, thus establishing the intimacy that fresh asparagus deserves— without dripping butter all down your shirtfront, which *always* happens when you try to maneuver whole spears into your mouth. And the problem of how to consume the butter that remains on the plate is neatly resolved. However, the reason that I love this dish is because of the sopped toast. It's so delicious that it can almost get you past the usual conclusion to a meal of asparagus: self-pity. It's the only vegetable of which it can be said that too much isn't quite enough.

ASPARAGUS IN A BOWL
[*serves 1*]

1 bunch asparagus, carefully rinsed
1 tablespoon butter
½ teaspoon salt
1 thickish slice good bread, trimmed to fit the bottom of a
     shallow soup bowl
freshly ground black pepper to taste

Peel the bottom third of the stalks. Slice off the tough ends, using the edge of the knife to locate the point where the tender part begins. Cut the trimmed stalks into bite-sized pieces, leaving the tips whole. Put the butter into a large skillet and add the salt and about ¾ cup of water. Bring to a simmer and add the asparagus, reserving the tips to add a minute later. Bring the liquid back to a simmer and, stirring frequently, cook the asparagus to the tenderness you like. Meanwhile, slowly but thoroughly toast the round of bread.

Set the toast into the bottom of the shallow soup bowl. Spoon over the asparagus and the remaining cooking liquid—there should be just enough to moisten the piece of bread thoroughly. Generously pepper and eat at once.

PÊCHES MELBA

For those of a certain age, "Pêches Melba" may lift the lid of memory's dusty recipe box—the one in which such dishes as Turkey Divan, Chicken à la King, Beef Stroganoff, and Oysters Rarebit were long ago filed away and forgotten. The mind nudged, you may recall that this was a dessert whipped up around the turn of the last century by Auguste Escoffier at London's Savoy Hotel in homage to Dame Nellie Melba, the glass-shattering Australian soprano (whom we also have to thank for Melba toast). But, as for the dish itself, what most likely comes to mind is a vague impression of ice cream and canned peaches topped with some kind of fruit sauce, whipped cream, chopped nuts— a confection, that is, exuding all the bogus hauteur of a "company dessert."

I have yet to find a cookbook that offers the dish exactly as Escoffier presented it, and many recipes are such depressing travesties that it's little wonder that peach melba has fallen not only out of favor but out of mind. Most contemporary cookbooks ignore it, even those that specialize in fruit. In this instance, the banishment is wildly undeserved. Escoffier created a dessert that ought to be made only on a few rare summer days—and that was his fatal error. Chefs and food writers found it too wonderful to exercise any such restraint. To keep it on the menu, they poached the peaches, cooked and thickened the raspberry pulp, and then, when the result no longer seemed all that special, resorted to those instruments of the devil: whipped cream and chopped nuts.

So, forget all you ever knew about *pêches melba*. Then, if chance should bring your way a perfectly ripe peach this summer, do this with it—as Escoffier directs in *Ma Cuisine*—and just call it:

SUMMER PEACH AND FRESH
RASPBERRY DESSERT
[*serves 4*]

4 fragrant, fully ripened peaches
1 pint fresh raspberries
1 pint premium vanilla ice cream

Dip each peach quickly into boiling water to loosen its skin and then into icy cold water to keep the flesh from cooking. Slip off the skin, cut the peach in half, remove the pit, and set each half, cut side up, in a small chilled dish. Put the raspberries in a sieve and, if they are from the supermarket, give them a quick rinse in cold water. Use a rubber spatula or the back of a spoon to press out their pulp into a bowl, discarding the residue of seeds. Scoop a ball of vanilla ice cream (its size is up to you) and put it on top of a peach half. Press the other half of the peach on top of this, and spoon over a quarter of the raspberry puree. Prepare the other 3 servings in the same manner and serve at once.

❦ ❦ ❦

One Maine winter's day, Matt was prepping a pile of grapefruit for marmalade, and cutting all that citrus rind into tiny slivers brought back memories of her brief stint in the late 1970s making desserts at the Harvest Restaurant in Cambridge. Joe Hyde was the head chef, and while he was a brilliant cook, he was not much of a dessert enthusiast. His idea of the most refreshing conclusion to a meal was fresh fruit, artfully cut up and swimming in booze. Consequently, Matt's pastry skills were hardly put to the test; she spent most of her time replenishing the restaurant's bottomless fruit cup and slivering orange rinds for Joe's special favorite—*Oranges à l'Arabe*. As it happened, we had some navel oranges at hand, and so, once the grapefruit sections were bubbling in the pot, she whipped up a batch for that evening's dessert. Here's the recipe, adapted from Joe's too-little-known book, *Love, Time & Butter*.*

---

*I should note that this recipe should not be taken as typical of this work. As its subtitle suggests—*The Broiling, Roasting, Baking, Deep-Fat Frying, Sautéing, Braising, and Boiling Cookbook*—this is a book about cooking technique from a gifted and practiced professional. Indeed, Joe Hyde is a chef's chef, which is one reason why his book did not receive the attention it deserved: the recipes demand first-rate ingredients and some skill as a cook, and the prose has the taut control of someone who earns his living working in a restaurant kitchen and not at a typewriter. This isn't to say he can't write. Every time I open the book, which is often, I find myself unable to resist reading once again the book's preface, in which Hyde describes with great gusto his memorable adventures as an apprentice cook at places ranging from local dives to Ferdinand Point's La Pyramide.

ORANGES À L'ARABE
[serves 4 to 6]

8 seedless oranges
⅔ cup sugar (or to taste)
1 vanilla bean
2 to 3 tablespoons Grand Marnier

Remove the zest (the thin outer peel) from 4 of the oranges and cut this into toothpick-sized slivers. Cover these with water and bring to a boil in a saucepan. Drain and re-cover with cold water. Boil and drain. Cover a third time with cold water. Stir in the sugar, add the vanilla bean, and simmer until the slivers become translucent threads and the liquid is syrupy. Reserve.

Carefully pare away the peel and pith from all 8 oranges to expose the flesh of the fruit. Then use the knife blade to free each segment from its membrane, putting the pieces (and any juice) into a shallow bowl. Remove the vanilla bean from the syrup and pour this, the zest, and the Grand Marnier over the orange slices. Cover and refrigerate for at least 1 hour. This dessert can be prepared up to 24 hours in advance.

TALES FROM
THE OLD COOKSTOVE

POT ON THE FIRE

❀ ❀ ❀

pot-bouille. In the *Grand Dictionnaire universel* Pierre Larousse defines this word as "everyday household cooking." It was used in this sense by Flaubert, Richepin, Huysmans, and Vallès; Zola used the expression as the title for one of his books (1882). The term *pot-bouille* is no longer in use but the more colloquial *tambouille,* derived from *pot-en-bouille,* is still found.

—*Larousse gastronomique*

Although he is all but forgotten by most readers today, a quarter of a century ago Roy Andries de Groot was a romantic if also intimidatingly formidable presence in the food world, a man of grand gestures and summary judgments, possessing an awesome palate and an even more awesome gift of describing what it encountered. If Samuel Johnson was the Great Cham of literature, de Groot was surely the Great Cham of food writing. Everything about him was larger than life, not least the fact that his intricate evocations of place and plate flowed from the pen of a blind man—a condition that, to my memory, he never once directly referred to in print.

I was not one of his admirers, but I understood why others were so enchanted by him. He demanded a lot from life, and, at least by his report, life was impressed enough to deliver. In one typical de Grootian narrative—it appears in the posthumous collection of his essays, *In Search of the Perfect Meal*—his driver gets lost on a trip through the endless marshland along the western shore of the Gironde estuary in southwest France. They had planned to lunch on the famous local oysters, *les gravettes,* at Arcachon, but after a morning of hard driving under a fiery sun they were grateful to find themselves in the lime-tree-shaded central square of a small country town.

The square was entirely deserted; it was high noon and everyone was at home eating lunch. However, they noticed a tiny café and, peering through its window, spotted two *petits fonctionnaires*, the town postal clerk and the stationmaster, waiting to be served their meal—exactly the sort of men, de Groot was well aware, who "in any town always know the best place for lunch."

As, indeed, it proved to be. Madame bustled out of the kitchen to seat them herself. Perhaps they would like to begin with *les saucissons truffés bordelais* . . . followed by an *omelette aux fines herbes* . . . then some chops of *agneau pré-salé*—local lamb that had grazed on the salt marshes and was consequently already seasoned . . . ? Monsieur came over from the zinc-topped bar and gestured toward the café's back door, through which could be heard the cackling of chickens; if they preferred, he said, in a few moments one of those could be ready for the sauté pan.

All this sounded very good, but de Groot had picked up an unfamiliar but delicious aroma wafting from the kitchen. What, he asked Madame, was that? She hesitated a bit before responding. It was, she finally said, a family dish, an ordinary sort of stew, too plain a thing for gentlemen like themselves. De Groot demurred; it was *just* the sort of thing for a gentleman like himself. And the reader knows, even before he describes what happens next, that he is about to enjoy one of the best meals of his life.

> When the unknown dish was placed in the center of the table, it appeared as an enormous earthenware *toupin*, radiating warmth. The steaming fragrance, when the lid was lifted, made waiting almost unbearable. The gently bubbling stew appeared to be a close cousin of boeuf bourguignon but was cooked in the red wine of Bordeaux. The flavor of the wine was as if it were concentrated and yet softened. This effect was achieved, I was to learn later, by the use of sweet figs. The chunks of beef, pork, carrots, mushrooms, and onions were all covered and unified by a wine sauce thickened, not with flour, but with a distillation of mashed vegetables. Intrigued, I asked our host how long the dish had been cooking. "It has been on our fire for ten years, Monsieur!" Unbelievingly, I prodded: "In that time, how often has the pot been refilled?" "In ten years, Monsieur, the pot has never been

empty—each time we eat from it, we fill the pot up again with new ingredients, but the base remains the same—this is the concentration of flavor that forms the sauce." I asked about the wine in the pot. "It must be a good red Bordeaux, of course, and the vintage must be exactly as old as the dish."

It was at this point, I think, that I threw the book on the floor.

Even so, I've read a lot of culinary flummery over the years, and none of it has haunted me the way this passage has. The thing is, although every element of the story rings false, there is *something* beneath it that I nevertheless want to believe. Make no mistake, I have never thought that his story was true—it is more akin to wanting to believe in fairies. Except, in this instance, I'm not even sure what name to give to this longing: the best I've come up with is the romance of the pot.

It is the Cracked Pot that Lasts the Longest.

Excepting the harder vegetables the French boil absolutely nothing, in our meaning of the word at least. From Dunkerque to Bayonne, from Nice to Strasbourg, not one ounce of anything goes into the pot unless it be to make soup: but then the nation lives on soup. Roast meat costs too much for the everyday consumption of a population whose earnings average eighteenpence a-head: so they feed on a copious stew of bacon, sausage, cabbage, potatoes, and bread—and very good indeed it is.

—Frederic Marshall, *French Home Life* (1873)

Unlike, say, the pan or the kettle, the pot is less an implement of the home kitchen than its emblem—at least, of that room as it once was, dark and smoky, its walls coated with grease, and permeated with the smell of food. Because of this, the pot takes on an amorphous shape in our imagination, which is why it lends itself so easily to such compounds as *teapot* or *beanpot* or *potherb* or *potholder*.

Or, for that matter, *crackpot, fusspot*, and *stinkpot*. The connotations of the word *pot* in English often have an edge of condescension—even of contempt—about them. A *potshot*, for example, was originally an unconscionably easy shot fired out of hunger, not sport; a *potboiler* is a work written strictly for the money; *potluck* once meant a supper where you got what happened to be caught by the ladle and now means something thrown together any which way to feed the neighbors; and a *potwalloper* was a commoner who could gain the right to vote only by proving he had a fireplace in which to do his cooking.

Compare the image of a pot simmering on the stove with a spitted haunch of beef roasting over the fire: the meat, large, seared an appetizing brown, glistening with fat, fills the room with its presence; with it on the table before you, you can eat until you drop. The pot, on the other hand, hunches over its contents like a despotic cook. You can see nothing; only a whisper of aroma is allowed to escape from its confines. It will strike you as stingy, since the amount it contains is predetermined; as secretive, since there is no telling what is hidden inside it, even if you are allowed to lift up the lid and look; and as insubstantial, cooked into boneless, diluted stuff that lacks anything into which to really sink your teeth. There are few epithets as stinging as *potlicker*—a person so debased and doglike as to be willing to lap up the remains at the bottom of the pot.

Of course, nothing could be more spineless than a pot, which is all belly and—at least until recently—lacks any perceptible brawn. Traditionally, pots were made of fired clay. They started out fragile, and cooking made them more so—hence, the old adage "No water spilt nor pot broken," only half of which makes sense today. Because of this, they were given a bulbous—potbellied—shape to make them stronger and expose more of their surface to the heat. But that shape also underlined their vulnerability. To "go to pot" is to surrender unresistingly to a slide into self-indulgence—to let yourself go soft.

Sometime in the late 1860s, the British historian Frederic Marshall, author of *Population and Trade in France in 1861–62*, published a series of entertaining and insightful articles on French home life in *Blackwood's Magazine*. In them, he explains to his English readers how the French raise their children, conduct their marriages, dress themselves, furnish their homes, and manage their households, and, with great relish and much detail, how they go about preparing their meals.*

In fact, Marshall uses this account as an opportunity to lambaste the culinary habits of his native land, especially the British tendency to regard any food that cannot be roasted as somehow unworthy of no-

---

*This series of articles was itself collected into a book, *French Home Life*, published in 1873.

tice. He is particularly scornful of the English habit of boiling food and then tossing out the cooking liquid, which he calls "one of the most senseless acts to which human intelligence can descend; it is an inexcusable, unjustifiable, wanton folly."

How much better the French, who, with their unique culinary marriage of parsimony and gastronomy, have produced a cuisine in which even the water that has cooked the cauliflower is treated with respect; in which meat is bought in small portions and then has every atom of nutritional value cleverly extracted from it; and in which the first rule of cooking is, as might be expected from a nation gone to pot, *go softly.*

> French kitchen-ranges do not resemble those which are still so generally in use in England, where the same vast mass of coal goes on blazing itself away, whether its heat be employed to boil a kettle or to roast a sheep. In France, cookery is carried on with wood or charcoal fires, roused up to activity in five minutes when the time comes to use them. A fire to roast a chicken is made just big enough to serve the purpose; the combustion of a pennyworth of charcoal boils or stews the contents of two saucepans at the same time; directly the operation is complete the fire is covered up with ashes, or is put out. In the case of soups, and of the few other dishes which require hours of gentle simmering, the very nature of the process prohibits strong flame and its accompanying loss of fuel. *"Cuisinez doucement"* is the first counsel given to a beginner; and that means, amongst other things, never have a bigger or a hotter fire than you really want; for if you do you will waste money, and will burn your casseroles and their contents.

A hot fire will also crack your pot—at least if it is one of those clay pots that, in so many forms, were for generations an absolute familiar in the French kitchen. These pots must be handled gently and set over a gentle flame, and what emerges from them has itself been gentled: it is, in every sense, *bien cuit.* Such a pot in such a kitchen, rather than proving a hindrance, is a reflection and an abettor of a culinary philosophy based on the firm belief that haste makes waste. If a cracked pot does last the longest, it is because the cracking has served as an effective chastisement to the cook.

THE POT SITS ON THE STOVE
BUT IT DREAMS OF THE GARDEN.

Potage: a Jumblement of several sorts of Flesh and Fowl boil'd together with Herbs, and served up in the Broth, mix'd together after the French Fashion.

—Edward Phillips, *The New World of English Words*
(5th edition, 1696)

And therefore the French do well to begin [their dinner] with their
herbaceous pottage.

—John Evelyn, *Acetaria: A Discourse on Sallets* (1699)

The looming presence of the pot in the French culinary imagination is
revealed through a simple enumeration of some of the famous dishes
prepared in one—*petit salé aux lentilles, daube de boeuf à la provençale, navarin d'agneau printanier, blanquette de veau, boeuf à la
mode, haricot de mouton, bouillabaisse, boeuf bourguignon, cassoulet,
poulet en cocotte.* Add to this list such items as confit, pâtés and terrines, and the innumerable daubes and *garbures*, not to mention that
backbone of French peasant cooking the *potée*—the "copious stew" of
bacon, sausage, beans, cabbage, and the like, whose ultimate realization is the *pot-au-feu*—and the case is closed.

This, then, is the basic conjugation of French home cooking: *pot,
potage, potager,* with *pot* being the present, *potage* the future, and
potager the past tense. In current parlance, a *potage*—a thick creamy
soup that could serve as a meal but is usually eaten as a first course—
lies somewhere between the elegantly delicate consommé and the
heartier, gut-filling *potée.* But the original meaning was closer to that of
the English word *pottage,* which my dictionary still defines as "a thick
soup of vegetables [what the above-quoted writers meant by the words
Herbs and *herbaceous*] and often meat."

The word *potager* is more complicated, but it has always had something to do with the vegetables that are the essential part of a *potage*:
sometimes it referred to the person who cooked them, sometimes to the
person who grew them (an English writer described Monsieur de la
Quintinie, who abandoned the law to become head gardener at Ver-
sailles for Louis XIV, as "that haughty *potager*"), but most usually,
and now almost always, to the garden in which they are grown. As
Georgeanne Brennan, author of two books on the subject, explains:

A *potager* is a year-round garden whose purpose is to supply the kitchen on a daily basis with fresh vegetables and herbs. It is cyclical not linear, because even while being harvested in the current season, it is continually being replanted for the coming season. *Potagers* are an integral part of the French food tradition, and although their numbers are diminishing, a trip through France will reveal plots of land planted to vegetables in front of houses, along streambeds and railroad tracks, and behind blocks of urban flats.

A *potager*, then, is a kitchen garden, but a kitchen garden with a difference. American gardeners, even if they won't admit it, are in love with surfeit. The word that *garden* immediately brings to mind (second only, perhaps, to *weeds*) is *bounty*—the basket overflowing with tomatoes, the armload of cabbages, the garbage bags stuffed with zucchini or pole beans.

Although garden writers claim that this hoarding impulse is a remnant of our pioneer heritage, it may originate from the fact that in this country gardening is generally associated with growing flowers, not vegetables or fruit. And with flowers, massed effects are very pleasing, with one crowd of blooms following another as the seasons progress. This, though, is not the French way. As Brigitte Tilleray says in *Recipes from the French Kitchen Garden,*

> given a small piece of land, the French countryman will prefer to plant vegetables rather than flowers. The sight of leeks growing in a modest front garden may invite the foreign visitor to smile at such true French pragmatism, but it is only the result of a long history of social order. . . . Every Frenchman knows that passionate and constant work in the well-groomed kitchen garden will feed his family throughout the year.

Furthermore, in most American gardening households it is the gardener who sets the tune and the cook who must dance to it—one day dealing with a plethora of Kentucky Wonders and on the next a glut of summer squash. No wonder tomatoes and sweet corn are our favorite garden produce—vegetables on which almost everyone delights in gorging. In France, the gardener almost always *is* the cook, and it is the garden that is made to dance the jig.

The French are masters of the intensive gardening technique whereby what is to be eaten is always crowding on the heels of what is being eaten now—bean rows, for instance, taking over the pea patch, and bell peppers going in where the carrots have come out. More interesting still is the way certain plants provide food from the moment their sprouts start to appear: overplant your peas and you have lots of tiny, tender pea shoots; onion plants first offer up slender, chivelike spears, then small green onions, and, finally, the mature onions themselves. All this from a plot that is, by American standards, surprisingly small. As Tilleray explains—

> A family of four might require a space of only nine feet by twelve feet to provide leeks, tomatoes, beans, herbs, cabbages, radishes, and lettuces on a seasonal basis, [as well as] potatoes, onions, and winter squashes to be stored in a cool place and used as needed.

The relationship between the gardener/cook and the *potager* is both intimate and spontaneous, especially if, as is ideal, the plot lies just outside the kitchen door. In the morning, when the cook steps out to snip some calendula, nasturtiums, or sweet peas, she sees what is ripe and ready to eat, and these observations nudge themselves into the day's menu. Later, she will return to fill her *panier* with fennel, eggplant, some tomatoes, and a handful of herbs. If it is late spring, she might also pick some strawberries; if it is summer, a fat Charentais melon. And so it goes, all through the spring, the summer, the fall, and well into the winter months. Because, as the proverb says . . .

NOTHING IS HUNGRIER
THAN AN EMPTY POT.

> But the French cook, as frugal as she may be, requires that each dish shall be itself, with its full aroma, its full essence, its own character. She knows, by long experience, that poverty does not prevent the exercise of skill: it sets the latter off against the former—it replaces money by intelligence.
> —Frederic Marshall, *French Home Life* (1873)

In his meditation on our subject in *Figues sans barbarie* (1991), the noted French chef Alain Senderens argues that whereas the cooking of the skewer or the spit epitomizes the masculine domain of display (the successful hunter, the dispenser of bounty), the cooking of the pot symbolizes the feminine domain of the kitchen, family economy, and, by extension, the civilizing process itself:

> By boiling in water in a vessel, man brought food from the realm of nature to that of culture. Preparing food in this way leads to a genuine transformation of a raw ingredient, since boiling yields food that is usually very thoroughly cooked. From this instant, cooking came to indicate the cultural, intellectual, and technological level of a society.

Although you have to admire the ability of the French male to use the praising of women as a way to praise himself, this seems more clever than true—especially when you consider that in French *le pot* is masculine, while *la broche*, the spit, is feminine.

It is probably no more intellectually sound to approach this duality—the roasted versus the boiled—as a matter of temperament rather than of gender, but it is curious that the word *pot*—unlike, say, *marmite, daubière, poêlon, cocotte, bassine,* or *toupin*—has a stubborn, even cloddish, bluntness to it. It strikes one, that is, as coming not from the part of the French character that derives from the Latinate, Mediterranean south but from the part that has its origins in the dark and tribal north.

Etymologists commonly trace the word *pot* from the Latin *potare*, "to drink"—from which comes the noun *potus*, which means "a drink" and, by association, both a drunkard and the tankard that got him into that condition. This use of the word, although now obsolete, is a venerable part of the English language, but the Reverend Walter W. Skeat, Professor of Anglo-Saxon at Cambridge University, thought that the word *pot*, meaning "a cooking vessel," came from another source. In his *Etymological Dictionary of the English Language* (1898), he wrote, "This is one of the homely Celtic words: Irish *pota, potadh*, a pot, vessel; Gaelic *poit*; Welsh *pot*; Breton *pôd*."

Whether this is literally true we shall probably never know, but as an insight it is rich with suggestiveness. As it happens, none of the Spanish or Italian words for that vessel are related to *pot*. The Celts, however, not only do use it but have a cuisine based on its use. To think of Irish, Welsh, or Scottish dishes is most likely to think of something cooked in a pot, whether it is stew, porridge, boiled potatoes, cabbage, or soda bread. The center of the Celtic cottage is a fireplace, and in the center of the fireplace sits a pot.

The English, of course, don't think much of the Celts, whereas the French have always romanticized them. It is as if the particular temperament the cooking of the pot represents has been stripped by the English of all its admirable qualities and by the French of all its less savory ones. Or perhaps it is simply a matter of opposite perspectives on the same qualities. Here, I think of a comment made by Norman Douglas in *Siren Lands*:

> Bouillabaisse is only good because it is made by the French, who, if they cared to try, could produce an excellent and nutritious substitute out of cigar stumps and empty matchboxes.

This, depending on how you look at it, can be read as either a high compliment or a rather devastating insult, since who is to say that they never *have* cared to try? Certainly, such suspicions about the French have fueled English humor over the centuries.*

Not all Englishmen have felt this way, of course. There has always been a minority that has looked longingly at the French way of managing the things of the kitchen. I think especially of John Evelyn's gentle, touching sentence in the preface to his *Acetaria*, "I content myself with an humble Cottage, and a Simple Potagere"; and of that king of the Francophiles Ford Madox Ford, who wrote of Gringoire, the protagonist of one of his later novels, *No Enemy* (1929), and a thinly disguised stand-in for himself:

> But only Mme. Sélysette who had accompanied him into his English wilds from the distant South could have told you whether Gringoire was as economical in his cuisine as he professed to be. For he swore that the saviour of society would be the good but excellently economical cook. . . . How Gringoire proposed to save the world by intensive kitchen gardening and exquisite but economical cookery may appear hereafter.

---

*Here, for instance, is Jonathan Swift, in his *Directions to Servants* (1745): "If a lump of soot falls into the soup, and you cannot conveniently get it out, stir it well in, and it will give the soup a high French taste."

And the letters Ford wrote to his lover, Stella Bowen, from the rural laborer's cottage in Sussex to which he retreated after the war are a veritable paean to the *potager*:

> The beans flowered today—& I like their scent best of all scents—
> & an orange tree appeared, and the borage & thyme & sweet
> marjoram are all hard at work growing & there will be oceans &
> oceans of vegetables & eggs & things.

In his plot he had put—besides the beans—peas, radishes, carrots, onions, lettuce, beets, marrows, fennel, parsley, cress, mint, sage, and spinach, and he wanted more.

I have planted many gardens in my life, but none of them has ever resembled a real *potager*. The reason is that to manage one properly, you have to work like the devil. Intensive gardening is just what it sounds like—there's always something to be rooted out and discarded and fresh seedlings to be planted in its place. The plot needs to be watered and weeded, the vegetables need to be picked and eaten, that day, every day.

And not just one vegetable either. To the French gardener/cook, the fact that today the garden has provided a cabbage, a turnip, and a leek or two, as well as celery, green beans, peas, white haricot beans, and potatoes, comes as good news. It means that a hearty *potée lorraine*, complete with pig's tail, saltback, and a chunk of pickled pork, will soon be bubbling in the pot. Chances are, however, that such vegetable-laden fare will seem a tempting notion to me maybe once or twice a year, and then in the middle of winter. On the whole, when it comes to vegetables, I want "or or or or," not "and and and and."

Here, then, is the paradox. What John Evelyn's "humble cottage and simple potagere" calls to my mind is something peaceful and quiet, an image of a little house with flowers in every room and a bowl of fresh-picked tomatoes on the kitchen table. For me, *pot, potage, potager* is the litany of a quiet life, the slow time of the countryside—a respite from the battle fatigue brought on by the hurlyburly of today. For the French, many of whom still nurture their rural roots, however far they may have moved away from them, there is certainly this aspect, too. But the phrase coheres around a hunger for a sort of eating that I, in my heart of hearts, have no real comprehension of nor appetite for.

A Well-Seasoned Pot Needs no Meat
to Make the Broth Taste Good.

It is a fact that great eaters of meat are in general more cruel and
ferocious than other men.

—Jean-Jacques Rousseau, *Émile* (1762)

The French would be the best cooks in Europe if they had got any
butcher's meat.

—Walter Bagehot, *Biographical Studies* (1880)

When it comes to meat, it is the French who are pragmatic and the
British wildly idealistic. The French eat as much meat as anyone; their
failure from the Anglo-Saxon perspective is in not regarding the idea of
it with proper deference. To eat frogs' legs or horse meat (as the French
still do) is to treat meat-eating with insufficient seriousness—in fact, it
seems to treat it almost as if it were a joke. A cuisine with real respect
for meat constantly strives to serve the best meat in the best way possible—not to toss in a chunk of this and a chunk of that and a chunk of
something else, depending on what is on hand or cheap at the market
that day.

In American cooking, too, it is the meat that is always put first. The
question "What's for dinner?" is really asking "What *meat* are we having for dinner?"—and if the answer includes specific cuts that are to be
grilled or roasted, we are all the happier.

The pot, by its very nature, can only blur such distinctions. In this
regard, it is like the stomach: it doesn't worship meat, it merely digests
it. Hence, from the French perspective, it civilizes it. More important, it
civilizes *us*.

One of my earliest serious efforts as a cook was to make a classic
French dish called *gigot d'agneau à la sept heures*—leg of lamb cooked
for seven hours. If you aren't familiar with this dish, the meat is roasted
for about an hour and then cooked for six hours more in a bath of
herb-and-garlic-suffused white wine. The result, I was promised, would
be lamb as I had never tasted it before, so tender and succulent it could
be eaten with a spoon.

This image swept away all before it—until, at the end of cooking, I
opened the heavy, blue-enameled Le Creuset casserole . . . and anticipation gave way to a mixture of rage and grief. I had transformed some-

thing from which I could have carved and eaten thick slices of pink, juicy meat edged with crispy fat into a huge gray lamb *pot roast*. I don't remember how it tasted, how spoon-tender it was or wasn't, only that I ate it with actual tears in my eyes. I was poor then, and that leg of lamb was so very, very expensive.

The truth is, I just didn't get it—a realization that now comes as no surprise. You can master countless recipes for French dishes and still have not a clue as to what French cooking really is. It's exactly like the language: it's hard enough to speak it like a native, but not nearly as hard as it is to *understand* it like one.

Take this business of meat. The Anglo-American pursuit of it is really about the pursuit of status. There are only so many prime cuts around, so every time you eat one you confirm your place in the hierarchy—and not only the social hierarchy. When I was a child, my parents would often eat steak, while we kids were fed hamburgers. We *liked* hamburgers, but the point wasn't the meal but the message. To this day, the sight of a porterhouse or strip steak in the butcher's case fills me with powerful feelings of covetousness and deprivation—not such a bad way, perhaps, to describe what it is like to live in a meat-obsessed culture.

As I discovered with my leg of lamb, the pot inverts the conventional hierarchy. In it, the cheapest cut works the best. The pot offers the cook the safest form of subversion, thumbing its nose at the establishment not by revolting against it but by living well despite it, and that same inversion is bestowed on the family as well. Even if Papa claims the largest pieces of meat for himself, they have already surrendered most of their flavor and nutrition to the broth. Everybody gets their share.

In other words, whereas a piece of grilled meat represents the last bastion of the rights of the individual, the cooking pot is the paternal protector and arbiter of the family and the family appetite. Listen to Jane Grigson writing in *Good Things* about pot-au-feu, literally "pot-on-the-fire," the most majestic of all French boiled meals:

> Many Frenchmen, it seems, have a button labelled pot-au-feu. Press it, and you'll be swamped with nostalgia—cosy kitchen, fire on the hearth, pot bubbling as it hangs from the pot crane, mother flinging in vegetables, the pervading smell, the wonderful beef, wonderful mother, those were the days.

Going home: that is what the romance of the bubbling pot is all about. What it promises is that within its depths what has been lost and missed is still there, decades of simmering having mellowed out any lingering bitterness or regret. Instead, it has been refined into something richly and subtly delicious—the taste of not only your own childhood but that of your father and of your father's father.

At least, such is the myth. In reality, of course, such a pottage, no matter the quality of its original ingredients, would have soon cooked down into a sourish, flat-flavored mush. De Groot knew this, too. His dish is no more suited for eternal cooking than is any other pottage. He surely was also aware that this story was a trope already worn to tatters by French food writers, however unfamiliar it might have been on this side of the Atlantic. Was he himself still susceptible to its spell? Or did he hope that it would touch the imagination of American readers wholly unaware of the resonance to be found in an old cooking pot?

Perhaps it was a bit of all these things, tinged with regret for the passing, in France as everywhere else, of that emblematic center of kitchen life. Even those with the most modest of incomes can now afford a more up-to-date *batterie de cuisine*—tossing the old clay and cast-iron pots, along with all the memories that have soaked into their pores, on the rubbish heap. As for those that have replaced them . . .

NOTHING IS AS LOST IN THE KITCHEN AS A NEW POT.

POT-AU-FEU

You have to be at least 30 years old to enjoy Pot-au-Feu. Before reaching this prophetic age, you cannot appreciate good things. You may consider the pot-au-feu commonplace, and as you do with its old pal, boiled beef, scorn it. This is a terrible mistake, but it is rectified as the years pass by. There is nothing better than a well made pot-au-feu when cooks deign to give it all their attention and care.
—Marthe Daudet, *Les bons plats de France* (1919)

For the French, pot-au-feu is many things before it is a recipe: an eating experience, a philosophy of cooking, a spiritual restorative, an exercise in nostalgia. It offers the chance to sustain a state of pious innocence while gorging with gluttonous abandon, since to feast on the food that ordinarily provides basic sustenance is to feel prodded by the hunger of poverty, the knowledge that such a feast is merely a moment's release from a lifetime of fasting.

Our own American boiled dinner of corned beef, turnips, potatoes, and cabbage springs from similar origins, and, if properly prepared, is quite equal to it in deliciousness, especially if made (as we do) with a good cut of braising beef instead of commercial, mass-produced corned beef. Unsurprisingly, then, Matt and I found ourselves more interested in a version of pot-au-feu that might be made with other vegetables and prepared in another way than one that essentially replicated a dish with which we were already intimately familiar.

Wean a pot-au-feu away from the caloric density that once served as its *raison d'être*, and what remains is the deliciousness of a homemade, deeply flavored beef broth—and the vegetables that have been gently simmered in it. Such a pot-au-feu, we felt, would work best if the flavor of the vegetables were not allowed to dominate the dish, and so, essentially, we turned the traditional version on its head. The recipe that follows is selective rather than inclusive, market- rather than garden-oriented, and, especially, geared to make less rather than more.

Even today, most pot-au-feu recipes call for two or more cuts of beef in order to achieve a broth with rich flavor and gelatinous depth. In the beginning, this is how we made ours, until we discovered that a top blade roast by itself produced just this sort of broth and—unlike many pot-roast cuts, no matter how long you cook them—was amazingly tender as well.

POSTMODERN POT-AU-FEU
[*serves 4 to 6*]

To make this dish, 3 pieces of cooking equipment are all but essential: an instant-read meat thermometer, a heat diffuser, and a heavy covered pot about 5 or 6 inches deep and 8 or 9 inches wide. This is a two-day recipe, so plan accordingly.

DAY ONE:
1 3-pound top blade roast (see note)
coarse sea salt or kosher salt

1 teaspoon olive oil

3 small onions, peeled and halved

a bouquet garni consisting of 3 whole cloves, 12 peppercorns, ½ teaspoon dried thyme, and an imported bay
leaf, tied together in cheesecloth

DAY TWO:

1 tablespoon olive oil

1 clove garlic, minced

2 or 3 carrots, peeled and cut into bite-sized chunks

2 large or 3 small leeks, trimmed well

1 celery root, the size of a softball (see note)

4 to 6 thick slices of crusty peasant-style bread (see note)

The day before: Put the beef into a Dutch oven or similar heavy pot—if possible, one large enough for the meat to lie flat. Fill the pot half-full with cold water. Stir in a teaspoon of salt and bring everything to an active simmer over high heat. When the water begins to bubble, lower the heat and let cook, bubbling gently all the while, for 5 minutes. Then remove the meat to a plate, discard the cooking liquid, and scrub the pot clean of scum. Rinse any scum from the meat itself and return it to the clean pot.

Meanwhile, heat the olive oil in a small skillet and place the onion halves in it, facedown. Sauté over medium-high heat until the cut surfaces are tinged with brown. (Don't let them scorch.) Remove the pan from the heat.

Press the sautéed onion halves and the bouquet garni into the spaces between the meat and the pot, then add just enough fresh cold water to cover the meat, about 3 cups. Sprinkle over another teaspoon of the coarse salt. Rest the top of an instant-read thermometer on the edge of the pot, making sure its tip reaches into the cooking liquid but doesn't touch the bottom. Then cover the pot with the lid, using its edge to hold the thermometer in place. Turn up the heat, bring the temperature of the contents of the pot up to somewhere between 170°F and 175°F, and keep it there, using a heat diffuser as needed. Cook the meat for 8 hours, checking the thermometer occasionally and adjusting the flame to keep the temperature constant.

At the end of the 8 hours, congratulate yourself if the temperature has never reached 180°F. Remove the meat and place it in a large, non-reactive loaf pan, discarding the onions. Pour the broth over the meat, and let everything cool down for 15 minutes. Then transfer to the refrigerator and cover with plastic wrap when entirely cool.

The day of the pot-au-feu: Take the pan with the meat and broth from the refrigerator and scrape the hardened beef fat from the surface, reserving a tablespoon or so. Remove the meat from the broth and set it on a cutting board. Put the broth in a small pan, bring it to a boil, and reduce it by a third.

Put the tablespoon of olive oil and the reserved beef fat into a large (12-inch) skillet and set this over medium heat. Add the minced garlic and, stirring, cook this in the hot fat until translucent. Add the carrots and let these cook for 10 minutes, stirring occasionally with a spatula.

Meanwhile, prepare the leeks. If the stalks are ½-inch thick or less, cut them whole into 1-inch lengths. Otherwise, slice them in half vertically and cut these halves into 1-inch lengths. Put these into a colander and rinse thoroughly, drain well, and add to the carrots. Stir the pan contents occasionally while preparing the celery root.

Use a stiff-bristled kitchen brush to scrub any loose dirt from the celery root, then pare it down to the white flesh with a sharp knife. Cut the flesh into chunks about the same size as the carrot pieces. Add these to the carrots and leeks, stir well, and pour in half a cup of the hot beef broth. Cover, lower the heat, and gently simmer until the vegetables are just tender, about 20 minutes.

In the meantime, cut the beef into generous bite-sized pieces, cutting out and discarding the wedge of cartilage. When the vegetables are all but done, add the beef to the sauté pan and gently stir until well heated.

Lightly toast or grill the thick slices of bread and set each at the bottom of a large soup bowl, trimming them, if necessary, to fit. Heap these with the vegetables and meat. Finally, apportion the remaining beef broth equally among the bowls. Serve at once, with extra slices of toasted bread on the side and a hearty but not too fruity red wine. Traditional accompaniments include a bowl of coarse salt, Dijon mustard, and cornichons.

Cook's Notes. The top blade roast is not often found in supermarkets, since it is usually cut into blade steaks—small boneless chuck steaks with a wedge of cartilage running through their center. People are used to trimming a piece of steak as they eat it but don't care to excise cartilage from their slices of pot roast. Ask the supermarket butcher to cut the roast from the same part from which he takes the steaks—and don't give the cartilage a thought; the long cooking will soften it nicely.

Celery root (also called celeriac) is a root vegetable with the texture of artichoke heart and the taste of celery, only more delicate. Peeled and cubed turnips, a more traditional choice, may be substituted (and added to the pan at the same time).

The bread needs to have a dense, chewy texture to stand up to its soaking in the broth. As an alternative (or in addition), steam new potatoes separately and serve them with the pot-au-feu.

POTATOES & POINT

🌿 🌿 🌿

1

When evening sets in Paddy puts on the pot,
To boil the dear praties and serve them up hot.
                              —*Whistle-Binkie* (1832)

The poor peasants, men, women, and children, were gathering
seaweed, loading their horses, asses, and backs with it, to manure
the wretched little patches of potatoes sown among the rocks.
"Three hundred and sixty-five days a year we have the potato,"
said a young man to me bitterly. "The blackguard of a Raleigh
who brought 'em here entailed a curse upon the labourer that has
broke his heart. Because the landholder sees we can live and work
hard on 'em, he grinds us down in our wages, and then despises
us because we are ignorant and ragged."
  —Asenath Nicholson, *Ireland's Welcome to the Stranger* (1847)

Their universal sustenance is the root named Potato, cooked by
fire alone; and generally without condiment or relish save an unknown condiment named *Point*, into the meaning of which I have
vainly inquired; the victual *Potatoes-and-Point* not appearing,
at least with specific accuracy of description, in any European
Cookery-Book whatever.
                      —Thomas Carlyle, *Sartor Resartus* (1871)

Tradition has it that Sir Walter Raleigh planted the first potato in Ireland in 1585, but tradition does not explain why anyone cared. What
was it about the potato that made a whole people not only take to it
but become so dependent on it that, centuries later, more than a million

of them would starve or flee when the crop began to fail? For that matter, why, *after* the Great Famine, did they continue to plant them and eat them to the point that to think of Irish food is to think of potatoes—even before the images of fresh sweet butter and soda bread. But what does one think even so? There's a bit and more of Irish in me—my mother's mother was a Doyle—but it was all washed out of us before I came along. I love potatoes, I eat them often, but I don't taste them with an Irish mouth.

To start to think about potatoes like an Irishman, one has to ask first not about the potato but about Sir Walter—what was *he* doing in Ireland at all? Answer: The aggressive acquisitional spirit of the Elizabethan Age that impelled the English to explore the New World also fired their conquest of the Emerald Isle. Indeed, it is from about 1600 that historians date the beginning of modern Ireland. The English, then, encountered the Irish and the American Indian at the same time, and were confounded by them both. Any civilization that had little use for cities or for the cultural values that make cities necessary seemed to them to be no civilization at all.

Like the American Indian, the Irish had a sense of propriety and a sense of property, but the demarcations of these were fluid—and less hierarchical than the English were prepared to recognize. The Irish counted their wealth in horses and wanted space to graze and ride them, so they marked property boundaries with ditches instead of walls. Irish women drank alcohol, presided at feasts, and—to English discomfort—greeted strangers with a social kiss. Under Irish law, they could keep their own names after marriage, and divorce was easy. The children, it was commonly agreed, were too much indulged and too little disciplined.

All the Irish loved poetry. At heart theirs was an oral culture, and poets were powerful participants in it. Their eloquence still made and unmade the reputations of both the living and the dead. In the shadowy, firelit halls, they touched their harps and sang of love and war; the English professed to hear songs of lust and vulgar brawling.

Cattle were also wealth, and Irish land law allowed for seasonal shifts in their grazing. The Irish were not nomads, but there was the great summer "booleying"—the movement of the herds to and from the upland pastures. The Irish ate beef but did not like to slaughter their young cattle to get it; their diet was essentially dairy-based or, in some instances—to English horror—dairy mixed with blood taken from the living beast, something African Masai herdsmen still do (and, as Sir Edmund Spenser noted at the time, a practice of the ancient Scythians as well). The Irish historian R. F. Foster writes of this diet:

> With their griddle-cakes, mutton, curds and buttermilk, the food of the native Irish in 1600 would have been rather like that in pastoral regions of India today. The dietetic balance was good, and descriptions of the people's physique bear this out: well-shaped, agile, rarely overweight. English observers were surprised that the rich and various resources of fish and wildfowl were not tapped by the natives: fishing, for instance, tended to be monopolized by foreigners. . . . Similarly, although surrounded by deer, the Irish were not great eaters of venison, nor great hunters. Although the Normans introduced cereals and pulses, the preference in the Gaelic diet was for raw salads of watercress.

The ordinary Irish enjoyed their bit of mutton or goat and the occasional chicken but did not hunger for meat with the anxiety of the English, upon whom it conferred status and gentility. Instead, they got their protein and much of the rest of their nutrition by drinking milk: fresh milk, sour milk, clotted milk, and buttermilk, and they ate cream, butter, curds, and cheese. This milk came from cows, yes, but the Irish also savored the milk of deer, goats, and sheep. *Bán-bhia*, they called it, or "white meat." As the eighteenth-century traveler and writer John Stevens noted:

> The Irish are the greatest lovers of milk I have ever met, which they drink in about twenty different ways, and what is strangest they love it best when it is sourest.

Best of all was buttermilk. "The most refreshing drink in the world," says Irish food writer Bríd Mahon in *Land of Milk and Honey: The Story of Traditional Irish Food and Drink*:

> Full-cream milk was rarely if ever drunk, except by the young, the elderly or the ill. Adults invariably drank skim milk or buttermilk. The young . . . up to the age of nine or ten years were fed *leamh-nacht* or fresh [whole] milk. As they got older they were gradually introduced to mixed milk: two thirds sweet milk and one third

sour milk. This last was not sour milk as we know it today but the milk left over in the timber churn when the *bainne géar*—sour whole milk—had been churned and the butter removed. . . . The addition of the churned milk made a very pleasant drink, wholesome and easy to digest with a slight flavor of tartness: "something to go down through your tongue," as the saying goes.

Buttermilk: the Irish were connoisseurs of it. Irish women washed their faces in it; turf cutters buried a pot of it in the bog to keep cool until they thirsted for it. It was considered a cure for hangover drunk straight and a cure for whatever else ailed you heated with a clove of garlic. It leavened the Irish hearth breads. The English called it "bony-clabber" and blenched when it was offered to them, as it often was, for in prosperous times visitors were greeted at even the poorest hovels with bumper mugs of it, served up still warm and frothy from the churn.

Not surprisingly, the invaders cut down the forests through which the Irish loved to wander (and into which Irish resisters easily vanished), walled up the grazing land into estates, and helped themselves to the cattle and the horses. In return, they gave the Irish the potato— although *gave* is much too generous a term, since they had no idea what they were about. The potato had only just arrived in England, and when Raleigh, out of curiosity, brought some over to plant at his Irish plantation, legend has it that he wasn't at all sure what part of it to eat.*

The English wouldn't work that out for another hundred years. (Stephen Switzer may have helped turn the tide when, in 1733, he wrote in the first volume of *The Practical Husbandman and Planter* that the potato was actually an "exceedingly useful and delightful food, not only for the vulgar, but also for the tables of the curious" and "that which was heretofore reckon'd a food fit only for Irishmen, and clowns, is now become the diet of the most luxuriously polite.") In Ireland, however, the pratie, as they came to call it (pronounced PRAY-dee,

---

*Historians now speculate that the Spanish may have first brought the crop to Ireland. Trade was brisk between Spain and Ireland in the seventeenth century, and the newly introduced plant became an important agricultural crop in Ireland long before it did so in England. It wasn't grown in the United States until Irish immigrants brought it over in the eighteenth century.

from the Gaelic *práta* or *préata*), prospered from the beginning. The land was soft and moist and the climate the same ("gardens full of rosemary, laurel and sweet herbs, which the cold of England often destroyeth," noted Fynes Moryson enviously in 1626). Everything here suited the potato, including poverty. Luxuriousness had little to do with it—and would soon have even less.

You can see it slipping in: like *bán-bhia*, the pratie was also "white meat," and it made a delicious complement to Irish food, while, at the same time, it gradually began to *supplant* Irish food. As each century passed, less and less common land was available for grazing. Forced to find their living on smaller and smaller plots of land, able only to support a single cow or a handful of goats, the rural Irish could no longer subsist on dairy. The potato, flourishing all the while, began to bulk larger and larger in their diet.

❊ ❊ ❊

As recently as two hundred years ago, the patterns of Irish rural life were much more diverse and occupations less defined than we can today easily imagine. Ireland was not originally a feudal land of squires and serfs; rural life was more of a piece. Sheep and goats were brought to pasture, pigs driven into the forests to eat mast, geese and ducks herded to nearby wetlands in the morning and home again at sunset. Wild berries were gathered, wild greens picked, rabbits snared, and turf cut for fuel.

Such a rural culture is something different from—and more interesting than—a culture of farmers. Farmers are land owners. We are so accustomed to rural land as owned land that we forget that it isn't for the herdsman's benefit that cows and horses are bound in by fences. When land becomes owned, definitions sharpen: between landed and landless, rich and poor, the "responsible" and the "shiftless."

This is what happened in Ireland, an event that was accelerated, strangely, by the Napoleonic Wars. With all of mainland Europe torn by strife, Eire became granary to the continent and prospered accordingly. With plenty of farm work for all, the population soared. Then Napoleon was exiled for good on Saint Helena; the war was over; the Irish economy collapsed. Suddenly there were too many people with little means of support; landlords plowed over the wheat fields and turned to cattle. Farm laborers became a glut on the market.

Even so, for a time, to the dismay—even rage—of the landlords, the beloved potato allowed some of the old fluidity to remain. Miraculously prolific, it is also the only single cheap food that can support life as a sole diet—especially if there is something like milk on hand to supplement the potato where it is nutritionally weakest. Furthermore, potatoes are extremely easy to grow. In his study of the potato in Ireland, Kenneth Connell wrote:

> For the lazy man there was no crop like it. It needed merely a few days' planting in the Spring, possibly earthing in the Summer, and a few days' digging in the Winter.

Notice the condescension in that "lazy man." Better to say, "For survival, there is no crop like it." Potatoes, in the Irish climate, yielded nine tons an acre; half an acre would feed a family—with the husband, if he did laboring work, alone eating ten pounds or so of them a day. Once they were put in, he was free to go to work where he could find it: sometimes right at home spinning, weaving, and sprigging linen; elsewise away. Bríd Mahon writes:

> The restless, ambitious man might spend his summer lifting the harvest on an English or Scottish farm, or hewing stones in an American quarry, for it was not unknown for men to emigrate to the New World for half the year and then make the long and arduous journey back home. The families of the absent worker often took to the roads to beg or seek seasonal work, but made sure to return home when the days began to shorten.

Still, there was one problem with the potato, which helps explain why the family might be forced to take to the road. A supply of potatoes never lasted the whole year, since at a certain point, no matter how carefully kept, they would sprout and rot. Nine months was the average time they would last, eleven the best that could be hoped for.* This

---

*In her memoir of growing up on an Irish farm, *To School Through the Fields*, Alice Taylor describes the potato harvest being stored away in an outdoor potato pit. This was "a six-foot-long trench that was about two feet deep and three feet wide. Butt loads of potatoes were poured into it and stacked high, and then thatched with straw to ward off the rain and frost."

meant that July was the terrible month. Those with a few pence bought oats or barley or Indian meal; those without lived on wild herbs— shamrock (here meaning sorrel), nettles, and, notoriously, wild mustard (*praiseach*). Biddy White Lennon explains in *The Poolbeg Book of Traditional Irish Cooking*:

> As a sole food, [*praiseach*] is unwholesome and turned their complexions as yellow as the flowers of the plant. The clergy recognised it as poor food and banned it in some places. July became known as "the yellow month," "hungry July" or "staggering July."

Despite such problems, the rural Irish poor had no real choice. On a small plot, nothing else could keep them fed and support as well a pig and a few chickens, who ate what was not wanted or not found edible by the family. For good and ill, as the nineteenth century progressed, the potato not only dominated the diet of the poor—by the time of the Great Famine, it *was* the diet.

There had already been fourteen partial or complete potato famines in Ireland between 1816 and 1842. But in the autumn of 1845 a new fungus disease—*phytophthora infestans*—struck the Irish potato, spreading with cruel rapidity and unpredictability in moist, mild conditions. In a matter of days, it could turn a healthy green field of potato plants black; within a few weeks the buried tubers themselves collapsed into a rotten, putrefying mass.

It would be a hundred years before the rot was correctly identified as a fungal infection; in the meantime, the British blamed the disease on Irish laziness—their shameful dependence on the single, easy crop. The Peel administration sent cornmeal to Ireland as emergency relief, which the Irish soon came to hate—as well they might, since, as sole sustenance, it gave them pellagra. Whether intended or not, the emergency measures worked to the advantage of the landed; by the time the worst had passed, well over a million Irish poor had died or fled. Many things vanished entirely, like the art of Irish wine- and cheesemaking, and, worst of all, the heart was cut out of the living rural culture.

2

"And all you have for your labour is the potato?" "That's all, ma'am, that's all; and it's many of us that can't get the sup of milk with 'em, no, nor the salt; but we can't help it, we must be content with what the good God sends us."

It was nearly three o'clock when I reached my destination, and made my way to the cabin through a muddy lane. There were two pigs, two dogs, two cats, and two batches of chickens just introduced upon the theater of action, enclosed in a niche in the wall, a huge pile of potatoes had been poured upon the table for the workmen and children, a hole in the mud floor served for the pigs and poultry to take their "bit," wooden stools and chairs to sit down upon, and a pot not inferior in size to any fire's made up my environment. . . . When my thoughts were a little collected, I said, "Well, my boys, the lumpers I see are ready."

—Asenath Nicholson, *Ireland's Welcome to the Stranger* (1847)

On May 16, 1844, a solitary woman stood on the deck of the steamer *Brooklyn* as it set sail from New York City to Ireland. She was nearly fifty, a widow, living in Manhattan on a small income, keeping herself busy with various good works (a disciple of Sylvester Graham, she opened a Graham Temperance Boarding-House and wrote *Nature's Own Book*, which advocated a militant, nuts-and-berries vegetarianism). Her name was Asenath Nicholson, and she was about to produce one of the great travel narratives of her century, *Ireland's Welcome to the Stranger, or Excursions through Ireland in 1844 and 1845 for the Purpose of Personally Investigating the Conditions of the Poor.* We shall simply call it *Ireland's Welcome to the Stranger.*

The book's full title tells much. She had become shocked and disturbed at the condition of Irish immigrants—half-starved and in total poverty—who were fleeing the Famine. She visited them in their New York City garrets and cellars, and decided—as far as I can discern, completely on her own—to go to Ireland and investigate conditions there for herself,

to sit down in their cabins, and there learn what soil has nurtured, what hardships have disciplined a race so patient and so impetuous, so revengeful and so forgiving, so proud and so humble, so obstinate and so docile, so witty and so simple.

Contemptuous of the popular Irish travel narratives of the time, where all was viewed through the reverse telescope of affluence, she determined to go to the Irish poor in their very hovels and to eat, live, and sleep with them there. And this is exactly what she did; more even, perhaps, than she planned. Unwilling to carry any but the smallest amounts of money on her person and not understanding the (at best) erratic nature of transcontinental mails, she often found herself dependent on the generosity and compassion of the people she had come to help. She would travel miles on foot through the worst imaginable weather, with only a penny to her name, hoping that an expected letter containing funds might be waiting for her at her next destination. There often wasn't, and she had to either walk on or back, this time with nothing in her pocket.

I wish there were space here to do credit to this wildly eccentric and wholly admirable woman, who against all advice climbed mountains on her knees so as to see the view, wandered in the most dangerous of places in the dead of night because she was bored or disgusted with her lodgings, and hobnobbed with paupers, convicts, and—to her fellow Protestants, far worse—Catholic priests. She came away full of admiration for some of them, and dared to write about it. What she has given our narrative is an observant and sympathetic view of Irish cottage life, tempered by a vegetarian sensibility that saw nothing strange—only admirable—in a potato-based diet. Through her eyes we are able to penetrate to a deeper level of empathetic insight into the intimate relationship between a foodstuff and those who depend on it for their very lives.

One of her many descriptions of meals shared in the cabins of the Irish poor begins when she is caught in a raging storm on foot on the road to Galway and realizes that she simply cannot go on.

In despair I stood; when looking to my left I saw at a distance a cabin, and a little girl standing in the door. She was gazing at me, as I supposed, from idle curiosity, and, as the last alternative, I hesitatingly turned towards the dreary abode. "Welcome, welcome, stranger, from the stawrm; ye're destroyed. I told the little gal to open the door and stand in it, that ye mightn't think we was shuttin' ye out in the stawrm; we've got a good fire and plenty of turf; and though the cabin is small, and not fittin' for sich a lady as ye, I'll make it better than the mad stawrm without; and I'll soon heave over a pot of potatoes, and get ye a sup of milk, and I wish my wife was here. I'm but a stranger; but here since Monday." All this passed before I had time to tell my country, pedigree, or business in Ireland. A huge pile of blazing turf soon dried my clothes, and I was sitting "high and dry" against the heels of a coach horse, who was taking his lunch from a pile of straw at the foot of a bed. In an hour the potatoes were ready, and the kind little girl brought me a broken soup-plate with two eggs on it, and a "sup of milk." The eggs I gave to a coachman who had dropped in to exchange horses, and took some salt and my tea-spoon, which I carried in my pocket; and upon a stool by the side of the pot, on which a basket was placed containing the lumpers, I ate my supper with the family and coachman, not only with a cheerful, but a grateful heart.

Very likely, the house is built of stone and the roof of thatch. There is a fireplace and possibly a chimney—otherwise, the smoke simply makes its way out the door. The floor is dirt and the room almost empty of furniture: there are some stools and a bed. Against one wall is stacked a pile of cut turf or peat. We already understand what the host means when he says that "I'm but a stranger; but here since Monday"—he has been off working somewhere distant and just recently come home.

Before we discuss the meal, a word should be said about the presence of the horse. Asenath Nicholson discovered that the Irish gave house room to a wide range of animals, not only what we call house pets—dogs and cats—but goats, chickens, geese, cows, horses, and pigs. This was not out of the ignorance of poverty; they genuinely enjoyed their company.

The English were particularly shocked by the presence of the pigs, but the truth is, given the chance, pigs are cleanly animals, and smart—they can learn their place:

> The family pigs snored snugly in their cribs, and, in all justice, I must say that these pigs were well-disciplined, for when one of them awoke and attempted to thrust his nose into a vessel not belonging to him, he was called a dirty pig, and commanded to go to his own kettle, which he did as tamely as a child or a dog would have done.

Another pig encounter occurred when she spent the night atop a pile of oat straw in a spare room. At cockcrow, a side door to the outside flew open with a bang, and in walked

a majestic pig, weighing three hundred-weight, and moving towards my bed, elevated his nose and gave me a hearty salute. I
said "Good-morning, sir," and he turned to the oaten straw and
made himself busy, till the mistress entered, and I asked her if she
would do me the favour to lead out my companion. She heeded it
not, but walked away. In a few moments she returned, and a little
more entreatingly I said, "Madam, will you be so good as to take
out this pig?" She was angry at my repeated solicitations, but finally took away the pig into the kitchen, with a mutter, "what
harrum?" and violently shut the door.

What I love is that the good woman, instead of shooing the pig back
outside to the yard, takes the monster back into the kitchen with her.

❧ ❧ ❧

No discussion of such a meal can begin without noticing what is prominently missing: a table. Tables are not universally absent in her visits to
the cottages, but one learns from Claudia Kinmonth in *Irish Country
Furniture: 1700–1950* (see pages 269–72) that they were a relative
rarity and often viewed as an encumbrance. The focal point of Irish
cottage life was the hearth: a turf fire provided heat, light, and company. It was the custom of household intimates to sit before it. As anyone who has regularly eaten before a fireplace will know, in such a
situation a table only gets in the way, and consequently, even in prosperous rural Irish households, a table for eating was often seen as af-
fectation and out of place.

   Nor was such a table needed. The centerpiece of a cottage's *batterie
de cuisine* was a huge cast-iron pot: huge because it had to cook very
many potatoes indeed (twenty pounds of them or more were easily required for a meal); so huge that it regularly performed the duties of a
table itself. Depending on the season, a child was sent either to dig up
the potatoes from the ground or to gather them from under the bed.
Sometimes they were scraped (*not* peeled, an act that slices away too
much of the nutritious layer next to the skin), but often they were not.
They were scrubbed clean of dirt and put into the pot; the pot was put
directly on the fire and the potatoes were boiled until they were done.

   When they were tender, someone held a shallow wicker basket
called a skib (from the Gaelic *sciobóg*) over a hole in the floor and the
potatoes were poured out. The potato water, when cooled, was—with

the peels and any leftovers—for the pig. The other, human, eaters gathered on their stools around the skib, which was set down before the fire

on top of the now empty pot. In the poorest households, the buttermilk, if there was any, was likewise shared from a single mug.

> The potatoes must be eaten from the hand, without knife, fork, or plate; and the milk taken in sups from the mug. I applied my nails to divesting the potato of its coat, and my hostess urged the frequent use of the milk.

As we shall see, the Irish have always been particular about how their potatoes are cooked; Irish cookbooks still have much to say on so simple-seeming a matter as boiling them.* This particularly extends to the flavor of different varieties, and Nicholson's reference to "lumpers" shows that we are in the presence of dire poverty. Those who could afford to planted such low-yield but flavorful varieties as "apples" and "minions." Lumpers were large and prolific rather than choice; a companion variety, "cups," was described in an American seed book of the time as "strongly flavored when cooked. Unfit for table use."

Salt was a valuable commodity and kept carefully in a salt-box hung beside the fire. This had a sloping lid that lifted up to allow the cook easy access and then fell shut again to keep out smoke smut and dust. When there was a table, salt would be sprinkled on it for pressing the potatoes in; when there was no table, it was put into a common bowl.

---

*And on the etiquette of eating them: "Our English visitors have difficulty in manipulating potatoes in their jackets. What they call a 'cheese' plate we call a 'skin' plate. The potato is first put on this and skinned with the knife and fork, then lifted on to the dinner plate. These skin plates are replaced by cheese plates later when required." This in a book on Irish *country* cooking!

This act of seasoning was known as "kitchening," a word used as both verb and noun to describe the sparing addition of some savory element to a basic food like bread or porridge or potatoes, and that accompaniment itself. A pinch of salt was a basic kitchening, but a good meal offered that plus a drink and a bite of something else—the "sup" and the "bit." When there was none of either—and sometimes no salt, as well—the meal was jokingly called "potatoes and point," a dish for which there was no recipe in cookery books because—as Thomas Carlyle well knew—the phrase meant not a dish but the *absence* of one.

A meal of potatoes and point meant that the eater was to take his or her potatoes and just point at the sup and the bit; it was not for them. Sometimes the pointing was metaphoric—in the sense of the old proverb "Hunger is the best kitchen"—because there was literally nothing else to eat at all.* At other times, as another old saying had it, one was to "Dip in the dip and leave the herring for your father." Here a savory broth of boiled salt herring was provided for dipping the potatoes into, but only one person got the piece of fish that had seasoned it.

In more prosperous times, however, the sup was a mug of buttermilk and the bit a mouthful of something savory: a strip or two of bacon, some salt fish, or perhaps a boiled egg. On a special occasion, if some fresh milk was to be had (and could be spared), the sup and bit might all be mashed up with the potatoes into a single dish. Indeed, since a pile of boiled potatoes can hardly be called a *dish*, we come to what is possibly to many Irish the basic, essential dish of their cuisine, a comfort food that any lover of potatoes can see their way fit to eating as a humble but filling and tasty supper. Asenath Nicholson encountered it at Mendicity, a Dublin poorhouse where paupers picked oakum to earn two meals. The breakfast was stirabout;

> the dinner, potatoes and some kind of herbage pounded together, well peppered, put into barrels, shovelled out into black tins, and set out upon the floor—there were no tables.

---

*Not that anyone did any actual pointing—the phrase "potatoes and point" is meant not as a description of reality but as a kind of bitter joke—in the manner of the Irish saying "Sauce of the poor man—a little potato with a big one." As P. W. Joyce explains in *English As We Speak It in Ireland*, "You will sometimes read that each person, before taking a bite, *pointed* the potato at a salt herring or a bit of bacon hanging in front of the chimney, but this never occurred in real life."

3

Potatoes were introduced into this country in 1587. After their cultivation became general they became a national food—in the 18th and early 19th century practically the sole food of the peasants. They were invariably "boiled in their jackets." Those living by the sea preferred to boil them in sea-water. There are old people in County Down today who talk of the "good old days" when this was done. No matter how "floury" the potatoes are, if boiled in sea-water the skin does not crack, and so none of the mineral content is lost. However, well-salted fresh water has much the same effect. This is how the country-woman boils her potatoes today. . . . Perhaps the most popular potato dish is champ. It is a favorite Friday dinner for those who keep Lent, and a popular dish with all old-fashioned folk.

—Florence Irwin, *The Cookin' Woman*

Now another remarkable woman enters our narrative. Florence Irwin was born in Ireland in 1883, and, as she explains with typical economy and vigor, as a young woman, after studying "Cookery, Laundry Work and Housewifery,"

I went straight to County Down, as Itinerant Cookery Instructress under the Department of Agriculture and Technical Instruction for Ireland, spending 6 to 8 weeks in each centre, which might be in a small town, a village, or just a populous town-land. I carried round with me a "Mistress" American stove and equipment for taking practical classes of 20–24 women, or children sometimes, for cookery, laundry-work, and dressmaking. This work I did from 1905–1913. My adventures were many.

The fruit of this work was her 1937 cookbook *Irish Country Recipes*, which a decade later was republished in expanded form as *The Cookin' Woman*. With its sympathetic evocation of rural Irish life and its wealth of authentic country recipes with their carefully written instructions, it is the best of all Irish cookbooks and possibly the best loved of them—certainly it remains in print there to this day. Irwin had a deep respect for her clients and an enviable natural rapport in her dealings with them. The book is full of mutual appreciation that can be at once funny and touching; she always knew that she was learning as much from them as they were from her.

Indeed, you can be lulled easily by her self-deprecatory ways for a long time before you realize that only a woman of great and independent spirit could have so resolutely shrugged off the culinary snobbery of her time and profession not only to recognize the value of the country dishes that she encountered but to make the effort to write them down, and so save for the record humble food that has been pushed to the back of the cupboard in most other Irish cookery books. About champ, the amalgam of all the basic elements of Irish cuisine—potato, milk, butter, and the taste for wild greens—she is positively eloquent.

> In a farmhouse, two stones or more of potatoes were peeled and boiled for the dinner. Then the man of the house was summoned when all was ready, and while he pounded the enormous potful of potatoes with a sturdy wooden beetle his wife added the potful of milk and nettles, or scallions, or chives, or parsley, and he beetled it until it was smooth as butter, not a lump anywhere. Everyone got a large bowlful, made a hole in the center, and into this put a large lump of butter. Then the champ was eaten from the outside with a spoon or fork, dipping it into the melting butter in the center. All was washed down with new milk or freshly churned buttermilk.

Champ is the name of the dish in Northern Ireland; in Eire itself it is known as cally, poundies, or stampy. Most if not all of these names derive from the thorough drubbing required to make it. A beetle was a thick wooden pestle that in Irish households was used for, among other things, softening straw before it was twisted into rope, thumping the dirt out of the laundry on washing day, and mashing potatoes in the big iron pot. This approach was necessary given the enormous amount of potatoes then consumed at a meal; for us, a sturdy potato masher is more than sufficient.

In contemporary Irish food writing, champ is more and more presented as a side dish, an elaborated mashed potatoes. For Florence Irwin, on the other hand, there is no question but that champ is a meal in itself. Not only does a piping hot bowl of it make a delicious, filling meal, but to prepare it this way is to begin to understand that, like all basic peasant dishes, champ is a strategy as much as a recipe. Irwin gives recipes for five "separate" versions—champ made with nettles, scallions, chives, parsley, and peas—but this is because she wants, in her typically careful fashion, to call attention to the different cooking of the greens. However, she concludes her recipe for pea champ with the following observation:

> The main thing about champ is it must be kept very hot while being made and served on very hot plates, and accompanied with good butter, and milk or buttermilk to drink. I have known of carrot, cabbage, and even lettuce being made into champ in the same way.

In other words, a bowl of champ depends partly on the inspiration of the moment, partly on which flavoring greens are in season, and partly on the particular contents of the cupboard. If you want a bit more, eat it with some sausage or strips of bacon, or follow one of her subsidiary recipes. For instance, "champ and scrambled eggs" takes an ordinary mound of champ (scallion, nettle, chive, whatever), makes a good "dunt" in the center, and fills it up with the scrambled eggs; "champ and poached eggs" does the same with a poached egg or two, but this time sprinkles the whole thing with grated cheese and slips it under the broiler until the cheese is melted and the mashed potato is crusted and flecked with brown. This is about as fancy as it gets.

CHAMP
[serves 2 as a meal or 4 as a side dish]

6 medium or 4 large all-purpose potatoes
sea salt
about 1 cup of milk
flavoring green (see below)
black pepper

Peel the potatoes and set in a pot with a tight lid. Mix half a teaspoon of sea salt into a cup of water and pour over the potatoes. Cover and bring to a boil, lower the heat until the water just seethes, and cook for about 20 minutes, or until the water is gone and the potatoes are cooked through. Experience will teach the exact amount of water to use; the trick is to catch the potatoes just before they scorch. If this seems too risky or bothersome, the potatoes can be boiled in the usual way, then covered with a clean cloth and "dried" over very low heat for a few moments.

Meanwhile, prepare the milk-and-greens mixture, as directed below.

When the potatoes are ready, mash them by hand until they are free of lumps. Then, over the heat so that the champ remains piping hot, work in the milk-and-greens mixture. The consistency should be thick but creamy—add more milk if necessary. Season well with salt and black pepper. Eat your bowl of champ with plenty of butter and wash it down with a glass of buttermilk—if you can get hold of the real thing.

Flavoring Greens

Scallion. Use 1 bunch (6 to 8), minced, including the part of the green that isn't wilted or damaged. While those who love scallions can mash them into the potatoes uncooked in the traditional Irish fashion, Irwin suggests that anyone bothered by their acrid aftertaste (and digestive effects) should not only cook them in the milk but first put them into a bowl, sprinkle them with a little salt, and pour boiling water onto them. Drain this away and add the scalded scallion bits to the milk. Bring this just to a simmer and hold it there for 5 minutes until the flavor has suffused through the milk. Proceed as directed above.

Chive. Use ¼ cup, minced. Again, these are traditionally beaten into the potatoes uncooked, but those who would like them a little tamed should simmer them in the milk for 5 minutes before working the mixture into the potatoes. Proceed as directed above. (Irwin notes that a chive patch ensures "green onion during the winter for broth and champ. . . . No matter how small the garden, a corner should still be found for a clump of chives.")

Green Pea. Use 1 cup baby peas. Cook in the milk until tender, about 6 minutes. Then, as you prefer, either mash these into the champ with the milk or strain out and reserve to be stirred in whole just before serving. Proceed as above.

Parsley. Use ¼ cup, finely minced. Heat for 3 minutes in the simmering milk and proceed. Other herbs to consider include watercress, lovage, and mint.

Nettle. Choose only the tender tops; wash and chop these finely. Simmer for 10 minutes in the milk and proceed as directed above.

And so on. Our own favorite champ is made by finely chopping a leek or a bunch of scallions and sautéing the result over low heat in melted butter with a minced clove of garlic until everything is soft and golden. Beat hot milk into the potatoes, stir in the buttery mixture, and serve and eat at once.

Like any dish that has long existed on the before side of a written recipe, the art of presenting it on the page is not to strive for exactitude but to attempt a kind of evocation. Champ is the mashed potatoes of the Irish rural poor, lifted out of insignificance by the sheer amount of labor that went into making them. There was that huge pot, remember, filled with sufficient potatoes to meet the hunger of all who sat waiting, a main dish to be dressed up, if it could be, with a bit of greenage and some lovely rich milk. Here is the one time Asenath Nicholson ate mashed potatoes in an Irish cottage; see how the passage radiates a kind of occasion, of special comfort:

> Mary now added a pile of dry turf to the fire, lighting up a white-washed cabin, and white-scoured stools, table, and cupboard. She had nothing but the potato and turnip, and "Sure ye can't ate that." "Put on the pot," said Will, "it's better than nothin' to her cowld and wet stomach." When the potatoes and turnips were boiled, they were mashed together, some milk and salt added, put upon a glistening plate, a clean, bright cloth spread upon the deal table, and Mary sat down.

This is the sort of dish where hunger itself is happy to provide the recipe.

So, too, with another dish she briefly mentions: "The next day I dined on kale and excellent potatoes [no lumpers here!] at the house of a Roman Catholic." Called colcannon, it is an Irish dish so much like champ that at first it seems hard to understand how they are told apart. As Bríd Mahon describes it in *Land of Milk and Honey:*

> Traditionally the first crop of new potatoes was a cause for cele-bration. A special meal was prepared. A basket of potatoes was dug and the tender skins rubbed off. A three-legged pot was filled

and the potatoes mashed with a pounder or beetle. Salt, pepper, finely chopped onions, cooked green cabbage or kale were mixed in to make that most delicious of all traditional dishes, the much-loved colcannon, known in Donegal as *bruitín*.

According to the *Oxford English Dictionary*, "cole" comes from *Kohl*, the German word for cabbage (as in *coleslaw*); to "cannon" into something is to smash into it. The Irish differentiate between champ and colcannon by calling the one a potato dish and the other a kale or cabbage dish. But what truly makes the difference, I think, is the intro-duction of a skillet, which lifts the latter dish one small social step above its ruder brother. (Perhaps because of that, colcannon has been elevated to holiday fare. It is traditionally served on Halloween, with a wedding ring tucked in, its finder, if eligible, to be married within a year.) Unlike most contemporary recipes, which simply mash the pota-toes and cabbage together, Florence Irwin's coarser-textured version produces a magnificent skillet-sized potato-and-cabbage pancake.

FARMHOUSE COLCANNON
[*serves 4 to 6*]

4 to 6 medium all-purpose potatoes, boiled and peeled
milk as necessary to moisten
1 small head of cabbage, cooked until just tender and grated or chopped as if for making coleslaw
2 tablespoons bacon drippings or butter
1 medium onion, chopped
salt and freshly ground black pepper to taste

Mash the potatoes until there are no large lumps, adding just enough milk to make the mixture pliable but not creamy. Stir in the chopped cooked cabbage and season to taste with salt and pepper. Meanwhile, melt the fat in a large skillet and add the chopped onion. When this has turned translucent, spread the cabbage and potato mixture on top of it, and sauté until the bottom begins to brown. Then cut it roughly with a spatula, turn it over, and continue cooking until that side, too, is touched with brown. Serve hot.

❋ ❋ ❋

It is impossible to read about traditional Irish food without a shifting of understanding—about dairy-based cultures versus meat-based cultures; about rural-based cuisines versus "civilized" city-based ones; about who gets to write the history books and, consequently, how we might then choose to read them; and also, perhaps, about what all this might mean for ourselves, whether we be vegetarian or carnivore, restrictive or permissive of appetite.

A bowl of mashed Kerry Blues and scallions has more in common than I ever imagined with a bowl of *dandan* noodles or vegetables and pasta. Irwin tells us to keep champ "very hot," but in my experience the real trick is to cool it down enough to not burn your mouth. Mashed potatoes hold heat; they demand to be eaten slowly. They fill the stomach with warmth. That they also feed it well is something my culturally biased culinary instincts have resisted believing, but it is true and I am starting to come around.

Interestingly, neither champ nor colcannon seems ever to be made by mashing buttermilk into the potatoes, although it is traditionally drunk while eating them. I would like to think that this fact reveals, buried deep in the communal memory, an awareness that buttermilk was there before the potato and remains, however long dethroned, the spiritual center of all Irish food. The role of the potato is not so easy to place. At times, reading through the texts that underlie this narrative, I felt it to be—as the bitter young farm laborer, quoted at the beginning of this chapter, described it to Asenath Nicholson—a kind of curse.

However, in time I came to think the opposite. The potato, in Ireland, soon separated itself from the English who brought it there and aligned itself with the poor and the oppressed. It flourished in Ireland as it did in no other place, among a people who were as easygoing and generous as it was. And when the landowners wanted to starve out the poor to get rid of them altogether, it was potato and point that allowed them to hold on, and, sometimes, to do more than that.

> The Irish peasant dogs, like their masters, are patient and kind; many a one has met me at the door of a cabin, and instead of barking as a surly dog would, by the wagging of his tail and invit-

ing look of the eye, said, "Walk in, walk in; my master will make ye welcome to our fire and our potato."

—Asenath Nicholson, *Ireland's Welcome to the Stranger*

A WORD ON THE IRISH COTTAGE

We all know the thing: its oversized format, its glossy pages, its brilliant color photographs, its come-hither text, its title with the word *style* always in it and usually the word *country*—*French Country Style, English Country Style,* and so forth, on and on. The idea, of course, is that for the perceptive home decorator, the belongings of the world are there for the plucking—if not the things themselves, then certainly their shapes, their colors, and the unstudied, harmonious interplay of these that can make the interior of a rustic cottage or a Caribbean shanty as pleasing to the eye as any country estate.

Claudia Kinmonth's *Irish Country Furniture: 1700–1950* is a brilliant if unintentional rebuttal to that kind of empty-headed chatter, that shameless theft. At first you might pick up the book thinking it another of the same: same coffee-table size, same glossy paper, same luscious photographs, same evocative prose. But Kinmonth's love of the beauty of her subjects—the ordinary chairs, tables, beds, cradles, storage bins of the Irish country cottage—is tempered with a sadness that is an awareness of loss, and an appreciation that is no prelude to appropriation but a deepening respect for roots.

In fact, I suspect the book's title was the publisher's idea, not the author's, since she limits herself to the household items of rural cottagers, which means almost entirely the working poor. Apart from clothing and tools, these things were all they possessed, and as each was passed down from generation to generation, repaired, adapted, expanded, put to new use, it became more and more a repository of the family's sense of itself.

In other words, a house has life to the extent that its inhabitants and its contents are able to nurture each other, thus gradually sustaining a larger, jointly shared identity. From this perspective, it might even be said that a chair also possesses a psychology, affecting, by its size, shape, and comfort, our relationship to the table it is pulled up to or another, different chair it is set beside.

Kinmonth is skilled in the verbal art of taking a thing apart to show how it is made and where it comes from and why this particular piece is shaped the way it is, but she is even better at explaining the role each plays in helping to define a home. As ordinary as any one of these items may be, it plays a part in a story that grows in complexity and richness as piece is set next to piece. In this, an Irish room is not unlike an Irish song: here the fiddle, there the pennywhistle, the accordion, the drum. As lovely as the song is when the singer starts alone, how much more is added as each of the other instruments joins in.

Consider, for instance, the dresser. Apart from the fireplace, it was the most important part of the cottage kitchen and often the most imposing piece of furniture in the house. It also seems rather complicated, since its role embraced both protection and display. It had a closed cabinet below; a work counter, known as the "bed," for tasks like cutting bread; and open shelves above, designed to display prized pieces of table- and servingware: platters, plates, bowls, jugs.

What display and protection have in common is the cottager's house pride. In essence, the dresser was the domain, the representative place, of the *bean a ti*, the woman of the house. Understanding this, you can see why the bottom of the dresser was often not a cabinet per se but a poultry coop, providing a safe, warm, dry nesting place for egg-laying geese and hens. Not only would a hen, fed on potato scraps and kept warm in the kitchen, lay eggs in the winter when otherwise it would not, but these same eggs were the woman's personal source of income, her wealth, and their place in the dresser affirmed this—as did, in other instances, a butter churn and pails of cream and milk.

Above all this, she displayed—in the words of the old song—the treasures she bought with this money:

> *Three noggins, three mugs, a bowl and two jugs,*
> *A crock and a pan something lesser,*
> *A red fourpenny glass, to draw at for mass,*
> *Nailed up to a clean little dresser.*

As she acquired more, the dresser grew to accommodate the new. To it were added wooden strips with hooks for suspending decorated mugs, guardrails against which platters might lean, and a rack for displaying silver teaspoons (often the only tableware in the house). In a dark and undecorated cottage, the dresser radiated brightness, cleanliness, and grace. Although such dressers have long been sought by collectors as desirable antiques, once they are ripped out of this living context and put to merely decorative ends, each becomes nothing more than its own elegant sarcophagus.

Food writing has a similar suspect habit of persuading indigenous cooks to surrender recipes for their most treasured dishes and then presenting these trophies ("discoveries" is the preferred term), torn from their surroundings, in cookbooks as pretentiously glossy as their style-book cousins. With food and furnishings as with persons, heedless possession can quickly snuff out first spirit and then life itself.

Irish Country Furniture, however, is full of both, because it is, at bottom, a book about the life of rooms, and especially—because Irish cottages had few rooms—about the aliveness of the Irish cottage kitchen. Most of us are already aware of how much the changing nature of kitchen work, however justified, has robbed that place of vitality; it is all the difference between sitting down by the hearth with a basket of peas to pod and slipping a heat-proof plastic bag of peas and butter sauce into the microwave.

What Kinmonth teaches us is how much has also been lost by crowding that room with stock players from culinary central casting— all eminently replaceable, and so all without any individuality or depth. In the Irish kitchen, the *dramatis personae* make up instead a tight-knit repertory company. In these pages, chair, bed, and table (or often, as noted above, *absence* of table) speak out eloquently, as do the settle, the meal chest, the food press, and the creepie. And what tales they tell.

Finally, and by the by, in her chapter on tables, Claudia Kinmonth records that a local historian, Patrick Hennessy, recalled

> that some of these tables had special holes drilled in their tops, near the edge, for eating boiled eggs out of. In many poor households, eggs formed an important part of the diet, and such a detail made more sense than spending precious money on eggcups.

A nice detail and a persuasive explanation. But some explanations become less convincing when an alternative case is offered, and it seems to me that Thomas Carlyle does just this when, in *Sartor Resartus,* he quotes a visitor to an Irish cottage observing the use its occupants put to just such a table.

> The family, eleven in number, at dinner: the father sitting at the top, the mother at the bottom, the children on each side, of a large oaken Board, which was scooped-out in the middle, like a trough, to receive the contents of their Pot of Potatoes. Little holes were cut at equal distances to contain salt; and a bowl of Milk stood on the table: all the luxuries of meat and beer, bread, knives and dishes were dispensed with.

CUISINE OF THE CRUST

❧ ❧ ❧

Il est loin le temps ou l'on mangeait du pain avec un petit bout de quelque chose: aujourd'hui on mange quelque chose avec un petit bout de pain. [It's been a long time since bread was eaten with a little mouthful of something else; these days, the little mouthful is the bread.]

—Madame Guinandeau-Franc,
Les secrets des fermes en Périgord noir

When I first wrote about *bruschetta* back in 1984, despite the title of the piece—"Bread & Olives"—my eye was on the olive.* At the time, I was intoxicated by the realization—as naïve as it may seem almost ten years later—that what gave extra-virgin olive oil its throaty, complicated richness was its direct connection to the olives from which it was pressed. However one gets corn oil from corn, it isn't from simply squeezing the kernels; consequently, corn exists in one cupboard of the mind, corn oil in another.

Thanks to such early investigations as Maggie Blyth Klein's *The Feast of the Olive*, what had once seemed equally separate concepts—olives and olive oil—were now joined in my imagination, filling my mind with vivid images: the vat of olives crushed under the huge millstones; the resulting fragrant, coarse-textured mass spread on mats set in a hydraulic press; the dribble of deeply perfumed, dark green oil emerging from the spigot. That crust of bread thrust under it to sop it up and bring it to the nose, the mouth, was so immediately understood,

---

*See *Simple Cooking*, pages 33 through 40.

seemed so entirely necessary, that I didn't absorb, then or later, how arbitrary was its presence there, how much it was a gift.

I can imagine *it* well enough: a dense, coarse-crumbed crust, sawed or ripped from a hefty country loaf, itself baked a deep mahogany, the top incised with circular ridges left from its final rising in a wicker *banneton*. But what is it doing here? This isn't a kitchen or a café but a workplace, full of men in dirty overalls carrying things in and out, making adjustments to clanking bits of machinery, standing and talking and flicking cigarette butts out the open door. Someone stopped at a *boulangerie* to buy it—today, yesterday, perhaps even the day before—and brought it to work, tucked under his arm, thinking nothing at all about it. A place was cleared for it on a table otherwise covered with tools, empty bottles, stacks of labels. And so here it is, sitting on a greasy, crumb-scattered copy of *Nice-Matin*, completely at home.

The richness of this situation can't be reduced to a single idea, nor do I wish it to be. But there is something important to be noticed here, and it reminds me of the famous portrait Van Gogh painted of his bedroom in the yellow house at Arles. You remember it: two humble chairs, a washstand, and a bed. This picture radiates presence. Every object in it has the same fullness, an uncomplicated, unquestioned solidity of being. Even the homely pitcher and basin that sit on Van Gogh's washstand speak of a physicality not yet distanced to a bathroom down the hall. But it is the bed that dominates the room, filling the painting with luminous self-assurance. The other pieces of furniture turn toward it, regarding it in awe. Such a bed is a room within a room, a place of ultimate refuge.

We do not need to ask if this bed is comfortable in order to be comforted by it. In fact, part of the power of the painting comes from the fact that we intuit, even if we don't consciously articulate this intuition as a thought, that the bed is *not* comfortable. The high head- and footboards cramp the sleeping space between them; the undulating lines of the bedclothes suggest an old-fashioned dense and lumpy horsehair mattress, the kind that holds the shape of the sleeper long after he or she has gotten out of bed . . . or tries to assume a different position while lying on top of it. No mattress company or bed-frame maker would use *Bedroom at Arles* as advertising material for their product. The painting is not about beds but about physical and spiritual exhaustion; about the great healing oblivion of sleep.

❦ ❦ ❦

Here was the cupped board floor, the long table of the same color, two old straight-backed chairs, a few plates in a rack by the sink, a loaf of bread hanging from the ceiling.
—W. S. Merwin, *The Lost Upland*

This, then, is where I began: with an image of a loaf of bread sitting on a factory worktable and radiating the same density of being, the same "thereness," as Van Gogh's bed, and with my awareness that that loaf possessed something that my own bread did not. This was because, although I made all our bread myself, and in the simplest of ways, the constraints of my own cultural conditioning had taught me that *bread is good only if it is fresh*. Consequently, the one time I could allow a loaf of bread to sit on my counter was when it had just come out of the oven. The peasant loaf—which a visitor can still find hanging from the ceiling—made me anxious.

There was, of course, a good reason for this. In my world, freshness of bread has always been the most important gauge of its realness. A loaf of bread straight from the oven is, like a roast chicken, best devoured while it is still crisp on the outside and warm within. (Leftovers . . . yes, there were things to be done with them, good things, but they still were what they were.) I was now faced with a difficult, even paradoxical, task: letting go what had made my bread real for me, what I had fought so hard to obtain—the privilege of always having it fresh—so that I could enter into a larger, more complicated, but also liberating relationship with it. I would have to understand that for bread there is also an *aesthetics of staling*.

In almost all peasant cultures, the original sustaining food was some kind of gruel—which is to say, grain boiled in water. This porridge is filling and nutritious; it is also dreadfully monotonous. Peasant cooks have expended endless culinary ingenuity over the centuries in improving upon it. Bread, in Europe at least, was the end result. Even so, many of the intermediary dishes retain their particular niches: cooled polenta sliced and fried in fat, pastas made of unleavened pastes, thick pancakes made of flours—like that ground from chestnuts—that are not amenable to bread-loaf baking.

In France, before the Revolution, the nobility not only controlled the major source of cooking fuel—wood—they also forbade peasants the possession of millstones or a bread oven. It was one of the privileges of both lay and ecclesiastical overlords to own the gristmills and the bakehouses and to collect a fee for their use. Consequently, communal bake ovens were fired only at intervals, and the bread baked in them was meant to last. This didn't mean that the bread wasn't tempting to eat hot, but that the frugal peasant knew better than to yield to that temptation. As Jeanne Strang wrote about such bread in her book on the foodways of southwest France, *Goose Fat and Garlic*:

> After less than an hour golden crusty loaves emerged, and the one we brought home, almost too hot to hold, looked so good we cut into it straightaway, although we knew it would keep well for up to a week. (In peasant families, they would resist the temptation to eat the fresh loaf, knowing that too much would disappear quickly, leaving none for the end of the week.)

Perhaps the word that better helps us understand this process from the peasant's perspective is *aged*. A newly baked country loaf is not so much "fresh" as "green." It was (and, to the extent that it still has pretensions to authenticity, remains) densely textured and minimally leavened. In contrast, its city cousin, inflated out of as little dough as artifice can manage, is a loaf where crust is everything and crumb the airy architecture that holds it all in place. A city loaf, like a roast chicken, is meant to be torn apart and devoured at once; a country loaf is—like a country ham—meant to be eaten slowly, bit by bit, its thick crumb retarding spoilage. In the classic manner, it is sliced by the head of the family, who clutches it under his arm and cuts it by drawing the knife in a sawing motion upward toward his chest. It is treated with the respect that we usually bestow on a piece of roast meat.

Again and again, we read in cookbooks written about Spanish, Italian, and French cooking, in reference to the wealth of dishes in those cuisines that utilize the sustaining crust, that "these were devised to utilize stale bread that might otherwise have been discarded." This phrase expresses a city way of understanding, completely at odds with peasant reality. On the contrary, *the peasant loaf was made for these dishes*. It was no more "stale" than Cheddar cheese is stale milk or a country ham stale pork. These are entities with their own identity, integrity, *rai-*

son d'être. To find my way to it, I had to make my loaf in the usual manner . . . and then resist it. I had to let it cool, wrap it up in a clean, dry dish towel, and put it away in the bread tin. The struggle then becomes not only resisting the urgency of ignorance but also mastering its sheer bafflement. What about this loaf do I expect to be different? What, really, do I want from it?

The first thing to be said is that my experience with the staling of what, for lack of a better term, I'll go on calling "city bread" had always been very much a one-note affair. One day it is fresh; the next day (if left out) it is a rock-hard lump that, when cut, crumbles into shards of rusk. I expected this. My image of stale bread was one gleaned from our shared cultural commons, where the distinction between hard bread and soft, between eaters of crust and eaters of crumb, is, first of all, a class distinction. Gentility trims away the crust from even the softest bread. In a brief fling with teatime, I myself once cut perfectly edible crusts from butter sandwiches.

"Some doe plenteously glut themselves, and others some live with gnawing of poore crusts." That word *gnaw* tells it all. Even so, the crust of the fairy tale wasn't yesterday's bread but last month's. It was a symbol of adversity, of hard times. According to the *O.E.D.*, the word *crust* means not only the dry hard skin of a loaf of bread but, by extension, "a scrap of bread which is mainly crust or is hard and dry: *often applied slightingly to what is much more than crust.*" (My italics.) Example: " 'To have a "crust " as she calls it, or in reality a good deal of cheese and bread and beer.' "

"Slightingly," I think, is not quite right. I would say, instead, "deprecatingly." Crumb is luxury; crust is poverty . . . and worse. Still, it is better to find a crust at the bottom of the cupboard than a raw turnip. Stale bread has three virtues: it is already cooked; it has substance; and it can absorb liquid. These are what make it a restorative. A crust dipped in broth softens, opens itself up, becomes almost a delicacy. By implication, it suggests that the hardness of one's fate might similarly change. Affectingly, a sopped crust comforts directly and by example. It reminds us what will happen when we are dipped into the warm broth of good fortune: we will soften . . . expand . . . become warm again.

Remember the bed in Van Gogh's bedroom. We are talking of the comfort hunger seeks from sustenance, a consolation that comes as much from what the food says as from what it tastes like. The difference between the fresh and the stale loaf is the same as that between the *petit pois* and the dried pea. You eat the former fresh and sweet and young. That is living for the moment. The latter you soak to soften and then eat with the comfort of knowing it is something that is always there. The dried pea is reanimated, yes; rejuvenated, no. You do no good service to a dried pea by pretending that by cooking it you have brought back its youth. That is the realm of the frozen pea, which possesses neither the bloom of true freshness nor the comforting solidity of that which endures. What we are giving back to bread when we recall—reinvent, really—the cuisine of the crust is the dignity of maturity.

Mediterranean peasant cuisine places bread at the center of the meal. Because of this, the weight and density of the crumb, besides retarding the staling process, also serves to fill the eater. Like country ham, country bread exists in a category separate from the raw and the cooked: the *preserved*. The field hand who takes a slice of it from his meal pouch expects, as he does with ham, to revivify it by water or by fire.

To think differently about bread is to make bread differently. Peasant bread is not especially delicious fresh. As Edward Behr once noted about his own slow-leavened loaf:

> I would rather eat my bread after it is a day old, when for a couple of days it makes good eating plain. On the day of baking, the bread smells magnificent, but to my mind it takes a day for the taste and texture to compose themselves.

Such a loaf does not necessarily meet expectations we bring to bread that *is* best when freshly baked: the crackling crust, the sour-sweet fragrance of hot yeast. But there are other expectations: complexity of taste and, especially, variability of texture. This is chewy bread; not only slow to stale but slow to eat, and it is this slow eating that makes the meal.

❋ ❋ ❋

> My mother can remember her childhood in Tuscany when the sea was so unpolluted that the bread was dipped in the sea, wrapped in a clean cloth, to soak it through.
> —Valentina Harris, *Recipes from an Italian Farmhouse*

As I write these words, summer has arrived with full force in Maine and we are already anticipating the first tomatoes of the season. Fresh tomatoes and bread: for the past several years, whenever I think of this combination, I remember a passage in Tom Stobart's *Herbs, Spices and Flavorings*:

> Where I lived on the Italian Riviera the common snack consisted of a crusty roll split and filled with sliced tomato, salt, olive oil, and a few leaves of fresh basil—no butter of course—just squashed to make the oil and juice impregnate the bread.

I first read this in the early 1980s, and it immediately defined for me the course of a pamphlet I was then writing: *Aglio, Oglio, Basilico*. I had begun it because I wanted to write about pesto; I ended up writing about summer. The clinging, assertive fragrance of basil; the pulpy sweetness of the tomato; the rich, thick olive oil with the hint of burning bitterness in its aftertaste . . . in a sense, *I* was the soft crusty roll, wanting to sop all this up, unable to get enough.

When I subsequently came across a recipe for *panzanella*—a salad made by refreshing bits of stale country bread by soaking them in water, then wringing them out and tossing them with chunks of tomato, cucumber, and so on in a simple oil-and-vinegar dressing—I felt I had finally found the dish that might make this possible.

I was right then making a salad, very trendy at the time, of fresh ripe tomatoes. These were cut into wedges and tossed in olive oil and a little red wine vinegar along with torn bits of basil, minced onion, and cubes of fresh mozzarella. Allowed to sit in a cool summer kitchen for a few hours before serving, the cheese softened to the point that it simply melted in the mouth. This same resting process filled the salad bowl with a delicious liquid composed of the dressing and the tomato juice. What *panzanella* did was give me permission to tear a loaf of fresh Italian-style bread into bite-sized chunks and toss these in. The result was delicious, but it wasn't *panzanella*. Let's call it . . .

PANZANETTA
[*serves 4*]

1 red salad onion, thinly sliced
4 large ripe tomatoes
4 to 6 ounces fresh mozzarella
a few sprigs of fresh basil
1 clove garlic
4 tablespoons fruity olive oil
½ tablespoon red wine vinegar
salt and freshly ground black pepper to taste
loaf of *fresh* peasant-style bread

Soak the onion slices in cold water for an hour, changing the water every 15 minutes. (This tempers the onion's rawness without affecting its crispness.) Then cut the tomatoes into chunks, cube the mozzarella, and toss these together in a large salad bowl. Tear the basil into little bits and scatter over. Mince the garlic clove to near-molecular consistency (easiest done with a good pinch of salt) and mix this with the olive oil and vinegar. Season to taste with salt and pepper. Cover with plastic wrap and let sit for a few hours in a cool place until the tomatoes release their juice. Now, bit by bit, tear the loaf into bite-sized chunks and stir these into the salad until the juices have been absorbed and there is a pleasing balance of ingredients. Adjust the seasoning before serving.

Cook's Note. This salad is also good with torn bits of brine-cured black olives added at the same time as the fresh basil. If the tomatoes are not fully sweet, use a balsamic-style vinegar instead of the wine vinegar.

I offer this recipe not only because I still like it but because it's a good illustration of how unexamined culinary inspiration tends to work. Encountering a recipe embodying an unfamiliar idea—the durable loaf—I simply tried to detach the recipe. Without in any way realizing what I was doing, I reimagined *panzanella* into a dish that not only incorporated fresh bread but focused on what, for me, was the important ingredient: fresh tomatoes.

The first time I made *panzanella*, I did try soaking the bread. It

turned into mush, and rather than wonder why, I simply decided to ignore such instructions in the future. This lesson on the difference between country and city bread not only failed to sink in, it didn't even
register. Nor did I wonder, as the years went on, why I never encountered a recipe for *panzanella* that included fresh cheese. This is because,
even if my "*panzanetta*" can be delicious, compared to the real thing it
is also as evanescent as a summer breeze. *Panzanella*, true to its peasant
origins, is a dense and chewy dish, and mozzarella would be as appropriate in it as in a batch of bread stuffing—which is a very good description of what *panzanella* is like . . . if you can imagine bread
stuffing as a hot-weather salad.

PANZANELLA
[*serves 4*]

1 red salad onion, thinly sliced
8 ounces or so stale country bread
3 large ripe tomatoes
1 cucumber, peeled and cubed
a few sprigs of fresh basil
4 tablespoons fruity olive oil
1 tablespoon red wine vinegar
salt and freshly ground black pepper to taste

Soak the onion slices in cold water for an hour, changing the water
every 15 minutes. Cut the bread into bite-sized cubes and soak them in
cold water just long enough to be sopped through. Drain the bread
cubes in a colander and squeeze gently but firmly to wring out as much
water as possible. Cut the tomatoes into chunks and mix these together
with the bread, the drained onion slices, and the cubes of cucumber in
a large salad bowl. Tear the basil into little bits and scatter these over
the salad. Drizzle over the olive oil and vinegar and season with salt
and pepper. Toss and then let sit for an hour or two on a cool counter
before serving. Adjust the seasoning before serving.

    Cook's Note. Other possible additions include celery, anchovy fil-
lets, capers, et cetera. Proportions are relative, with some versions
of *panzanella* favoring the bread and others the tomato. Likewise, a

decision to shred the bread and cut everything else into smallish dice produces a very different dish from one in which everything is cut large.*

There it is. Compare these two dishes and you have in perfect contrast the hunger of the clerk and the hunger of the peasant. For the latter, fresh tomatoes are no special novelty. Their meals, whether made in summer or in winter, require substance, whether that substance be pasta or bread. *Panzanella* is an uncooked version of *pappa al pomodoro*, a dish that is usually described as "bread and tomato soup." However, the actual Italian—roughly, "bread sopped in tomato sauce"—brings to mind its culinary equivalent: pasta dressed with tomato sauce. In peasant cooking, sopped bread and pasta are close kin, and, as we know, in rustic Italy it is the pasta, not the sauce, that dominates the dish. So, too, with bread.

PAPPA AL POMODORO
[*serves 4*]

8 ounces slightly stale country bread
4 cloves garlic, cut in half
basil stems
salt and freshly ground black pepper to taste
4 large ripe tomatoes
4 tablespoons fruity olive oil
3 or 4 sprigs of fresh basil, separated into leaves and stems

Cut the bread into cubes and place them in a bowl. Make a simple broth by boiling together the garlic and the basil stems in 2 cups of water, seasoning it to taste with salt and freshly ground black pepper.

Set a colander over the bread and put the tomatoes into it. Pour the

---

*Carol Field, in *The Italian Baker*, tells us that in the middle of the sixteenth century, the Mannerist painter Bronzini composed a rhyme in praise of bread salad. This pre-tomato *panzanella* was made of onion, cucumber, basil, purslane (*porcellina*), and arugula. Any salad of mixed bitter greens, tossed with torn chunks of our grilled and oiled slice, remains a dish worthy of a poem.

broth over the tomatoes to loosen their skins. Then remove the tomatoes from the colander and peel and coarsely chop them, discarding the
skins with the debris from the broth.

Heat the olive oil in the same pot used to make the broth. When it
is hot, stir in the tomatoes and cook, stirring occasionally, until they
have thickened into a sauce. Tear up the basil into tiny pieces and stir
this in.

Pour the bread into the colander and, using the back of a wooden
spoon, press out as much of the broth as possible. Stir the bread into
the tomato sauce and season again with salt and black pepper. It will
look like a red bread pudding.

❦ ❦ ❦

> Bread rubbed with tomato has been described as the essence of
> the cultural identity of Catalonia—the last word in gastronomic
> pleasure. The large, dense loaves, called peasant bread, are baked
> without salt and have a cross cut into the top. The bread is cut
> into thick slices, then briskly massaged with tomato on both sides,
> bathed in that most penetrating balsam extra-virgin olive oil and,
> by the way of a blessing, sea salt. . . . Eating *pa amb tomàquet* is
> an experience which requires full concentration.
> —Alicia Rios, *The Heritage of Spanish Cooking*

According to Colman Andrews, writing in his masterly *Catalan Cuisine*, Catalans characterize themselves as having an enormous appetite
for bread. They even have a word—*panarra*—for those who devour it
by the loaf. If *pa amb tomàquet* is for them the essence of their cultural
identity, this may be because it is also the ultimate reduction of a classic Spanish peasant dish, *sopa seca*, or "dry soup." Although its variations are many, a *sopa seca* is basically a soup in which crusts of dry
bread have drunk up all—or almost all—the broth, producing a kind of
savory bread pudding enhanced with everything from seafood to leafy
greens. *Pa amb tomàquet* is *sopa seca* for anytime when cooking is in-
convenient, but especially during the long, hot Spanish summers. In
many ways, it is the ideal summer meal.

I have to admit that, for the longest time, I didn't myself think of it
that way. In fact, my imagining of it is nicely captured in the least effective photograph in that magnum coffee-table production *France: A*

Culinary Journey, where it is depicted as a pathetically skimpy slice of toasted French bread wiped with the single half of a *plum* tomato.* My first suspicion that I might have got *pa amb tomàquet* wrong came when I read Leopold Pomés's *Teoria i pràctica del pa amb tomàquet*, which, although written in Catalan, comes with an (occasionally surrealistic) English gloss. Pomés, a playful, heavily bearded Catalan intellectual, argues many things about *pa amb tomàquet*,† but the one that struck me most was his insistence that it is ideally eaten with *knife and fork*.

Pa amb tomàquet looks rather silly broken down into the standard recipe format, so let's just present it so:

PA AMB TOMÀQUET

Have at hand a large, densely textured, slightly stale country loaf; plenty of ripe tomatoes; a cruet of fruity olive oil; a jar of sea salt.

Begin by cutting the tomatoes in half, discarding any that are not quite ripe (the pulp is not yet soft and wet) or too ripe (the pulp has turned to water). Gently squeeze out the seeds and gelatinous juices so that nothing is left but pure, soft pulp. Slice the bread into half-inch-thick slices. Rub the cut side of the tomato gently but firmly against the bread, slowly enough so that the crumb can soak up the pulp (it shouldn't be coated with it as if the pulp were jam).

Do the same with the other side of the bread, discarding the tomato halves as soon as they are exhausted and making sure that every part of the surface has received its share. Lightly drizzle both sides with the olive oil and then sprinkle them with the sea salt. The bread slice should be neither wet nor dry, but at once firm and moist. The way to describe a properly made *pa amb tomàquet*: it glistens.

What you are left with, after it has been coated, oiled, and salted on both sides, is still a piece of bread, but a piece of bread so unctuous and

---

*If you wonder what a Catalan dish is doing in *that* book, you forget that Catalonia extends across the French border into the *pays Catalan* of Roussillon.

†The book is worth seeking out if only to enjoy his riff on the *non*universality of *pa amb tomàquet* (accompanied by an illustration of a fantasy New York City fast-food place serving nothing but).

juicy that it is best enjoyed cut into bite-sized morsels and eaten with a fork. Not because it will fall apart into a mush; not even, as Pomés himself says, because it will get your fingers greasy; but for the same reason you don't hoist a steak off your plate and eat it with your fingers: *because that isn't the best way to enjoy it.*

After this essay appeared in our food letter, *Simple Cooking,* subscriber Maurice Frechette told us about the Maltese version of *pa amb tomàquet,* called *hobz iz zejt,* or "bread and oil."

> My wife, Lynn, is Maltese, and we spent a week a few years ago on that island with her great aunt Rose. She would take us to the beach (rock—the Maltese think sand beaches are "dirty") to swim, making us a picnic lunch of *hobz iz zejt* in the morning before we went. Here's how I described it in my journal at the time:
>
>> cut a tomato in half, rub it on the bread, then dip the bread in
>>   a plate with oil add pepper and salt
>> tastier: minced garlic in the oil
>> traditional: use the tomato husk by chopping it up and putting
>>   it on the bread
>> Aunt Rose: adds capers, olives, tuna, onions
>
> Maltese expatriates weep for this. We ate it every day on the beach that had no sand. It improves if you cover it with a towel and put in on a hot rock next to the sea in Sliema. Always by the sea.
>   A few additional pointers (and a caveat). The tomato should be big and juicy (of course, it's the cut side that is rubbed on the bread). The bread is the large, crusty, round loaf that Mediterranean bakers make from Portugal to Greece. I'm sure the toppings are a matter of local dispute, but not knowing more than two Maltese cooks, I can't really comment on what the disputes are about. I know Aunt Rose would always make them with tuna, capers, and the chopped husk of the rubbed tomato. Sometimes, we'd see garlic.
>   Now the caveat: no matter how carefully we make it, *hobz iz zejt* never tastes quite as good here as it did there. Maybe this is why Maltese expatriates really *do* weep when it is mentioned. The problem may lie in the nature of the ingredients, but my hunch is that the fat, soggy slices need to sit wrapped in a towel on a hot rock at the beach in a Maltese August until you are hungry enough to eat them.

❋ ❋ ❋

> A Frenchman once told me, "A piece of crusty *pain ordinaire* may be a spoon for your soup, but a slice of *pain de campagne* is like a plate."
>
> —Joe Ortiz, *The Village Baker*

This image of a bread "steak"—of a thick slab of bread, dressed and eaten off a plate with silverware—did more to break the hold that fresh bread had on my imagination than any number of bowls of soup in which chunks of dry bread have been allowed to soak. If one equivalent of *panzanella* is pasta tossed with fresh tomatoes, *pa amb tomàquet* edged me into the neighborhood of the pizza slice. But if the similarity opened the necessary door, it was the possibilities inherent in the difference that propelled me through it.

When I began to follow my appetite rather than the usual formulas in the composing of pizza toppings (see the essay "Existential Pizza" on page 129), I soon discovered that there were certain things that I yearned to eat on a crust that did not do well baked onto a pizza. Among them were freshly made compounds like pesto, *olivada, tapenade*, or *peperonata*, which, even if some pizza recipes utilize them, are really not meant to be eaten hot (or not meant to be heated at all).*

Others, like eggs scrambled with fresh tomatoes and basil or a *brandade* of white beans, are simply antithetical to such treatment. Not so with *bruschetta*, or *frotté d'ail*, as it is known in Provence. A dense country loaf does not, in my opinion, make good sandwich bread, but a slice of it grilled and brushed with olive oil makes an unmatchable edible *plate*.

Borne on this image, the crust has found a durable place in my culinary imagining. Consider: a bottle of wine, a loaf of country bread, and the most basic of outdoor grills, under which a large handful of twigs has burned to a tangle of glowing embers. Throw on these a sprig of rosemary and grill slices of the bread in the aromatic heat. Brush them

---

*This is not meant to deny the concept of the *cold slice*—the piece of pizza eaten the next morning for breakfast . . . and found good. If *pa amb tomàquet* is the hand that reaches out from the durable loaf to the instant crust that is pizza, the cold slice is the hand that reaches from the opposite direction to clasp it firmly in a fraternal grip. But the toppings on a cold slice were baked onto it, so this does not invalidate the comments above.

with olive oil (or not, as circumstances dictate) and generously—this a meal, not an hors d'oeuvre—top.

Recently, food writers have discovered that *bruschetta*—or its little brother, *crostini*—is an ideal medium for easy summer dishes (see the booklist below). However, I suggest that, before consulting them, you first turn to your own instincts. A good starting place is to enhance the olive-oil rub with a little crushed garlic, anchovy (*anchoïade*), or minced or puréed black olives (*tapenade*), and use this in conjunction with one of the many Mediterranean summer dishes—grilled eggplant, *piperade*, ratatouille—that will moisten and enrich a grilled crust. Instances are legion: from *anchoïade* spooned over coarsely chopped broccoli to *tapenade* mixed with wedges of tomato, slices of hard-boiled egg, or the traditional can of tuna . . . and on to fresh green beans dressed with garlicky *aïoli* and pesto stirred into a bowl of cooked tiny white navy beans.

ANCHOÏADE

Versions for this abound in Mediterranean cookbooks, but the simplest—described by René Jouveau in *La Cuisine provençale de tradition populaire*—directs that for each serving you rinse and remove the backbone from 1 or 2 salted anchovies and set these in a small skillet, pour over some olive oil and a touch of wine vinegar, and, on the lowest possible heat, allow everything to gently meld into a sauce.

TAPENADE

The Provençal shepherd or field hand might not have had a flask of olive oil with which to anoint his grilled slice, but he could rub it with olives and sprinkle it with bits of fresh herb. To my mind, the best *tapenade* still has the feel of that olive-rubbed crust. To make it, prepare *anchoïade* as above but omit the vinegar, and mix into it a large quantity of coarsely chopped black brine-cured olives, a much smaller amount of minced capers and garlic, and a pinch of crumbled *herbes de provence*. It is all the better when made with two or three different types of cured olive.

❧ ❧ ❧

The bed in Van Gogh's painting possesses density of being because it is at once ordinary and durable, an object that promises always to be there. We look at it and see sleep. To those who know and value it, the peasant loaf offers this same gift. It radiates a density of being precisely because it calls no attention to itself. The peasant who reaches for it is instantly assuaged by its familiar presence, a touch as familiar to his hand as that of his own body. Hunger has already begun to fall away; the spirit is resuscitated by anticipation of the revivified crust.

Our culture no longer values what is durable. Intimations of mortality discomfit us: the cheese that deliquesces, the country ham that molds, the bread that crusts. We turn instead to the instantly eatable, the always fresh—which is also how we want to think about ourselves. We are what we eat. The peasant loaf asks us to decide which metaphor we want to appropriate for ourselves: the tired crust revived in hot and soothing broth . . . or the plastic-wrapped slice that never stales.

Further Reading

As anyone not residing in Ultima Thule must by now know, in the past few years trend-conscious American chefs and cookbook writers have seized hold of the rustic Italian snack of grilled country bread rubbed with garlic and dribbled with olive oil, most commonly called *bruschetta* (which we are slowly learning to pronounce "broos-KET-ta"). This is because such a tasty slab of bread can—as much as any pizza crust—stretch a little savory topping a long way. Italians well understand this, as witness, say, the way that farmworkers regularly enhance their morning snack of *bruschetta* with some slices of salami or prosciutto or the flesh of a few black olives before they wash these down with plenty of cool white wine.

Of the many writers who have tackled this subject, my personal favorites are Ann and Franco Taruschio, who, in their unjustly overlooked *Bruschetta: Crostoni and Crostini*, bring to the subject great culinary talent, an easy familiarity with authentic Italian cooking, and some dogged backroads research on *bruschetta*'s home turf, and so return us to the inspiration of the original.

In their recipes—many of them traditional—one enticing combination follows another: anchovies and ripe figs; fontina and spring onions; ricotta and walnuts; soft scrambled eggs and Gorgonzola; cockles and fresh basil; black olives and mushrooms. Always, the ingredient list is as short as the flavors are long. The authors also share a very unusual method for making *pane pugliese* that was taught them by a farmer's wife, and they devote a whole chapter to the little-discussed topic of *bruschetta* made with polenta or flatbreads.

Perhaps my favorite moment in the book came when I discovered that the cheeseburger has a wealthy uncle in Rome: a filet mignon set on a grilled slice of bread and topped with mozzarella and an anchovy, then drizzled with a sauce made of the steak drippings and a reduction of Marsala and white wine. This one I'll wait to try until I visit the authors' country *albergo* in Wales, The Walnut Tree (said to have been Elizabeth David's favorite British restaurant), but others—the *fettunta* with cannellini beans and pancetta or the *bruschetta alla Giudia* with marinated green tomatoes—I can't wait to make for myself.

Otherwise—to select a few from a wealth of titles—anyone interested in summer bread dishes should start with Pino Luongo's *A Tuscan in the Kitchen*; among its many bread dishes is the Tuscan version of *pa amb tomàquet: fettunta al pomodoro*. Robert Freson's photographs in *Savoring Italy* are an education in Italian breads and bread dishes, further explored in the recipes and essays on Tuscany (by Leslie Forbes) and Sardinia (by Louis Inturrisi). Robert Carrier writes eloquently on bread and olives in *Feasts of Provence*. And Carol Field devotes a chapter in *The Italian Baker* to traditional peasant bread dishes. Finally, three books with strong discussions of the role of bread in peasant cuisines are Jeanne Strang's *Goose Fat and Garlic: Country Recipes from South-West France*; Colman Andrew's *Catalan Cuisine*; and Mary Taylor Simeti's *Pomp and Sustenance*.

CIOPPINO IN THE ROUGH

❋ ❋ ❋

In California the Italians have a dish known as cioppino, which, as it becomes better known, will undoubtedly have quite a vogue in this country.
    —Evelene Spencer and John N. Cobb, *Fish Cookery* (1921)

Cioppino is often condescended to in historical studies of our national cooking. Read, for example, what Waverley Root and Richard de Rochemont say about it in one of the first genuinely thoughtful surveys of our national cuisine, *Eating in America*:

> Cioppino sounds authentically Italian, but both the dish and the name were invented in San Francisco, with the freest of fantasy in both cases. Cioppino is a seafood stew which admits of infinite variations, oftenest built around crab, and the Italian-looking word is explained as a reduction of the English word "chop" to its Italian phonetic equivalent.

For much of my cooking life, passages such as this succeeded in establishing cioppino in my mind as something bogus—that is, not only vulgar but, worse still, *touristy*. And, certainly, cioppino was once the *piéce de résistance* of San Francisco seafood restaurants, where the diner was ceremoniously draped in an apron and presented with a tureen heaped with giant Dungeness crabs, whole jumbo shrimp, clams, mussels, squid, and chunks of assorted fish. With this came a loaf of the famous local sourdough bread for soaking up the garlicky, spicily seasoned wine and tomato sauce in which all this seafood swam.

A little reflection might have led me to the realization that such a meal is not the worst fate that might befall the unwary traveler, but until a year or so ago I never had any reason to take heed of cioppino at all. Then, on the cookbook shelf of a used-book store up in Maine, I happened upon a vintage (1921) seafood cookbook, *Fish Cookery*, by Evelene Spencer and John N. Cobb, which contained the first of two narratives that would have the peculiar synergistic effect of turning my opinion of cioppino on its head—and in the process giving me a far more complex perspective on the dish.

If its authors are to be believed (Cobb was director of the University of Washington's College of Fisheries and Spencer the fish cookery expert for the United States Bureau of Fisheries), Americans were much more adventurous in their tastes for seafood seventy-five years ago, when regional tastes remained strong and certain species had not yet become endangered. (For instance, there are several recipes here for whale meat, including one for whale pot roast and another for whale curry.)

The book contains a fascinating discussion of cioppino, and, more importantly, quotes at length from what must be one of the earliest printed descriptions of the dish, written by H. B. Nidever for the July 1917 issue of *California Fish and Game*:

> The cioppino (pronounced chipeno) is one of the simplest, healthiest, and cheapest ways of cooking fish. Originated by Italians, it is cooked and eaten by them almost exclusively. Cioppino is a great dish among the fishermen, some practically living on it because of its healthfulness and muscle-building qualities, and the ease with which it is prepared. When fishermen are out on trips for days at a time the only supplies that are taken are bread, wine, a little coffee, and the ingredients that are used to make up a cioppino, depending on their luck to catch the needed fish.
>
> Butter is never used in the preparation of the cioppino, olive oil taking its place. There are a great many kinds of cioppino; that is, most of the people that cook it prepare the dish in a slightly different way. Sometimes it is what one might call fancy—shellfish, celery, parsley, wine, etc., being used in its preparation. But the kind generally prepared by the fisher folk is very simple and inexpensive, the olive oil used being the most expensive ingredient. Some prefer salad oil, which is less expensive and not quite so rich.

The cioppino is neither a roast, a chowder, nor a fry. In America, it would probably be nearer a pot roast than anything else. In preparing a cioppino the whole fish is used, including the head, which contains some of the best part of the fish. The large-sized fishes are generally preferred on account of the size of their bones. Most any of the larger-sized ocean fishes, such as the rock fishes, rock bass, sea bass, halibut, and barracuda, can be used. The wings of the skate are highly prized among the Italian fishermen for a cioppino; striped bass are very fine. Several different varieties of fish are sometimes used.

Cioppino, such as is made by the fishermen, is prepared as follows. For five people use from three to five pounds of fish sliced in fairly large pieces, then prepare one or two onions, depending on size, by chopping them up quite fine. Place in a stewpot one-half cup of olive oil (salad oil may be used) and add the onions, frying them until yellow, in the meantime adding several cloves of garlic, and a little parsley. Add a can of tomatoes (raw tomatoes may be used) and cook for about ten minutes. If potatoes are used (a great many never use potatoes in the preparation), they should then be added and cooked for five or ten minutes. Add the fish, covering it well with the tomatoes, onions, etc., season with salt, and rather highly with pepper or paprika, put on the lid, and let simmer until done. Don't stir. A little water may be added if desired. Serve in a deep plate. Cioppino may be poured over French or Italian bread.

Reading the sentence that named the few things the fishermen brought with them—bread, wine, coffee, the ingredients (minus the fish) for their stew—I felt that pleasantly eerie sensation of a mental nickel dropping into its slot. In *A Tuscan in the Kitchen* Pino Luongo tells of the *materassai* who once came every spring to Italian households to air the stuffing of the mattresses. They carried with them for their lunch a flask of wine, a loaf of bread, a cold *frittata di pasta*, a flask of *condimento per insalata*, and an empty salad bowl, knowing they would find all the greens they needed in the neighboring fields.

So, too, with these Californian *pescatori* on their wave-tossed wooden boat out in the immensity of the Pacific. The net is hauled in and emptied onto the deck, which is immediately awash with a shimmering pile of wildly thrashing fish. Even as this catch is being sorted through, one of the fishermen is coaxing a pile of kindling into a fire in the tiny galley stove while he chops up an onion or two and minces some garlic cloves with his scaling knife. These he tosses with some salt, dried oregano, and hot pepper flakes into the olive oil awaiting them in the bottom of the large, soot-coated cast-iron pot. He sets this over the flames, and as the mixture begins to gently sizzle he selects several of the fish from the catch around him. He guts and scales them, then cuts them into chunks and tosses them, heads and all, into the pot. When that is full, some tomato paste is added, and promptly diluted with an ample ration of wine.*

Soon the air is full of the savory aroma of wood smoke and simmering fish. As the rest of the crew gathers around, the cook adds the final touch, tipping the flask of olive oil over the pot and anointing his creation with a delicate drizzle of oil, which floats on top of the stew in a lace of golden drops. A large loaf of staling bread is drawn from a canvas sack and passed from hand to hand, each eater tearing off a piece to be dunked and refreshed in the rich, sea-salty broth. The meal is eaten directly from the pot, the chunks of fish falling apart into delicate flakes the moment they are captured by a spoon.

Leonard Bernstein once remarked that the mark of a great artistic achievement is that it is at once fresh and inevitable, and this neatly encapsulates what is so special here. This cioppino is fresh—and not only for the obvious reason that its major ingredients still drip of the sea. It is fresh because each time it is made the choice of fish is both spontaneous and unique. Every day the catch is different, every day the dish is invented anew—this time with a single fish large enough to feed the crew, the next with a mess of assorted fry, and on and on.

Inevitability in a dish is often a matter of—in the best meaning of the term—economy. This shipboard cioppino, for all its offhand simplicity, is—in the way it makes the best possible use of what is at hand and in the way that what is at hand has been pared down to a few care-

---

*The paste may have been scooped from a crock, cut from a sausage-shaped roll of tomato leather, or dumped from a can cut open with a scaling knife. As Andrew Smith tells us in his preconception-puncturing *The Tomato in America*, recipes for making tomato paste and tomato leather appeared in American newspapers long before the Civil War. In one of the examples he provides, the November 1834 edition of the *New York Farmer* printed an eyewitness account of the way tomato paste was made in Turkey, which concluded with the writer's astonishment at how far a small amount of it would go: "A small pot which I brought with me, containing about half a pint, lasted my family more than a year, and we used it very freely."

fully chosen essentials—as tightly argued as any philosophical proposition. Those who see cooking merely as a chore can never know how a dish like this—however often it's made—can continue to offer the cook intellectual satisfaction so intense as to be almost sensual.

❀ ❀ ❀

As Sherlock Holmes was wont to complain, the more brilliant the deduction, the more self-evident it will seem once explained. The second of the two documents that entirely reversed my opinion of cioppino was an essay on that dish by Johan Mathiesen, which he has kindly allowed me to reprint here (see pages 302–4). As you will see, he relates how, when he lived on the Pacific coast of Oregon, he learned to make cioppino from Chuck, a biker-cum-fisherman, who had himself picked it up from other fisherman in California and who then brought it with him when he moved up the coast. Chuck, he writes, "taught me that cioppino was not something holy and sacrosanct, but rather the natural result of cooking together what you probably had around the house anyway."

Shift Bernstein's "inevitable" from the passive to the active and what you have—at least when applied to cioppino—is something along the lines of "compellingly obvious." Chuck was neither a studier of cookbooks nor an amateur chef. He had absorbed the making of cioppino because, once he saw it done, he felt right away not only that he could do it himself but that he definitely wanted to. And Johan, although he *was* a cookbook reader, underwent the same epiphany—because to watch Chuck prepare cioppino put it not in the category of recipe perceived but of experience lived, a very different kind of apprehension.

I remember feeling something similar when, in a visit to a Manhattan Gallic expatriate hangout called Pierre au Tunnel, I first encountered *soupe à l'oignon*—an encounter that eventually prompted my first bit of culinary writing*—and then again when I first met up with rice and beans. There needn't be any educative intention: something contagious passes from the cook to you, leaving your hands itching to go straight to your own kitchen to make the dish yourself.

A Treatise on Onion Soup: Its History, Powers, and Modes of Proceeding, a small (sixteen-page) pamphlet published in 1979.

That this kind of nonverbal culinary transmission can happen at all
is amazing enough, but what really astonishes is its nearly genetic ability to breed true. Put Johan's encounter with cioppino beside that of
H. B. Nidever's and you can't help but notice how much the grandson
resembles the grandfather, despite the fact that in the generation between, social mobility has been paid for in the usual dilution of character. (It would make a great movie, with Al Pacino cast as the
all-too-prosperous restaurateur dad, John Cusack as the rebellious
grandson, and Robert Duvall as the rough-hewn family patriarch, Il
Cioppino.)

Once such a dish is appropriated into the realm of recipe, it becomes codified, and so its consistent replication comes as no surprise.
But in vernacular cooking, when the bloodline of a dish runs true generation after generation—as, say, that of hoppin' John has in the Deep
South—it is a sure sign that it has reached a state of enduring perfec-
tion.

This is doubly the case with cioppino, where the same thing has
happened on both the Mediterranean and Pacific coasts, at least if one
accepts the argument that cioppino's origins lie in a traditional Genoese
seafood soup called *il ciuppin.** Usually, these days, this is prepared as
a purée, but in *The Classic Food of Northern Italy*, Anna Del Conte offers a cioppino-like version that is the specialty of the house at the Ristorante Angiolina in Sestri Levanti on the Italian Riviera. Del Conte
makes no mention of—and may never have encountered—"cioppino," but she might as well have been taking photographs at a
Ciuppin/Cioppino family reunion, so clearly does her recipe reflect their
common features.

IL CIUPPIN DI SESTRI LEVANTI
(adapted from *The Classic Food of Northern Italy,* by Anna Del Conte)
[*serves 4*]

*The author notes that when the dish was served to her at the Ristorante
Angiolina the chunks of fish still contained "their bones and other bits*

---

*In *Flavors of the Riviera*, Colman Andrews, noting this same commonality, explains that
the word *ciuppin* itself is "simply a corruption of the Genoese word *sûppin,* meaning 'little
soup.' " So much for the "Italian phonetic equivalent" of *chop.*

*and pieces, only the head being removed, something that Italians, like
the Orientals, do not mind, but that annoys the British." This is exactly
how I imagine our shipboard fisherman's cioppino, fish head included.*

¼ cup olive oil
1 medium onion, 1 celery stalk, and 1 carrot, all cut small
2 garlic cloves, minced
½ cup dry white wine
1 pound assorted white-fleshed fish, such as hake, dogfish,
    whiting, or haddock, cut into large chunks
4 cups boiling water
½ cup canned plum tomatoes, with their juice, chopped
salt and freshly ground black pepper to taste
4 thick slices of country-style Italian bread
1 to 2 tablespoons minced fresh parsley

Add 2 tablespoons of the olive oil to a large saucepan and gently sauté
the vegetables and all but ½ teaspoon of the chopped garlic in it for 10
minutes over medium heat, stirring frequently. Pour in the wine, turn
up the heat, and cook for another 5 minutes, until the wine is reduced
by one-third. Add the pieces of fish and sauté gently for 5 minutes,
turning them frequently.

Pour over 4 cups of boiling water and add the tomatoes and seasoning. Bring the soup back to a simmer and cook for 15 minutes. Taste
and adjust the seasoning.

Meanwhile, toast the bread in the oven broiler. Mix the reserved ½
teaspoon garlic into the remaining olive oil. Lightly brush the toasted
bread with this mixture, placing the slices in the bottom of individual
deep soup bowls. Ladle the *ciuppin* over the bread. Drizzle on any remaining garlic-flavored oil, sprinkle with the parsley, and serve.

Can any firm distinctions be drawn between cioppino and *ciuppin*—or
any of the many other similar native Italian or Mediterranean fish
stews? The answer is probably no, although cioppino is usually made
with red rather than white wine, and without water, so that it is notably dense with fish. Also, the bread that accompanies cioppino is—if
one can get it—a sourdough loaf, and it is torn apart at the table and
dunked into the broth rather than being sliced, toasted, and served as a
chapon at the bottom of the bowl.

This lack of a unique identity, however, is a mark of cioppino's authenticity. Like any vernacular dish that has endured through the years, it is able to generate at need a new member of the tribe—niece or nephew, grandchild, or cousin once removed—that is appropriate to the demands of the moment but that also exhibits those inherited characteristics that set the family apart.

If cioppino as flashy impresario of the old-time San Francisco restaurant scene was no one I wanted to invite into my kitchen, this other cioppino, natural child of the fishing boats, had won first my interest, then my sympathy, and finally my appetite. However, before I could set out to make a version that might possess any claim to this same birthright, I had to follow the logic of the dish through one last, unexpected twist.

❋ ❋ ❋

> The first time my father went to Italy to visit his family there, they sent us some olive oil and it was like nothing I'd ever had. We started using it to make the same marinara sauce that my father remembered my grandmother making. There was a world of difference in that sauce between using plain olive oil, which was easily obtained, and this extra-virgin olive oil.
> —Nancy Verde Barr, *We Called It Macaroni*

For me—as, I expect, for any reader who might have already chanced upon this dish—cioppino is about seafood. What seems so special about it—especially when concocted onboard a fishing boat—is the freshness and abundance and choiceness of the fish. For the fishermen themselves, however, that aspect of the dish was so ordinary, it was hardly worth noticing. A net full of fresh fish is to them what a bin heaped with grain is to the peasant who farms the land—nothing to be scorned, certainly, but the dish's necessary foundation rather than its defining ornamentation.

To see cioppino through their eyes, then, I had to shift my gaze from the bubbling kettle of fish on the deck of the tiny fishing boat to the flask held carefully by the fisherman cook as he anointed his stew with a dribble of precious golden oil. At first, I wasn't exactly sure what I was looking for, until a certain sentence of H. B. Nidever's account—"But the [cioppino] generally prepared by the fisher folk is very simple and inexpensive, the olive oil used being the most expensive ingredi-

ent"—collided with a passage written by Spencer and Cobb, which reveals how a touch of condescension can dull even a lively and curious
palate.* (On the other hand, in their favor, the two authors are
adamant in their defense of garlic.)

> As to the oil used in this dish, the Italian, of course, would scorn
> any other oil than that of the olive, for this is the one luxury
> which is his necessity, no matter how little he has to spend on
> food. To the average American, who is no connoisseur, fortu-
> nately for his purse, so far as oil is concerned, corn oil, cotton-
> seed, or any preferred brand of salad oil may be used with equal
> results.

This peculiar edginess regarding the cost of olive oil—and I suspect we
are hardly talking about extra-virgin olive oil—inadvertently points us
to an important distinction between the dishes of the working poor and
those that spring from our own middle-class foodways.

Peasant food is rooted as a matter of course in what is abundant
and cheap, enhanced when possible by calculatedly careful touches of
the expensive: the grating of Parmesan, the paper-thin sliver of prosciutto, the drizzle of olive oil. Our cooking lays its emphasis on ample
provision of the relatively expensive and relegates what is abundant
and cheap to the background—where it is sometimes not eaten at all.
This means that very expensive items traditionally used primarily to
point up what we ourselves push to the back of the plate—say, the
forty-dollar truffle shaved over the bowl of pasta—make us anxious,
since they fly in the face of our sense of value. This is why the "average
American," who would think nothing—should the cash be at hand—of
treating himself to a sixteen-ounce sirloin, be he connoisseur or no, still
considers it only sensible, even today, to replace "costly" olive oil with
that pressed from cottonseed.

My point is not that this bias is wrong—what we are talking about,
after all, is competing conceptions of extravagance—but that if you call
it into consciousness you begin to grasp the inversion that cioppino had

---

*The absence of *wine* both in Spencer and Cobb's discussion of cioppino and in their recipe
for it is also a matter of interest. The book was published early in the Prohibition Era
(1920–1933) and so can be trusted on that subject about as much as cookbooks published today are reliable when they touch on the subject of fat.

to undergo in order to grace a San Francisco restaurant table. The emphasis no longer fell on the preciousness of the oil, the ethnic signatory power of the tomato paste and the garlic, but on an opulence more likely to appeal to the *amour-propre* of the most desirable patrons, and so loosen their wallets.

As I began contemplating how I would make this dish myself, I found that I was under the sway of neither the one nor the other of these contrary visions, but held in a state of tension between them. If I could not return to a world where extra-virgin olive oil is measured by the drop and tomato paste lovingly put up by hand, I was at least freed from the image of a dish swollen with the highest-ticket items in the fishmonger's case. All the necessary components—the fresh seafood, tomato, wine, garlic, olive oil, bread—had now achieved equal weight. "To make cioppino" became an act of finding the delicate—and, for us, the right-seeming—balance among them.

❋ ❋ ❋

As I began searching out cioppino recipes in contemporary cookbooks, I was a little taken aback to learn that it is now often considered a crab dish (by which I mean, when prepared at its simplest, it is made *solely* of crab). However, such a transition was inevitable the moment cioppino stepped ashore, and this did not at all mean that it stepped out of character. Crab is abundant on the Pacific Coast, and for many years it was there for anyone's taking—the next best thing to having the perks of a fisherman's wife.

Although at the time that I wrote this we lived on the Maine coast, where fresh-picked crabmeat was available down the road almost three whole seasons of the year, and despite the fact that something about the slightly pungent edge to even the freshest of crabmeat means that it stands up well to the robust flavors of tomato and wine, we soon discovered that we preferred to make our cioppino with fish—either cod, haddock, or pollock. This is partly because crabmeat is already cooked and so must be added at the end of the cooking process, while the fish is poached in the sauce and so adds more of its own flavor to the stew. But there is also that matter of balance, of emphasis. A cioppino made with crab is a crab cioppino; one made with cod is cioppino, pure and simple, since the fresh fish melds deliciously into the whole.

This elementalness is also reflected in the sauce that provides our cioppino's base. Sea-made cioppino might originally have depended on tomato paste—perhaps augmented with canned tomatoes—but, as H. B. Nidever attests, onshore it was prepared in a simple, classic marinara sauce. This is usually distinguished from other tomato-based sauces by a quick preparation, one that allows tomatoes, if fresh, to retain some of their texture and simple garden sweetness. It is thus an ideal medium in which to cook seafood, since it, too, should remain in the pot for as short a time as possible. (Indeed, marinara sauce reputedly takes its name from the fact that fishermen's wives could have it ready the moment their husbands arrived home with the day's catch.)

As Matt and I worked our way to our own version of cioppino, we hoped to find some aura of marinara freshness in the new all-natural, organic tomato sauces that had started to appear in our local natural foods store. However, these turned out to have the same tomato-paste-thickened texture and overcooked taste of their supermarket predecessors—which too much dominate any seafood dish. Consequently, when fresh tomatoes are not available, we turn to imported Pomì chopped tomatoes, which—because the aseptic packaging allows them to be minimally processed, without any addition of salt or calcium chloride—are surprisingly light, clean-tasting, and tomato-y. Finally, most cioppino recipes we found added a green bell pepper to the sauce. We liked this touch but prefer a red or yellow bell pepper, which adds texture and sweetness without any vegetative sharpness. Here, then, is our own addition to the family album—cioppino as a delicious, swiftly and casually prepared everyday dish.

MAINE COAST CIOPPINO
[serves 2]

¼ cup extra-virgin olive oil, plus a little for anointing
    purposes
1 medium onion, chopped
1 red or yellow bell pepper, cored, seeded, and chopped
1 large garlic clove, finely minced
¼ teaspoon ground hot red pepper
½ teaspoon dried oregano

⅔ cup zinfandel or other dry but fruity red wine

2 pounds fresh tomatoes, peeled, cored, and roughly chopped or 1 28-ounce container of peeled Italian tomatoes (Pomì by preference)

1 teaspoon salt

freshly ground black pepper to taste

¾ to 1 pound fresh firm-fleshed, white-meated fish, such as cod, haddock, or pollock (see note)

1 small loaf good sourdough or Italian country bread

Put the olive oil into a heavy-bottomed cooking pot and set over medium-low heat. Add the chopped onion and bell pepper. Sauté gently, stirring occasionally, for 10 minutes, adding the minced garlic, ground hot red pepper, and dried oregano during the last 3 minutes of cooking.

Pour in the wine and increase the heat to medium-high. Cook until the wine is reduced by one-third. Stir in the tomatoes and add the salt and freshly ground pepper to taste. When this begins to simmer, lower the heat to keep it there, and cook, stirring occasionally, for 5 minutes.

Add the fish to the sauce. Bring everything back to a simmer and cook until the fish is no longer translucent and begins to fall apart, about 5 minutes or so if the pieces are thin, or up to 10 minutes or so if they are thick. Immediately remove the pot from the heat and, with a spatula or cooking fork, gently separate the fish into flakes, keeping these as whole as possible. Ladle the cioppino into 2 large soup bowls and dribble a little olive oil over its surface. Serve with the wine and the loaf of bread, which should be pulled into pieces to dunk into the broth.

Cook's Note. Here are Spencer and Cobb's comments regarding the fish to be used for this recipe:

> When purchasing fish for this dish, it is well always to bear in mind that a dry-meated one is best for this purpose, as it may be stewed without falling to pieces. Also that it should be of the larger fish, free from bones and skinned. On the Atlantic Coast, such fish as cod, haddock, pollack, grouper, or red snapper are suitable; the wings of the skate when obtainable are highly recommended, as they are greatly esteemed by the Italian fisherman for this dish. On the Pacific Coast, shark, ling cod, red, black, or

brown rockfish, halibut, etc., can be used. Inland, the buffalo fish, also the frozen grouper, will answer the purpose.

CIOPPINO
Johan Mathiesen

Chuck and Mary lived in a cedar-shaked shack off the road out to Bastendorf Beach. Cloistered by the impenetrable rain forest, ready at any moment to be swallowed up by the salal, Oregon grape, and salmonberries, their one-bedroomed fisherman's shanty stood as scant protection against the gales screaming off the Pacific; the wind outside would rustle the curtains inside and drive the rain under the still. In the dark, though, in the storm, the least of shelters can seem the securest of harbors. It was there in that rude abode with the smells of sweat, wet wool, burning wood, and the sea mingling with those of tomato, oregano, and red wine that I first learned of cioppino.

Chuck had brought cioppino with him from the fishing ports of California, San Diego, and Half Moon Bay, where he'd mingled with the "Portegees." It was the Portuguese and the Italians who had re-created their Mediterranean seafood soup with what they'd found in the Golden State: crabs, clams, cod, and shrimp from the endless coast and cranky red wines from the inland valleys, coupled with intense tomatoes and garlic grown under the relentless sun. Somewhere in the process the soup took on the name of cioppino. It was all familiar fare for Latins who had grown up under very similar conditions back home. It's not the dish that's so surprising, it's the name.

Chuck was the perfect ambassador. Cioppino engenders arguments the way bouillabaisse does—not only as to what goes in it but, more importantly, where it comes from. The name is obviously Italian, and John Mariani (we can expect a guy with a handle like that to be impartial, no?) in his *Dictionary of American Food and Drink* claims that the word comes "from a Genoese dialect, *cioppin*, for a fish stew . . . the dish seems to have originated with the Italian immigrants of San Francisco."

But Helen Evans Brown in her definitive *West Coast Cook Book* is less than sanguine over that opinion. In her estimation, "this is one of California's most famous dishes, and one that we can claim is ours, all

ours. . . . One story says that San Francisco's fishermen did *not* introduce cioppino to California, but that an Italian named Bazzuro, who
ran a restaurant on a boat anchored off Fisherman's Wharf, is responsible. What's more, it was supposed to have been an old recipe, well
known in Italy. This back in the 1850s. I refuse to believe it!"

Neither Mariani nor Brown understood what Chuck understood.
Chuck didn't even know there was an argument about cioppino; as far
as he knew, cioppino was simply a fish stew he'd learned to make from
other fishermen, Portuguese for the most part. Hell, Chuck himself was
neither Italian nor Portuguese; he was a Hell's Angel.

For a while I spent a lot of time with Chuck. His was the push that
got us rolling downhill to Charleston in the first place, and for a couple
years there he was part of our "karass." We spent a lot of time doing
things I shouldn't mention and were both a little amazed at each other.
I was the anarchist radical and he was the biker fisherman. That our
lives crossed was a matter of chance, but it was largely because of
Chuck that I was allowed into the rough, tough bar-fighting world of
renegade, testosterone-fueled pitbulls—men for whom beer-driven
brawls were a contact sport like football. If you didn't want to play,
they certainly wouldn't pass the ball to you.

It was Chuck who introduced me to this signature dish of which I
knew nothing. It was he who taught me this dish for which there was
no recipe, only a concept. It was he who taught me that cioppino was
not something holy and sacrosanct but rather the natural result of
cooking together what you probably had around the house anyway.
Every fisherman has a fridge full of fish, a jug of Dago red, a half head
of garlic, a couple onions, and some dried herbs in the cupboard from
two years ago. It doesn't take a whole lot of imagination to throw them
all into a pot together, especially when there's nothing else in the house.
Thank God I learned cioppino from someone who had no idea where
the water came from.

Surely Mariani and Brown were both right—or, perhaps, both
wrong. By hook or by crook, the name was appropriated from the Italian; the *c-i-o* part guarantees that. None of my Italian reference books
support this claim, but none of them even discuss it, which leaves the
question begging. Mariani gives no sources, so we're left to our level of
trust (a trust you've got to worry about when he's the guy who says to
put saffron in your cioppino). On the other hand, no one fisherman

"invented" cioppino in San Francisco or any other place. The nameless Mediterranean fishermen who migrated to California simply went on making the same soup they'd always made, concocting it from the materials at hand, just as they and their ancestors had done for hundreds of years, without benefit of cookbook or authority beyond their mothers. It was bound to be different from its European cousins because the raw materials were different, but they were all born of the same stock. Surely the recipe is ancient; surely it's as new as the New World. To pretend that it was invented out of whole cloth by the fishermen of San Francisco, though, flies in the face of history—and common sense.

Chuck went off to Alaska when the fishing died here in Oregon. Mary got left along the way. She was a fishermen's groupie with big breasts and an appetite for guys who smelled like cod liver oil. She was destined to get left in lots of ports. I left the world of the coast altogether, moved to the big city, and found out that all sorts of people had opinions about cioppino, something we'd never even heard of in Wisconsin. By that time it didn't matter; I was immune. I'd learned it at the source. I'd learned it from an acid-dropping, booze-swilling, loose-fisted, rebel biker turned fisherman who was happiest drifting out on the ocean far from the reach of the law. He taught me that cioppino was something you could throw together dead drunk, high as the mastheads, in a houseful of boisterous friends and family at ten at night. This was strong food for strong people. It worked.

And it didn't have no saffron.

KHICHRI/KUSHARI/KEDGEREE

❊ ❊ ❊

1

Back in 1989, the literary magazine *Granta* printed an essay by Bruce Chatwin describing his experiences following Indira Gandhi on the election trail the last time that she would seek election as prime minister of India. In one of his interviews with her, the following exchange took place:

> "You have said the Janata Government is a *khichri*. In England we have the same word, 'kedgeree.'"
> "Yes, we used to have it for breakfast at Teen Murti [her father's house, now a museum]. Lady Mountbatten taught my father's cook how to make it: smoked haddock, rice, and hard-boiled eggs. But in India *khichri* means a 'mess.' I'll say it again and again: 'The Janata is a mess.'"

Reading it, I felt that gentle seismic tremor that indicates a moment of culinary enlightenment and, on its heels, a sense of wry amusement at the serendipitous ways such illuminations occur. You may read the collected works of Madhur Jaffrey from cover to cover without a hint as to India's current political morass, but clues about Indian cooking—any kind of cooking, really—can come your way from the unlikeliest of sources.

Indira Gandhi, of course, was the daughter of Jawaharlal Nehru, and the image of Lady Mountbatten, wife of the last viceroy of India, teaching Nehru's cook how to make kedgeree—as emblematic a dish of the British Raj as ever there could be—has a certain deliciousness. It is also ironic that Indira Gandhi was apparently unaware that, in India, *khichri* is also the name of a dish, a nourishing gruel of rice and lentils that is a staple of the very poor. The Nehrus, it seems, did not eat much of *that*.

However, amusing as all this may be, what set off that tremor was the word *mess*. It suggested that *khichri*, like most dishes of the poor, is more a strategy than a recipe. After all, it is hard to imagine a single recipe for something called a "mess."

Food like *khichri* attracts me for two reasons. The first is that, while it is almost always inherently simple, it offers the attentive maker a wealth of interesting options. As protean as its distant Caribbean relation, rice and peas, *khichri* has learned over the centuries to adapt itself to many different situations and ingredients, while retaining its identity and dignity. The second reason, which is obviously related to the first, is that such a dish can make you think.

❉ ❉ ❉

At its most elementary, *khichri* (which can also appear as *kitchri, khichdee, kitchree*, etc.; I have standardized the spelling in the quotations that appear in this essay) is a gruel made of rice and any one of a number of different legumes, but most usually *moong dal* (split and hulled mung beans), seasoned with *ghee* (clarified butter), salt, and pepper. Gruels are the foundation of the cooking of the poor. They are hot, thick, and nourishing. They extract the maximum mileage from their ingredients, because more liquid can be added to "stretch" them without violating their integrity. They hold heat and so must be eaten slowly. In sum, gruels offer the most comfort for the least amount of money.

Because all cultures begin poor, some form of gruel provides the base note of all cuisines, including our own. And, in cooking as in the evolution of the species, ontogeny recapitulates phylogeny. Our roots are in our baby food. As Julie Sahni writes in *Classic Indian Vegetarian and Grain Cooking*,

> [*Khichri*] is the first solid food given to an infant in India because it is mild flavored and easy to digest. It is also the basic diet of a person home with a cold or the flu. I love the creamy consistency and subtle flavor of this dish.

Even in these few short sentences you can pick up the fondness that native Indians feel for *khichri*—a feeling that we will encounter again and again as we follow it on its strange and fascinating wanderings.

We who are neither babies nor down with the flu can yearn for comfort, too, but we want, even so, some kind of stimulation to spark the appetite and entertain the palate. For us, it is the milk that we pour and the sugar that we sprinkle over the cereal, the pat of butter and dab of jam we spread on the piece of toast. These additions are without any edge; other cultures like their mouthfuls less dulcet. When the Chinese sit down to *congee*, for instance, the table is set with little bowls of such enhancements as minced scallion, shredded ginger, chopped fresh coriander, pickled turnips, boiled eggs, sesame oil, chili-spiked vinegar, and soy sauce.

Similarly, Indians eat *khichri* with an assortment of chutneys and vegetable pickles. However, as you will see in the first recipe, the gruel can itself receive enough spicing to make it interesting when eaten as a simple one-bowl meal.

SOME INTRODUCTORY NOTES

Those of us who are approaching *khichri* for the first time need to bear in mind that this is not a dish its Indian eaters think of in terms of a recipe; it is pulled together in response to those mysterious fields of force by which, somehow, countless palates spontaneously create and sustain a native cuisine. Indian cooks vary the proportion of *dal* to rice in their *khichri*, some using more rice, others more *dal*. When making *khichri* as a gruel—compare the two recipes that follow immediately below—they also vary the proportion of *dal* and rice to water (as we do when making oatmeal or grits) to produce different consistencies. A small amount of the *dal*/rice mixture cooked a long time in a lot of water makes a more glutinous, *congee*-like soup, while a larger amount makes a thicker, grainier-textured one.

The seasoning of the dish similarly shapes itself out of deft use of, among others, turmeric, cumin, coriander seed, clove, cinnamon, and fenugreek; fresh garlic, ginger, and hot green chile; bay, parsley, and coriander leaf. Here, too, we must feel our way, letting taste learn to find a pleasing balance. All the seasonings given in the recipes should be treated as variations on what can only be a suggested theme.

Dal. Indian cookery utilizes a wide varieties of lentils, beans, and peas, some familiar—chickpeas, kidney beans, black-eyed peas—and others not. The preferred way of preparing many of these is to reduce them to a smooth purée, and any legume that has been processed with such treatment in mind is called *dal*, as is the prepared dish itself. So, the tiny, olive-drab *moong* (mung) bean, when it has been dried, split, and hulled, or "washed," now looking like a little rectangular yellow split pea, becomes *moong dal*. This is the traditional *dal* for making *khichri*. It cooks quickly and requires no prior soaking, which is obviously helpful with *khichri* pilaf, since the rice and beans cook together in the same time. *Khichri* is also made with lentils and split peas, so readers unable to find *moong dal* should substitute as they see fit, making necessary adjustments for cooking times.

Ghee. Unlike clarified butter, its closest Western equivalent, *ghee* is cooked until all the moisture has evaporated and the butter solids have darkened, imparting a golden color and a nutty, caramel flavor to the liquid butterfat. This, when strained clear, can then be heated to 375°F before smoking, making it an ideal frying medium. A good-flavored vegetable oil such as peanut or sunflower seed can be substituted.

To make *ghee*, heat unsalted butter over a moderate flame in a thick-sided pot that will evenly distribute the heat. When the butter froths up, turn the flame down low. Cook until the solids have sunk to the bottom of the pan and turned from white to a tawny gold (do not let them brown). This will take some time. At that point, remove the pot from the heat and gently skim off the thin, dry crust on top of the butterfat. Reserve this. Very carefully spoon the *ghee*, which should be a light golden color, into a sieve lined with cheesecloth and set over a bowl or jar. Do not disturb the solids at the bottom of the pan. Let the *ghee* cool, then cover with a tight-fitting lid. The solids, any remaining *ghee*, and the crust can be combined and used to flavor soups and vegetables, or just eaten on bread. *Ghee* will keep in the refrigerator for at least a month.

Rice. The standard rice for making *khichri* is Indian basmati (see rice notes on pages 21–22), widely available in natural foods stores, Oriental groceries, and many supermarkets. Indian cooks pick over the rice, removing detritus and spoiled grains, and rinse it carefully in several changes of water. Some then soak the rice for a period of time before cooking it, but we have not found this necessary.

GEELI (WET) KHICHRI
(adapted from Madhur Jaffrey's *World-of-the-East Vegetarian Cooking*)
[*serves 2 to 4*]

¼ cup *moong dal*, picked over and rinsed
⅓ cup long-grain rice, picked over and rinsed
2 thin slices of fresh ginger, peeled
1 teaspoon salt plus freshly ground black pepper to taste
2 tablespoons *ghee* or vegetable oil
¼ teaspoon whole cumin seeds

OPTIONAL ACCOMPANIMENTS:
assorted Indian chutneys and vegetable pickles

Place the *moong dal*, rice, and ginger slices in a heavy pot and pour over 4 cups of water. Bring to a boil, stir once, lower heat until the gruel just simmers, and cover. Cook for about 1½ hours, or until the mixture has the consistency of a thick porridge. Stir occasionally with a wooden spoon during the last half hour of cooking to keep the *khichri* from sticking to the bottom of the pot. Remove the ginger and season to taste with salt and black pepper.

Heat the *ghee* or vegetable oil in a small skillet over a medium-high flame. When the *ghee* is hot, add the cumin seeds and fry them until they begin to turn dark and release their aroma. This will take only a few seconds—do not let them burn. Pour this mixture over the hot *khichri*, cover for 1 minute, then mix well and serve in bowls, with, if you like, various Indian chutneys and vegetable pickles to be spooned over to taste.

Khichri is often eaten with vegetables. Sometimes these are incorporated directly into the gruel—in her *World-of-the-East Vegetarian Cooking*, Madhur Jaffrey does this with spinach. Other times they are cooked separately but eaten together, as Julie Sahni shows in this thicker *khichri* served with potato (a favorite Indian vegetable) and bell pepper.

GEELI KHICHRI WITH POTATOES AND PEPPERS
(adapted from Julie Sahni's *Classic Indian Vegetarian and Grain Cooking*)
[*serves 4*]

1 cup *moong dal*, picked over and rinsed
½ cup long-grain rice, picked over and rinsed
¼ teaspoon ground turmeric, divided in half
1½ teaspoons salt
freshly ground black pepper to taste
4 tablespoons *ghee* or vegetable oil
2 medium potatoes, peeled and cut into small cubes
2 green bell peppers, cored, seeded, and diced
1 teaspoon whole cumin seeds
½ teaspoon ground hot red pepper

Place the *moong dal*, rice, half the turmeric, and 1½ teaspoons salt in a heavy pot and pour over 6 cups of water. Bring to a boil, stir once, lower the heat until the gruel just simmers, and cover. Cook for about 1 hour, or until the mixture is smooth and thick. Stir occasionally with a wooden spoon during the last half hour of cooking to keep the *khichri* from sticking to the bottom of the pot. Season to taste with black pepper.

Heat 2 tablespoons of the *ghee* or vegetable oil and the remaining turmeric in a skillet over a medium-high flame, stirring constantly. When hot, add the potato cubes and fry these for about 5 minutes. Add the diced green pepper and, still stirring, cook until the peppers are wilted, another 5 minutes. Reduce the heat, cover, and cook until the potatoes are soft. Season to taste with salt and black pepper and transfer to a warm bowl.

Wipe the skillet clean, add the remaining 2 tablespoons of *ghee*, turn the heat back up to medium-high, and, when the *ghee* is hot, add the cumin seeds. Fry them just until they begin to turn dark and release their aroma. Sprinkle over the hot pepper and immediately pour this mixture over the *khichri*, cover for 1 minute, then mix well and serve in bowls, accompanied by the potatoes and peppers.

The next step in the evolution of *khichri* is its transformation into a pilaf. Madhur Jaffrey writes that this form of *khichri* is called "*khili hui khichri,*" or "*khichri* that has bloomed," since the rice is allowed to cook until it is dry and puffed up. Although still inexpensive to make, a *khichri* pilaf is a more "civilized" dish. The amount is fixed rather than flexible; it requires more skill and attention to make well; and, while Indians sometimes eat it as a simple repast with a salad of cucumbers dressed with yogurt, it is more often served as a side dish to a larger and more varied meal.

Lazy cooks prepare the beans and rice separately, stirring them together just before the *khichri* is served. However, this not only breaks up the cooked rice kernels but impedes the subtle blend of flavors that is one of the pleasures of the dish—another being the contrast as the mouth encounters the smooth, waxy bits of bean among the softer, rough-textured grains of rice. As has already been mentioned, there is no set formula for the proportion of rice to *dal*—and a *khichri* that is, say, half one and half the other is a very different dish from one that we offer here, in which the rice predominates and the *moong dal* is given the supporting role.

KHICHRI
[*serves 4*]

4 tablespoons *ghee* or vegetable oil
½ cup *moong dal*, picked over and rinsed
1 cup long-grain rice, picked over and rinsed
1 teaspoon salt
½ teaspoon whole cumin seeds
¼ teaspoon each ground turmeric and hot red pepper
crispy onion shreds (see pages 312–13)
4 hard-cooked eggs, peeled and sliced (optional)

Heat the *ghee* or vegetable oil in a small skillet over a medium flame. When hot, add the *moong dal* and rice and fry, stirring constantly, for a few minutes. Add the salt, cumin seeds, turmeric, and hot red pepper, and continue stir-frying for another 2 minutes. Add 3 cups of water and bring to a boil. Turn the heat to low, cover, and simmer for 15 minutes. Then remove the pot from the heat and let stand, covered, for another 15 minutes. Serve warm, topped with the crispy onion shreds and garnished, if you like, with the rounds of hard-cooked eggs. (Many Indian cooks would sharply disagree with the addition of the hard-boiled eggs, which do not usually appear in recipes for *khichri*. But they are an occasional and very tasty accompaniment and, as we shall see below, they open a door to one possible origin of the dish.)

Cook's Note. Split peas, if substituted for *moong dal*, should be precooked for about 30 minutes; lentils, unless very small, for about 15 minutes. Use any remaining cooking liquid as part of the rice-water measurement.

Variation. Khichri with fresh ginger and cashews: Add to the above list of ingredients a healthy pinch of ground clove, 1 tablespoon finely minced fresh ginger, and ½ cup coarsely chopped cashews, preferably raw. Divide the *ghee* in half and use the first half to stir-fry the *moong dal* and rice as directed above, adding the clove and ginger at the same time as the turmeric and hot pepper. While the *khichri* cooks, heat the remaining ghee in a small skillet over a medium flame. When hot, add the cashew pieces and cook until they are golden-colored and aromatic. Mix these into the finished *khichri* and serve topped with the crispy onion shreds.

CRISPY ONION SHREDS

If I had come away with nothing but this delicious fried garnish at the end of the explorations recounted here, I'd have still felt myself richly rewarded. The traditional use for these crisped onions is to lend a caramel color and sweet fried-onion flavor to sauces—the onion slivers, cooked to a crackly dark brown all through, will dissolve when stirred into hot water. A generous handful on top of a bowl of the simplest khichri *or* mujaddarah *can make it into a satisfying repast, and once you master the recipe you will almost surely find that crispy onion shreds will become an integral part of your cooking.*

This method takes pointers from Julie Sahni's Classic Indian Cooking, *Copeland Marks's* The Varied Kitchens of India, *and Madhur Jaffrey's* World-of-the-East Vegetarian Cooking. *While the concept is quite simple, the trick is never to let any of the onions actually burn, since this will impart an acrid taste to the dish. (I remember a pot roast recipe from my youth famous for the flavor that burned onions gave to*

*it during the long cooking. I was unimpressed. Now I understand that
the idea was to stop just this side of burning.) Like Cajun cooks, Indian
cooks push the envelope, trying to get the onions super crackling
brown. Resist the temptation to hurry things by cranking up the heat.
Be patient and alert, turning the onions gently and continuously with a
spatula so that they cook evenly. Then whisk them out of the pan the
moment they are done.*

> 3 large onions
> ½ teaspoon fine sea salt
> ½ cup peanut or other frying oil

Peel the onions but leave the root ends untrimmed. With a razor-sharp
knife, cut them into the thinnest possible rings, starting from the end
opposite the root end (this will hold the onion intact). When the onion
becomes too small to slice thin, discard the remnant.

Toss the onion rings with the salt in a bowl, making sure the rings
are all separated. Let rest for 15 minutes. Then spread them on paper
towels and cover with another layer of towels. Press firmly to remove
as much liquid as possible.

Heat the oil in a wok or large skillet over medium-high heat. Add
the onion rings and turn with a spatula until all are coated with oil.
Continue turning them gently as they cook. First they will release any
remaining moisture, then wilt, and then begin to turn brown. Watch
them carefully at this point, stirring all the time, until they are a deep-
colored reddish brown, with darker brown (but not black) bits. Then
quickly remove the pan from the heat and, with a spatula or slotted
spoon, scoop the onions out onto a plate. From there, scatter them over
paper towels and let them drain for 15 minutes. When they have
cooled, they should be very crispy.

Cook's Note. These onions can be used at once or kept in an airtight
container in the refrigerator for a few days. Larger batches can be
frozen until needed. Copeland Marks points out that the frying oil now
has an aromatic onion flavor and can be reused to good purpose.

2

> Their ordinary diet [is] kitsery, which they make of Beans
> pounded, and Rice, which they boile together. Then they put
> thereto a little Butter melted.
>
> —John Davies (1662)

Khichri can at times seem almost as central to Indian national identity as the Upanishad, and Indian food writers can be fiercely possessive about it. Certainly, it is an ancient dish. As early as 1340, Arab travelers described it much as it is now—"a dish of rice cooked with *dal*, usually that of *moong*." At least one Indian food historian places its origin in the kingdom of Gujarat, now an Indian state, which lies just north of Bombay and south of Pakistan, with a coastline on the Arabian Sea.

If you go to read about Gujarat, one of the first things you are told is that this is where the Parsi settled when, long ago, they first arrived in India. Although these people were familiar to me as members of an Indian religious sect that had provided the British Raj with a corps of skilled government administrators, I didn't realize until I began reading about *khichri* that the word *Parsi* actually means "Persian."

In the eighth century, when Islam swept into Persia and began to extirpate the religion of the Zoroastrians, many of these persecuted believers fled east into the area that is now Pakistan. Eventually, when this refuge, too, became threatened by the Moslem advance, a group of Parsi set out from the port of Hormuz in seven junks, sailing first to the island of Diu and then to the mainland, which was even then called Gujarat. There, agreeing that their men would bear no arms and their women would don the sari, they were given a tract of sterile land, which, according to some early writers, they turned into a "garden of heaven."

Over the centuries, the Parsi evolved from a farming folk into an increasingly urbanized, artisanal class of weavers and carpenters and, eventually, merchants. Although they are now scattered all over India, their largest community—about eighty-five thousand people—resides in Bombay, with a much smaller one in Calcutta. They continue to follow the teachings of Zoroaster, a creed based on "good thought, good word, and good deed," worshiping in fire temples and burying their dead in towers of silence.

The Parsi have a distinctive cuisine, one that exhibits a Persian taste for nuts and dried fruit. They also have a rich repertoire of egg dishes and a long tradition of combining legumes with rice. According to the Indian food historian K. T. Achaya, in Persia they used the *rajmah* bean, but in India they abandoned it for the lentil.

Did the Parsi introduce *khichri* to India? If so, I'll probably be the last to know. The important thing is that as this suspicion—and a suspicion is all it is—began to grow, I again felt one of those little seismic tremors, a moment or two of that delicious sense of certainty dissolving into mystery. Or, not to be so romantic about it, into a *mess* . . . into a *khichri*. Because, whatever else you want to say, here is one of those subversive dishes whose goodness and appeal quietly goes about undermining nationalistic possessiveness.

Of course, every culture that has encountered rice and beans has learned to put them together in single dish. That the inhabitants of Osaka and New Orleans both sit down to red beans and rice doesn't mean the two dishes are the same. In other instances, however, the family resemblance is obvious. When Middle Eastern food writers discuss the rice-and-lentil dish that today is mostly known by the Arabic word *mujaddarah* (as we shall spell it), they can matter-of-factly note, as Arto der Haroutunian does in *Middle Eastern Cookery*, that "it is known as *kitry* in Iraq, *adas pollo* in Iran, *muaddas* in the Gulf States, and in far away India as *khichri*."

India, as we are learning, wasn't all *that* far away, even hundreds of years ago. Sometime after the Parsi emigrated, the Mongols united Persia and India into part of a single kingdom. There, the Moghul emperor Akbar the Great was so entranced by the taste of *khichri* that it (or, rather, a highly elaborated version of it) became a favorite palace dish. Much later still, in the late sixteenth century, Sephardic Jews began to emigrate in large numbers from Baghdad to Calcutta. Even more than the Parsi, these newcomers were drawn to Indian flavorings. Copeland Marks describes it in *The Varied Kitchens of India* as "love at first sight," and the resultant melding of their cuisines as a "culinary marriage between the cooking of Baghdad and that of Calcutta."

One Indian dish that they immediately took to was *khichri*. Gradually, it began to make its way to the parent Sephardic community in Baghdad, where, as Claudia Roden told us, "Iraqi Jews . . . ate it every Thursday night as part of a meatless meal to prepare their stomachs for the rich Friday night meal." It then spread from Baghdad Sephardic kitchens to neighboring Moslem ones, where it was received with such approval—the shade of Akbar the Great must have smiled—that it is today perceived as an Iraqi, not a Sephardic, dish.

In an essay read at the 1984 Oxford Cookery Symposium, Sami Zubaida remembers *khichri* as a favorite dish from his boyhood in a Jewish household in Baghdad. Most Iraqi main dishes, he notes, combine at least some meat with such dairy products as yogurt and butter, something forbidden to Jews.

> *Khichri* was the only "proper" main dish which had no meat, and as a result all dairy products were lavishly used: not only was it cooked in butter but melted butter was added at the table; yoghourt was used as a sauce and as an accompanying drink; and as an extra refinement, fried slices of cheese would also be added on occasion. *Khichri* then was a culinary compromise in the clash between the general culture and the subculture. It rectified a deprivation and as such becomes a remarkable dish, a candidate for inclusion in the Ideal Cook Book!

Here, slightly adapted, is Zubaida's very buttery Sephardic version of *khichri*.

KHICHRI AL-BAGHDADI
[serves 4]

8 ounces (about 1½ cups) long-grain rice
8 ounces (about 1½ cups) red "Egyptian" lentils (see note)
4 to 6 ounces (8 to 12 tablespoons) butter or *ghee*
4 to 6 cloves of garlic, minced
1 to 2 teaspoons ground cumin
1 tablespoon tomato purée
salt to taste

OPTIONAL GARNISH:
1 onion
2 tomatoes
4 ounces Haloumi cheese (see note)
more butter or *ghee*

Rinse the rice and lentils separately and soak in cold water, rice for 30 minutes, lentils for 1 hour. Melt half the butter or *ghee* in a saucepan and gently fry the minced garlic for a few minutes, or until soft and translucent. Add the cumin and fry for another minute. Mix in the drained rice and lentils (if using larger lentils, it might be wise to boil these for 10 minutes before adding to the rice), and sauté these for a few minutes in the hot butter. Add the tomato purée and mix well. Pour in water to cover by about half an inch, and salt to taste. Bring to a boil on a high flame, then reduce heat and simmer uncovered until the liquid is absorbed. When only a few bubbles remain on the surface of the rice-lentil mixture, cover tightly and allow to steam over a very low flame for another 15 minutes. Turn out onto a platter. Cut the remaining butter into pieces and distribute it over the hot *khichri*.

For the garnish: Cut the onion into thin rings and the tomatoes and cheese into slices. Melt more butter or *ghee* in a skillet and fry the onion rings over medium heat until they begin to brown. Place the cheese slices on top of the onions. When these turn soft, lay the tomatoes on top of them. Continue frying until the tomatoes soften. Then slip the contents of the pan on top of the *khichri* before serving.

Cook's Notes. Red lentils are available at Middle Eastern and natural foods stores. Interestingly, Zubaida says his own preference for this dish is the Indian split *tur dal* (also *toor dal* or *toovar dal*), which although called a lentil in India is, in fact, the pigeon pea—unknowingly, he has devised an Iraqi version of rice and peas!

Haloumi is a hard Middle Eastern cheese. An aged Gruyère is a possible substitute, but the Greek cheese Kefalotyri, if available, would be an even better one.

Sephardic Jews, by the way, brought *khichri* to other parts of Asia as well. Copeland Marks told us that "the Jews of Uzbekistan combine rice and mung beans and call it 'khirch-iree.' " They consider it a *Chinese* import!

Mujaddarah shares many characteristics with *khichri*, including the fact that it is prepared both as a thick *congee* or gruel, where it is eaten like hummus, and as a pilaf, where it is cooked until dry and eaten as a side dish. And it resonates in Arab cuisine with similar evocative force. As Claudia Roden recalls in *A Book of Middle Eastern Food*:

It is such a great favorite that although said to be for misers, it is a compliment to serve it. An aunt of mine used to present it regularly to guests with the comment, "Excuse the food of the poor!"—to which the unanimous reply always was: "Keep your food of kings and give us *mujaddarah* every day!"

Although Arab cooks vary the proportion of rice to lentils, the recipes are astonishingly consistent in their simplicity, whether they come from Saudi Arabia or Lebanon; *mujaddarah* seems not to be elaborated into the extravagant variations that Indian cooks have devised for *khichri*. However, in areas where rice is expensive or not a traditional grain, bulgur is used instead. The following recipes are good examples of the *congee* and pilaf styles of *mujaddarah*.

MUJADDARAH (1)

(adapted from Mary Laird Hamady's *Lebanese Mountain Cookery*)

[*serves 4 as a meal, 8 as a side dish*]

⅓ cup olive oil
2 large onions, sliced thin
1 tablespoon salt
¼ teaspoon black pepper
¼ cup short-grain rice, picked over and rinsed
2 cups lentils, picked over and rinsed
olive oil for drizzling

ACCOMPANIMENTS:
pita bread, slivered scallions, radishes, lemon wedges, ground black pepper

Prepare crispy onion shreds as directed on pages 312–13, but remove only half of the browned onions from the pan. Add ½ cup of water to the onions in the pan and stir until the water is absorbed. Return to the heat and stir in another ½ cup of water. Let this simmer until it is almost absorbed and add a final ½ cup. The onions should now be reduced to a sauce. Stir in the salt, pepper, rice, and lentils, and add 1½ quarts of water. Bring to a simmer, cover, and cook for 1 hour, or until the consistency is very thick, like oatmeal. Remove from the heat, put in a serving dish, and let cool to room temperature. Drizzle with olive oil and serve with the accompaniments, including the reserved crispy onion shreds.

MUJADDARAH (2)
(adapted from George Lassalle's *East of Orphanides*)
[*serves 4*]

1 cup whole (brown) lentils, picked over and rinsed
⅓ cup olive oil
2 large onions, sliced thin
1 teaspoon ground cumin
1 cup long-grain rice, picked over and rinsed
1¼ teaspoons salt
black pepper to taste

Put the lentils in a pan with 2 cups of water. Bring to a simmer and cook for 15 minutes, or until the lentils are almost cooked. Prepare crispy onion shreds as directed on pages 312–13, but remove only half of the browned onions from the pan. Add the cumin and ½ cup of water to the onions in the pan and stir until the water is absorbed. Return to the heat and stir in another ½ cup of water. Let this simmer until it is almost absorbed and add a final ½ cup of water. The onions should now be more or less reduced to a sauce. Add to this any remaining cooking liquid from the lentils and sufficient water to make 2½ cups. Stir in the rice, lentils, and salt and pepper. Bring to a boil on a high flame, then reduce heat and simmer uncovered until the liquid is absorbed. When only a few bubbles remain on the surface, cover tightly and allow to steam over a very low flame for another 15 minutes. Serve with the remaining crispy onion shreds scattered on top.

❋ ❋ ❋

Then out into the [streets of Cairo] again for a final nibble, *kushari.* The dish is a mélange of spaghetti, rice, and lentils; as the chef spoons it into the bowl he sprinkles flakes of fried onion on top and adds a bit of hot tomato sauce. The counters of a *kushari* stand bear bottles containing two kinds of sauce, one of vinegar with cloves of garlic floating in it, the other based on hot red peppers. Either sauce turns a bland dish into a fiery treat.

—Harry G. Nickles, *Middle Eastern Cooking*

If *khichri*'s appearance in the kitchens of Baghdad seems strange, its recent emergence as the Egyptian street food *kushari* strains credulity entirely. But there it is, being sold from brightly painted baby-blue and cotton-candy-pink pushcarts and tiny, hole-in-the-wall eateries. No one is sure how or why this happened—only that it has. Claudia Roden told us that when she left Cairo in 1952 she had never encountered *kushari*; when she returned thirty years later she found it everywhere. Here is her description of these *kushari* sellers at work.

Vendors put a plate of *kushari* together on demand—taking a ladleful from each of three different pans: one of short tubular macaroni (not spaghetti), another of rice, yet another of lentils. They do that at full speed, in seconds, the proportions depending on the relative cost of ingredients at the time and "*la tête du client.*" As far as I know there is always pasta; otherwise it becomes *mujaddarah* (or *mega-dara* in the local dialect). Pasta is cheap, while lentils have become expensive because many have left the land to work in Saudi Arabia, Kuwait, or Libya.

Apart from macaroni, what distinguishes *kushari* from both *mujadarrah* and *khichri* is that the basic ingredients are all already cooked. And this isn't the case only at the fast-food carts. Here is a home recipe for *kushari*, adapted from Samia Abdennour's *Egyptian Cooking*.

KUSHARI
[*serves 4*]

1 cup brown lentils, picked over and rinsed
1 cup rice, picked over and rinsed
4 ounces short tubular macaroni
2 large onions, sliced fine
¼ cup olive oil
2 cups tomato sauce
ground hot red pepper

Separately cook the lentils, rice, and macaroni. Prepare crispy onion shreds as directed on pages 312–13. As soon as they are removed from the pan, add the lentils, rice, and macaroni to the hot skillet with the remaining oil and cook for 7 to 10 minutes, stirring often to prevent their sticking. Then serve, topping each plate with some of the crispy onion shreds, a share of the tomato sauce, and a sprinkle of hot red pepper.

This dish, with its multiplicity of precooked starches, its multinational blend of ingredients, its mimicry of an *idea* of a dish with less regard to authenticity than to cost-saving, and, especially, the ease with which it can be portioned out, has the feel of the steam table to it, and, even more specifically, the army mess line. All of our informants generally agree that *khichri* evolved into *kushari* thanks to the British presence in Egypt—the dish possibly picked up by local cooks hired to work in the mess hall of some Indian regiment stationed in Cairo during World War II.

The important thing to notice, though, is how quickly this Creole cousin of *khichri* found a place in the hearts of the Egyptians who mob the lunch carts for it every day. The word has also worked its way into the Egyptian language as an affectionate synonym for "jumble" or "mess." As Charles Perry explained to us:

> *Hashîsh kushari* is a mixture of powdered hashish and tobacco (to judge from the composition of the rice and lentil dish, probably longer on tobacco than hashish). *Shây kushari* is tea made in a glass by adding water to leaves, rather than steeping it in a pot and straining out the leaves.

Of course, this was not the first time *khichri* had become the camp follower of an invading army, only to soon find itself dressed in foreign clothing, speaking a foreign language, and answering to what a foreign mouth believed to be its native name.

3

> Kedgeree (*khichri*) of the English type is composed of boiled rice, chopped hard-boiled egg, cold minced fish, and a lump of fresh butter: these are all tossed together in the *sauté*-pan, flavoured with pepper, salt, and any minced garden herb such as cress, parsley, or marjoram, and served in a hot dish.

The Indian *khichri* of fish is made like the foregoing with the addition of just enough turmeric powder to turn the rice a pale yellow colour, and instead of garden herbs the garnish is composed of thin *julienne*-like strips of chilli, thin slices of green ginger, crisply fried onions, etc.

—Col. A. R. Kenney-Herbert,
Wyvern's Indian Cookery Book (1869)

Natives of India tend to roll their eyes when the word *kedgeree* is mentioned, seeing it as yet another Western misreading of their cuisine. Let one native commentator, Julie Sahni in *Classic Indian Cooking*, speak for all (emphasis mine):

The boiled rice-and-fish preparation known as "kedgeree" is **not** an Indian dish, for a proper *khichri* **must** contain *dal* and does **not** contain fish. Kedgeree, very popular in British countries, was originally concocted by the British stationed in India to suit the Western palate.

Since *everyone* says this, it must be true. Still, Col. A. R. Kenney-Herbert was a keen observer of Indians and their kitchens, curious about and appreciative of their food, and he was there in the 1860s and Julie Sahni and company were not. The second paragraph quoted above—excised by Kenney-Herbert when he revised and expanded *Wyvern's Indian Cookery Book* into the better-known *Culinary Jottings for Madras* (first published in 1879)—requires, it seems to me, a slightly more complicated reading of the situation. It is, after all, apart from the fish, a dead-on description of *khichri*, with no sense at all of any adaptation "to suit the Western palate." The fact that the recipe was pruned from the later book reinforces this interpretation, since, to make room for other recipes, Kenney-Herbert trimmed matter he felt would not interest English cooks.

Perhaps because my initial encounter with *khichri* was in that exchange between Bruce Chatwin and Indira Gandhi, I find it hard to believe that a dish with the name of "mess" has its list of ingredients set for all time. Certainly, pilafs made with fish are not unknown in India—see the recipe for *pilau matabak* in *The Varied Kitchens of India*. And remember the Parsi predilection for using eggs in their cooking. Dishes like *khichri*, before they suffer hardening of the arteries, adapt themselves to situations as they find them. Since bits of fish do the same thing that legumes do—provide nutritional balance and textural contrast—it's not impossible to imagine the one leading the way to the other.

Imagine a native of Bombay visiting New England sometime in the last century and sampling a Yankee vegetable hash. On returning home she prepares the dish with the addition of *garam masala* and chopped coriander leaf. This hash is embraced as a novel vegetarian dish and endures well into this century, when an American food writer casts doubt on its purported lineage, since American hash is *always* made with meat and never with spices.

A dish like kedgeree often ends up far more a reflection of the culture that adopts it than the one that gave it birth, because—as was the case with chili con carne or spaghetti and meatballs—it is adopted only because it gives an exotic twist to something already familiar. The recipe that Kenney-Herbert gives directly above kedgeree in *Culinary Jottings for Madras* is one for a simple dish of leftover fish mixed into mashed potato:

> "Twice-laid," as this dish is called at Home, cannot be sent up better than . . . streaked with a fork outside, and baked till it takes on a pale brown tint. Chopped hard-boiled egg may be stirred into the fish and potatoes with advantage.

Substitute rice for the potato, and the route to kedgeree is all but inked onto the map.

Certainly, kedgeree, whatever its Anglo-Indian pedigree, was welcomed in England because it was at once novel, savory, digestible, inexpensive to make, and easy to keep hot under a chafing dish—and thus ideally constituted to take its place among the constellation of favored dishes that make up that great institution the British breakfast.

"Wyvern" himself published a book devoted to this subject—*Fifty Breakfasts*—but perhaps its greatest theorizer was another anonymous, retired military man, Major L, whose *Breakfasts, Luncheons, and Ball Suppers* (1887) offers an elaborate treatise on the subject, with menus for different seasons, occasions, and lifestyles. One of his menus sets out the following (not counting the cold meats on the side table or the various breads and cakes): "Kedgeree of Cod, Devilled Pheasant à la Perry, Broiled Ham, Mutton Chops, Eggs *aux Fines Herbes* . . ."

Sixty years later, when Dylan Thomas was commissioned to write the libretto to a (never made) film operetta, *Me and My Bike*, he opened it with Sir Gregory Grig, "fiercely moustached, ensanguined, vintage-portly, with poached eyes and mulberry nose," coming down to just such a morning repast:

> Sir Gregory goes to the sideboard, raises, one after the other, the covers of the huge silver dishes, commenting as he does so, in a rich North Country voice: "York ham. Cold pheasant. Game pie. Lamb chops. Devilled kidneys. Curried eggs. Kedgeree." He shakes his head. "Pot luck again!" He rakes a generous helping of each onto his great silver plate and goes down the sideboard to an array of bottles.

Although fewer Englishmen today have the opportunity to exercise it, the taste for such breakfasting remains—or, at least, the complaint does that things are not as they were and still ought to be. Here, for instance, is Nicolas Freeling speaking out of his 1972 charmer, *The Cook Book*:

> Even the Ritz is apt to offer you the small pallid parsley omelette. Whereas I want fish-cakes, and mutton chop, and kedgeree, and kidneys.

A possible solution to this problem of time and appetite for breakfast is offered by Clement Freud in *Below the Belt*, another curmudgeonly masculine Brit culinary epic. He suggests that the best meal of the day—breakfast—be moved to the best time of the day to enjoy it—late evening, using among other arguments the fact that a decent kedgeree takes "an hour to make, which is absolutely all right for an evening meal." (The particular kedgeree he had in mind was made of leftover roast pheasant.) This points the way for us lesser mortals, for whom one of these "light" dishes can provide a very filling supper.

The classic kedgeree is made exactly as Kenney-Herbert describes, except that smoked fish is now generally preferred to plain. Indeed, Eliza Acton had already remarked in *Modern Cookery for Modest Families* (1845) that "the best of all 'Kidgerees' to my mind is made with smoked haddock." However, as the dish's popularity spread, some cooks felt that if it *were* truly an Indian dish, it ought to have "Indian" ingredients. So, in went curry powder and sultanas, and the result was sent to the table with the chutney bottle. Our own feeling is that if a *khichri*-type kedgeree is wanted, the cook should follow the line laid out by Kenney-Herbert, seasoning it with turmeric, fresh ginger, and hot green chile, and serving it topped with crispy onion shreds.

Those who feel otherwise have Elizabeth David on their side, which should be solace enough. However, Jane Grigson, who writes of kedgeree with genuine enthusiasm in several of her books, while starting out in the curry powder, sultana, and chutney party (see, for instance, her 1973 recipe in *Fish Cookery*), switched her allegiance by the time she wrote *The Observer Guide to British Cookery* (1984). The recipe she offers there "came from someone who had spent years in India and retired to Cheltenham. The only spice is mace; indeed, the whole thing is simple and fresh." We have adapted it as follows.

KEDGEREE
[serves 4]

8 ounces (about 1½ cups) long-grain rice, cleaned and rinsed
2 blades of mace or a pinch of nutmeg
8 ounces smoked haddock fillet
2 tablespoons unsalted butter
2 hard-cooked eggs, peeled and chopped
salt and pepper to taste
½ cup all-purpose (whipping) cream
sprig or two of fresh parsley, minced

Cook the rice in your usual way with the two blades of mace (if using nutmeg, add this later, when the cream is stirred in). Cover the smoked haddock with water and gently poach, turning once, until the fish begins to flake. Remove from the poaching liquid and break apart with a fork. Melt 1 tablespoon of the butter in a large skillet and add the fish, stirring gently for a few minutes. Mix in the rice—discarding the mace—and, when the mixture is hot, the hard-cooked eggs. Season with salt and pepper to taste. Remove from the heat and quickly stir in the cream, the minced parsley, and the rest of the butter. Turn into a heated serving dish and serve at once.

Cook's Note. Those who find this dish a little rich might moisten the mixture partly with cream and partly with some of the fish-poaching liquid.

SMOKED SALMON KEDGEREE
[serves 4]

Smoked haddock is often marketed in the United States as "finnan haddie," whether it is the authentic Scottish article or not. If the product is a strange fluorescent yellow, it is artificially smoked and should be approached with caution. Englishmen under duress have used smoked herring instead (in this instance, perhaps a little curry powder is advised). We ourselves tried a small amount of smoked salmon and were led by a chain of association—salmon . . . eggs . . . cream . . . baby peas—to the following very pleasing results.

> 8 ounces (about 1½ cups) long-grain rice, cleaned and rinsed
> 8 ounces frozen baby peas
> 2 tablespoons unsalted butter
> ½ teaspoon salt
> ¼ teaspoon ground hot red pepper
> 1 onion, chopped
> sprig or two of fresh parsley, minced
> 2 hard-cooked eggs, peeled and chopped
> 4 ounces smoked salmon, cut into small strips
> salt and freshly ground black pepper to taste
> ½ cup all-purpose (whipping) cream

Cook the rice as you usually do. Meanwhile, simmer the frozen baby peas in ½ cup water for 5 minutes and remove from the heat. Melt the butter in a large skillet. Sprinkle in the salt and hot red pepper, add the onion, and sauté until translucent, stirring in the minced parsley toward the end of the cooking time.

When the rice is done, add the peas and their cooking liquid to the onions, and stir well. Turn in the cooked rice, the chopped hard-cooked egg, and the strips of smoked salmon, stirring to distribute the ingredients evenly throughout the rice. Taste for seasoning, adding salt as necessary and plenty of black pepper. Moisten well with the cream, and turn into a heated serving bowl. Serve at once.

  Cook's Note. A piece of fresh salmon may be substituted for the smoked. Poach it just until done, flake it with a fork, and proceed as above, using some of the poaching liquid instead of that from the peas to moisten the dish, adding to this a squeeze of lemon.

Wherever *khichri* has wandered, it has always managed to offer its eaters the solace of essential sustenance—however peculiar that may seem to the noninitiate. In a piece that appeared in his "Waiting for Dessert" column in *The Village Voice*, Vladimir Estragon (Geoffrey Stokes) wrote about a time when his wife—aka "The Woman Warrior"—was ordered by her doctor to spend a few days in bed. Estragon considered himself the ideal nurse—"I make custards, read aloud, disappear if asked, stuff like that"—but was nearly confounded when she asked him to prepare her favorite comfort food.

> What is to be done when one's n&d, sad-eyed as a bloodhound, requests *khichri*? One is to cook it, and that's that. It did, however, seem an odd choice for a *comforting* food. Spiced rice garnished with hard-boiled eggs and fried onions is, let's face it, a long way from tea and toast.

The Woman Warrior knew differently. Now we do, too.

Author's Note

I would especially like to thank Claudia Roden, Charles Perry, and Copeland Marks for kindly taking the time to write me informative letters in response to my queries regarding *khichri*. Thanks are also due to Alan Davidson, Barbara Wheaton, and Barbara Haber, for their prompt and generous assistance in providing me with information vital to completing this essay. Readers interested in pursuing more elaborate versions of *khichri* should start with Yamuna Devi's *Lord Krishna's Cuisine: The Art of Vegetarian Cooking*, which contains several of them.

CAPONATA SICILIANA

❧ ❧ ❧

Caponata came into my life in a rather offhand way. About ten years ago, I was chatting with a friend over the telephone about our different cooking adventures, and he mentioned that he had come up with a secret ingredient that vastly improved his standard pasta sauce—he stirred in an entire can of Progresso eggplant appetizer, a *condimento* also known—I was to discover—as caponata.

I had never noticed these cans before—small wonder, since they're even tinier than cans of tomato paste—but they were right there at the Stop & Shop. I bought a couple and took them home. However, since I didn't make tomato-based pasta sauces except to feed company, and then only when I was broke, those two cans sat on the kitchen shelf for a long time. Finally, one night, hungry and with not much in the house to eat, I glanced over the list of ingredients—eggplant, onion, celery, olives, and so on—and decided that a can of the stuff all by itself might do just fine stirred into a plate of spaghetti. After that, until I moved to Maine, where they proved not much in evidence, a succession of those little cans regularly moved through my kitchen.

An impression of a dish can be very different when you first encounter it as an eater, rather than as a cook. For anyone *making* caponata, the largest presence in the dish is the eggplant. However, spooning caponata out of the can (and marveling at how Progresso manages to get just one single green olive into each of them), I had the impression of a kind of vegetable *sweetmeat*—the mouth lingering not on any particular ingredient but on the syrupy sweet-and-sour savor and distinctly meaty texture of the whole.

At the time I knew even less about Italian cooking than I do now, and I had no idea that caponata was a Sicilian specialty. But I was surprised and intrigued by the complexity that was somehow bestowed on what was, after all, nothing more than a bunch of ordinary vegetables. It seemed exotic in what I took to be a very Mediterranean way, something you might be served in a Greek or Turkish taverna, or on the table of an exiled Sephardic family anywhere in the Levant.

As we shall see, there was some truth to this. But, more to the point, and unbeknownst to me, that mouthful of canned eggplant appetizer succeeded in capturing something, muffled and tinny though the echo was, of Sicilian cooking, where nearly every dish seems a medley of Mediterranean flavors. Turks, Greeks, Spaniards, Africans, Sephardic Jews: all have had their turn at stirring the pot.

❧ ❧ ❧

If you've never encountered caponata, you should imagine a delicious mélange of vegetables cooked and served, usually at room temperature, in a slightly viscous sweet-and-sour sauce—the vegetables' own cooking liquid plus a touch of wine vinegar and sugar. Eggplant provides the substance, augmented and highlighted by celery and sometimes sweet red pepper; tomato and onion melt into a sauce. The Mediterranean aspect comes from the flavorings, which at their simplest include capers, olives (green, but sometimes also black), garlic, and parsley. Further additions include, most usually, raisins and *pignoli*.

Mary Taylor Simeti explains in her book on Sicilian cooking, *Pomp and Sustenance*, that caponata is an elaboration of a humble preparation that occurs all over the Mediterranean. This, she writes, "consists of frying small pieces of eggplant in oil, then simmering them or simply covering them with a sauce or dressing." As an illustration, she offers a version from Ustica, a tiny island off the Palermo coast. In it the fried eggplant is put into a serving dish, sprinkled with white wine vinegar, sugar, minced fresh mint, and slices of raw garlic. Then it is allowed to sit until the flavors mingle and the dish has cooled.

About as far out to sea to the south of Sicily as Ustica is to the north lies another island, Malta, a former British colony and now an independent state. In her *Mediterranean Vegetable Cookery*, Rena Salaman gives a Maltese recipe for a caponata-like dish called *bringiel agrodolce*, where pieces of eggplant are sautéed in olive oil, then crushed tomatoes, garlic, and fresh mint are added and cooked into a sauce. The *agrodolce* of wine vinegar and sugar is mixed in, and the dish, again, is allowed to rest. Salaman writes: "Sweet-and-sour dishes found their way along the North African coast and into Europe during the Arab invasions of the seventh and eighth centuries. . . . Similar dishes are found in Sicily, Spain, and the Arab countries." They are found in Greece, too, where *melitzanes stifatho* is a near clone of the Maltese dish, except that the herbs are often sweet basil and bay instead of mint.

At some point in the past, this still simple dish reached Sicily, where it was embraced, and bestowed with a uniquely Sicilian—even Palermitan—personality. Palermitan means "of or from Palermo," and I would never have had the insight, or nerve, to make so exact a connection, despite a few clues I found pointing to it, had Matt not been reading to me—from *The New Yorker*—an account of Palermitan life and architecture by Fernanda Eberstadt. I was just then mulling over the origins of caponata, and this picture portrait of Palermo put in my hand the key piece to the jigsaw puzzle. Suddenly, all the parts fell together in seamless, illuminating fit.

Sicily has belonged at one time or another to every powerful Mediterranean civilization, without ever possessing a defining culture of its own, and Sicilian taste is a confusing but heady *tutti-frutti* of bits and pieces taken from them all. This is nowhere more apparent than in Palermo, the provincial capital, where churches built at the time of the Crusades by Norman rulers out of the same sober gray stone as their counterparts in France and England sport pink stucco domes instead of slate roofs and reveal interiors where polyphonic Islamic and Byzantine motifs run riot. And its history ever since has only built on and compounded this fecund cultural confusion.

Today, located out of the mainstream of both modern Sicilian commerce and a booming tourist trade, Palermo seems less an important city than an old, battered wardrobe, a repository for all the fancy costumes of that island's bizarrely complicated history, left there in a careless jumble for the current inhabitants to root around in for anything that claims their eye. Consider, for example, the decor of a shiny red food stall that Eberstadt noted in Vucciria, one of Palermo's many outdoor markets:

wallpapered in gold-and-brown coffee-bean wrapping paper; fes-
tooned with crimson poinsettias and with branches of mistletoe
and bittersweet, sage and laurel; lit by strings of green and blue
bulbs overhead; furnished with chairs, curtains, a television set,
votive candles illuminating a tiny red altar to the Madonna, and
covered with sepia photographs of the vendor's stout, unsmiling
mother and father, mother and grandparents, father and uncles
circa 1920.

This, all in the background; in the foreground are the vendor's wares
themselves: a panoply of olives, whole and stuffed, all different types
and colors, set out in pails; mammoth three-liter, chrome-yellow tins of
salted anchovies; and stacked jars of scarlet roasted peppers.

Translate this promiscuous flamboyance into pottery and you have
majolica; into theater and you have Palermo's life-sized puppet shows;
into cuisine and you have . . . caponata. In *Itinerari palermitani*, Gaetano
Falzone attributes its invention to just this Palermitan flair for mixing up
different culinary influences in a single dish, and Antonio Cardella, in *Sicilia e le isole in bocca*, puts caponata in this kind of neighborhood:

> At last we are in Via Alloro, a narrow street, main artery of the
> ancient ward of Palermo called Kalsa, crowded with phantasms of
> a more or less remote but still impressive past. If you happen [to
> come here] at noon during spring, you will smell a pleasant sweet-
> sour scent fluttering through the alleys swarming with people:
> women in the humble kitchens of their even more humble houses
> prepare the well-known "caponata" of eggplants or else yellow
> pumpkin in sweet-sour sauce.

As advocates of the "Mediterranean Diet" have been drumming
into our heads recently, few countries bordering on the Mediterranean
can support a meat-rich diet. Even today, fresh meat remains a luxury
for the less affluent.* The sheep flock is weeded of surplus lambs in the

---

*Although that is changing fast. Even as prosperity-oppressed Americans fantasize about sub-
sisting on the spare but putatively life-prolonging diet of the Mediterranean poor, the rising
income level among those who have traditionally eaten such food has brought about a diet
revolution of its own: fast-food meals, fat-intensive snacks, and lots and lots of fresh meat.
Each package of imported pasta, bottle of olive oil, or tube of roasted garlic paste the
Mediterranean diet enthusiast adds to the grocery cart brings some *contadino* one step closer
to his first Big Mac.

spring and chickens that stop laying go straight to the pot, and that, for the less affluent, is mostly that. The passion that Italians have invested in making salami and prosciutto is as much testimony to the culinary mileage that can be gotten from such *salume*—all served in paper-thin slices—as to the need to preserve without waste every bit of the slaughtered pig before the advent of refrigeration.

Consequently, southern Italian cooking depends, as do other Mediterranean cuisines, on such protein-supplying substitutes as legumes and cheeses, which are put to lavish and imaginative use. But, as if to prove that a meat-spare diet springs from no inherent dietary prudence but from a keenly felt deprivation, it is also rich in meat analog.* Brine-cured olives may start the list, but it quickly expands into the fleshy-textured vegetables that, grilled over charcoal, take on a resemblance to animal flesh, an impersonation heightened still further by a lavish anointing of olive oil.

Perhaps the simplest, and hence most astonishing, of these analogs is a dish of sweet red peppers grilled, peeled, and served at room temperature, dressed in their own juices enriched with just a dribble of olive oil. In color, sweetness, and succulent texture, the roasted pepper flesh is not so much "like" rare roast beef as what rare roast beef might aspire to, if a cut of meat could have an aspiration.

Eggplant, of course, can be prepared in the same way—roasted over a fire and the flesh then tossed in oil—and the result is also delicious, but no one would ever confuse it, in this state, for meat. What it is more like, really, is chunks of *fat*. This connection is all the more obvious when you think of how it is used as a sop for olive oil in many Italian—and other Mediterranean—dishes. We, with our meat-rich and, especially, fat-rich diet, tend to accuse these dishes of being "drenched" in oil, but in their proper context they are sublime—as good as any mouthful of roast pork, and probably no more caloric.

It is only in keeping with our understanding of the Palermitan culinary sensibility to imagine its cooks enriching not so much the dish as

---

*Colman Andrews, in his sympathetic but clear-eyed assessment of the "Mediterranean Diet" in *Flavors of the Riviera*, notes that a pioneering nutrition study on the island of Crete in the years following World War II revealed that while fish, meat, and dairy products made up only 7 percent of the diet, some 72 percent of the families surveyed identified meat as their favorite food, and I'll bet it still is.

its metaphorical implications. The synergistic combination of oil and eggplant provides the fat; the celery (especially) and olives add a generous portion of meaty, slightly gristly flesh. Finally, the *agrodolce*, plus the seasonings and tomato, combines sweet, salt, and sour to produce a thick, rich, and darkly colored blood. Effect is added to effect, until before us lies the savory interior of an entirely edible, fabulously rococo beast.

※ ※ ※

In *Classic Techniques of Italian Cooking*, Giuliano Bugialli argues that the word *caponata* derives from medieval ways of cooking capons, which were often prepared with an *agrodolce* sauce. This preparation was then applied, he suggests, to the cooking of eggplant. Perhaps, however, he has got the cart before the horse. As we have seen, the dish most likely arrived in Sicily not from Italy but from the Middle East; Sicilians might have given the dish its name simply in recognition of its similarity to the delicate, moist, and tasty flesh of the bird.

"Little capon" it may well be named, but some Sicilian cooks have seemed more intent on transmogrifying it into a miniature basilisk, cockatrice, hippogriff, or whatever you would call the monstrous beast assembled from the parts that make up the following definition of caponata, given by Spike and Charmane Hughes in their *Pocket Guide to Italian Food and Wine*:

> an elaborate dish of aubergine [eggplant], olives, celery, capers, hard-boiled egg, baby octopus, lobster, prawns, smoked tunny-fish roe and swordfish, all covered with a sweet-sour sauce made of almonds, olive oil, bread, anchovies, orange juice, sugar, grated chocolate, and vinegar.

Give the weight of literal transliteration to an evanescent gesture, and you're likely to end up with a heavy, indigestible, and misunderstood dish. Sicilian cooking, with its love of dramatic flourishes, is especially vulnerable to bad translation. Add to this the effect of its sensual abandon on Anglo-Saxon imaginations, which fail to understand the essential simplicity of means that underlies it, and you have a surefire recipe for disaster. Waverley Root, for example, devotes three whole pages to caponata in his *Food of Italy*: they are at once informative, entertaining, and perversely wrong-headed.

To make a true caponata, Root insists, you must sauté all five of the chief ingredients—eggplants, peppers, tomatoes, onions, and celery—separately; season each with its own appropriate herbs and spices; and cook each an exactly determined time. These separately and perfectly cooked vegetables are then finished up in an "enormous iron skillet with vinegar, capers, olives, a little tomato sauce and a hint of anchovy juice" and served "still sizzling in the skillet." The result is a dish with "as many different flavors as it has ingredients" that "melts away in the mouth almost as literally as ice cream."

While I doubt that Spike and Charmane Hughes ever tasted a version of caponata that matched their definition of it, I do believe that Root had eaten one made the way he describes and that it tasted as good as he says. But it was served to him in a restaurant; it was a chef's bravura creation, and from it Root deduced several rules that, on soberer reflection, he should have realized were really exceptions to them—starting with the fact that caponata is usually served at room temperature, precisely in order to allow the ingredients time to cool together and thus give their flavors a chance to meld.

Instead, this passage, with its sizzling skillet and mouth-watering flavors, makes such heady reading that few food writers who encounter it escape unscathed. Donaldo Soviero, in *La Vera Cucina Italiana*, quotes it approvingly at length, and Jo Bettoja, although she never specifically mentions it, echoes it almost word for word in *Southern Italian Cooking*, including these instructions: "[W]hen more than one vegetable is used in a caponata, each one is cooked separately and seasoned with its own herbs and spices, so they retain their own distinct flavors." But what *are* these separate herbs and spices? When Root gets around to giving a recipe for caponata in *The Best of Italian Cookery*, he says not one word about them.* And, even more tellingly—since her recipe follows directly after this advice—neither does Jo Bettoja.

However, she does make a point of sautéing the eggplant, celery,

---

*I may be unfair here. A careful reading of the small print on the copyright page suggests that this book is a translation of an Italian cookbook to which Root provided the introduction and the notes—some explanatory, some expository—that appear in boxes here and there throughout the book. If so, Root might never have prepared *any* of the recipes in this book that bears his name—which would explain why the commentary has the feeling of floating in from the dining room.

and onion separately. For some cooks, this has become an *idée fixe*. Consider Carlo Middione's rather bullying imperatives in *The Food of Southern Italy:* "The three major ingredients, eggplant, celery, and onions, are cooked separately. Use the same pan, cooking one after the other. This is extremely important. Do not try to make this dish otherwise." Oh, Carlo, come on.

At this point it is worth recalling that many Sicilian cooks gain the same effect simply by timing when the vegetables go into the pot. Nor does everyone agree that the ingredients of caponata should be *à point*. Arthur Schwartz, restaurant critic for *The New York Daily News*, writes in his cookbook *What to Eat When You Think There's Nothing in the House to Eat:* "American cooks don't seem to understand that the eggplant is supposed to be soft, not firm; that the chunky mixture should hold together, not fall into separate vegetable pieces." And, if the idea is to keep the flavor of each major ingredient separate (which makes sense only if the caponata is to be eaten, as Root suggests, directly from the skillet), why not go all the way and follow the example of Jacques Médecin, who in *Cuisine niçoise* insists on cooking each of the basic ingredients of his *ratatouille* in its own skillet?

I have never been to Sicily, and, even if I had, I doubt if I would have wheedled out of anyone the secret of "true" caponata. After all, it is by its very nature a dish to which ingredients can be added with abandon, and every Sicilian town and village—and possibly every family—has its own way of making it. But understand its power over the appetite—which has nothing to do with separate sautés or secret flavorings but with the way that the *agrodolce* enhances and transforms its voluptuously meaty texture—and you can safely wend your way through the shouting and posturing of the various recipe writers, as vehement in their own way as an aisle of Sicilian fish vendors competing for your custom.

❊ ❊ ❊

We ourselves began to make caponata with the idea of resurrecting my use of it as a simple pasta sauce—not at all a traditional use!—along the lines of the vegetable pastas discussed on pages 197–204. In other words, we wanted to eat a lot of it, and thus wanted to make it as lean as we could without denying it any of its essential succulence.

Even at this simple level, there are still decisions to be made, starting with the preparation of the eggplant. Many recipes encourage you to do without the salting, soaking, and subsequent wringing out of that vegetable, supposedly to rid it of its bitter juices. We do it, however, because the process gives the eggplant a denser, chewier texture. The eggplant can be peeled or not, as you choose. We like it with the peel.

Also, we decided to add the flesh of a sweet red pepper, which is not generally considered an essential ingredient, because it increases the impression of meatiness, allowing us to decrease the amount of olive oil. (If you plan to serve it as an appetizer, you may want to use more olive oil.) You may also choose to add other traditional ingredients, like raisins, pine nuts, or even a teaspoon or so of cocoa, all of which would be added during the last few minutes of cooking. Finally, Giuliano Bugialli, in *Classic Techniques of Italian Cooking*, offers a tomatoless Tuscan version of caponata in which, instead, two tablespoons of tomato paste are blended into half a cup of water and mixed with the sugar and vinegar to make a sauce at the last minute. This produces a thicker, more syrupy caponata that is more emphatically a relish.

We find that caponata freezes well, and we put aside half of each batch in this way. The following amount, served with four ounces of pasta per person, makes a generous meal for four. (We eat it without cheese.) It is also delicious on plain boiled rice. But the easiest way to turn it into a meal is to empty a can of chunk tuna on top of it—a dish that Arthur Schwartz says he has been eating regularly for twenty years. Carlo Middione suggests serving it with roast meat or poultry or stuffed into hollowed-out, medium-sized tomatoes, which are then heated in the oven until their skins start to soften. Sicilians often eat it simply with some bread and a glass of red wine.

CAPONATA CASA NOSTRA
[*serves 4 to 8*]

2 pounds eggplant (about 2 large)
1 tablespoon coarse kosher salt
1 pound yellow onions (about 3 medium)
1 large red bell pepper
5 or 6 stalks celery, with leaves
6 tablespoons olive oil

1 teaspoon crushed hot red pepper
3 or 4 cloves of garlic, peeled
1 28-ounce can tomatoes in juice
about 10 Kalamata-style black olives, pitted
about 5 large green olives, pitted
2 tablespoons salted capers (see note)
a handful of fresh Italian parsley, minced
¼ cup red wine vinegar
2 tablespoons white (or brown) sugar
salt and freshly ground black pepper to taste

Wash, dry, and trim the stem end from the eggplant. Cut it, skin included, into ½-inch dice, place in a colander, and sprinkle with the coarse kosher salt, spreading this through the eggplant pieces with your hands. Set over a large bowl and let rest for at least a half hour and preferably up to 2 hours. Then discard the collected liquid and dump the eggplant cubes in a sink full of cold water. Swirl them around to rinse them well, then lift them out, handful by handful, squeezing them hard. Put them back into the colander, into which you have already spread an expendable dish towel. When all the eggplant pieces are in the towel, gather its ends together and twist it progressively tighter and tighter, forcing as much liquid out of the eggplant as possible. Put the cubes in a large bowl.

Peel and coarsely chop the onions. Core, seed, and coarsely chop the red pepper. Cut the celery into bite-sized pieces. Pour the olive oil into a large pot and heat over a low flame until it begins to ripple. Stir in the crushed hot red pepper and then the celery. Cook this, stirring occasionally, for 5 minutes, then add the onion, garlic, and red bell pepper pieces. Cook these, still stirring, for another 5 minutes, or until the onion is soft and translucent. Stir in the eggplant. Sauté this mixture for 20 minutes. At this point, taste the eggplant. The flesh should be soft and tender. If not, continue cooking another 5 minutes and taste again.

Add the tomatoes with their liquid, dividing them into chunks with a heat-proof rubber spatula. Reduce heat, cover, and simmer about 10 minutes, while you cut the pitted black and green olives into small bits and rinse and chop the capers. Add these, stir in well, and cover again, continuing the simmering until the eggplant skin is tender, about 15 more minutes. Taste the caponata for doneness: the vegetables should all be soft but retain some texture; the liquid should be syrupy. Stir in the minced parsley, the vinegar, and the sugar. Cook just long enough to dissolve the sugar, then remove from the heat. Add salt and pepper to taste. Serve warm or at room temperature.

Cook's Note. The true caper comes from a small bush (*Capparis rupestri*) with tough oval leaves that grows wild around the Mediterranean, its buds producing lovely, short-lived flowers. Brine these buds and you have capers, their pungent flavor coming from the capric acid (named after that slightly goaty taste) that develops during curing. Capers are cured either in a salty vinegar solution or in plain salt, and anyone—like myself—used to only the pickled version will find dry-salted capers an eye-opener: plumper, firmer in texture, and intensely flavored. In fact, they are almost like a nutmeat, and I find it hard to resist eating them straight from the container. Look for them at better fancy grocers.

Of the many sweet-and-sour Mediterranean eggplant dishes these researches uncovered, one of the most appealing is the Turkish *patlican ve biber salatasi*, which transforms our mythological vegetable beast into a delectable, fire-breathing dragon. This version has been worked up from Ayla Algar's *Classic Turkish Cooking* and the Turkish-influenced Bulgarian-Sephardic cooking of Suzy David in *The Sephardic Kosher Kitchen*.

GRILLED EGGPLANT AND PEPPER SALAD
[*serves 4 to 6*]

2 medium-sized eggplants (about 2 pounds)
1 green bell pepper
2 red bell peppers
2 fresh poblano (or other mildly hot) chile peppers
1 large tomato
1 clove garlic, minced
salt and black pepper to taste
1 teaspoon sugar
1 to 2 tablespoons wine vinegar
4 to 6 tablespoons olive oil

a handful of flat-leaf parsley, chopped
hot red pepper flakes or powder to taste

Grill the eggplant and peppers over an open flame, if possible, or otherwise under a broiler until they are seared and black on all sides. The
eggplants will turn soft and sag slightly. Peel the still warm eggplants
and set in a colander to drain for at least a half hour. Then chop the
flesh into small pieces and put into a medium-sized bowl.

Meanwhile, peel away the blackened skin from the peppers. Slice
them open and remove and discard the seeds. Reserve all juices. Cut the
flesh into small pieces and mix both these and the reserved juice with
the eggplant.

Pour boiling water over the tomato to loosen its skin, then peel and
seed it. Cut the flesh into pieces and mix this and any juice into the
pepper-eggplant mixture.

Stir this well and add the minced garlic, salt, and black pepper to
taste. Dissolve the sugar in the wine vinegar and stir this into the mixture. Add the olive oil, minced parsley, and hot red pepper flakes or
powder to taste. Let the flavors mingle for an hour or so before serving.
Serve with wedges of pita bread. The salad will keep for several days in
the refrigerator.

Further Reading

Cooks seeking more adventurous versions of caponata might consider
the grilled version in Johanne Killeen and George Germon's *Cucina
Simpatica*, the Italian Sephardic Jewish one in Edda Servi Machlin's
The Classic Cuisine of the Italian Jews, or the recipe for "Island Eggplants" in Rosemary Barron's *Flavors of Greece*. And while eggplant is
certainly the traditional foundation of caponata, it is hardly mandatory.
Among the books consulted for this piece, we discovered versions made
with potatoes (in Mimmetta LoMonte's *Classic Sicilian Cooking*), arti-
chokes, and cauliflower and escarole (in Jo Bettoja's *Southern Italian
Cooking*).

CAKES ON THE GRIDDLE

❦　❦　❦

Cakes made of a batter so thin that it flows easily upon a griddle, and that can, therefore, be quickly baked and served hot, are griddlecakes, and great favorites they are. . . . Cold days are the gala days for hot cakes.

—*New England Cook Book* (1905)

Pancakes were an event in my family, and it was a very special Sunday—as Sunday it almost always proved to be—when my mother would consent to make them. This was because she believed that they should be eaten straight from the griddle—which meant that she would have to stand at the stove before a collocation of skillets, turning out batch after batch of them, while four hungry children and an equally hungry husband eagerly awaited their turn to be served . . . and served . . . and served again. It was only when appetites waned (and the level of batter in the pitcher had dropped precipitously) that she could load up the frying pans one last time for herself, knowing that she who ate last at least ate in peace . . . and had the table to herself.

We North Americans have no patent on the pancake, but we do hold one for the pancake *breakfast*—and most certainly for the flavor combination of griddlecakes, syrup, and sausage links or bacon. If a forkful of hot cake dripping butter and maple syrup now brings me back to my childhood kitchen, with all the anticipatory bustle of a pancake morning, I'm reminded that its evocative force was just as keen when I was still a child. Then, my little Log Cabin syrup tin linked me directly to the exciting world of the winter forest, where lumberjack camp cooks flipped their flapjacks high into the air and smoke belched from the stovepipes of maple-sugar shacks, sending the sweet smell of boiling sap floating over the deep drifts of snow.

Here, I know, I speak for myself, but surely not only for myself. Fried or scrambled or three-minute eggs, hash brown potatoes, buttermilk doughnuts, steaming bowls of oatmeal, hot buttered toast, fresh-brewed coffee poured straight from the percolator, each has its place at the traditional American breakfast table. But none of them—except the coffee—has left in its wake as much appreciative prose as the griddle-cake.

Breakfast may be only a breaking of the night's fast for many of us, a matter of a bowl of cereal and a glass of juice. But for those who will soon be pulling on their work boots, it has always been the day's most important meal, filling the stomach and energizing the spirit. Let the old cowboy song say it for anyone ever dragged from a warm bunk into the icy morning air by the aroma of griddlecakes wafting from the cookshack or farmhouse kitchen:

> *Wake up, Jacon, day's a-breakin'*
> *Fryin' pan's on an' hoecake's bakin'.*
> *Bacon in the pan, coffee in the pot,*
> *Git up now and git it while it's hot.*

Why? Why pancakes? Why for breakfast? Why with syrup? I realized, not for the first time, that with a much made dish, as with an old friend, our sense of familiarity may come less from intimate knowledge than from casual assumptions we have never bothered to challenge. When we finally do, we discover in them unfathomed and unguessed-at depths.

A trip to the cookbook shelf, rather than helping to resolve my questions, only added to my confusion. I discovered that, a hundred years ago, it was not uncommon for "pancakes" to be dropped like doughnuts into boiling fat, rather than fried flat in a skillet. Nor were griddlecakes universally served with syrup. Sometimes they were eaten as is, at other times with a dab of butter, a sprinkle of sugar, a grating of nutmeg. Most perplexing of all, however, was the freewheeling attitude cooks at that time had toward naming their creations. Pancakes, griddlecakes, flannel cakes, feather cakes, drop cakes, flapjacks, slap-jacks . . . as soon as you think you have sorted out one from the other, the next cookbook you turn to muddles up everything all over again—even if it was written by the same author.*

Still, I did learn something. The griddlecake has its origins in the porridge pot, and in these books, with their plethora of recipes, ranging from the primeval hoecake (cornmeal plus water) straight through to the feathery-textured, genteel flannel cake, we can trace its efforts, all through the last century, to escape from that pot for good.

In the beginning, the cook would take some cold gruel, pat it flat, and either set it among the ashes in the fireplace to bake or slip it onto a hot, greased griddle. As primitive as the method was, that brief, direct contact with the fire made all the difference in its status. For it might almost be called a universal culinary law that the baked and the fried is of a higher order than the boiled. This is partly a matter of texture—of buttery and crisp, crusty and light, versus wet and sludgy. And it is also because the baking or the frying particularizes each spoonful of gruel/batter as it cooks it, transforming an amorphous mass into an assortment of individuals—fritters, jollyboys, doughnuts, griddlecakes—each with its own crisp crust and light, tender interior.

The griddlecake, simple as it is, can absorb an enormous amount of such attentiveness. It thus allows any cook, however poor or ill-equipped, an opportunity to shine. And nothing, as the nineteenth century would slowly but surely discover, abets this more than possession of a tin of baking powder.

❋ ❋ ❋

My woman wants to set some [griddlecakes] and she took a notion she must have risin' to put in 'em.
—C. M. Kirkland, *Forest Life* (1842)

The baking powder, or "saleratus" (the grandest word in the trappers' very abridged dictionary), cannot be found.
—W. A. Baillie-Grohman, *Camps in the Rockies* (1882)

---

*For instance, Marion Harland's recipe for flannel cakes in *Common Sense in the Household* (1873) calls for flour, milk, egg, and yeast; the one she gives in *Breakfast, Luncheon, and Tea* (1892) calls for cornmeal, milk, yeast, and no egg; and, finally, the one in her *Complete Cook Book* (1903) calls for flour, egg, milk, and baking powder.

When Congress created the United States Patent Office in 1790 to encourage and protect American ingenuity, the first patent it awarded was to a Vermonter named Samuel Hopkins for an improved method of producing pearlash, a leavening agent made of chemically treated wood ash. Although European bakers bought it by the shipload for leavening highly spiced cakes like gingerbread, its soapy aftertaste was no boon to American griddle breads. But pearlash's limitations only spurred on other inventors, and a patent self-rising flour would appear in 1852 and commercial baking powder in 1856.

Although this same ingenuity was soon to be applied to the production of bread yeast—Gaff, Fleischmann & Co. would market foil-wrapped compressed yeast in 1870—most home cooks depended on various sourdough concoctions. These could produce excellent bread, but even the most dependable could not do so on demand. Baking powder, on the other hand, was nothing if not fast-acting, and, as the various formulas were perfected* and cooks learned to take their measure, it transformed home baking. All the foods we associate with that phase, saving only yeast breads and pies, have become what they are because of it.

To the breakfast table baking powder gave the doughnut, the biscuit, the muffin or gem, and, of course, the griddlecake. Where the last of these had it over the biscuit or the muffin as a breakfast bread (and it was not at all unknown, at least in Maine, to use the griddlecake as a kind of Yankee wheat tortilla, "wrappings for the more substantial victuals [being] stowed away . . . cod-steak or pork-chop or beef-steak") was that it could be produced nonstop, requiring neither tricky kneading nor rolling out and cutting nor a set amount of time in the oven.

To the eater, this meant a veritable river of batter pouring from a bottomless pitcher, an endless procession of freshly baked griddlecakes,

---

*I include here baking soda, first known as saleratus or "aerated salts," which came into use around the same time. Although it is a component of baking powder, it possesses leavening power of its own, which can be set off by an acidic ingredient in the batter (most famously, buttermilk), and many cooks preferred to utilize it alone. Baking powder could be made at home by mixing baking soda and cream of tartar (a by-product not—as I once thought—of teeth-scrapings but of winemaking), but increasingly it was scooped from a tin container holding a patent mixture, in which case it might well be made with much cheaper, if harsher, aluminum salts.

served up one after the other after the other, until appetite cried, "Hold, enough!" If the difference between a dollop of gruel and a griddlecake was that between a penny and a silver dollar, then to have a bagful of self-rising flour was to own the mint. This is why, in pancake iconography, the basic unit is the *stack*.

A feeling for the logistics such a breakfast entailed can be found in *Prairie Kitchen Sampler*—a kitchen-by-kitchen recollection of Nebraska farmhouse cooking by E. Mae Fritz. She remembers that in the 1920s farmers could still bring their grain to the local mill. There,

> as the miller milled the wheat, he would, upon request, add dry leavening agents to one or two bags turning the flour into "pancake flour." Pancake flour, in its day and in its way, was the forerunner of all the many boxed baking mixes that now take up more and more grocery store shelf space with each passing year. . . . So far as I know, there wasn't a recipe for making pancakes from pancake flour. If there was, I never saw a copy of it. I didn't need a recipe to stir up a batch of pancakes, all I needed to know was how many people I'd be feeding [and] the size of their appetites.

Note that she calls this "pancake flour," not "biscuit" or even "self-rising" flour. Each of these sacks weighed fifty pounds. Even so, it would probably take her no more than three months to work her way through two of them. Her pancake formula mixed four cups of this leavened flour with two cups of milk and four beaten eggs to make twenty-four six-inch pancakes. Her calculation was that a hungry farmer—or farmhand—would eat four to six for breakfast,

> slathered with butter and drizzled with syrup, [along with] several strips of home-cured bacon or a slice of ham or pork sausage patties, hash browned potatoes, and fried eggs, and he drank milk along with cup after cup of hot coffee.

Furthermore, baking powder catalyzed the cook as much as it did the pancake batter. The moment the liquid was added to the mix, the cook was racing against time: it wasn't only the hungry men around the table who urged her on but the very stuff of the griddlecake itself. (I speak of single-acting baking powder; the double-acting variety came much later.) In the chapter "Down-East Breakfast" in his 1950 book

Maine Doings (whence came the pancake-as-wrapper quote above), Robert P. Tristram Coffin paints a vivid portrait of the result:

> The flapjack cook uses no effete pancake-mix. She uses plain buckwheat or wheat flour, sour milk, salt, two even teaspoons of cream-o'-tartar, one of saleratus, a tablespoon of sugar, elbow grease, a tablespoon of shortening, a large duck's egg, and vigor, to mix it up. She pours it out of a gallon pitcher into an old-fashioned, thick-iron frying pan, sending up volcanoes of blue smoke from its sizzling pork fat, and she fills the spider full of her dough from rim to rim. She sears her dough-flap brown on its port side . . . tosses it high into the air, big as the frying pan itself, catches it exquisitely as it comes hurtling down . . . without smearing the rim of her pan, sears it, this side, to a light mahogany, and tosses it tablewards to her hungering man. The parade of flying flapjacks is continuous. The good cook keeps the kitchen air full of them.

Fanciful as this portrait is, it nicely captures a moment in our culinary history, now lost to our everyday experience, when old-fashioned artisanship made its brief but happy marriage with modernity's sense of business urgently needing to be done. The practiced skill of the cook set a rhythm that looks forward to the hurry-scurry of the short-order grill; the meal she produced, however, looked back to the old-fashioned farmhouse breakfast, where frugal ingredients were transformed by intensive labor into a morning feast.

In fact, the griddlecake breakfast is an ideal example of what—now that it has almost entirely vanished—we're beginning to realize we once actually had: authentic American peasant cooking. The meat is of secondary importance (and from the family-raised pig), the meal being built instead around a humble bread, made palatable with a coarse-flavored, homemade syrup of boiled-down sugar-maple sap or the juices crushed from the sorgo plant.

Today . . . well, what history intends to abandon, it first dilutes. Now, at too many breakfast tables, the syrup has only a touch of maple—if that—and the pancakes are made from a mix, if they aren't bought frozen to be heated in the microwave. The sound of bacon spluttering in the skillet summons as much fear as it does appetite. Close behind all this treads the question: Why bother? And the pancake breakfast begins to fade away.

This is not how it has to be. In our own two-person, two-griddle household, pancakes are a regular affair, mixed from scratch, cooked, and served—with no sense of hurry—in about the time it takes to brew the coffee. Matt makes and pours the batter. Then, while she washes up, I tend to the cooking, as the plates warm in a slow oven below. Good sweet butter and a pitcher of Maine maple syrup wait on the breakfast table, but these are not the real extravagance here—or, rather, they are the lesser part of it. To our immediate ancestors, what a baking-powder-activated pancake batter gave was instant access to plenty. To us, for whom plenty is not an issue, it bespeaks instead the luxury of just enough room in our morning for all this to take place.

PANCAKES' PROGRESS

Matt Lewis Thorne

It was obvious I had to teach my old pancakes some new tricks. I had no trouble getting them to roll over and they were great at playing dead, but that was it. In fact, since they no longer came from a box, they weren't even "my old pancakes" anymore. When the spirit moved—less and less often—I'd consult one cookbook or another, stir up a bowlful of batter, and John and I would have ourselves some pancakes. I felt better about the ingredients, but in every other respect I might just as well have been using a mix. And, even on good days, I'm not sure the pancakes I produced ever surpassed the ones made with Bisquick I'd happily downed as a kid. I guess it was *me* who needed to learn a few tricks.

It's odd that, right then, I was really fired up about a group of other dishes based, like pancakes, on simple batters of flour, milk, and eggs— things like popovers, puffy oven-baked pancakes, and clafoutis. These were, for the most part, new cooking experiences for me, and that, I suppose, was the difference. I was used to keeping my thoughts and feelings about foods I had known all my life quite separate from those about new foods I was exploring.

But this time, a small spark of interest and excitement eventually leapt the break, and I found myself wondering about the connections between the formulas for these new batters and the various basic pancake recipes I'd been following. Maybe I could make our pancakes lighter . . . more tender . . . crisper at the edges . . . if I pushed the batter in the direction—richer in eggs, say, or more the consistency of heavy cream—of those I'd been using for popovers or clafoutis.

Eager to find out, for starters, whether the secret to a light pancake might be a loose, eggy batter, I cooked up a batch right away. Perhaps I shouldn't have been surprised—but I was—that the resulting pancakes were more like some kind of mongrel crêpe than anything else. Forget "light"! These were limp, sprawling, anxious-seeming things, hardly able to stand up to a fork, much less to the assertive flavors of maple syrup and bacon.

As it happens, my recent work with batters had also involved an occasional foray into crêpedom. John and I were most comfortable when we were at a far remove from the likes of crêpes suzette. (I should say *I* was most comfortable. John now tells me that he would have *swooned* if I'd presented him with crêpes suzette.) So, we made cheese blintzes, in memory of the near-perfect ones we'd eaten at Theresa's on the Lower East Side; diminutive Swedish pancakes, which, topped with tart, sugared lingonberries, traditionally follow a Thursday night supper of split pea soup; buttery crêpes dressed with just a squeeze of lemon juice and a sprinkle of sugar, eaten from our fingers.

It would be a simpler and more likely story if I could say that *these* had been the inspiration for, the direct antecedents of, the strange creatures that now confronted us. And it's true that the qualities we liked best in the atypical crêpes we were drawn to—the tantalizing play of textures in the cheese blintzes, the admirable way the Swedish *pankakkor* held their own in such savory company, the uncomplicated goodness of the lemon-and-sugar crêpes—had a lot to tell us about what we might shoot for in our pancakes. But you'll get a more accurate sense of the way my mind works, not to mention a clearer picture of how these pancakes turned out, if I admit that actually I was curious to see what a griddled, baking-powder-leavened buttermilk popover would be like. At any rate, now I knew.

No matter. The important thing was that we had taken the first step. Even these bland, self-effacing pancakes had more life in them—and certainly more thought behind them—than the standard cookbook variety with which I'd just been going through the motions. From now on, full of ideas about the pancakes we wanted to end up with, we would be working our own way toward them. The following is a brief report on our current whereabouts.

BUTTERMILK GRIDDLECAKES
[makes 8 4- to 5-inch griddlecakes]

*The ideal pancake must attain to that golden mean where substance strikes a balance with delicacy, crispness, and feathery lightness. For us, this pancake achieves just that, earning both halves—"griddle" and "cake"—of its sobriquet. Many cooks have found—and we agree—that a separated egg adds an extra touch of lightness. The blend of flours is a time-honored one, including just enough whole wheat to accentuate the taste of the grain and a big spoonful of cornmeal to lend a pleasing husky whisper to the texture. This pancake batter is not as thin as many, but it pours well and spreads out smoothly. We find no need for the sugar that is often called for to promote browning, to mask the strong taste of some commercial leaveners, and, frankly, to boost the flavor of highly processed flours. And the judicious use of three different fats—peanut oil in the batter, a touch of bacon fat on the griddle, and sweet butter to melt on top—contributes a final note of special savory goodness.** *

bacon fat (or peanut oil or butter) for the griddles (see
     note)
3 ounces (about ¾ cup) unbleached all-purpose flour
½ ounce (about 2 tablespoons) whole-wheat flour
½ ounce (about 2 tablespoons) stone-ground cornmeal
½ teaspoon cream of tartar
½ teaspoon baking soda
¼ teaspoon salt
1 tablespoon peanut oil
1 large egg, separated
¾ cup buttermilk

To SERVE:
sweet butter and maple syrup

Set the oven to its lowest temperature and put in the plates to warm. Dip the end of a finger into a small amount of bacon fat and fill in 4 5-

---

*Should anyone be interested, there is an extensive discussion of homemade baking powder, buttermilk (and the self-renewing Swedish dairy culture we substitute for it), and weighing versus measuring in the chapter on cornbread making in *Serious Pig*.

inch circles on each of 2 two-burner griddles with a light film of grease.

Measure the dry ingredients into a mixing bowl—preferably one with a handle and a spout—and give them a couple of turns with a whisk to mix them thoroughly and break up any lumps.

Measure the oil into another bowl. Add the egg yolk and whisk gently, then add the buttermilk and whisk again. Now scrape the buttermilk mixture into the bowl of dry ingredients and whisk just to blend.

Separately, beat the egg white until it forms soft peaks, then fold it into the batter with a rubber spatula.

Preheat the first griddle over a medium-high flame. When the griddle is hot and the grease entirely melted, start the second griddle heating and portion out half of the batter to make 4 pancakes on the first. Then, move on to the second and do the same, scraping the bowl clean. As soon as each pancake has puffed up and the bubbles on its surface burst and stay open, flip it over to cook on the other side. As soon as all are turned, reduce the heat to low. When done, bring them at once to the table on the preheated plates. Serve with the butter and syrup.

Variation. In the summer, we like to fold half a cup of wild blueberries into the batter just after the beaten egg white. Avid blueberry pancake fans often resort to frozen berries during the other three seasons, but they might consider following Edna Lewis's lead and stew these into a syrup instead. This is served *in combination with* the maple syrup—something she describes as the tastiest pancake topping anyone could imagine.

Cook's Note. When John and I began to get serious about pancakes, we treated ourselves to a pair of two-burner Silverstone-lined Nordic Ware Griddle Kings. Now we can sit down at the same time, each with a full ration of pancakes laid out on warmed stoneware plates. Although we own both soapstone and cast-iron griddles, we prefer the aluminum griddles because they heat up quickly and are easy to clean. They require no greasing, so that the small amount of bacon fat we use is strictly for flavor and to aid in the crisping process. (On the down side, they don't diffuse heat very evenly, which requires some attentive spatula work.)

SILVER DOLLAR GRIDDLECAKES

When this essay first appeared in *Simple Cooking*, subscriber Maggie Rogers wrote to share a childhood recollection of her neighbor:

Mrs. Stuckey, mother of twelve, standing at a huge black wood-stove, making *perfect* "dollar" pancakes. So rich that we two add-ons, hungry from our mile's walk to catch the school bus, lost any recall of propriety lessons and moved into the fracas—probably unnoticed! What a warm family of Mennonites they were: dairy-ing, thirty-five cows, only recently moved from hand to machine milking. But back to pancakes. These were spooned right onto the stovetop; no griddles meant more space and productivity. I don't remember what we poured over them—if anything—since they were a size for picking up in the fingers, no fork needed. Butter? They seemed as though they were *made* of it. . . . I've never found such since, although my sourdoughs are close. Best with sweet salted butter and the strange slatey-sweet taste of elderberry jelly. They marry perfectly.

SIMPLE FRENCH FOOD

❦ ❦ ❦

My copy of Richard Olney's *Simple French Food*, a first edition, was bought off a remainder table at Barnes & Noble in the late 1970s. I can still remember the table—it had nothing else on it but piles of the book—and I can still remember my excitement when I picked it up and began leafing through its pages. As well I might: *Simple French Food* is one of the books that changed my life. In my mind, it sits not in the cookbook library but on another, more private shelf, whose inhabitants must sometimes look at each other and wonder how on earth they ever all arrived at this same destination.

Consequently, one of the reasons I have never written about the books is that I really didn't want anyone else in the world to know about it. And there is something about the slightly shameful feeling that comes of meeting a book on a remainder table that abets that kind of selfishness; the world had its chance and, as usual, didn't know what to make of it. Book and reader exchange at the remainder table the cynical, mutually recognizing glance of the cultural exile.

Richard Olney, however, is the real thing. Born in Marathon, Iowa, in 1927 and educated at the University of Iowa and the Brooklyn Museum Art School, he went to France at the age of twenty-four. Ten years later, "in love with the light, the landscape, and the odors of Provence," he bought an abandoned property near Solliès-Toucas, around which he has since built his life.

The writer to whom Olney immediately demands comparison is Elizabeth David. The prose of each is characterized by an aesthetic sensibility enmeshed in the stabilizing regimen of a strictly imposed self-discipline. The resulting intellectual toughness (in *Simple French Food*, Olney dispatches that *monstre sacré* and insufferable old windbag Brillat-Savarin with a single, savage saber thrust) can distance both authors from their readers. It is an unusually self-confident cook who, opening one of Olney's books, doesn't soon feel something like a naïve and frisky puppy edging up to a clever, battle-scarred, and not particularly charitable old tomcat.

> Eels live for a long time out of water and should be alive when purchased. . . . Rap the back of the head sharply against the edge of a table to knock the eel unconscious, cut a circular incision all around the base of the head, cutting slightly into the flesh, grasp the head firmly in one hand, holding it in a towel to prevent its slipping, and peel the skin, glovelike, from the body, turning it inside out; it is difficult to get it started and pliers can be useful, but once begun, it slips off easily.

The very exactness of his instructions has a peremptoriness to it that announces in advance that we are not to expect any hand-holding, even when it comes to cutting an incision around the head of a still-living eel.

It helped that I first read the book not as a potential instruction manual but as a uniquely intelligent and boldly stated culinary autobiography. What transfixed me then, and what returned in a sweeping rush when I sat down to reread it recently, is how at ease he is with a seriousness that, in this country, is itself suspect. What he expresses with rigor, clarity, and grace is an argument for the life spent in contemplative self-gratification.

Simple French Food is genuinely subversive not only because it articulates such a sensibility but because it does so without shame—or shame's usual appurtenances: diffidence, joviality, confession. Jim Harrison is the only other American writer who comes to mind who is as unflinchingly forward in his philosophical hedonism, and he, unlike Olney, has the excuse of being a novelist. Olney, of course, is a food writer, but he never hides behind the fig leaf of that profession, pretending that this is all somehow just a *job*.

Instead, Olney goes directly from the efflorescence of experience to the printed page, defiantly ignoring the reader's resisting prudishness. No one who hasn't tried can understand the courage it takes to write a passage as unguarded as this:

[G]iven the fanciful but far from frivolous presence of flowers and a sufficient variety of green things, presented in a vast, wide ceramic or earthenware vessel . . . nothing in the entire repertory of food possesses the same startling, vibrant visual immediacy—the same fresh and casual beauty. It is a concentrated, pulsating landscape of garden essences and must absolutely be tossed at table, for, no matter how delicious, the visual explosion of joy [mixes] inextricably and lastingly with your guests' memories of mingled flavors. . . .

    This salad, in the seasonal round of my own life, symbolizes the happiest time of the year—that which is lived almost entirely out of doors with the table set daily on the terrace in the shade of a grape arbor, the sparkling play of light heightening the effect of the table display of variegated greens and bright-colored punctuations. . . . [O]ften, preceded by melon or figs with ham in the Italian manner and followed by cheeses, it is the principal course, and sometimes it represents the entire meal.

Am I wrong to think that many of us feel something more akin to unease than relief when we come across such prose, with its self-possessed concentration on a *salad*? We have been brought up to think that intelligence used in this fashion is intelligence misused, especially when it is, as here, utterly unqualified by explanation or apology. He is obsessed by neither gluttony nor health. Nor is he an aesthetic butterfly flitting among the herbs and vegetables ("knock the eel unconscious"). The disquieted reader's only recourse is to speculate on what secret unhappiness could drive a writer so smart, so aloof, so *tough*, to such a life, to such a subject.

My own conjecture is that our culture's implacable resistance to the legitimacy of such a life helps explain Olney's lifelong expatriation. France is still a country where you can sit down at their midmorning snack with the workers who have come to fix your plumbing and talk seriously about Grandmother's daube; it is also a place where you can then write about it with what can only be called rigorous sensual intellectuality.

Intelligence in a food writer, even more than upfront sensuality, may be the ultimate provocation. Cookbook editors who are endlessly permissive when it comes to bad writing and stolen recipes come down fiercely on the slightest hint of intellectual *hauteur*. Olney flaunts it; he is the food world's Gore Vidal. Who else would dare set forth this daunting definition of culinary simplicity—

the more elaborate the set of rules—that is to say, *the better one understands and is able to define an intricate framework of limitations*—the greater is the freedom lent one's creative imagination

—and then apply it to something as humble as a parsnip? His improvisational flight on *that* unsexy root will leave you breathless. More than any other food writer, Richard Olney makes me want to move to France. Not to learn how the French cook and eat, but to learn how *I* might—if my appetite and mind were similarly set free.

This is why, thirty years after its original publication, *Simple French Food* remains a dangerous book. It may also explain why its latest publisher has felt it necessary to add an introduction by Patricia Wells to the original foreword by James Beard. (With Olney himself contributing a preface, this book lacks nothing in prolegomena.) I suggest you just push past this crowd and go right through the door. You'll find it quiet inside; the master is in the kitchen scrambling some eggs. Take your courage in hand and go on in.

RICHARD OLNEY: IN MEMORIAM

I was dismayed far more than I thought possible when Matt and I learned that Richard Olney had passed away on August 3, 1999, at his remote hillside home in Solliès-Toucas in Provence. Part of the shock came from the fact that I had not known, as Ed Behr would tell me later, that Richard had been failing in recent years and was no longer able to manage the steep climb up and down the driveway that wound down the hill from his small house to the road into town. Since he didn't drive, he must have known that his days at his beloved retreat were coming slowly to an end; that he died in his own bed before he was forced to leave would serve as a comfort to those who knew how passionately he would have hated any alternative.

But mostly I was dismayed because more than any other food writer—with the single exception of Patience Gray—Richard served as a touchstone for me, the personification of what, with courage, discipline, intelligence, and, yes, a broad streak of idiosyncrasy, a food writer might hope to accomplish in his life. The name of my food letter, *Simple Cooking*, is an undisguised tribute to him, and no culinary award I've had bestowed on me has meant—or could mean—as much to me as his assenting to write a blurb for *Outlaw Cook*. (And the blurb he wrote made me literally dizzy with pleaure.)

It would be both presumptuous and inaccurate to describe him as my mentor, but I did sometimes consider myself as a kind of wayward nephew—in whom he might, every now and then, admit with a sigh seeing some slight family resemblance. (And, quite honestly, that sigh would have been as important to me as the assent.)

We never met, but we did correspond—sometimes by letter, some-times by postcard, and, most often, by fax. Consequently, I was moved to read in *The New York Times* obituary—splendidly written by R. W. Apple, Jr.—that while "many saw Mr. Olney as a hermit . . . he kept in constant touch with friends and family in the United States by fax." This was, I expect, a way of having his cake and eating it, too—faxing, after all, offers a hermit an ideal way of keeping in touch.

The arrival of one of those faxes was quite an event in this house-hold, not least because we no longer owned a fax machine and had to catch his transmissions on our computer. When I suggested that he try e-mailing (faster, cheaper, easier), he reacted as if I had suggested that he switch over to instant béarnaise sauce.

With a fax machine, you see, he could still *write* letters—by hand, if it were simply a note; otherwise on a manual typewriter—and then ac-tually *send* them. He probably felt guilty enough having surrendered to the ease of faxing—like giving up the woodstove for a gas range, when everyone else had long ago turned to the microwave. He was resolutely wedded to the physicality of things—and he lived a life that allowed him to savor that corporality in full. For this and many other reasons, he inspired first awe and then affection; Matt and I will miss him sorely.

LAST GLEANING

LAST GLEANING

❧ ❧ ❧

> The time for such apples is the last of October and the first of November. They then get to be palatable, for they ripen late, and they are still perhaps as beautiful as ever.
> —Henry David Thoreau, *Wild Apples*

It is an evening in October. I'm back in Maine, right now walking down the road from the site where my parents have long planned to build a new house. My mother has already been landscaping there for several years, and along with the rose bushes, flowering shrubs, and flower beds she has also put in a small vegetable garden. A light frost has been forecast for the night, and I have volunteered to go cover the tomato plants with a tarp.

The house—the nineteenth-century Maine farmhouse they live in now—is at the top of a small rise. The drive loops up to it and back down to exit a dozen or so yards away. Tonight, instead of heading up the part closest to me, I cut across the patch of lawn between, passing among the crab apple trees, laden with ripe fruit. On the morning of my departure, I will pick a sackful of these, to bring home for making one of our favorite jellies. This crab apple picking has become an annual tradition for my parents as well as for Matt and me, but tonight I'm on another errand. I'm headed toward the field on the far side of the house, where a small orchard, restored by my father, bears Wolf River apples, an antique variety that is most notable for its large size. These apples, above all else he has grown here, are my father's pride and joy.

The sun has set, but the sky is still that deep, cold blue which rather than casting light on things wraps them in a dreamlike luminosity. By the time I reach the trees, the grass beneath my feet is already lost in shadow, but looking up through the branches I can see the apples, as big as grapefruits, faintly glowing above my head. I reach up and touch them, cool and smooth in the crisp night air, feeling for ones that are firm and whole, not soft or worm-riddled. I pluck three such, tucking each into my jacket as I do, and carry them back to the house.

My father is dying of small-blood-vessel disease of the brain. This is a disease that neither I nor anyone I know has ever heard of, and it has no cure. As the blood vessels started to collapse inside his head, all his faculties began to fail, at first slowly, almost imperceptibly, then at a frighteningly accelerating pitch. When, moving out of Maine in mid-August, Matt and I stopped to say good-bye, it was obvious that something was seriously wrong. But he could still drive a car, walk a few miles, hold a lucid conversation.

A month later he could no longer make it down to the mailbox at the end of the driveway or remember how to write a check. My mother grew frantic with concern, especially since his doctor was incommunicative and vague. Finally, she took my father to a neurologist and changed doctors. By the time everything was made clear, things had gotten so bad that she had had to call the local First Responders, the town's volunteer ambulance service, several times to lift him off the floor—often in the middle of the night, when he had fallen trying to make his own way to the bathroom. He was too weak to get himself up and far too heavy for my mother to lift.

Now, barely two months since I last saw him, he lies in the town's single hospital bed (it goes from house to house and last held a young neighbor recuperating from a motorcycle accident), with the side rails raised to keep him in. He still mostly knows who I am and remembers Matt, but he thinks I'm a professor at Amherst College and that Matt and I live on Cape Cod, both of them touchingly understandable confusions. And all but his simplest sentences become hopelessly muddled or—as frustration suffuses his face—fade into silence.

When I enter the house, I come into dark. My mother, whose daily routine has tumbled down around her, has finally found a moment to go upstairs and take a nap. My father is seventy-seven and she seventy-four; she is a remarkably energetic woman, but the strain of caring for him—nurses come only three mornings a week—has pushed her to the edge of her limits.

The absolute mistress of her kitchen, she has never allowed me—or any other family member—to cook there. But on this visit I'm permitted to make our lunches and dinners, an experience both revelatory and eerie. This kitchen has been familiar to me as an eater for almost thirty years; as a cook, I'm a complete stranger to it. I simply do not know what equipment she has or where she keeps what she does have. Dishes that I regularly make in my own kitchen must be reimagined, improvised, here. I even work with a microwave oven for the first time in my life (excellent, it turns out, for making instant couscous).

This night's cooking challenge, however, is still some time away. I make my way silently through the gloom to the far corner of the living room, once my father's office and now his sick room, and settle into the chair beside the bed. My father turns his head toward me in the dark. I reach over and switch on the lamp.

"Hi, Dad," I say.

"Hi, John," he replies. "Good to see you." This phrase, now his standard greeting, masks his confusion as to when we might last have met. He regards me with gentle inquisitiveness—his manner now, except when he is trying to escape from bed to "get back home." His face lights up when I show him the apples.

"I used to grow those," he whispers. "They're delicious."

"You grew *these*," I answer. "Let's eat some."

"Okay," he says. "Good idea."

It is a conceit of mine to pare an apple so that the peel falls off in one single coil, but this is too much of a challenge with a Wolf River, especially with my father watching. I peel it strip by strip instead and drop the parings into one of his little plastic drinking cups. Soon I have peeled enough to cut us both a wedge. As I hand him his, he has to adjust once again to a missing part of his anatomy. A few years ago he cut off the tip of his right index finger with a band saw. Now, each time he uses that hand, the little stump is new to him, another of the many inexplicable obstacles that have come to fill his life. But he ultimately gets a grip on his piece of apple and slips it into his mouth. I do the same with mine, savoring the taste, even as I begin peeling and cutting the second round.

My father is right. These apples are delicious, their flavor fresh and tartly bright. It's their texture that keeps them from being the perfect eating apple; the flesh is spongy rather than dense and crisp. This same quality makes them an excellent pie apple—they hold both their shape and their flavor, while the cooking makes them succulent—and, as it now appears, an easy one for an invalid to eat. We sit there silently for a spell, me peeling and cutting, then the two of us eating, wedge following wedge. When his interest flags, I sit with him some more, just holding his hand. The house is absolutely silent, and the bedside lamp casts the only light. The darkness moves in around us, not ominously but as if tucking us in together for the night.

🌿 🌿 🌿

> Indeed, I have no faith in the selected lists of pomological gentle-men. Their "Favorites" and "None-suches" and "Seek-no-farthers," when I have fruited them, commonly turn out very tame and forgettable. They are eaten with comparably little zest, and have no real *tang* or *smack* to them.
>
> —Henry David Thoreau, *Wild Apples*

My father lies calmly, slightly dozing, his eyes fluttering open and shut. Between the two of us we have managed to eat only a little more than half of one of the Wolf Rivers, but I know that I have made him happy. Indeed, these days it is difficult not to make my father happy; his whole affect is one of disarmingly innocent love. In this regard, he is like the apple we have just eaten, now so soft and sweet, but so green and sour when I first knew him that I could scarcely bear the taste.

He was a hard father, and all I have to do is see a photograph of him in those days to remember this: there isn't a one in which you don't either see anger or sense it rippling just below the surface. Merely to catch his attention was to risk a blow, often enough a blowup. The only time I ever felt at ease with him was when the family was watching television. When he and I first started to get along a bit when I was in my teens, that's exactly what we did: watch old horror movies together late on Friday nights.

Dinnertimes were the worst. The rigor of army life meant that he was usually gone by the time we kids had breakfast, and we had lunch at school. But dinner was dangerous territory—like a picnic that was *always* spread out in a pasture that somewhere harbored a bull, already snorting and pawing the turf. Our childhood appetites made things that much more dangerous—generous portions goaded him, and requests for seconds made him see blood. I still don't know whether it was hunger or terror that made us keep asking for them; sometimes the psyche finds the strain of fear worse than what is feared itself.

Every Christmas brought an explosion. My mother loves that holiday and all the trappings that go with it; my father inevitably erupted with anger sometime during Christmas Day, often storming out of the house and slamming the door behind him. What none of us knew as children—or, indeed, for many years afterward—was that his parents had died, one after the other, during a single Christmas season when he was still a boy. He was then separated from his brother and sisters and sent to live with relatives who took him only as a Christian duty, which they didn't for a moment allow him to forget.

His life with them was so miserable that he left them the instant he was old enough to do so and never spoke a word to them again. He enlisted in the army, whose institutional paternalism would give him a sense of security he felt nowhere else. Fighting with distinction during World War II in Africa and Italy, he rose in the ranks from a lowly private to the officer corps; he retired a lieutenant colonel. Even so, he did not become "army" in the sense that many of the fathers of my friends had, dressing their sons in miniature army fatigues and running the household with barracks discipline. His anger was entirely personal.

I was too afraid of my father to hate him; indeed, he had me so frightened that, if he had let me, I would have placated him any way I could. But I was part of the problem, not the solution; we, his children, were a constant rub on a rawness that never healed. The only way we could change that was by growing up; then, slowly, he grew comfortable with us, began to enjoy our company. It took me, at least, much longer to become fond of his.

I remember the first time I felt an intimate bond arise between us. I was in my late twenties, a high school teacher; he was in his late forties, about to retire from the military. We had gone out together to do an errand for my mother in his brand new MGB, a canary-yellow, open-topped British sports car. That he had even bought such a spiffy car had had its effect on me (in fact, I would buy it from him a few years later), because it made me realize that while in one way I knew everything about him, in another I knew hardly anything at all.

In any case, this was the time (around 1970) when McDonald's franchises had begun springing up in earnest on the East Coast. I had visited only one or two, but I was already enamored of their fries, which, aficionados will remember, were then deep-fried in beef suet. This is the perfect potato-frying medium, and McDonald's fries, especially if you could get them straight from the fryer, were the stuff of legend. My father and I happened to pass by one of their locations, and I was inspired to suggest that we stop to sample some.

To my delighted astonishment, he immediately complied, whipping the MGB straight into the parking lot. I went in and bought us two large servings, and we sat and ate them together in the car. It was the happiest eating experience I had ever had with my father, but for a very long time it never occurred to me to wonder why.

❀ ❀ ❀

> To appreciate the wild and sharp flavors of these October fruits, it is necessary that you be breathing the sharp October or November air. What is sour in the house a bracing walk makes sweet. Some of these apples might be labelled, "To be eaten in the wind."
> —Henry David Thoreau, *Wild Apples*

It wasn't until my parents moved to Maine that my father really began to mellow. With the farmhouse came a large tract of land. This he came to love more than anything else in his life besides my mother, his constant companion and only real friend, and he loved it entirely for itself. Once you got up the hill from the house and the fields around it, the land became boggy where it wasn't rocky, the soil thin and acid. It was useless except for some modest lumbering potential, but my father treated it as if he had bought a stand of sugar maples or prime bottom land beside the Penobscot River.

Soon there was an ambitious vegetable garden, an asparagus patch, a henhouse, a dew pond, a flock of sheep. He had someone come in to mow the meadow for his winter hay, but he himself loaded the bales onto the trailer he hauled behind his tractor and piled them up inside his new barn. He drove the same tractor up into the woods to haul back the logs he had felled and trimmed, then proceeded to cut them into lengths and split them into the firewood that would heat the house all winter.

I visited my parents in Maine, but not often. When I did come to visit, much of what I encountered I simply couldn't understand. Both my parents had been yearning to put down roots, and when they

moved to Maine they did, quite strong ones. Not only were they at-
tached to their old farmhouse and the land it sat on but to the town of
Searsmont as well. They got to know their neighbors, joined in local
events, became active in town politics—my father was for years the
town's first selectman, my mother serving on, among others, the school
board, the town planning commission, and the local Democratic com-
mittee.

All this was alien to me. Unlike them, I had grown up an army brat,
moving somewhere new every few years, my roots floating in hydro-
ponic solution. As an adult, it's only during those rare times when I
happen onto an army base that I feel, and then with great ambivalence,
that burst of recognition—half pang, half joy—that one feels before a
long-relinquished childhood home.

Then I, too, moved to Maine. My mother was happy to have me
close, but my father was thrilled: he saw first me, then Matt and me
both, as potential converts to the same complete devotion he felt toward Maine for the life it let him live. When we drove over to visit he
would load us up with packages of frozen lamb, cartons of eggs, bags
of apples, boxes of tomatoes. After a nudge or two, we could also get
him to give us some asparagus. His bed never produced enough to satisfy him, let alone to share with others. But he did with us.

Above all, he loved to talk about Maine itself and to advise me on
how to live there. He taught me how to season our firewood, insulate
our cottage with bags of raked-up leaves, nurse our tomatoes through
Maine's erratic growing season, and find the right local bean for our
bean pot.

He also came to my rescue several times when my ten-year-old
Honda Civic, a car never meant for long-distance heavy-winter driving,
began a series of periodic and eventually terminal cold-weather collapses. One dark and lowering night, he drove through snow showers
all the way to Augusta to get me, without complaint.

We didn't become friends exactly—our lives were too different for
that—but we were finally finding a way to become father and son. I
started to notice—and then, more slowly, to accept—how much I was
like him. I had his sense of humor, his dislike of ceremony, and, alas,
more than a little of his easy irritability. I, too, started tasks with an enthusiasm that always seemed to falter about three-quarters through.
However, there was one similarity that, once I learned it, I couldn't

keep out of my mind. My father and I were not only overweight but, although I was three inches taller, the *same* weight, sometimes to the pound.

Indeed, as observation, once alerted, made crystal clear, my father was, like I was, a secret eater. For each of us, food eaten unobserved provided a pleasure so distinct from public eating that it might as well have been an entirely different act. To the outsider, that pleasure may seem to come from eating in excess—which, when no one is watching, is easy enough to do. In truth, though, it is the reverse: eating in private is so pleasurable, so charged with feelings of release, that once you get started it can be very hard to stop.

The problem with secret eating is not so much overeating as *double* eating—finding yourself compelled to have the same meal twice. This, in the right circumstances, can be done simultaneously ("Let me go refill that platter"), but usually the secret meal is eaten either before the others come to table or later, after everyone has left it—say, when doing the dishes (my father's job).

On family occasions, as we sat talking in the den, my father would float off to the dining room, where my mother had just set out the smoked salmon appetizer. He would eat some, come back, then steal back and eat some more, before the rest of us, caught up in the conversation, even realized it was there. At other times, I would come into the kitchen, where he was carving the ham or the roast beef, and catch him slipping the trimmings not into the garbage—as my mother thought he was doing—but, as I also do in that situation, into his mouth.

This recognition, although never acknowledged, was mutual. We secret eaters know each other, and when we eat together, by tacit mutual decision, we keep the secrecy intact. In the summer of 1992, I asked my father if he would take some photographs of Duffy's Restaurant for me, in return for which I would buy him lunch. As it turned out, it poured rain all day, but we did it anyway—and the photo went on the cover of the next issue of my food letter.

I forget what I had for lunch, but I can clearly recall what my father ordered: a grilled cheese sandwich with a side of fries. The sandwich, grilled to a crunchy, buttery brown, was made of two thick slices of their home-baked bread; the fries were crisp and golden and so numerous that they spilled off his plate. "This is *great*!" he said, looking as if he had just been wafted off to heaven. Then he lost himself in his plate, just as I did in my own.

There were other moments that are more important to me: the deep pleasure he took in my writings about Maine; my admiring delight in the humorous but no-nonsense way he ran a town meeting; and, most of all, the open, unreserved love for each other that we had both begun not only to feel but to find ways to express. But that lunch, until I sat down by his bed with those Wolf River apples, was the best time I had ever spent alone with him.

On reflection, I see that our meal at Duffy's meant so much to me because of a mutual admission of helplessness before a certain kind of pleasure. There was nothing admirable about this: my father's secret eating made it all but impossible for him to deal with adult-onset diabetes (a warning signal of the disease that killed him was his—to us inexplicable—inability to master the blood-sugar monitoring device). Still, it was real, and it gave me a kind of explanation of my childhood that my father never had been able to put into words.

The only story that I remember hearing of my father's life as an orphan was that every day of the school year he was given as his lunch two pieces of bread held together with a smear of "sandwich spread"— a mayonnaise-and-sweet-pickle mixture meant to be used as a condiment with cold cuts, not by itself. This sandwich was a message, not a meal, and it eventually became a form of torture. It was hardly the only thing his foster parents did to him, but it explains it all. And it left him—as he left me—with a hunger too visceral for public show.

❋ ❋ ❋

> By the middle of November the wild apples have lost some of their brilliancy, and have chiefly fallen. A great part are decayed on the ground. . . . The note of the chickadee sounds now more distinct, as you wander amid the old trees, and the autumnal dandelion is half-closed and tearful.
>
> —Henry David Thoreau, *Wild Apples*

I hear footsteps above my head; my mother is awake. It's time for me to start the supper prep. I let go of my father's hand and bend down to kiss his forehead. I gather up the apples and, before heading to the kitchen, take them to the back door and toss them far out into the darkness for the deer.

I leave the following morning. Two weeks later, he's in a nursing home, where, in another few weeks, he'll suffer a massive stroke. Then, two days after that, the phone call from my mother. "This is the call," she said, fighting back the tears. "Your father is dead."

I come back, of course, to attend the memorial service. During it, the minister invites the members of the congregation to rise and share their memories of the deceased. Neighbors and friends stand up and speak, but none of his children do—not out of bitterness, I think, but because our memories are too complex . . . and certainly too private. For the longest time, I thought my father intentionally refused to talk about his past. But I came to realize he simply couldn't. All he ever wanted was to escape from it, a process that to his mind never had anything to do with words. So, I had to get to know my father by discovering how much of me was him, as I hope he himself came to understand during our last years together how much of him was me.

BIBLIOGRAPHY

❋ ❋ ❋

The exact quotation? Alas, that would be found in a book borrowed by a friend who never returned it, marked by a slip of paper that fell out long ago.

—Nigel Strangeways, *Babblings of a Bibliophile*

Abdennour, Samia. *Egyptian Cooking: A Practical Guide.* Cairo: The American University in Cairo Press, 1984.

Achaya, K. T. *Indian Food: A Historical Companion.* New Delhi: Oxford University, 1994.

Acton, Eliza. *The Best of Eliza Acton.* Edited by Elizabeth Ray. London: Longmans, Green, 1968 (excerpts from *Modern Cookery for Modest Families*, first published in 1845).

———. *The English Bread Book.* Lewes, England: Southover, 1990 (reprint of the 1859 edition).

Alford, Jeffrey, and Naomi Duguid. *Seductions of Rice.* New York: Artisan, 1998.

Algar, Ayla. *Classic Turkish Cooking: Traditional Food for the American Kitchen.* New York: HarperCollins, 1991.

Anderson, Burton. *Treasures of the Italian Table.* New York: Morrow, 1994.

Anderson, E. N. *The Food of China.* New Haven: Yale University, 1988.

Anderson, Jean. *The Grass Roots Cookbook.* New York: Times, 1977.

Andoh, Elizabeth. *At Home with Japanese Cooking,* New York: Knopf, 1980.

Andrews, Colman. *Catalan Cuisine.* New York: Atheneum, 1988.

———. *Flavors of the Riviera.* New York: Bantam, 1996.

Artusi, Pellegrino. *Science in the Kitchen and the Art of Eating Well.* Translated by Murtha Baca and Stephen Sartarelli. New York: Marsilio, 1997.

Baillie-Grohman, William A. *Camps in the Rockies—Being a Narrative of Life on the Frontier, and Sport in the Rocky Mountains, with an Account of the Cattle Ranches of the West.* Sampson Low, Marston, Searle & Rivington, 1882.

Barr, Nancy Verde. *We Called It Macaroni*. New York: Knopf, 1990.

Barron, Rosemary. *Flavors of Greece: The Best of Classic and Modern Greek Culinary Traditions*. New York: Morrow, 1991.

Bastianich, Lidia. *La Cucina di Lidia*. New York: Doubleday, 1990.

Beeton, Mrs. Isabella. *The Book of Household Management*. London: Ward, Lock, and Tyler, 1869.

Behr, Edward. "In Pursuit of the Fundamental Loaf." *The Art of Eating*, no. 18 (spring 1991).

———. "Maryland Crab." *The Art of Eating*, no. 23 (summer 1992).

———. "Pizza in Naples." *The Art of Eating*, no. 22 (spring 1992).

Bettoja, Jo, with Jane Garmey. *Southern Italian Cooking: Family Recipes from the Kingdom of the Two Sicilies*. New York: Bantam, 1991.

Bianchi, Anne. *From the Tables of Tuscan Women*. Hopewell, NJ: Ecco, 1995.

Boni, Ada. *Italian Regional Cooking*. New York: L. P. Dutton, 1969.

Bradney, Gail, ed. *Best Wines! Gold Medal Winners from the Leading Competitions Worldwide 1999*. Bearsville, NY: Print Project, 1999.

Brennan, Georgeanne. *In the French Kitchen Garden*. San Francisco: Chronicle, 1998.

———. *Potager: Fresh Garden Cooking in the French Style*. San Francisco: Chronicle, 1992.

Brennan, Jennifer. *Curries and Bugles: A Memoir and Cookbook of the British Raj*. New York: HarperCollins, 1990.

Brown, Helen Evans. *West Coast Cook Book*. Boston: Little, Brown, 1952.

Brown, Rose, Cora Brown, and Bob Brown. *America Cooks*. New York: Norton, 1940.

Bugialli, Giuliano. *Bugialli on Pasta*. New York: Simon & Schuster, 1988.

———. *Classic Techniques of Italian Cooking*. New York: Simon & Schuster, 1982.

———. *The Fine Art of Italian Cooking*. New York: Times, 1978.

Buonassisi, Vincenzo. *Pasta: The History and Preparation of One of the World's Most Popular Foods*. Wilton, CT: Lyceum, 1973 (translation of *Il codice della pasta*. Milan: Rizzoli, 1973).

Butazzi, Grazietta. *Toscana in bocca*. Milan: Il Vespro, 1979.

Caggiano, Biba. *Italy Al Dente*. New York: Morrow, 1998.

Calingaert, Efrem Funghi, and Jacquelyn Days Serwer. *Pasta and Rice Italian Style*. New York: Scribner's, 1983.

Campbell, Helen. *In Foreign Kitchens*. Boston: Roberts Brothers, 1892.

Cardella, Antonio. *Sicilia e le isole in bocce*. Milan: Il Vespro, 1978.

Carlyle, Thomas. *Sartor Resartus: The Life and Opinions of Herr Teufels-drockh in Three Books*. Berkeley: University of California, 1999.

Carrier, Robert. *Feasts of Provence*. New York: Rizzoli, 1993.

Chang, K.C., ed. *Food in Chinese Culture*. New Haven: Yale University, 1977.

Chatwin, Bruce. "On the Road with Mrs. Gandhi." *GRANTA* 26 (spring 1989).

Chu, Woul Young. *From Traditional Korean Cuisine*. Seoul: Jim Min Chang, 1985.

Cipriani, Arrigo. *The Harry's Bar Cookbook.* New York: Bantam, 1991.

Claiborne, Craig. *Craig Claiborne's Southern Cooking.* New York: Times, 1987.

Coffin, Robert P. Tristram. *Maine Doings.* Indianapolis: Bobb-Merrill, 1950.

Contini, Mila. *Milano in bocca.* Palermo: Editrice de "il Vespro," 1976.

Copley, Esther. *Cottage Cookery.* London: Groombridge & Sons, 1849.

Cornfield, Robert. *Lundy's—Reminiscences and Recipes from Brooklyn's Legendary Restaurant.* New York: HarperCollins, 1998.

Cost, Bruce. *Bruce Cost's Asian Ingredients.* New York: Morrow, 1988.

Cunningham, Marion. *The Breakfast Book.* New York: Knopf, 1987.

Czarnecki, Jack. *A Cook's Book of Mushrooms.* New York: Artisan, 1995.

Dahl, Roald. *Roald Dahl's Revolting Recipes.* New York: Viking, 1994.

Dahl, Roald, and Felicity Dahl. *Memories with Food at Gipsy House.* New York: Viking, 1991 (republished in Britain as *The Roald Dahl Cookbook.* London: Penguin, 1996).

David, Elizabeth. *English Bread and Yeast Cookery.* London: Penguin, 1977.

———. *Italian Food.* Rev. ed. New York: Harper & Row, 1987.

David, Suzy. *The Sephardic Kosher Kitchen.* Middle Village, NY: Jonathan David, 1984.

Davidson, Alan. *North Atlantic Seafood.* New York: Viking, 1979.

De Groot, Roy Andries. *In Search of the Perfect Meal.* New York: St. Martin's, 1986.

Dean, Sydney W. *Cooking American.* New York: Hill & Wang, 1957.

Del Conte, Anna. *Gastronomy of Italy.* New York: Prentice Hall, 1989.

———. *The Italian Pantry.* New York: Harper & Row, 1990.

della Croce, Julia. *The Vegetarian Table of Italy.* San Francisco: Chronicle, 1994.

Della Femina, Jerry. *An Italian Grows in Brooklyn.* Boston: Little, Brown, 1978.

der Haroutunian, Arto. *Middle Eastern Cookery.* London: Century, 1982.

Devi, Yamuna. *Lord Krishna's Cuisine: The Art of Vegetarian Cooking.* New York: Dutton, 1987.

Douglas, Norman. *Siren Lands.* New York: Dodd, Mead, 1924.

Eberstadt, Fernanda. "Annals of Place: The Palace and the City." *The New Yorker,* December 23, 1991.

Ervin, Janet Halliday, ed. *The White House Cookbook.* Chicago: Follett, 1964 (a slightly adapted reprint of the classic 1887 publication originally written by Mrs. F. L. Gillette and Hugo Zieman, a former White House steward).

Estragon, Vladimir. *Waiting for Dessert.* New York: Viking, 1982.

Evelyn, John. *Aceteria: A Discourse of Sallets.* London: Prospect, 1982 (a facsimile of the 1699 edition).

Farah, Madelain. *Lebanese Cuisine.* Portland, OR: 1986.

Field, Carol. *The Italian Baker.* New York: Harper & Row, 1985.

Forbes, Leslie. *A Table in Tuscany.* San Francisco: Chronicle, 1991.

Ford, Ford Madox. *No Enemy.* New York: Macaulay, 1929.

Foster, Robert Fitzroy. *Modern Ireland: 1600–1972.* London: Allen Lane, 1988.

Freeling, Nicolas. *The Kitchen Book & The Cook Book: Two Culinary Classics.* Boston: Godine, 1991.

Freson, Robert (photographer), and Alexandra Arrowsmith (recipe editor). *Savoring Italy: A Celebration of the Food, Landscape, and People of Italy*. New York: HarperCollins, 1992.

Freud, Clement. *Below the Belt*. London: Robson, 1982.

Fritz, E. May. *Prairie Kitchen Sampler*. Phoenix, AZ: Prairie Winds, 1989.

Fu, Pei Mei. *Pei Mei's Chinese Snacks & Desserts*. Taipei: 1987.

Garmey, Jane. *Great British Cooking: A Well-Kept Secret*. New York: Random House, 1981.

Gibbons, Euell. *Stalking the Blue-Eyed Scallop*. New York: David McKay, 1964.

Giusti-Lanham, Hedy, and Andrea Dodi. *The Cuisine of Venice & Surrounding Northern Regions*. Woodbury, NY: Barron's, 1978.

Graham, Harry. *Ruthless Rhymes for Heartless Homes*. New York: R. H. Russell, 1901.

Gray, Patience. *Honey from a Weed: Fasting and Feasting in Tuscany, Catalonia, The Cyclades, and Apulia*. New York: Harper & Row, 1987.

Gray, Peter. *The Mistress Cook*. New York: Oxford University, 1956.

Grigson, Jane. *Fish Cookery*. London: Penguin, 1975.

——. *Good Things*. New York: Knopf, 1971.

——. *Jane Grigson's Fruit Book*. New York: Atheneum, 1982.

——. *The Observer Guide to British Cookery*. London: Michael Joseph, 1984.

Grossman, Loyd. *Loyd Grossman's Italian Journey*. London: Vermilion, 1994.

Guinaudeau-Franc, Zette. *Les secrets des fermes en Perigord noir*. Paris: Berger Levrault, 1980.

Hamady, Mary Laird. *Lebanese Mountain Cookery*. Boston: Godine, 1987.

Hambro, Nathalie. *Particular Delights: Cooking for All the Senses*. London: Macmillan, 1981.

Hansen, Barbara. "New Vietnamese Cuisine—One Last Coffee Before I Go." *Los Angeles Times* (food section): Thursday, July 28, 1994.

Harland, Marion. (Mary Virginia Hawes Terhune). *Breakfast, Luncheon, and Tea*. New York: Scribner's, 1892.

——. *Common Sense in the Household: A Manual of Practical Housewifery*. New York: Scribner's, 1883.

——. *Marion Harland's Complete Cook Book*. Indianapolis: Bobbs-Merrill, 1903.

Harris, Valentina. *Recipes from an Italian Farmhouse*. New York: Simon & Schuster, 1989.

Hazan, Marcella. *The Classic Italian Cookbook*. New York: Harper & Row, 1973.

——. *Essentials of Classic Italian Cooking*. New York: Knopf, 1992.

——. *More Classic Italian Cooking*. New York: Knopf, 1978.

Hazelton, Nika. *The Regional Italian Kitchen*. New York: Evans, 1978.

Heritage, Lizzie. *Cassell's Universal Cookery Book*. London: Cassell, 1901.

Hess, Karen. *The Carolina Rice Kitchen*. Columbia, SC: University of South Carolina, 1992.

Hibben, Sheila. *A Kitchen Manual*. New York: Duell, Sloan & Pearce, 1941.

————. *American Regional Cookery*. Boston: Little, Brown, 1947.

————. *The National Cookbook*. New York: Harper & Brothers, 1932.

Hom, Ken. *Easy Family Recipes from a Chinese-American Childhood*. New York: Knopf, 1997.

————. *The Taste of China*. New York: Simon & Schuster, 1990.

Hughes, Spike, and Charmane Hughes. *Pocket Guide to Italian Food and Wine.* New York: Simon & Schuster, 1986.

Hutchins, Sheila. *Grannie's Kitchen: Recipes from the North East of England*. London: Granada, 1979.

Hyde, Joe. *Love, Time & Butter: The Broiling, Roasting, Baking, Deep-Fat Frying, Sautéing, Braising, and Boiling Cookbook*. New York: Baron, 1971.

Irwin, Florence. *The Cookin' Woman*. Edinburgh: Oliver & Boyd, 1949.

————. *Irish Country Recipes*. Belfast: The Northern Whig, 1937.

Jackson, Annabel. *Café Vietnam*. Chicago: Contemporary, 1998.

Jaffrey, Madhur. *Madhur Jaffrey's World-of-the East Vegetarian Cooking*. New York: Knopf, 1981.

Jones, Pamela Sheldon. *Pizza Napoletana!* Berkeley: Ten Speed, 1999.

Jouveau, René. *La Cuisine provençale de tradition populaire*. Berne: Éditions du Message, 1963.

Joyce, P. W. *English As We Speak It in Ireland*. London: Longmans, Green, 1910.

Kasper, Lynne Rossetto. *The Splendid Table: Recipes from Emilia-Romagna, the Heartland of Northern Italian Food*. New York: Morrow, 1992.

Kennedy, Diana. *The Art of Mexican Cooking*. New York: Bantam, 1989.

Kenney-Herbert, Colonel A. R. *Culinary Jottings for Madras*. Totnes, Devon: Prospect, 1994 (a facsimile edition of the 1885 edition).

————. *Fifty Breakfasts*. London: E. Arnold, 1894.

Keys, Ancel, and Margaret Keys. *How to Eat Well and Stay Well the Mediterranean Way*. New York: Doubleday, 1975.

Killeen, Johanne, and George Germon. *Cucina Simpatica: Robust Trattoria Cooking*. New York: Harper Collins, 1991.

King, Shirley. *Pampille's Table: Recipes and Writings from the French Countryside*. Winchester, MA: Faber & Faber, 1996 (a translation and adaptation of Marthe Daudet's *Les Bons Plats de France*, 1919).

Kinmonth, Claudia. *Irish Country Furniture: 1700–1950*. New Haven: Yale University, 1993.

Kirkland, C. M. *Forest Life*. New York: C. S. Francis, 1842.

Klein, Maggie Blyth. *The Feast of the Olive*. Berkeley: Aris, 1983.

Kuo, Irene. *The Key to Chinese Cooking*. New York: Knopf, 1977.

L, Major. *Breakfasts, Luncheons, and Ball Suppers*. London: Chapman and Hall, 1887.

Lassalle, George. *East of Orphanides*. London: Kyle Cathie, 1991.

Lee, Karen. *Chinese Cooking Secrets*. New York: Doubleday, 1984.

Lennon, Biddy White. *The Poolbeg Book of Traditional Irish Cooking*. Dublin: Poolbeg, 1990.

Leung, Mai. *The Chinese People's Cookbook*. New York: Harper & Row, 1979.

————. *The Classic Chinese Cookbook*. New York: Harper & Row, 1976.

Lin, Florence. *Florence Lin's Complete Book of Chinese Noodles, Dumplings and Breads*. New York: Morrow, 1986.

LoMonte, Mimmetta. *Classic Sicilian Cooking*. New York: Simon & Schuster, 1990.

Luongo, Pino. *A Tuscan in the Kitchen*. New York: Clarkson Potter, 1988.

Machlin, Edda Servi. *The Classic Cuisine of the Italian Jews*. New York: Everest, 1981.

————. *The Classic Cuisine of the Italian Jews*, Vol. II. Croton-on-Hudson, NY: Giro, 1992.

Mahon, Bríd. *Land of Milk and Honey: The Story of Traditional Irish Food & Drink*. Dublin: Poolbeg, 1991.

Mariani, John F. *The Dictionary of American Food and Drink*. Rev. ed. New York: Hearst, 1994.

Marks, Copeland. *Sephardic Cooking*. New York: Donald I. Fine, 1992.

————. *The Varied Kitchens of India*. New York: M. Evans, 1986.

Marks, Copeland, with Manjo Kim. *The Korean Kitchen: Recipes from the Land of the Morning Calm*. San Francisco: Chronicle, 1993.

Marshall, Frederic. *French Home Life*. London: Wm. Blackwood & Sons, 1873.

————. *Population and Trade in France in 1861–62*. London: Chapman and Hall, 1862.

Martini, Anna. *The Mondadori Regional Italian Cookbook*. New York: Harmony, 1983.

McNair, James. *Vegetarian Pizza*. San Francisco: Chronicle, 1993.

Médecin, Jacques. *Cuisine Niçoise: Recipes from a Mediterranean Kitchen*. London: Penguin, 1983.

Merwin, W. S. *The Lost Upland: Stories of Southwest France*. New York: Knopf, 1992.

Michell, Alexandra, ed. *France: A Culinary Journey*. San Francisco: Collins SF, 1992.

Middione, Carlo. *The Food of Southern Italy*. New York: Morrow, 1987.

————. *La Vera Cucina*. New York: Simon & Schuster, 1996.

Nearing, Helen. *Simple Food for the Good Life*. New York: Delacorte, 1980.

Ngo, Bach, and Gloria Zimmerman. *The Classic Cuisine of Vietnam*. Hauppauge, NY: Barrons, 1979.

Nicholson, Asenath. *Annals of the Famine in Ireland in 1847, 1848, and 1849*. New York: E. French, 1851.

————. *Ireland's Welcome to the Stranger; or, An Excursion Through Ireland in 1844 and 1845, for the Purpose of Investigating the Condition of the Poor*. London: Gilpin, 1847.

Nickles, Harry G., and the editors of Time-Life Books. *Middle Eastern Cooking*. Alexandria, VA: Time-Life, 1969.

Olney, Richard. *Simple French Food*. New York: Atheneum, 1974.

Olney, Richard, and the editors of Time-Life Books. *Dried Beans & Grains* (a volume in *The Good Cook Series*). Alexandria, VA: Time-Life, 1982.

Ortiz, Joe. *The Village Baker: Classic Regional Breads from Europe and America*. Berkeley: Ten Speed, 1993.

Owen, Sri. *The Rice Book*. New York: St. Martin's, 1993.

Parker, Robert M. *Parker's Wine Buyer's Guide*. 4th ed. New York: Simon & Schuster/Fireside, 1995.

Pellegrino, Frank. *Rao's Cookbook—Over 100 Years of Italian Home Cooking*. New York: Random House, 1998.

Pham, Mai. *The Best of Vietnamese & Thai Cooking*. Rocklin, CA: Prima, 1996.

Pomés, Leopold. *Teoria i pràctica del pa amb tomàquet*. Barcelona: Tusquets Editors, 1985.

Read, Jan, and Maite Manjón. *The Great British Breakfast*. London: Michael Joseph, 1981.

Renner, H. D. *The Origin of Food Habits*. London: Faber & Faber, 1944.

Rios, Alicia (text), and Lourdes March (recipes). *The Heritage of Spanish Cooking*. New York: Random House, 1992.

Roby, Norman S., and Charles E. Olken. *The Connoisseurs' Handbook of the Wines of California and the Pacific Northwest*. 4th ed. New York: Knopf, 1998.

Roden, Claudia. *A Book of Middle Eastern Food*. New York: Knopf, 1972.

Root, Waverley. *Food of Italy*. New York: Atheneum, 1971.

———. *Waverley Root's The Best of Italian Cooking*. New York: Grosset & Dunlap, 1974.

Root, Waverley, and Richard de Rochemont. *Eating in America*. New York: Morrow, 1976.

Rorer, Sarah Tyson. *Mrs. Rorer's New Cook Book*. Philadelphia: Arnold, 1902.

Routhier, Nicole. *The Foods of Vietnam*. New York: Stewart, Tabori & Chang, 1989.

Sahni, Julie. *Classic Indian Cooking*. New York: Morrow, 1980.

———. *Classic Indian Vegetarian and Grain Cooking*. New York: Morrow, 1985.

Salaman, Rena. *Mediterranean Vegetable Cookery*. London: Collins, 1987.

Scaravelli, Paola, and Jon Cohen. *Cooking from an Italian Garden*. New York: Holt, Rinehart and Winston, 1984.

Schrecker, Ellen, with John Schrecker. *Mrs. Chiang's Szechwan Cookbook*. New York: Harper & Row, 1976.

Schwartz, Arthur. *Naples at Table*. New York: HarperCollins, 1998.

———. *What to Cook When You Think There's Nothing in the House to Eat*. New York: HarperCollins, 1992.

Senderens, Alain. *The Table Beckons*. New York: Farrar, Straus & Giroux, 1993.

Sexton, Regina. *A Little History of Irish Food*. Dublin: Gill and Macmillan, 1998.

Shere, Lindsey R. *Chez Panisse Desserts*. New York: Random House, 1985.

Shields, John. *The Chesapeake Bay Crab Cookbook*. Reading, MA: Addison, Wesley, 1992.

———. *The Chesapeake Bay Cookbook*. Reading, MA: Addison, Wesley, 1990.

Simeti, Mary Taylor. *Pomp and Sustenance*. New York: Knopf, 1989.

Simonds, Nina. *China Express*. New York: Morrow, 1993.

———. *Classic Chinese Cuisine*. Boston: Houghton Mifflin, 1982.

Skeat, Walter W. *An Etymological Dictionary of the English Language*. Oxford: Clarendon, 1882.

Smith, Andrew F. *The Tomato in America*. Columbia, SC: University of South Carolina, 1994.

Soviero, Donaldo. *La Vera Cucina Italiana: The Fundamentals of Classic Italian Cooking*. New York: Macmillan, 1991.

Spencer, Evelene, and John N. Cobb. *Fish Cookery*. Boston: Little, Brown, 1921.

Stang, Sondra J., and Karen Cochran, eds. *The Correspondence of Ford Madox Ford and Stella Bowen*. Bloomington: Indiana University, 1993.

Stobart, Tom. *The Cook's Encyclopedia*. New York: Harper & Row, 1982.

———. *Herbs, Spices and Flavorings*. New York: Overlook, 1982.

Strang, Jeanne. *Goose Fat and Garlic: Country Recipes from South-West France*. London: Kyle Cathie, 1992.

Strangeways, Nigel. *Babblings of a Bibliophile*. London: Eidolon, 1921.

———. *Malone and the Motley Fool*. New York: Speculaas, 1932.

———. *Toaster Agonistes*. London: Eidolon, 1923.

Taik, Aung Aung. *Under the Golden Pagoda*. San Francisco: Chronicle, 1993.

Taruschio, Ann, and Franco Taruschio. *Bruschetta: Crostoni and Crostini*. New York: Abbeville, 1995.

Taylor, Alice. *To School Through the Fields: An Irish Country Childhood*. New York: St. Martin's, 1988.

Thomas, Dylan. *Me and My Bike*. New York: McGraw-Hill, 1965.

Thompson, Flora. *Lark Rise to Candleford*. London: Oxford University, 1948.

Thoreau, Henry David. *Wild Apples*. New Bedford, MA: Applewood, undated. (First printed in *The Atlantic Monthly*, November 1862.)

Thorne, John. *Simple Cooking*. New York: Viking, 1987.

———. *A Treatise on Onion Soup: Its History, Powers, and Modes of Proceeding*. Boston: Jackdaw Press, 1979.

Thorne, John, with Matt Lewis Thorne. *Outlaw Cook*. New York: Farrar, Straus & Giroux, 1992.

———. *Serious Pig*. New York: North Point, 1996.

Tilleray, Brigitte. *Recipes from the French Kitchen Garden*. London: Cassell, 1995.

Tropp, Barbara. *The Modern Art of Chinese Cooking*. New York: Morrow, 1982.

Turner, Alice M. (compiler). *The New England Cook Book*. Boston: Charles E. Brown, 1905.

Vitale, Gioietta, with Lisa Lawley. *Riso: Undiscovered Rice Dishes of Northern Italy*. New York: Crown, 1992.

Wade, Mary L. *The Book of Corn Cookery*. Chicago: A. C. McClurg, 1917.

Westrip, Joyce Pamela. "Some Persian Influences on the Cooking of India." Vol.

1 of *National & Regional Styles of Cookery, Proceedings of the Oxford Cookery Symposium 1981.* Edited by Alan Davidson. London: Prospect, 1981.

White, Florence. *Good Things in England.* London: Jonathan Cape/Cookery Book Club, 1969.

Wilson, C. Anne. *Food and Drink in Britain.* London: Constable, 1973.

Witty, Helen. *Mrs. Witty's Home-Style Menu Cookbook.* New York: Workman, 1990.

Wright, Jeni, general ed. *The Encyclopedia of Asian Cooking.* London: Octopus, 1980.

Wyman, Carolyn. *I'm a Spam Fan.* Stamford, CT: Longmeadow, 1992.

Yates, Dornford. *Adele & Co.* London: Hodder & Stoughton, 1931.

Yee, Rhoda. *Dim Sum.* San Francisco: Taylor & Ng, 1977.

Zee, A. *Swallowing Clouds.* New York: Simon & Schuster, 1990.

Zubaida, Sami. *"Kitchri."* A paper delivered at the Oxford Cookery Symposium in 1984 and published in *Cookery—Science, Lore and Books. Proceedings of the Oxford Symposium on Food, Cookery, and Food History 1984/1985,* edited by Tom Jaine. London: Prospect, 1985.

INDEX

※ ※ ※